Border Crossing in

MW01241896

China's transformation from a poor and underdeveloped country into a global market power has profoundly altered its socioeconomic power relations with the other countries in the Greater China region, namely, Taiwan and Hong Kong. Indeed, this economic shift has resulted in the massive flow of capital and people from Taiwan as well as Hong Kong to China, to seek business opportunities and new lifestyles. These flows have in turn completely transformed longstanding borderlines in the region.

This book examines the transformation of Taiwan and Hong Kong's socio-economic relationships with China as their economies have become more deeply integrated into Greater China. Across three key sections, it explores the impact of increasing social interaction and the shrinking of existing borderlines to ask whether these changes will bring about a convergence of identity among the people involved. "Production" examines how investments from Taiwan and Hong Kong to China have transformed production networks; "Community" explores the impact of cross-boundary mobility and the integration of migrants into Chinese communities; and finally, "Identity" engages with what is one of the most important issues in contemporary Taiwanese society.

Border Crossing in Greater China contributes not only to theoretical debates on border crossing issues, but also provides valuable insights on the practical concerns regarding social and political integration and tensions in the region. As such, it will be of great interest to students and scholars of Taiwan studies, Chinese studies, Chinese society, and Chinese economics.

Jenn-hwan Wang is Chair Professor of the Graduate Institute of Development Studies at National Chengchi University, Taiwan.

Routledge research on Taiwan
Series Editor: Dafydd Fell, SOAS, UK

The Routledge Research on Taiwan Series seeks to publish quality research on all aspects of Taiwan studies. Taking an interdisciplinary approach, the books will cover topics such as politics, economic development, culture, society, anthropology and history.

This new book series will include the best possible scholarship from the social sciences and the humanities and welcomes submissions from established authors in the field as well as from younger authors. In addition to research monographs and edited volumes general works or textbooks with a broader appeal will be considered.

The Series is advised by an international Editorial Board and edited by *Dafydd Fell* of the Centre of Taiwan Studies at the School of Oriental and African Studies.

Border Crossing in Greater China

Production, community and identity

Edited by Jenn-hwan Wang

Routledge
Taylor & Francis Group

LONDON AND NEW YORK

First published 2015
by Routledge
2 Park Square, Milton Park, Abingdon, Oxon OX14 4RN

and by Routledge
711 Third Avenue, New York, NY 10017

First issued in paperback 2017

Routledge is an imprint of the Taylor & Francis Group, an informa business

British Library Cataloguing in Publication Data
A catalogue record for this book is available from the British Library

Library of Congress Cataloging in Publication Data
Border crossing in greater China: production, community and identity / edited by Jenn-hwan Wang.
    pages cm. – (Routledge research on taiwan series; 13)
    Includes bibliographical references and index.
    1. Taiwan–Relations–China. 2. China–Relations–Taiwan. 3. Hong Kong (China)–Relations–China. 4. China–Relations–China–Hong Kong.
    5. National characteristics. I. Wang, Jenn-hwan.
    DS799.63.C6B67 2014
    337.51051249–dc23   2014000431

ISBN 13: 978-1-138-08960-0 (pbk)
ISBN 13: 978-0-415-74485-0 (hbk)

Typeset in Times New Roman
by Wearset Ltd, Boldon, Tyne and Wear

Contents

Figures

Tables

Contributors

Chang, Chia-ming is Professor of the Department of Sociology and Dean of Academic Office at the Soochow University, Taiwan. His research focuses on sociology of development and globalization, industrial and economic sociology, East Asia studies, as well as Taiwanese business. His most recent book is *Taiwanese Business in Suzhou, China: Investigation from the Viewpoint of Globalization and Localization* (The Laureate Books Co. Ltd., 2006). Email: ccm@scu.edu.tw.

Cheng, Chih-peng is Assistant Professor of the Center for General Education and the Institute of Sociology at the National Tsing Hua University, Taiwan. His research focuses on the production network of Taishang, economic development in Taiwan, and economic transition as well as regional development in China. Email: chengcp@mx.nthu.edu.tw.

Cheng, Ter-hsing is an assistant professor of the Department of Sociology at Soochow University, Taiwan. His research focuses on Chinese immigrants in Central and Eastern Europe, the development of Sinology or China studies in Central and Eastern Europe, issues on democracy, including civil society, collective memory, and transitional justice. His recent papers are "Civil Society and Participatory Democracy in the New Democracies: A Comparison between Taiwan and Czech Republic" (*Journal of Law and Public Governance*, National Chia-Yi University, 2013), "The EU's Common Immigration Policy and The Member States' Challenge: The Perspective of Czech 'Immigrants' Integration' and Chinese Case" (*European Moduel, Jean Monnet Program*, National Chengchi University, Taiwan, 2013). Email: jameseataiwan@yahoo.com.tw.

Chien, Shiuh-Shen is Associate Professor of Development Geography at National Taiwan University. His research interests cover development geography, the geography of globalization, transnational studies, and the political economy of urban and regional development, with empirical focuses on the Global South in general and post-socialist China in particular. His articles in print can be seen in the *Asian Journal of Political Science*; *Asian Survey*; *Environment and Planning C*; *Global Networks*; *Regional Studies*; *Urban Studies*; etc. He can be reached at schien@ntu.edu.tw.

Chin, Angelina is Associate Professor of History at Pomona College, where she teaches courses on colonialism, diaspora, and feminism in Modern East Asia. Her research interests revolve around transformations of urban identity and citizenship, as well as transregional connections in Hong Kong, Taiwan, and South China. She is currently working on a project on postcolonial memory and diasporic nostalgia of Chinese refugees from the 1940s to the 1970s. She is the author of *Bound to Emancipate: Working Women and Urban Citizenship in Early Twentieth-century China and Hong Kong* (Rowman & Littlefield, 2012). Email: Angelina.Chin@pomona.edu.

Chung, Robert is Director of the Public Opinion Programme, the University of Hong Kong. He is the founder of the Public Opinion Programme at the University of Hong Kong, which began in 1991. Under his leadership, POP is well known for its impartiality and professionalism in collecting, studying, and interpreting public opinion in Hong Kong and nearby regions. Email: robert.chung@hku.hk.

Deng, Jian-bang is Associate Professor and Chair of the Graduate Institute of Futures Studies at the University of Tamkang in Taiwan. His main research focuses on the impact of mobility and cross-cultural interactions on transnational professionals. He has published several papers on these subjects, with special reference to Taiwanese skilled workers in China. His recent paper "Immigration Policy in Taiwan Facing Challenges: Citizenship Arrangement for Families of Taiwanese Expatriates with Chinese Spouses" will be collected and published in the book *Assessing the China Impact*, edited by Gunter Schubert (forthcoming). Email: dengjb@mail.tku.edu.tw.

Hu, Richard Weixing is Associate Professor of Political Science in the Department of Politics and Public Administration, the University of Hong Kong. His teaching and research focuses on China's foreign relations, East Asian political economy, and cross-Taiwan Strait relations. His latest publications include "Explaining Change and Stability in Cross-Strait Relations: a Punctuated Equilibrium Model," *Journal of Contemporary China*, 21–7 (November 2012), 933–953; "Politics of Détente: Comparing Korea and Taiwan," *Pacific Review*, 26–2 (March 2013), 199–220; and *New Dynamics in Cross-Taiwan Strait Relations* (Routledge, 2013). Email: rwxhu@hkucc.hku.hk.

Keng, Shu is Associate Professor at the School of Public Economics and Administration, Shanghai University of Finance and Economics. His research interests include comparative political economic, government–business relations, and cross-Strait relations. He is also the co-editor of the book *Taishang Study* (with Ruihua Lin and Gunter Schubert, Wunan, 2012). Email: skeng0731@gmail.com.

Lin, Ping is an associate professor at the Department of Politics, National Chung Cheng University in Taiwan. He has published several journal articles on issues of Taiwanese migrants in China, such as in *Taiwanese Political Science Review*, *Journal of Population Studies*, *The China Review*, and *China Information*. Email: polpl@ccu.edu.tw.

Lin, Ruihua is Assistant Professor at the School of Public Economics and Administration, Shanghai University of Finance and Economics. Her research focuses on comparative political economic, immigration studies, and Taiwanese businessmen studies. She is also the co-editor of the book *Taishang Study* (with Shu Keng and Gunter Schubert, Wunan, 2012). Email: emmy388@gmail.com.

Shen, Hsiu-hua teaches at the Institute of Sociology, National Tsing Hua University, Taiwan. She is also a faculty member of the Center for Contemporary China at the University. Her areas of teaching and research are migration, gender studies, the sociology of intimacy, and everyday life of social class. Email: hhshen@mx.nthu.edu.tw.

Sonoda, Shigeto is a professor of sociology at the University of Tokyo. He is now working for the Institute for Advanced Studies on Asia (IASA) and Graduate School of Interdisciplinary Information Studies (GSII). He is also serving as Deputy Director of the International Center at the University of Tokyo. Prof. Sonoda is a board member of several academic associations including Japan Association for Asian Studies. He has taken initiatives in conducting researches including *AsiaBarometer 2003–2008*, *Asia Student Survey 2008*, and *Tianjin Annual Survey 1997–2011*. His special interest is in social stratification and globalization of cultures in Asia, and localization process of Japanese company in Asian countries. His latest publications include: *Emerging Middle Classes in East Asia* (editor, Keisho-shobo, 2012), *Can Education Solve Social Inequality?* (with Atsuko Shimbo, Iwanami Shoten Publishers, 2010), and *Social Inequality in Contemporary China* (Chuo Koron, 2008, awarded Special Prize of 20th Asia-Pacific Award). Email: shigetosonoda@ioc.u-tokyo.ac.jp.

Tai, Edward is Senior Data Analyst of the Public Opinion Programme, the University of Hong Kong. He is mainly responsible for the data analysis of the public opinion data, collected through surveys conducted by the Public Opinion Programme, and focusing on both time series analyses and indexes building. Email: edward.tai@hkupop.hku.hk.

Tseng, Sheng-wen is Assistant Professor of the Development of Leisure Management and also Director of the Leisure Business Consulting and Developing Center and Deputy Director of the Center for China's Economics and Trade Studies at the Yu Da University of Science and Technology, Taiwan (ROC). His research focuses on industrial innovation, industrial organization, cultural economics, and tourism industry in Taiwan, as well as China's regional development. Email: swtseng@ydu.edu.tw/g9261502@yahoo.com.tw.

Tseng, Yen-Fen is a professor of sociology at the National Taiwan University. Her research focuses on migration and city characteristics. Recent publications include "Reconfiguring Citizenship and Nationality: Dual Citizenship of Taiwanese Migrants in China" (*Citizenship Studies*) and "Shanghai Rush:

Skilled Migrants in a Fantasy City" (*Journal of Ethnic and Migration Studies*). She is a corresponding editor at the *International Journal of Urban and Regional Research.* Email: yftseng@ntu.edu.tw.

Wang, Jenn-hwan is Chair Professor of the Graduate Institute of Development Studies at the National Chengchi University, Taiwan. His research focuses on innovation and technology in Taiwan, South Korea, and China, Taiwan's economic development, as well as China's regional development. His most recent book is *The Limits of Fast Follower: Taiwan's Economic Transition and Innovation* (Chuliu Publisher, 2010). Email: wangjh@nccu.edu.tw.

Xiao, Suowei is an assistant professor in the School of Social Development and Public Policy at Beijing Normal University. Her research interests include gender, marriage, and family, social inequality, migration, and health. She has been published in *Men and Masculinities, Vaccine, China Journal of Social Work,* and *Sociological Review of China,* among other academic journals. She is currently working on a book manuscript on the contemporary second-wife phenomenon in China. Xiao received her Ph.D. in Sociology from the University of California at Berkeley and her B.A. in Chinese Literature from Peking University. Email: xiao@bnu.edu.cn.

Acknowledgments

This book originates from the study group of Taiwanese enterprises (called *Taishang*) in the Center for China Studies, National Chengchi University, Taiwan. The group consists of scholars from various universities in Taiwan, and we intensively discussed related socioeconomic issues regarding Taiwanese outward investments to China and their impact on social relations and national identity almost every month since early 2011. Because the issues are so significant in current China–Taiwan relations, we decided to hold a conference, and to invite scholars from Hong Kong, China, as well as from Japan to participate, so as to compare the similar cross-border issues and to highlight the theoretical significance of the phenomenon. The conference, called "Border Crossing in Greater China: Production, Community and Identity," was held on September 13–14, 2012, in National Chengchi University, Taiwan. All chapters in this book were and have been revised from the conference papers.

As the editor, I want to thank the TOP University Program of National Chengchi University for its financial support. It was due to this support that we have the resource to engage regularly in intensive meetings and debates. Of course, I also want to thank the authors who devoted their time in numerous weekends to engage in hardworking workshops in the Center for China Studies. If not for their hearty devotion, it would not have been possible for this book to be published. Also, I am grateful for those discussants of the conference who provided valuable comments to improve the quality of our chapters. They are: Te-Sheng Chen, Ray-may Hsung, Ruey-ling Tzeng, Shu-ling Hwang, Ching-hsin Yu, Yukihito Sato, Ming-chi Chen, and Fei-yu Hsieh. Finally, I also want to pay my deep gratitude to Ms. Yi-horng Chiang for her laborious assistance at almost every step in the preparation of this book; and to Ms. Yi-chih Huang, and Dr. Tsung-yuan Chen, for their editorial assistance of proofreading at the final stage of the whole book.

1 Introduction

Crossing borders in Greater China – a multidimensional perspective

Jenn-hwan Wang

Introduction

This book is about the transformation of borderlines in the Greater China region, defined as the socioeconomic region of China, Taiwan and Hong Kong, in which China has emerged as a super power in the world economy in recent years. China has changed from being a poor and underdeveloped country into a giant market power in the world within just about three decades, which as a consequence has altered the socioeconomic power relations among the parties involved within the region. Along with this sea change has been the massive flow of capital and people from Taiwan as well as Hong Kong to China to seek business opportunities and new lifestyles. The huge movements of people and capital across borders have as a result transformed the borderlines set up in the Cold War atmosphere (Hsing, 1997; Wang, 2001; Chang, 2006; Deng, 2009). Now, more and more people from Taiwan and Hong Kong are periodically working and living in urban China, immersing themselves in the rising middle class residential areas, which are in particular located in the prosperous cities of the Eastern coastal provinces. In addition, some of them may send their children to local schools in China to seek future opportunities in the rising economy. A more interesting question is: Will the increase in social interaction and the shrinking of borderlines bring about a convergence of identity among the people involved?

The purpose of this book is to describe and analyze the process of the transformation of borders in Greater China, with special attention being paid to the Taiwanese side, and to a lesser extent, Hong Kong. Borders or boundaries were initially conceived of as a manifestation of the territories of states, which are no more than legal lines separating sovereign jurisdictions (Newman and Paasi, 1998: 189; Anderson and O'Dowd, 1999: 594). Since the establishment of the Westphalia system in 1648, the modern state system recognizes that the nation state is able to exercise its sovereign power – the exclusive right to exercise legitimate violence within the limits of a territory – to allocate resources, forge a national identity, enforce its surveillance power even against its people's will and be immune from outside interference (Giddens, 1990; Weber, 1978). Borders or boundaries thus tend to be established by international agreements and mutual understanding among states. In addition, borders intimately related to the sovereign nation state simultaneously unify and separate, as well as include and exclude people.

Nevertheless, the ideas that connect borders with the territory and sovereignty of the state have been challenged in recent years. The challenges mainly come from (1) the globalization process that erodes the sovereign power of the nation state; (2) the social and cultural construction of space that highlights the social boundaries rather than the state boundaries; and (3) the construction of a local or ethnic identity as opposed to a national one that is mediated by narratives and discourses.[1] All the above challenges maintain that borders are products of social construction (Simmel, 1997; Newman and Paasi, 1998), which also relate to the issues of geographic scale in which the power of the nation state has been de-territorialized and re-territorialized in the age of globalization (Brenner, 1999; Jessop, 2002).

The recent transformation of the Greater China region is particularly illuminating regarding the above contesting of borderline issues. First of all, Taiwan's economy has been gradually integrated into the massive Chinese market that broke the borderlines set up in 1949. For example, the Taiwanese economy now depends much more on the Chinese counterpart for its current and future economic prosperity. In the early 2000s, China accounted for over 42 percent of Taiwan's total approved outward investment (Ministry of Economic Affairs, 2005). Since then, the major commodity export markets from Taiwan have rapidly shifted from the US to China (via Hong Kong). Now, Taiwanese investments in China account for their largest share, reaching as high as 62.8 percent during the 1991–2013 period, and the investments have spread to all areas of China, especially the Yangtze River Delta Area (Mainland Affairs Council, 2013). It is very clear that the economic border has been shrinking rapidly which engenders tensions with political borders.

Second, as more and more Taiwanese people live in urban China, some of them become rooted in Chinese soil and choose to stay there as residents. The borderlines between Taiwanese and Chinese seem to be becoming very blurred. Differing from the situation in the 1990s when Chinese brides chose to marry Taiwanese men and to stay in Taiwan, now more and more Taiwanese males work in China, get married there and stay (Deng, 2009). This outcome has become all the more common as many Taiwanese have sought job opportunities in China. It seems that social inclusion has followed the economic integration and become a new tendency.

In addition to the above phenomena, an even more delicate and complicated issue is the identity issue: Taiwanese or Chinese? Will those who stay in China for a long time identify themselves as Chinese instead of Taiwanese? This issue is particularly interesting because the Taiwanese consciousness has been rising due to the democratization process since the 1980s, as a result of which the Chinese identity has been in decline (Wu, 2005; Keng et al., 2006). However, concurrent with this rising Taiwanese consciousness has been the increase in economic integration across the Taiwan Strait. The divergent political and economic tendencies have triggered tension among people on the island regarding the issue of national identity. In the pre-democratization era, the Chinese identity prevailed due to the Kuomintang Party's (KMT) Mainland Chinese origin; in the process of democratization, the native Taiwanese identity prevailed; now, as the economic integration rapidly proceeds, a new wave of identity conflict is emerging along with the social inclusion phenomenon mentioned above. This is especially interesting when compared with the case of Hong Kong where the social and economic integration with China has proceeded more quickly and deeply than in the case of Taiwan following Hong Kong becoming a special administrative zone of China in 1997.

This chapter, and some other chapters in this book, will use the contesting concepts of borderlines or boundaries to explore the transformation of social, economic and identity issues in the Greater China area, especially concerning the Taiwanese side. Therefore, in a way that differs from most existing publications, which mainly deal with observable macro-political and economic issues, this book is chiefly concerned with the recent micro-social and economic transformation underlying the most observable surface tendencies. More precisely, if most existing publications in the Greater China region are by and large concerned with high-level politics and the macro-economy, this book is more focused on the micro levels of cross-border *production*, the daily routines of *community life*, as well as *identity* formation and transformation due to the increasing social interactions across borders.

The border as a contesting agenda

The idea that borders are conceived of as a manifestation of the territories of nation states has been largely amended in recent years. Now, borders are regarded as equally social, political, economic and discursive constructions. Economically, the digital revolution has compressed the geographical space into a "space of flows" that replaces the space of places (Castells, 1996). At a social level, more and more social groupings have constructed their "own" territories to include "themselves" and to exclude "others" (Agnew, 1994); Culturally, various social and ethnic groups have crafted their own narrations to create identities and boundaries of their own in order to differentiate between "us" and "them" (Somers, 1994; Simmel, 1997). All of these factors have changed the meaning of borders, which we will discuss as follows.

Globalization and border transformation

Recent discussions on the geographic transformation of contemporary capitalism have found that capitalist territorial organizations are constantly being reconfigured due to incessantly spatial movements of capital that have reconstituted the geographical landscape (Harvey, 1990; Brenner, 1999). This has especially been the case in recent decades when the telecommunications revolution largely shortened the distance between physically separated locations. The "space of flows" has replaced the "space of places," as Castells (1996) maintains, through which space has been conquered by time and has given rise to the effect of "time and space compression" (Harvey, 1990).

Indeed, current capitalist developments have unleashed the animal spirits of capital that has constantly sought to enlarge market profits, through which the traditional sovereign power of the nation state has been transformed. On the one hand, capital movements have sought to escape from the territorial trap and to expand to operate on a global scale, such as through the creation of global production networks or financial transactions via the Internet (Harvey, 1990; Castells, 1996). The state's power in this situation has thus been de-territorialized. On the other hand, capital still seeks to have a relatively fixed, provisionally stabilized territorial organization for which the elements of capital accumulation are easy to find, such as industrial clusters for manufacturing activities (Saxenian, 1994; Malmberg and Maskell, 2002; Maskell, 2005) or global cities for financial capital (Friedmann, 1986; Sassen, 1991; Brenner, 1999). To search for a "spatial fix" is therefore a constant moment of re-territorialization in the current capitalism (Brenner, 1999: 42).

Related to the above spatial reconfiguration of capitalism is the transformation of state power. The de-territorialization process of capital has eroded and relativized the territorial state power, through which the national geographical border is also being reconfigured. Capital movements have gone beyond the state's spatial enclosure and sought to find a new spatial fix elsewhere. Therefore, capital is not placeless or rootless, and always involves a reconfiguration of territorial infrastructure that is good for capital accumulation as the new re-territorialization process is embarked upon.

The de-territorialization and re-territorialization processes thus involve the creation of a wide range of policy and institutional developments designed to retain or attract capital investment. For advanced countries, the post-Fordist era has led to an erosion of the Keynesian Welfare State in favor of the Schumpeterian Workfare State (Jessop, 2002), through which internationalization, flexibility and innovation have become the major reconstruction principles in the search for global competitiveness. The developing countries, by contrast, have been able to use the de-territorialization process of capital to reconfigure the local infrastructure and new legal regimes to establish a "spatial fix" for capital flows from advanced countries (Wang and Lee, 2007).

Borderlines have been reconfigured and sovereign state power has also been transformed in recent decades. Unlike the conventional wisdom that assumes that nation states are "power containers," they are now struggling to reconstruct their containing power against the global power of the market. In this age of neoliberalism, global market power seems to be dominant, although political backfiring has always existed and is an empirical question that we will discuss later.

Social and cultural construction of borders

Globalization does not create a world of homogenization but rather fragmentization (Agnew, 1994; Castells, 1996). In recent years, the idea of borders has increasingly tended to be applied in a metaphoric sense and does not necessarily refer to the material physical space. It thus refers to the social and cultural construction of boundaries between social collectivities through which social distinctions are constructed (Simmel, 1997; Newman and Paasi, 1998: 188). Simmel thus argued that social space based on boundaries closes the social groups off from the rest of the world; however, it also holds them together subject to their own rules. A boundary strengthens the "psychological coherence of individual persons' and 'reinforces the unity and reality of the social group" (Simmel, 1997: 141). Therefore, the social boundary is "not a spatial fact with sociological consequences, but a sociological fact that is formed spatially" (ibid), indicating that boundaries provide spatial configurations for experience and interaction.

In urban areas, migrants and local inhabitants may develop different social gatherings and create various spatial organizations. In general, ethnic groups tend to use boundaries as a means to construct their own space in order to differentiate between "us" and "them." In this case, boundaries are institutionalized into norms that separate groups and communities from each other (Simmel, 1997). However, norms have both constraining and facilitating functions in relation to social actions; therefore, boundaries provide normative rules to regulate interactions between members of social groups; they also facilitate social exchanges as well. In some specific cases, boundaries may be determined by social sphere and shared by groups across physical state borders. This is especially found in border regions where communities have been divided by national borders but are unified by the same culture (Newman and Paasi, 1998; Brunet-Jailly, 2005).

In the contemporary world, borders and boundaries have become concomitant with the aims of various social groups to define and redefine the relations between social and physical space (Newman and Paasi, 1998: 188). Although some groups tend to have the desire to build spatial turf to maintain homogeneity and exclude others, still other groups may want to include other groups to build a melting pot. The social construction of a place and border thus reflects the power relations and the social struggles involved in the construction process.

Social construction of identities

The social constructions of borders and identities are the two sides of the same coin. The construction of identity, however, largely depends on discourses and narratives. As Somers (1994) notes, it is through stories that we come to know and make sense of the social world which constitutes our social identity. The construction of a national imagined community also takes place via the process of narration through which a collective identity is formed (Anderson, 1991).

The construction of identity narratives is itself obviously a part of political action, which may relate to power relations in a society where the dominant group has much more discursive power in hedging national hegemony. In other words, in the study of state boundaries, it is important to know whose "plots" or "turfs" dominate these identity narratives, what is excluded or included by them, and how the representations of "us" and "them" are produced and reproduced in various social practices, such as the media, education, etc.

(Newman and Paasi, 1998: 196)

The construction of identity is also a contesting process where various narrations and discourses are struggling for hegemonic status. The state, as Jessop (1990) suggests, is a social relationship and is an institutional ensemble that is opened to political struggle for various interests and advantages. However, as an institutional form, the state is not equally accessible to every interest, and it has a "strategic selectivity" characteristic, because the state is viewed "as a system whose structure and *modus operandi* are more open to some types of political strategy than others" (Jessop, 1990: 260). The state is thus the site of struggles where strategies are selected and elaborated. The dominant group that holds the state power will tend to construct "hegemonic projects" to build popular support. Such hegemonic projects have the "national popular" characteristic that has "political, intellectual and moral leadership" and which goes beyond short-term class interests (Jessop, 1990: 208). The discursive narration of each "nation" legitimizes its own territory and establishes its own border, which as a consequence reflects and constructs both its collective and individual consciousness.

In sum, state boundaries are equally social, political and discursive constructs as opposed to naturalized, physical lines drawn between nation states. As Newman and Paasi (1998: 187) argue, "boundaries and their meanings are historically contingent, and they are part of the production and institutionalization of territories and territoriality." Borderlines can shape and also be reshaped by market forces, and equally construct and be reconstructed by the social, cultural and powerful discursive narrations of specific ethnic groups. These different forces are not congruent with each other in the contemporary age of globalization, and can only be studied empirically as we will show in the Taiwanese case as follows.

Transformation of borderlines across the Taiwan Strait

In the year 1987, the KMT regime lifted the Martial Law which had been implemented since 1950 in Taiwan and officially ended the Civil War with the People's Republic of China (PRC) that had been waged ever since (Wang, 1996). From then on, the KMT regime began to relax its border controls, first of all to let Mainlander veterans visit their families in China, and then to allow Taiwanese businesses to invest and tourists to visit China in the early 1990s. In addition, Taiwan recently also began to allow Chinese tourists to visit Taiwan, students to study in universities and capital to be invested in Taiwan's market. All in all, the formidable territorial borders established by the Civil War era have been torn down. Now it is estimated that over one million Taiwanese constantly live in China and the trend is increasing. By contrast, there are also increasing numbers of Mainland Chinese constantly living in Taiwan either for marriage or for business purposes. The interactions between Taiwanese and Chinese in the territories of both China and Taiwan have changed the political, economic and social boundaries across the Taiwan Strait. As will be discussed below, while the Taiwanese economy has been integrated into the enormous Chinese market, the social and cultural constructions of borderlines and identities in Taiwan have proceeded in a direction that is not congruent.

The rescaling of borderlines: economic integration

Taiwanese outward investment to Mainland China started in the 1980s when Taiwanese business people used various channels, such as Hong Kong or the Cayman Islands, to indirectly invest in the four special economic regions of China due to the government's official restrictions (Wang, 2001). After the lifting of the ban on those restrictions in 1993, Taiwanese outward direct investment to China increased rapidly. In general, Taiwanese investments in China can be divided into four stages. The first stage was in the early 1990s when many traditional small and medium-sized enterprises (SMEs) and labor-intensive industries began to move to the area around the Pearl River Delta to manufacture their products for export. The second stage took place in the late 1990s when many Taiwanese high-tech firms were required by big global buyers to relocate their assembly activities to the Yangtze River Delta region in order to lower their costs to compete in the world market. Therefore, in a way that was different from the former stage, the movement of Taiwanese capital at this stage involved a higher level of technology. In the third stage, starting around 2005, many Taiwanese consumer service-oriented industries began to launch their businesses in the coastal area cities in order to take advantage of the booming domestic market in China. From this stage on, Taiwanese business people began to influence the lifestyle of the emerging Chinese middle class in big cities (Chang, 2006; Tseng, 2011). From the 2010s on, Taiwanese investments have begun to move again into the interior provinces, such as Sichuan, Hubei and Henan, as labor costs in the coastal areas have kept on rising in recent years (Chapter 8).

Overall, the electronics component sector was the largest category among the Taiwanese investments in China during the period 1991–2012. According to the Mainland Affairs Council (MAC), it accounted for 19.7 percent of the total investment, and was followed by computers and related opto-electronics, which accounted for about 13.8 percent of the total during the same period (MAC, 2013). In other words, the electronics category comprised about 33.5 percent of the total investment. Nevertheless, more and more investments in the service sector have also begun to follow suit in recent years, such as wholesale services, finance and insurance. Since 2010, there has been more than US$1 billion in investment in each year (ibid).

In terms of investment destination, Jiangsu has replaced Guangdong by becoming the most favorable investment province for Taiwanese businesses in recent years. It in fact has accumulated most of the capital investments during the whole of the 1991–2012 period (ibid). When Jiangsu, Shanghai and Zhejiang are added together, the Yangtze River Delta has accumulated most (50 percent) of the Taiwanese investment (Table 1.1). Nevertheless, because of the movement toward the interior provinces, Taiwanese investment in Sichuan has increased rapidly.

The increase in Taiwanese investment in China has transformed the trade relationship between Taiwan and the US. In fact, China has replaced the US in becoming the largest trading partner for Taiwan in 2001; and its share has increased year by year. Taiwan's trade dependency ratio in relation to China (exports to China/total exports) has kept on rising since the early 1990s. It rose from 28.4 percent and reached 41.8 percent in 2010 (MAC, 2013). China is now not only the largest trading partner, but also the largest source of Taiwan's trade surplus. In 2011, Taiwan has a trade surplus with China of as high as US$40.3 billion, and had a similar surplus with Hong Kong of US$38.4 billion. Adding these two together, the figure reached US$78.7 billion. In the same year, Taiwan recorded a trade surplus of about US$26.9 billion. It is obvious that Taiwan has generated most of the trade surplus from China so as to compensate for its deficit with several other areas.

Indeed, China has become Taiwan's largest outward investment destination, trading partner, source of its trade surplus and largest export market. Taiwan's economy is gradually being integrated into the Chinese market. Moreover, it is also because of Taiwanese investments in China that the Taiwanese electronics industry has been able to gain its irreplaceable status in the world market which in turn has contributed to China becoming the top exporter of high-tech industrial products in the world (Wang, 2011).

The shrinking of political borders due to the increasing economic integration and geographical rescaling can be shown in the trend toward the economic upgrading of Taiwanese investments in China. We can use the example of increasing investments in R&D in the electronics industry to reveal the tendency.

As for the upgrading of industrial investments, most existing studies have found that the tendency has been changing from traditional to high-tech

Table 1.1 Taiwanese outward investment in China, by area

Years/ Rank	2011		2012		1991–2012	
	Area	% of total capital	Area	% of total capital	Area	% of total capital
01	Jiangsu	30.79	Jiangsu	27.0	Jiangsu	33.1
02	Guangdong	15.34	Shanghai	16.8	Guangdong	20.6
03	Shanghai	15.13	Guangdong	11.1	Shanghai	14.8
04	Sichuan	6.45	Fujian	8.6	Fujian	7.0
05	Fujian	6.42	Zhejiang	7.8	Zhejiang	6.6
06	Zhejiang	5.04	Sichuan	6.0	Shandong	2.3

Source: MAC (2013).

industries and to professional services such as those provided by architects. Recent studies, however, have found that the tendency has moved upward from manufacturing to R&D segments, especially in the electronics and semiconductor industries (Chen, 2004; Ernst, 2006, 2010). Wang and Tseng's (Chapter 2) study on the cross-border integrated circuit (IC) design industry finds that there are three types of innovation networks: global firm-led, foundry-led and IC design firm-led innovation networks. In the first type of cross-border innovation networks, the global branding PC firms have outsourced all design works to key Taiwanese contractors. Taiwanese PC firms have thus set up R&D subsidiaries, including embedded software in China, to take advantage of the low costs to produce PCs for the branding firms. In the second type of cross-border innovation networks, which are constructed by Taiwanese foundries (TSMC and UMC), the networks have been built due to the motivation in expanding the market share by assisting local Chinese IC design firms so as to create new business clients and business partners. The third type of cross-border innovation networks have been created by both large and small Taiwanese IC design firms to fully explore the huge emerging telecommunications market in which the IC design giant MediaTek has had an especially significant role to play. Wang and Tseng (Chapter 2) have also found that the dominant power of the innovation networks is still in the hands of Taiwanese headquarters. In other words, the Taiwanese part has tended to engage in core, process technology and product development R&D activities, whereas the Chinese counterparts have tended to be involved in improving, localization and manufacturing R&D, as well as in performing the function of basic research by collaborating with major universities.

In addition, in a way that differs from the former enclave style when Taiwanese firms were mainly embedded within their own circles, now more and more Taiwanese firms have been localized. Cheng's (Chapter 3) study of the shoe industry also finds that, in a departure from the former stage when Taiwanese investments had few local partners, more and more Taiwanese firms are now incorporating local Chinese suppliers into their supply chains and are establishing local production networks. The re-territorialization process is also observed in the professional service sector. As Chien (Chapter 4) shows, Taiwanese architectural professionals, in addition to the industrial sector, have moved their ventures into the big cities in China and have contributed deeply to the new wave of urban spatial restructuring in China to serve the needs of the enormous domestic market. In order to do such business, establishing good social relations with local bureaucrats is said to be necessary in China. Shigeto Sonoda (Chapter 5) shows how businessmen have figured out ways to deal with local bureaucrats, or *guanxi*, in order to enable their investments to receive better treatment, regardless of whether they are Taiwanese, Japanese or Korean. Surprisingly, this chapter shows that Korean businessmen depend the most among the three groups on *guanxi* to do business.

In sum, the Taiwanese economy has been deeply integrated into the Chinese market, changing from investment mainly in manufacturing to R&D activities; and from traditional to high-tech industries. The political border has been compressed by the shrinking of economic boundaries. The territorialized economy in the former stage had been de-territorialized, and has recently been re-territorialized into the Chinese soil. This tendency moreover has been speeding up as more and more Taiwanese businesses in the consumer service sector have gone to China in recent years to take advantage of the booming Chinese domestic market, to which we now turn.

Reconstitution of social borders: across residential boundaries

Along with the physical and manufacturing investments is the cross-boundary mobility of people from Taiwan to Mainland China. The pattern of the social interaction of Taiwanese with the local Chinese community has changed along with the ways in which Taiwanese investment has taken place in the Chinese market. The general patterns of the transformation that can be roughly described as Taiwanese have changed from "enclave" to "immersion," and from isolation to adaptation in interacting with local society (Lin, 2009). The social borders have become murky along with the evolution of the economic integration.

At the initial stage of the cross-boundary mobility were the owners of SMEs and their cadres. Due to the backwardness of the Chinese urban environment at the initial stages of the economic reform, Taiwanese businessmen tended to live in the dorms of the factory and isolated themselves from the Chinese community. They went out from the dorms only in the evenings or on weekends, and sometimes they went to karaoke hostess bars in the cities where they were able to enjoy relaxation and commercial sex (Shen, 2008; Chapter 9). There were also many Taiwanese businessmen who built another family by having a mistress, or second wife (er nai), in the cities where they bought houses isolated from local communities and lived like families (Xiao, 2011; Chapter 10). A "second wife" is currently the popular name for a Chinese woman involved in a long-term relationship with a married man upon whom she depends financially. This residential isolation continued for some time as the Chinese economy continued to grow and the local real estate market started to boom. Sometimes, Taiwanese businessmen would bring their families with them. This situation continued until the late 1990s (Deng, 2009).

The enclave and isolated residential phenomenon changed radically around the turn of the new millennium when the Chinese domestic market nurtured the emergence of a middle class. Now a new group of small business owners went to China to open shops, such as those providing wedding photos, coffee shops and food chain stores, in the consumer service industry (Chang, 2006; Chapter 6). Differing from the former stage when the investments were concentrated in manufacturing, now the new tendency was focused on the domestic consumer service market. Consumer service markets are very different from manufacturing in that there is a need to reach the consumers and to know the local people. In addition, in a way that is different from the former stage when the owners (men) moved alone to China, now the new wave is family-oriented. As part of this new tendency, more and more Taiwanese have moved to China and have lived in the

Chinese urban community and integrated themselves into the Chinese neighborhood (Tseng, 2011).

Along with this process of new investments in consumer service products, now Taiwanese-style restaurants and wedding photo shops are everywhere in China and have influenced the lifestyle of the rising Chinese middle class, i.e., this can be clearly observed in the case of Suzhou where most Taiwanese ICT firms have been concentrated (Chapter 6). Kunshan city in the Suzhou municipality was even referred to as "little Taipei" due to its concentration of Taiwanese people and shops. "Taiwan" or "Taipei" has become quality brands in the Chinese market. Moreover, as income levels have rapidly risen in the coastal areas of China, more and more investments by Taiwanese in sophisticated consumer goods and services have also taken place in China and they have largely affected the lifestyle of the rising middle class.

Similarly, as China becomes more prosperous, many Taiwanese are beginning to migrate to China, not merely for economic reasons, but also for lifestyle purposes – pursuing a certain cultural imagination of the host country and enjoying a privileged lifestyle (Chapter 7). Indeed, in recent years, many Taiwanese have moved to prosperous coastal cities in China to enjoy the privileged status which they were not able to enjoy in Taiwan due to the differentiation of commodity prices. Some of them have also begun to move to inner cities where the cost of living is much lower, and they can still enjoy a high standard of living by having much lower living expenses as compared to those in Taiwan.

In contrast to the above lifestyle phenomenon is the ongoing new investments by Taiwanese firms in interior provinces due to the rapidly rising labor costs in coastal areas. Interestingly, Taiwanese firms are no longer building gated factories that are cut off from local communities. They have instead collaborated with the local communities in order to recruit local workers. A new type of locally embedded Taiwanese firm has been created which has not been seen in the coastal areas before. Now they have to build good relationships with the local community so that rural people may have the desire to work for the manufacturing firm. The rising labor costs in the coastal areas have dramatically changed the factory-community relations in China at present (Chapter 8).

Along with Taiwanese investments in China when male cadres had to work alone in China for long periods of time, more and more cross-border marriages have emerged. In the past, Taiwanese cadres (male) tended to bring their Chinese wives back to Taiwan to apply for Taiwan citizenship and stay in Taiwan. However, in recent years, as the Chinese domestic market has grown rapidly, female partners have tended to have more job opportunities in China than in Taiwan. Moreover, due to Taiwan's legal regulations, the female Chinese partner has to stay in Taiwan at least for two years in order to find a suitable job. Under this situation, the female Chinese partner thus does not have the motivation to apply for Taiwan citizenship and even does not have the intention to move to Taiwan. On the contrary, a new tendency has emerged where the Taiwanese male stays with his wife in China to work and remain there for the long term!

Furthermore, there are more and more Taiwanese students who have moved from the island to attend schools in China. Differing from the children of Taiwanese business people who have grown up in China and have to study there, those Taiwanese students who have voluntarily chosen to study in China are doing so mainly to enhance their career opportunities. China began to open its universities for Hong Kong, Macau and Taiwanese residents in 1985, and the first Taiwanese students went to study in China in 1987. In 2005, besides the decision that overseas Chinese would pay the same fees as local Chinese students, China also allowed Taiwanese to work in China after their graduation. According to Chinese statistics, there were 7,346 Taiwanese studying in China in 2012, with most of them studying Chinese medicine, business and law and being concentrated in Guangdong, Shanghai, Wuhan and Chengdu.

According to Lin (2010), the major reasons for those students deciding to study in China were: (1) to look forward to the future developments; or (2) to enter into the fields that they were not able to study in Taiwan, such as archeology or Chinese medicine. Lin (2010) also found that more and more Taiwanese college students were tending to stay in China to develop their own careers and work with their Chinese classmates. Returning to Taiwan was no longer the priority.

To sum up, along with the Taiwanese investments that have changed from being focused on manufacturing to consumer goods, Taiwanese residency in China has also switched from enclave-type living to immersion within the local communities. The spatial borders have been broken, thus allowing Taiwanese to be integrated into local residential areas. Moreover, cross-Strait marriages and study have also changed from being uni-directional to being bi-directional. Even more striking is the tendency for Taiwanese males to move together with their wives to China to stay there, which has created a new wave of residential inclusion and social integration.

In fact, more and more Taiwanese now are seeking opportunities to work in China, including professionals such as architects and cultural workers (Chapter 4 and Chapter 11). While they have tended to retain their professional pride because they have thought that they have better professional training, nevertheless, they have still had to use the market expansion opportunities in China to extend their professional careers. Indeed, the social borders across the Taiwan Strait have been changing in recent years, and the social distance between Taiwanese and Chinese has been shrinking rapidly. However, whether the change in social borders can be translated into identity transformation is another story to which we will now turn.

The transformation of the identity border: assimilation into Chinese society?

The identity issue is much more complicated as compared to the above two phenomena, especially when it refers to the border of national identity. National identity refers to an individual's self-perception of national and political belongings. This also relates to the construction of nationalism by way of narration and storytelling by specific groups to convey to people that they belong to the same nation (Anderson, 1991). The construction of nationalism involves a process of discursive struggle in which different groups contest for hegemonic status. The group that gains the state apparatus has the discursive power and enjoys the hegemonic status.

On the issue of identity, Taiwanese business people or migrants in China have faced a very awkward situation in recent years (Tseng and Wu, 2011). This relates to the change in hegemonic national identity in Taiwan following the democratization in the 1980s. Before the 1980s, the national identity constructed by the KMT regime, led by Mainlanders, was based on Chinese identity; therefore, in the old KMT regime's rhetoric, Taiwan was attached to the "Chinese" nation (Wang, 1996). However, after 1990, the new KMT regime, controlled by native Taiwanese, not only promoted Taiwanese consciousness but also treated it as a legitimate national identity. To use Jessop's (1990: 181) term, the new regime launched a new "hegemonic project" through which a new national identity was constructed. This new identity has become a hegemonic status after 2000 when the original opposition party, the Democratic Progressive Party that promoted Taiwan independence, gained state power. From then on, an institutional process of "de-China-lization" and Taiwanization in basic national education and mass media has been propagated. Taiwanese consciousness has now become a legitimate and dominant national identity. This transformation of national identity, however, has not progressed smoothly. There have been contested issues on the island that have revolved around "Taiwanese" versus "Chinese," or "Taiwanese nation" versus "Chinese nation," and which have also inevitably given rise to ethnic conflicts between Mainlanders and Taiwanese (Wu, 2005). Some Taiwan independence advocates regard Mainlanders and those who invested in China as renegades of the Taiwan nation; this ethnic tension was intensified during the era of DPP rule from 2000 to 2008.

In 2008, the KMT took over the state power again and began to relax many restrictions set by the former DPP regime on cross-Strait interactions, including letting Chinese tourists visit Taiwan, allowing Chinese students to study in Taiwan's universities, and welcoming Chinese capital for investment in certain industries in Taiwan. The radical transformation of social borders created by the state has increased the intensity of social interactions. Before, it was only the Taiwanese who went to China; now more and more Chinese have the opportunity to visit Taiwan.

Will the increase in social interactions across the Taiwan Strait heighten the Chinese identity in Taiwan? A poll on national identity, conducted by the Election Center of National Chengchi University, has shown that the Taiwanese identity (identifying oneself as Taiwanese) has been constantly rising (increasing from 17.6 percent in 1992 to 52.4 percent in 2010), while the Chinese identity has by contrast been declining. This of course has to do with the democratization process in which the Taiwanese identity has been upgraded to the national level. By contrast, the Chinese identity has lost its hegemonic status due to the fact that it has no institutional agents that can legitimize the narration and discourse. Therefore, as the Chinese identity lacks institutional support, it does not have the discursive power to influence the identity formation. In other words, the increase in social interaction has not translated into a convergence of national identity; on the contrary, it has strengthened the divergence.

Interestingly, Hong Kong has exhibited a similar tendency in strengthening its own identity. Different from Taiwan, which still maintains national sovereignty, Hong Kong was returned to China in 1997 and is regarded by the PRC as a showcase of its "One Country Two Systems" policy which may have political implications for Taiwan in the future. Robert Chung and Edward Tai (Chapter 13) use data from the Public Opinion Program at the University of Hong Kong to show that more and more Hong Kong people regard themselves as Hong Kongers than they do Chinese. This feeling of the distinctiveness of being Hong Kong people has become increasingly strong in recent years, particularly among the youth. In other words, the greater the interaction between Hong Kong and China, the higher the proportion of Hong Kong people who regard themselves as different from Chinese.

The rise of the Hong Kong identity as opposed to the Chinese one has been related to the rise of a stream of popular discourse in constructing Hong Kong as being different from Mainland China. As Angelina Chin (Chapter 14) shows, these discourses have gained widespread popular influence among the Hong Kong people who imagine themselves as being part of a transnational Diaspora which despises the Chinese immigrants who recently migrated to Hong Kong. They criticize the PRC for being authoritarian so as to show that Hong Kong has a different culture inherited from the British colonialist rule as compared to the Chinese authoritarian culture. The discourse is being contested and has triggered political debates that have influenced the ways in which Hong Kong people identify themselves. Currently, the formation of a Hong Kong identity continues to be ongoing and is being contested politically.

Compared to the identity issue that is being contested in domestic politics in Taiwan, it is very difficult and politically sensitive to directly study the same national identity issue in regard to Taiwanese business people in China. Lin et al's. (Chapter 12) study insightfully breaks down the identity issue into three dimensions of social assimilation: (1) the arrangements regarding the children's education; (2) the family's local friends; and (3) the plans for retirement. That is to say, the higher the possibility of sending the children to a local school, of making local friends and of planning to retire in China, the higher the degree of their being assimilated into Chinese society. By combining the above three dimensions, they find that although a self-claimed national identity is still important in explaining whether Taiwanese people have decided to identify with the local society, the social class factor indeed matters in explaining how Taiwanese in China make decisions regarding their children's education and make friends with local people. It implies that, as China grows richer, more Taiwanese will probably maintain stable and friendly working relations with the local Chinese rather than remain aloof from them.

In sum, as China becomes more prosperous than before, more and more Taiwanese are tending to accept the idea of working, studying and even retiring in China. However, the hardcore Taiwanese identity has not been changed, and instead has been strengthened. Interestingly, Hong Kong has exhibited a similar tendency, although it has been a part of China since 1997. The shrinking of social and economic borders has indeed strengthened the domestic national identity instead of moving in a congruent way.

Conclusion: the rise of a local identity and anxiety over integration

The changes in cross-Strait relations since the late 1980s have radically transformed the borderlines and political and economic boundaries between Taiwan and China. Economically, the Taiwanese economy has been rapidly absorbed into the enormous Chinese market and has depended heavily on it for prosperity. Socially, along with the change in the economic borderlines has been the increase in the number of Taiwanese business people staying and working in Mainland China. Some of those people have now tended to become local residents and to live in Chinese middle-class neighborhoods, which is very different from the situation in the initial stage when Taiwanese business people lived in enclave communities that were isolated from the local people. Moreover, more and more Taiwanese business people and students have chosen to take the opportunity to work in China to further their careers. The social borderlines have experienced shrinking and rescaling.

Nevertheless, the tendencies toward social and economic integration between Taiwan, Hong Kong and China have not been without resistance. As we have shown, the phenomenon of a rising local/national identity has become evident in both areas and has developed in a divergent manner in contrast to the social and economic integration. Furthermore, as a result of the shrinking of borders and the rise of a Taiwanese identity in Taiwan's politics, there has been an increasing sense of anxiety in recent years. Will Taiwan be merged by China? Will China use the leverage of economic integration to ask for political unification in the future? Moreover, because of the loss of economic dynamism in Taiwan in recent years, more and more young people regard working in China as both acceptable and inevitable. A sense of anxiety based on the complicated nexus of national identity and economic integration has thus been generated. This anxiety will continue as the geographic borderlines continue to shrink. In addition, it can be expected that China will continue to use its economic and social powers to influence Taiwanese society, i.e., such as through the setting up of Taiwanese business associations in

China (Keng and Schubert, 2010). However, as long as it is not able to generate institutional "discursive power," the sense of anxiety in Taiwan will continue for a certain period of time and the anxiety may generate an identity conflict as it faces the increased integration of its economy with the Chinese market.

Note

1 The cross-boundary identity issue has also been intensively discussed in the areas such as gender and various social groupings. However, it is not the focus of our discussion in this chapter.

References

Agnew, John. 1994. "The Territorial Trap: The Geographical Assumptions of International Relations Theory." *Review of International Political Economy* 1 (1): 53–80.

Anderson, Benedict. 1991. *Imagined Communities: Reflections on the Origin and Spread of Nationalism*. London: Verso.

Anderson, James, and Liam O'Dowd. 1999. "Borders, Border Regions and Territoriality: Contradictory Meanings, Changing Significance." *Regional Studies* 33 (7): 593–604.

Brenner, Neil. 1999. "Beyond State-centrism? Space, Territoriality, and Geographical Scale in Globalization Studies." *Theory and Society* 28 (1): 39–78.

Brunet-Jailly, Emmanuel. 2005. "Theorizing Borders: An Interdisciplinary Perspective." *Geopolitics* 10 (4): 633–649.

Castells, Manuel. 1996. *The Rise of the Network Society*. London: Blackwell.

Chang, Chia Ming. 2006. *Taiwanese Businessmen in Suzhou: Globalization and Observation of Localization*. Taipei: Crown books (In Chinese).

Chen, Shin Horng. 2004. "Taiwanese IT Firms' Offshore R&D in China and the Connection with the Global Innovation Network." *Research Policy* 33 (2): 337–349.

Deng, Jian Bang. 2009. "Making a Living on the Move: Transnational Lives of Taiwanese Managers in the Shanghai Area." *Taiwanese Sociology* 18: 139–179 (In Chinese).

Ernst, Dieter. 2006. *Innovation Offshoring: Asia's Emerging Role in Global Innovation Networks (East-West Center Special Report)*. Hawaii: East-West Center.

Ernst, Dieter. 2010. "Upgrading Through Innovation in a Small Network Economy: Insights from Taiwan's IT Industry." *Economics of Innovation and New Technology* 19 (4): 295–324.

Friedmann, John. 1986. "The World City Hypothesis." *Development and Change* 17 (1): 69–84.

Giddens, Anthony. 1990. *The Consequences of Modernity*. Cambridge: Polity Press.

Harvey, David. 1990. *The Condition of Postmodernity: An Enquiry into the Origins of Cultural Change*. Cambridge: Blackwell.

Hsing, You Tien. 1997. *Making Capitalism in China: The Taiwan Connection*. New York, NY: Oxford University Press.

Jessop, Bob. 1990. *State Theory: Putting the Capitalist State in Its Place*. Cambridge: Polity Press.

Jessop, Bob. 2002. *The Future of the Capitalist State*. Cambridge: Polity.

Keng, Shu, and Gunter Schubert. 2010. "Agents of Taiwan-China Unification? The Political Roles of Taiwanese Business People in the Process of Cross-Strait Integration." *Asian Survey* 50 (2): 287–310.

Keng, Shu, Lu Huei Chen and Kuan Po Huang. 2006. "Sense, Sensitivity, and Sophistication in Shaping the Future of Cross-Strait Relations." *Issues & Studies* 42 (4): 23–66.

Lin, Ping. 2009. "Do They Mix? The Residential Segregation of Taiwanese People in China." *Taiwanese Political Science Review* 13 (2): 57–111 (In Chinese).

Lin, Ping. 2010. "Home Alone: Taiwanese Single Women in China." *Journal of Population Studies* 41: 111–151 (In Chinese).

MAC (Mainland Affairs Council). 2013. "Cross-Strait Economic Statistics Monthly (No. 229 & No. 238)." www.mac.gov.tw/lp.asp?CtNode=5720&CtUnit=3996&BaseDSD=7&mp=1&nowPage=1&pagesize=30 (January 31, 2013) (In Chinese).

Malmberg, Anders, and Peter Maskell. 2002. "The Elusive Concept of Localization Economies: Towards a Knowledge-based Theory of Spatial Clustering." *Environment and Planning A* 34 (3): 429–449.

Maskell, Peter. 2005. "Towards a Knowledge-based Theory of the Geographical Cluster." In *Clusters, Networks, and Innovation*, eds. Stefano Breschi and Franco Malerba. Oxford: Oxford University Press.

MOEA (Ministry of Economic Affairs). 2005, 2006. "Investment Commission Statistics." http://investintaiwan.nat.gov.tw/zh-tw/opp/hdqtr.html (January 31, 2013) (In Chinese).

Newman, David, and Anssi Paasi. 1998. "Fences and Neighbours in the Postmodern World: Boundary Narratives in Political Geography." *Progress of Human Geography* 22 (2): 186–207.

Sassen, Saskia. 1991. *The Global City: New York, London, Tokyo.* Princeton, NJ: Princeton University.

Saxenian, AnnaLee. 1994. *Regional Advantage: Culture and Competition in Silicon Valley and Route 128.* Cambridge. MA: Harvard University Press.

Shen, Hsiu Hua. 2008. "The Purchase of Transnational Intimacy: Women's Bodies, Transnational Masculine Privileges in Chinese Economic Zones." *Asian Studies Review* 32: 57–75.

Simmel, Georg. 1997. *Simmel on Culture: Selected Writings*, ed. David Frisby and Mike Featherstone, London; Thousand Oaks, CA: SAGE Publications.

Somers, Margaret R. 1994. "The Narrative Constitution of Identity: A Relational and Network Approach." *Theory and Society* 23 (5): 605–649.

Tseng, Yen Fen. 2011. "Shanghai Rush: Skilled Migrants in a Fantasy City." *Journal of Ethnic and Migration Studies* 37 (5): 765–784.

Tseng, Yen Fen, and Jieh Min Wu. 2011. "Reconfiguring Citizenship and Nationality: Dual Citizenship of Taiwanese Migrants in China." *Citizenship Studies* 15 (2): 265–282.

Wang, Jenn Hwan. 1996. *Who Rules Taiwan: The Transformation of the State and Its Power Structure.* Taipei: Jiu-Liu Books (In Chinese).

Wang, Jenn Hwan. 2001. "Governance of a Cross-border Economic Region: Taiwan and Southern China." In *Regionalism and Subregionalism in East Asia: The Dynamics of China*, eds. Glenn Drover, Graham Johnson and Julia Tao Lai Po-Wah. Huntingdon, NY: Nova Science Publishers.

Wang, Jenn Hwan. 2011. "Rival States vs. Integrated Economies: Information and Communication Technology Industry." In *The Second Great Transformation: Taiwanese Industrialization in the 1980s-2000s*, ed. Reginald Yin-Wang Kwok. Taipei: Chengchi University Press.

Wang, Jenn Hwan, and Chuan Kai Lee. 2007. "Global Production Networks and Local Institutional Building: The Development of the Information Technology Industry in Suzhou, China." *Environment and Planning A* 39 (8): 1873–1888.

Weber, Max. 1978. *Economy and Society*. Berkeley: University of California Press.

Wu, Nai Te. 2005. "For Love or Bread: A Preliminary Inquiry into the Changes in the National Identity of the Taiwanese." *Taiwanese Political Science Review* 9 (2): 5–39 (In Chinese).

Xiao, Suo Wei. 2011. "The 'Second Wife' Phenomenon and the Relational Construction of Class-coded Masculinities in Contemporary China." *Men and Masculinities* 14 (5): 607–627.

Part I
Production

2 Managing cross-border innovation networks

Taiwan's IC design industry

Jenn-hwan Wang and Sheng-wen Tseng

Introduction

Most recent studies on the formation of global production networks (GPNs) in electronics argue that Taiwanese PC firms have been included in GPNs as turnkey suppliers to serve major multinationals, due to the Taiwanese firms' strong capability in utilizing China's cost advantages so as to maintain their competitiveness in the world market (Dedrick and Kraemer 1998; Wang and Lee 2007; Ernst 2010). Some studies also have found that a great transformation has been occurring in recent years (Chen 2004; Ernst 2006; Ernst 2010), that is, the emergence of cross-border innovation networks, or global innovation networks (GINs), which has underpinned the already salient global and regional production networks. Following the above studies, this chapter is particularly focused on one of the major sectors of the ICT (information and communication technology) industry, namely, IC (integrated circuit) design, as it describes and analyzes its recent development. A cross-border innovation network here refers to the formation of collaborated R&D activities which transverse national boundaries (Ernst 2006). This collaboration may take many forms, ranging from the intra-firm division of labor across borders, inter-firm R&D alliances, or cooperation between firms and R&D institutes across borders.

The globalization of innovation is not a new phenomenon. The international division of labor since the 1970s has already created an internal division of labor within firms, in which many of the R&D activities have been conducted both in firms in their home countries or in subsidiary firms in invested countries. What has been new in recent decades is that innovation activities have been outsourced to other firms across borders (Archibugi and Iammarino 1999; Quinn 2000). This increasing outsourcing of innovation activities has occurred not only from advanced to developing economies, on which most of the research is focused, but has also emerged from semi-peripheral or advanced developing countries such as Taiwan to lower developing countries such as China, which is the focus of this chapter.

This chapter will use firms in Taiwan's ICT industry, especially the IC chip design sector, as an example to discuss the ways in which these firms have formed cross-border innovation networks to compete in the world market.

Taiwanese ICT firms have been described by many as technologically fast followers (Ernst 2004; Tseng 2009; Wang 2010), indicating that these firms are not leaders in technology and innovation but are good and high-quality technological followers. A fast follower firm can be defined as a firm whose technology is not on the frontier, but has the technological capability to closely follow the technologies invented by the technology leaders (Ernst 2004; Tseng 2009; Wang 2010). Therefore, it is located in the upper middle level of the value chain. However, due to the nature of market competition, these firms have to continuously search for new innovation in order to either diversify their products or move to the cutting-edge technology of existing innovation in order to survive in the market. As for Taiwan's ICT firms, due to their status as subcontractors in the GPNs, very different kinds of innovation strategy have been adopted in encountering market competition. While some firms may have merely searched for cheap talent, other firms may have been intent on expanding their market shares, and yet others have been requested by global buyers to adopt an outsourcing of innovation strategy. As will be discussed later, although all kinds of R&D outsourcing are related to cost down and market expansion motives, nonetheless, those firms that have the power to construct cross-border innovation networks still affect the ways in which the networks are formed. Thus, we distinguish three major types of cross-border innovational networks, namely, global firm-led, foundry-led, and IC design firm-led innovation networks. These three types exhibit different network features and they have also evolved in various ways as China has become an emerging market in recent years.

The data used in this study have been collected mainly in Taiwan and also as a result of field trips conducted by both authors in China in July 2008 and February 2012. A total of more than 50 informants were interviewed face to face or by telephone. Some interviews were conducted in the field sites in China (mainly in Shanghai and Suzhou), where Taiwanese firms were located. Each interview was conducted by the authors, and was completed within one or two hours. Our informants were mainly composed of high-ranking executive managers of enterprises, industrial researchers, and university professors from both China and Taiwan.

The formation of global innovation networks

Innovation outsourcing has been a salient phenomenon in the business world over the past two decades (Quinn 2000; Hoecht and Trott 2006; Stanko and Calantone 2011). The increasing segmentation of the value chain of the goods and services has led companies to seek opportunities to possibly reduce costs and expand market share. Various theories have been used to explain the outsourcing phenomenon (Stanko and Calantone 2011). The first one is the transaction theory that asks very essential "make or buy" questions (Williamson 1985). What this means is that the internalization of R&D will be preferred where transaction costs are excessive; conversely, the market (i.e., outsourcing) will be selected when transaction costs are low. So if the firm can find higher margins when outsourcing R&D elsewhere than it does internally, this firm will outsource the R&D activities to other firms. The second hypothesis is the resource-based argument, which proposes that firms tend to outsource those activities that are not central to their resources (Odagiri 2003). It argues that firms have to protect their critical assets, otherwise they will lose out to their competitors over time if they are completely reliant on outside contractors.

Although cost saving is always one of the most important elements in a firm's decision making, research findings have consistently supported the relationship between asset specificity and internal innovation governance. Thus, even though reducing cost is very appealing to firms, it is much more important to protect the firms' core competence and engage in innovation internally (Stanko and Calantone 2011, 10). From a long-term competitiveness perspective, the nurturing of a firm's competitive core in order to maintain its ability to compete in unpredictable markets is much more important than the costs involved (Hoecht and Trott 2006, 673).

There are thus a number of good and bad consequences that may be derived from a company's outsourcing. As for the benefit side, a firm can gain from R&D outsourcing due to a reduction in cost, access to specialist talent, increased speed and flexibility, and a stronger focus on core competencies (Quinn 2000, 26–27; Hoecht and Trott 2006, 673). However, a firm can also take a risk of losing competitiveness associated with large-scale outsourcing, due to the tendency that it may become too dependent on a supplier, it may lose essential know-how, or it may nurture strong future competitors (Stanko and Calantone 2011).

In the current ICT world, the outsourcing of innovation has been a common practice. The main causes of this outsourcing are to access overseas talent, to lower R&D costs, and to speed up product development. Collectively, the outsourcing firms are able to generate high profit margins (Quinn 2000; Stanko and Calantone 2011, 14). This phenomenon has been well documented by Ernst (2006) when he described how the US firms outsourced their R&D activities to East Asian firms in the IT sector. It was the rising cost of R&D, high risk of innovation, the emergence of pools of talent overseas, and the prevalence of internet infrastructure that drove US IT firms to seek to outsource their innovation functions overseas as they faced severe market competition. The US firms responded to the intensifying competition for scarce global talent "by opening high technology operations in foreign locations, developing strategic international alliances, and consummating cross-national spin-offs and mergers" (Ernst 2006, 20). As a result, GINs have been formed that cut across national borders. Thus, innovation activities are dispersed from advanced countries to developing countries, through which multiple locations in the world are simultaneously engaged in innovation activities directed by global firms. It is also well-known that most IC or software design can currently be organized in a 24-hour-based working team around the globe, and thus venture capitalists in Silicon Valley have reportedly required start-ups to include some offshoring or outsourcing in their business plans in order to better leverage their resources (Brown and Linden 2006, 16).

The above perspective regarding outsourcing the R&D segment in the value chain from advanced firms to latecomer firms in industrializing countries (Ernst 2006; Ernst 2010) has insightfully described the emerging tendency of global capitalism. Nevertheless, the emphasis on a global firm's top-down perspective has resulted in little attention being paid to the issues related to how firms in industrializing countries cope with the new tendency. The purpose of this chapter is to fill this gap in the literature.

GINs in the global IT industry and the upgrading of Taiwan's IT industry

In the 1990s, when global firms outsourced all but marketing and R&D functions of the value chain to supplier firms in developing countries, new opportunities came within the reach of Asian firms to use network participation as a catalyst for further technology upgrading (Ernst 2006). Indeed, it was due to this outsourcing that electronics firms in Taiwan continued to upgrade their technological and organizational capabilities to fulfill the stringent demands imposed upon them by the global firms. Most of the Taiwanese electronics firms upgraded their operations from OEM (original equipment manufacturing), where they sold the products to global firms without having their own labels, to ODM (original design manufacturing) where they became engaged in designing new products for global firms (Chen 2002; Wang 2010). Their technological capability was upgraded from simply manufacturing products for the global firms to designing new products for them. Moreover, in order to fulfill the time-to-market demand from global firms, these Taiwanese firms developed a very strong organizational capability in managing those processes ranging from manufacturing to shipping the products in a very speedy way.

As Ernst (2010) argues, a GIN is a natural extension of GPN and hence shares most of their characteristics (Ernst 2010, 6). The continuous outsourcing of global firms has been extended from a function of merely manufacturing to encompass R&D, which is mainly due to the low cost of overseas engineers and the proliferation of overseas markets. Moreover, it is also due to the creation of local innovation clusters in developing countries that global firms have tapped into human resources in those areas that are able to fulfill their outsourcing R&D demands. As a result, many firms in developing countries have been incorporated into the innovation networks.

The current GINs have an international division of labor according to the nature of their R&D activities. The global innovation centers that are still in the US or other advanced countries are engaged in cutting-edge innovative ideas, concepts and the architecture of the products. By contrast, the innovation centers located in developing countries either combine diverse technologies to create new products (i.e., Taiwan or Korea), modify existing products for local markets (i.e., Beijing, Bangalore), or engage in contract R&D or repetitive detailed engineering tasks (i.e., second-tier cities in China). Through this new geography of innovation, a global "epistemic community," which shares a similar knowledge base and uses the same language and cuts across national boundaries, has been formed (Ernst 2006, 12). It is because global firms have to transfer knowledge and skills to local suppliers in order to ensure that product specifications can be met that knowledge sharing has thus become the glue holding the members around the globe together.

How have firms in the middle level of the global value chain, such as Taiwanese firms, coped with the newly emerging GINs? How do they, on the one hand, respond to the demands from the center and, on the other hand, actively pursue their own upgrading and interests in the new GINs? These are questions that this chapter wants to answer.

Taiwanese electronics firms can be broadly defined as technological fast followers whose technological capability still lags behind that of the leading firms but remains ahead of the firms that do not have much sophisticated knowledge, such as those in China (Wang 2010). Since fast follower firms are only ahead of their competitors by a small gap, they therefore need to continue to build a broader set of capabilities that include some aspects of technological and organizational innovation. The economies of speed, flexibility, and cost control are basic principles that enable the Taiwanese electronics firms to successfully survive and compete in the world market (Amsden and Chu 2003; Wang 2010). Outsourcing is naturally one of the best strategies that fast follower firms should implement to sustain their competitiveness.

Logically, fast follower firms in the electronics industry may have few possible strategies to adapt to the global innovation-outsourcing trend. They may continue to upgrade their technological capability and extend some of their R&D segments (within the firm) to other countries in order to lower their costs and expand their market shares. Alternatively, they may outsource some of their R&D segments in other countries in order to reduce cost or to benefit from strategic collaboration in expanding their market share. ODM firms may also be forced by global buyers to outsource some of their R&D segments to firms in lower-wage countries to fit the demands of the buyers. As will be discussed below, all of the above strategies have been adopted by Taiwanese firms in the ICT-related IC design industry. Because of the different types of technology and global linkages among firms, there are different combinations of strategies evolving over time. These are the issues that we will discuss next.

Technological transformation of the global semiconductor industry

The development of Taiwan's IC design industry has a strong relationship with the development of the global semiconductor industry. The development and manufacturing of semiconductors involve three primary activities in the value chain: design, fabrication, and testing and assembly. Before the emergence of the first pure play foundry, which fabricates ICs for the fabless design house, Taiwan Semiconductor Manufacturing Company (TSMC), the standardized feature of the semiconductor companies was to keep all activities in-house, which was also based on the IDM (Integrated Device Manufacture) model, and encompassed firms such as Intel, Motorola, and Texas Instruments. The emergence of the foundry sector caused more fabless design houses to emerge that could concentrate their efforts on innovative design and leave the fabrication part to other firms. The value chain of the semiconductor industry was further broken down into segments that could be located in different localities.

Since the 1990s, the semiconductor industry has experienced further structural change. The radical changes in the methodology of IC design referred to as "system-on-a-chip" (SoC), which combines "system-level integration" on a chip with "modular design" and "design automation," have facilitated the reuse of design building blocks (SIPs) to increase the level of design performance (Macher et al. 2002). In turn, this change has led to drastic changes in the organization of the value chain. The IC design sector has now been further disintegrated into electronic design automation (EDA) vendors, such as Cadence Design Systems, Synopsys, and Mentor Graphics, that provide super precise design tools; the silicon intellectual property (SIP) providers that offer services for collecting and offering SIP blocks which an IC design house needs; and IC design service companies, such as Global Unichip and Faraday (Taiwanese firms) that provide SIPs collecting as well as services to bridge IC design firms with foundry manufacturing services. Since the emergence of the SoC technology and its related reorganization of the value chain, the IC design industry has been transformed, as Ernst (2006) observes, from an integrated form of design organization, where (almost) entire ICs are designed within a single firm, to a form in which stages of chip design can be outsourced to other firms and relocated across national boundaries (Ernst 2006, 2). This vertical specialization of IC design has been transformed from an artisan-type of design activity into a highly routinized factory-type operation where most of the knowledge is codified and most of the stages of design can be automated (Ernst 2006, 2).

It is under the above technological transformation that Taiwan began to face new challenges. Taiwan has since the 1990s emerged as a power house of the semiconductor industry. However, it faces a new challenge arising from emerging GINs in the semiconductor industry through which global MNCs outsource their design functions directly to China and India to take advantage of the lower labor costs. Taiwanese IC design firms thus are sandwiched between frontier innovative firms (mainly US firms) that are seeking low production cost and catching-up firms (such as Chinese IC design firms) that have been upgrading their technological capability. Taiwanese IC design firms are thus seeking new opportunities, such as through forming their own global innovation networks, to sustain their competitiveness in the world market.

Indeed, the above trends have resulted in the Taiwanese IC design sector forming cross-border innovation networks since the late 1990s. In fact, a survey-based study conducted by Chen (2004) has shown that Taiwanese electronics firms have already built up their R&D networks since the late 1990s in China. He categorized Taiwanese R&D portfolios across the Taiwan Strait into five types. The first type is related to the division of labor across the Taiwan Strait in which product development is undertaken in Taiwan, while engineering support and manufacturing-related R&D is provided in China. This often entails the de-linking of R&D and manufacturing. The second type is where Taiwanese firms outsource their software development services to China partly because of the cheap cost of software development there. The third type of portfolio involves a tendency for some Taiwanese firms to conduct their basic research in China, which often involves collaboration with local universities and/or research insti-tutes. The fourth type is where some Taiwanese firms keep their upstream (core) R&D segment (or R&D for products at the development stage) in Taiwan, while leaving downstream and non-core parts (or R&D for products at the mature stage) to their subsidiaries in China. The final type is where Taiwanese firms carry out major R&D activities in China for systems-related products, while maintaining the development function for related peripherals, such as the moth-erboards of handsets in Taiwan (Chen 2002, 345–346).

In a sense, these five types of portfolios have involved three kinds of division of labor across the border. The first is the division between core and periphery, in which the Taiwan side is the coordinator of the innovation while the Chinese subsidiaries or partners are engaged in product development. The second type is that where the Taiwan side does the core design while the Chinese partners provide the supporting R&D. The third type is that where the Taiwanese firms collaborate with Chinese universities or research institutes seeking new ideas or new materials. Almost a decade has passed since such collaboration was intro-duced, and much transformation has taken place in the global market. China has now emerged as one of the power houses in the ICT industry in the world, and whether there have been new developments and what may have been changed deserves to be further analyzed. As will be shown later, the above five types of portfolios as well as the three kinds of division of labor in the cross-border innovation networks are still currently in existence. However, the new tendency is that the Chinese side is playing an even more important role than it did before due to the rise of the Chinese domestic market.

The formation of cross-border R&D networks

Differing from the above findings, which were based on survey data that lumped all industries together, our chapter is based on qualitative data that mainly targets the IC design industry. Our perspective follows the global com-modity chain approach (Gereffi 1999; Gereffi et al. 2005) that investigates the value chain of the commodity and power relations within the chain. As Gereffi et al. (2005) argue, the governance of a value chain involves the management of complex webs of inputs and outputs and the control of resources, especially intellectual property (Gereffi et al. 2005, 87). Those within the chain that control the essential resources have the power to effectively manage the chain as well as the capacity to retain most of the profits or rents. Based on this per-spective, we will differentiate the emerging cross-border innovation networks of the IC design industry into three major categories from the angle of the network controller. This is because the network controller has the power and capability to organize the network and link various actors together to produce a good, which has enabled it to retain most of the profits. Accordingly, the first type of cross-border innovation network is the one built by the global branding firm, especially by a global PC firm together with key component firms. The second type is constructed by Taiwanese foundries, especially by TSMC and UMC. The third type is created by large and small Taiwanese IC design firms of which the IC design giant MediaTek is especially significant in this category. Each type can be differentiated into sub-categories which we will discuss in detail below.

Type A: global branding firm-led GIN

The global branding firms' construction of GINs, via Taiwanese firms, occurs mainly in the PC industry in which global PC firms outsource the work of chip design to Taiwanese fabless IC design companies. This is because the PC system needs a large number of IC chips to be functional. Currently, Taiwanese PC firms produce over 90 percent of notebook PCs for the world market (MIC 2010) and many other components. The prosperity of the Taiwanese PC industry has thus generated the prosperity of the IC design industry.

Before the year 2005, major global PC branding firms on the one hand outsourced the design and manufacturing segments to Taiwanese PC turnkey suppliers, and on the other hand collaborated with Taiwanese IC design firms to develop IC chips for their PCs. These products included chipsets that had brand-specific features, for example, a quick turn-on function or sound control chips (Tseng 2009) that could be installed in the branded PCs. During this period of time, the global branding firm-led innovation networks (the global branding firm-IC design firms and their subsidiaries in China) were mainly targeting PC-related peripherals for which the technology levels were not very high. Due to cost down considerations, Taiwanese IC design firms built their own innovation networks across borders via intra-organizational mechanisms in order to develop these middle- to low-end products.

During the same period, many Taiwanese IC design firms also began to establish their own subsidiaries in big cities, such as in Beijing, Shanghai, Suzhou, or Shenzhen, where IT industries were concentrated. For example, one of the biggest IC design firms in Taiwan, VIA Technology, had already established its China headquarters in Zhongguancun, Beijing to take advantage of recruiting cheap and good talent from China's best universities, namely, Qinghua University and Peking University. Besides the VIA technology case, most of the Taiwanese IC design companies chose to set up their subsidiaries in Shanghai, Suzhou, or Shenzhen, where a large number of Taiwanese PC manufacturers were located. It was also because the IC design industry had just begun to take off in China during this stage that many Taiwanese firms sent their own Taiwanese engineers to China to train local engineers to engage in low-end work in R&D activities.

Due to the severe market competition and the shortening of the IC chip's life cycle, many global branding firms have outsourced some of their R&D segments to or collaborated with Taiwanese IC design firms. This type of collaboration usually involves teamwork from both sides, with the global branding firms usually providing the detailed technical layout for Taiwanese firms to follow. If there are problems, the branding firm may send its engineers to the Taiwanese counterpart to find the solution. Such R&D collaboration has of course given Taiwanese IC design engineers the opportunity to learn the most advanced frontier knowledge on application and layout designs. Nonetheless, in collaborating with the advanced firms, what the Taiwanese partners have learned consists mainly of non-core parts and not the core architectural segments. As one informant said, "We mainly interact with engineers sent out from the buyer (or the outsourcing company). With these interactions, we can merely learn from them the functions of SIPs and their applications. We also collect market information for the buyer" (Interview data D07-A-01; also Tseng 2009, 87).

The above type of network, however, has changed dramatically since 2006 when the global high-tech industry entered the post-PC or telecommunications era. Now the lag in Taiwanese IC design firms' capability behind the global leading firms has been shortened to merely half a year, and firms such as Mediatech, Realtek, Davicom, Ali, and Ralink have all upgraded their technological level to design and produce more sophisticated telecommunication, network, and multimedia products. Global branding firms have now set up R&D centers in Taiwan to engage in development work, with responsibility for the middle- to lower-end design segments.

The reasons why those global branding firms have set up R&D centers in Taiwan has been mainly due to the considerations of cost down and the clustering effect in the Hsinchu area where all needed services are concentrated. Take the R&D center of Broadcom in Taiwan as an example. It is located in Hsinchu Science Park, and has about 400 people, most of whom have graduated from Taiwan's top universities, such as the National Taiwan, Tsinghua, and Chiaotung universities. According to our interviews, Broadcom retains the most sophisticated knowledge in its headquarters and its Taiwanese R&D center is responsible for the middle segments of the design and for product development works. Even in these cases, Taiwanese engineers have to have very intensive interactions with their counterparts in the US, due to the complexity of the design, simulation, and testing processes. This is especially the case when designing analog type chipsets which are so complex that long-term experience and intensive face-to-face interactions between engineers are required to do the design work in order to avoid making mistakes. Through these interactions, much tacit knowledge has been transmitted from the US to local engineers. However, the engineers in Taiwan in those cases still do not have the opportunity to touch the core architectural part of the design. Therefore, in this type of GIN, the global branding firm is the leader, while the Taiwanese IC design firms are sandwiched in the middle, and the Chinese subsidiaries make up the tail in the international division of labor of IC design.

Type B: Taiwanese foundry-led GIN

Differing from the former case, where global branding firms contracted out the design to Taiwanese firms, the foundry-led case is one that is led by Taiwanese firms. Taiwanese foundries began their investments in China in 2001 when UMC utilized its overseas investment company to create a new foundry firm, Hejian, in Suzhou. During that time, this was considered to be an illegal act according to Taiwanese law due to the hostile cross-Strait relations. Nevertheless, it was also due to the global competition pressure that the Taiwanese government finally allowed another foundry firm, TSMC, to invest its manufacturing facilities in Shanghai in 2003.

The main purposes of the Taiwanese foundries' investment in China were to maintain their business clients and to explore the potentially very large market. Had they not invested in China, their clients might have sought new outsourcing manufacturing facilities in China; and they also stood to lose their competitiveness in China due to the booming semiconductor market there owing to the strategic support provided to the foundry industry by the Chinese government.[1]

There were many channels that TSMC and UMC used to create new business clients and business partners. The first one was to hold a technological forum that introduced the latest technological developments in IC design and process technology. By means of this forum, TSMC was able to allow potential clients to access its technology and services. In this initial stage of China's semiconductor industry, TSMC's technological forums played an important role of knowledge leadership for the emerging IC design companies in China. Second, TSMC also established the Service Center of IC design in Shanghai in 2005, which hired over 40 Chinese engineers, to assist the Chinese IC design companies to solve their design problems as well as to connect them to TSMC's process technology. Third, TSMC also very actively established a collaborative relationship with China's eight major IC design bases[2] starting from 2009, in order to share the knowledge with Chinese clients, and train and recruit potentially very talented engineers. Fourth, Taiwanese foundries also began to collaborate with Chinese universities to develop new products, which facilitated the building of closer relationships with local R&D institutes and trained potentially excellent engineers. One of the good examples was TSMC's collaboration with Qinghua University in Beijing that finally produced two 65 mm chips for the market. Through this firm-university collaboration, students acquired the knowledge of IC design, including putting their chips into the production process which only the foundry could offer. Through these channels, TSMC and other Taiwanese foundries were able to retain and create business clients in China, which were also the platform on which they were able to show their leadership in IC process technology to Chinese clients.

Due to the leadership provided by Taiwanese foundries in process technology, the cross-border division of labor has become very clear: the headquarters in Taiwan play the role of coordinator and decision maker. The technological levels of their subsidiaries in China are behind those of the Taiwanese headquarters. Therefore, the R&D activities in China are also led by Taiwanese, plus some Chinese engineers, and coordinated by those engineers in Taiwan. This is particularly evident in the case of chip design in the telecommunications sector. Due to the severe market competition in the handheld telecommunications sector, chips have become cheaper, shorter, and thinner, which forces chip design firms to rely even more closely on the foundry which is able to provide the needed process technology, manufacturing, and design services. In fact, foundry firms are currently creating new design service companies to serve the needs of IC design firms. Now Global Unichip Corp (created by TSMC) and Faraday Technology (created by UMC) are two major companies[3] that mainly engage in the chip design service work, for instance, trading Silicon Intellectual Property (SIP) for IC design firms, and they dominate the Chinese market. In this sense, the Taiwanese foundry's cross-border innovation network is still dominated by the headquarters of the foundry firm, whereas the Chinese clients are the downstream firms in the networks.

Type C: Taiwanese IC design houses-led networks

As discussed above, Taiwanese IC design firms began their investments in China in the early 2000s. VIA Technology was the first to collaborate with universities in China to develop chipsets for computers. In due course, VIA Technology also extended this firm-university collaboration to develop chipsets for third-generation cell phones and for notebook PCs in recent years. However, due to the concentration of Taiwanese foundries in the areas of Shanghai and Suzhou, most Taiwanese IC design companies began to form clusters in other areas than in Beijing.

More recently, due to its rapid economic growth and accession to the WTO in 2001, China has emerged as a huge consumer market for consumer goods, such as ICT products. This has generated a large demand for chipsets for third-generation communication handheld devices, LCD panel drivers, as well as other consumer goods. The severe competition among global firms in the Chinese domestic market has led to the transformation of the relationships between IC design firms and their subsidiaries in China. Now, Taiwanese IC design firms want to develop their own innovation networks, rather than be led by global branding firms; they also want to take advantage of the booming Chinese domestic market as an overseas market and intend to become branding firms themselves rather than just remaining in the OEM position.

Currently, there are different types of cross-border R&D networks led by Taiwanese IC design houses. The first type consists of those Taiwanese IC design companies that have invested in or acquired Chinese IC design firms to co-develop new products. In this category, MediaTek is the most active firm. MediaTek acquired Beijing Pollex Technology in 2006 in order to develop a cell phone chipset for the *Shanzhaiji* (copyphone). In 2010, MediaTek acquired AST wireless due to the latter's core competence in regard to the Chinese version of the third-generation telecommunication – TD-SCDMA, in order to quickly catch up with the Chinese version of the third generation technological standard.

Second, there has been a tendency for Taiwanese IC design houses to build R&D centers in China in order to lower their costs and to develop products for the Chinese domestic market. This has been particularly so in the telecommunications IC chipset area. For example, MediaTek spent RMB 745 million on building an R&D center in Zhongguancun, and at the same time it also expanded its R&D facilities in Shenzhen and Hefei in Anhui Province to co-develop third generation IC chipsets. Now MediaTek has over a thousand engineers in China, of which about half are located in Beijing. In these types of cross-border R&D networks, the headquarters in Taiwan still play a dominant role in coordination and chip design. Team members frequently communicate by visual telecom platforms or conference calls. Through these mechanisms, much detailed knowledge and design specificities have been transferred from Taiwan to the teams in China. Through these mechanisms-acquiring Chinese IC design firms, hiring huge numbers of Chinese engineers, and building cross-border innovation networks within its organization, MediaTek has been able to quickly develop IC chipsets specifically for the massive Chinese market and has sold these chipsets to that market. It is due to the above mechanisms that MediaTek has become the King of *Shangzhaiji* (copyphone), and also became the fifth largest IC design firm in the world in 2010.

Our interviews showed that some big Taiwanese IC design firms, such as MediaTek or VIA, have created an international division of labor in their design work. They have usually established a Knowledge Management Platform to support design teams that are scattered around the globe. Different teams have the right to various degrees to access the data which is distributed according to the level of authority. Teams regularly hold visual conferences to communicate with each other regarding the specific design work in order to speed up the design of the chipsets. The Chinese parts are at the lower end of the design networks, while those in the US are at the upper end. Therefore, Chinese engineers are not allowed to access the core parts of the design. This is also due to the high risk of piracy in China which has led the IC design firms to build firewalls to protect their own intellectual property. Therefore, team leaders sometimes have to fly to China to personally communicate with local engineers, rather than allow local engineers to access the core knowledge, in order to ensure that the design process has been followed or to do the debugging works. This is especially the case in the design of complicated analog chips. However, as time has gone by, the division of labor has gradually changed. As one manager of a major IC design company pointed out, "because the design capability in China has largely been upgraded in recent years, we have also begun to ask our engineers on the Chinese side to participate in some of the core parts of new projects" (Interview data D11-A-01, 3).

In order to access the most advanced knowledge in the US, many Taiwanese IC design firms have acquired small firms in Silicon Valley[4] and have transformed the companies into R&D centers of their own firms. Through such firms, new knowledge is transmitted from Silicon Valley to Taiwanese teams. One high-ranking engineer said to us, the purpose for which we set up an R&D center in the US was because this is the world center. You can more easily access the newest information and technology, as well as access those key component producers. By reducing the distance, we can communicate more easily, and sometimes access the most advanced technology at its very earliest stage.

(Interview data S04-A-01, 2)

Therefore, in this case, the Taiwanese IC design firms' headquarters constitute the core that do the design while the subsidiaries on the Chinese side follow the design structure to do the non-core parts. However, as the Chinese engineers' capability has been increasing, the division of labor has begun to change.

Summary

The above three categories of cross-border innovation networks have been the products of evolution through which Taiwanese firms have extended their R&D functions from mainly in Taiwan and the US to China. The path of evolution can be summarized as follows:

1   In the early 2000s, global branding firms in the PC industry still played an important role in the formulation of cross-border IC design networks. During that period, Chinese IC design firms were at their initial stage and, therefore, the networks were mainly established by Taiwanese firms through their own intra-organizational networks controlled by Taiwanese head-quarters.
2   Due to the concentration of IT industries in the eastern coastal regions of China, Taiwanese foundries were forced to invest and establish facilities in the area to retain existing and develop new business clients in the early 2000s. In the process, Taiwanese foundries also established a closer collab-oration relationship with local universities to develop products for the domestic market and attract new talent.
3   From 2006 onwards, or in the post-PC era, Taiwan's IC design firms have focused on telecommunications products to target the booming Chinese domestic market. Taiwanese firms have begun to acquire good Chinese IC design companies to join their cross-border innovation networks, in which the headquarters in Taiwan still play a coordinating role.
4   There has been a tendency for Taiwanese foundry and IC design firms to begin to establish closer collaboration relationships with Chinese univer-sities and R&D institutes in order to develop products for the domestic market and to recruit talent.
5   Through the above mechanisms, Taiwanese firms have worked out a pattern of cross-border innovation networks to maintain their market competit-iveness. The IC design firms can thus quickly respond to the market demand, and use cheap and good engineers to mass produce the second gen-eration innovation products for the market, such as *Shanzhaiji* (copyphone).

6   Nevertheless, there has been a tendency for the Chinese subsidiaries to have
      largely upgraded their technological capabilities in recent years; therefore,
      the existing division of labor across the Taiwan Strait has been modified in
      which the Chinese subsidiaries have begun to take part in the core design of
      new chips.

As compared to Chen's study (2004) a decade ago, some similarities are still
there. For example, there is the division of labor across borders in which the Taiwanese part still plays the leadership role. However, new tendencies have
occurred in particular with the rise of the Chinese market and its local IC design
industry. Taiwanese firms have been adjusting to the new situation by establishing more intensive linkages with local innovation networks. Given this new
development tendency, the dominant power is still in the hands of Taiwanese
headquarters. In other words, the Taiwanese part has tended to engage in core,
process technology and product development R&D activities, whereas the
Chinese counterparts have tended to be involved in improving, localization, and
manufacturing R&D, as well as performing the function of basic research by collaborating with major universities.

Discussion and conclusion

The chapter describes and analyzes the recent development of cross-border
innovation networks constructed by the Taiwanese ICT-related IC design industry. We construct three types of cross-border innovation networks: the first type
is established by global branding firms, in collaborating with Taiwanese foundries and IC design houses and their subsidiaries in China. The second type is
built by Taiwanese foundries, as they link up with their subsidiaries in China and
Chinese IC design firms or R&D institutions. The third type is founded by Taiwanese IC design houses, which network with their subsidiaries in China or
Chinese firms as well as R&D institutions (see Figure 2.1). While the first type
is the continuity of the top-down approach adopted by MNCs as described by
Ernst (2006), the rest are developed by Taiwanese firms in encountering the
newly emerging international market competition. The characteristics of the
three types of cross-border networks can be shown in Table 2.1.

      What are the theoretical implications of the emergence of Taiwanese cross-
border innovation networks in regard to the ICT-related IC design industry? We
maintain that there are at least three key findings that may contribute to the
current literature.

      First of all, in a way that differs from the GIN literature, as proposed by Ernst
(2006; 2010), which pays much attention to the issues regarding how MNCs
construct their global innovation networks, our chapter finds that Taiwanese
ICT-related IC design firms have also constructed their own cross-border innovation networks in order to escape from the trap of being merely manufacturing
contractors. In other words, Ernst pays attention mainly to type A of our three
categories; we instead argue that types B and C are especially important for firms

Table 2.1 Typology of cross-border innovation networks

Networks type	Global branding firms-led	Taiwanese foundries-led	Taiwanese IC design houses-led
Leader	Global branding firms	Taiwanese foundries	Taiwanese IC design houses
Player	• Global branding firms • Taiwanese IC design houses	• Taiwanese foundries • Taiwanese subsidiaries in China • Chinese firms or R&D institution	• Taiwanese IC design houses • Taiwanese subsidiaries in China • Chinese firms or R&D institution
Major IC product	• Before 2005: PC • Since 2006: telecommunication, networks, and multimedia	Silicon Intellectual Property (SIP)	Notebook, telecommunication, networks, multimedia, and LCD
Causes to form networks	• Cost down • Clustering effect	• Cost down • Market expansion • Customization	• Cost down • Market expansion • Customization • Clustering effect
Operations of networks	• Inter-firm teamwork between global branding firms and Taiwanese IC design houses • Product development • Intensive interactions	• Intra-firm teamwork between Taiwanese foundries and Taiwanese subsidiaries in China • Inter-firms teamwork between Taiwanese subsidiaries in China and Chinese firms or R&D institutions • SIP development • Intensive interactions	• Intra-firm teamwork between Taiwanese IC design houses and Taiwanese subsidiaries in China • Inter-firm teamwork between Taiwanese subsidiaries in China and Chinese firms or R&D institutions • Basic research and product development • Intensive interactions

Source: This study.

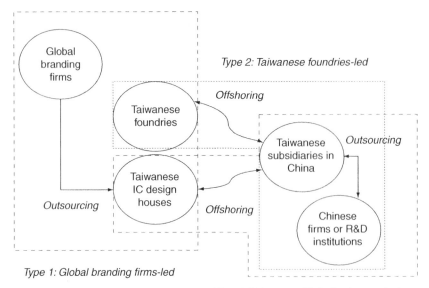

Figure 2.1 Three categories of cross-border networks (source: This study).

in advanced developing countries, such as Taiwan in our case, as they pursue their own global innovation networks.

In short, while Ernst's perspective is one that is from the angle of an advanced country, we instead highlight how fast followers build their own innovation networks in order to take advantage of the huge emerging market to expand their market share. Some of them, such as MediaTek and VIA, have wanted to become market leaders rather than take/receive orders from global firms. In fact, they have become successful in the emerging Chinese market. Therefore, our findings complement Ernst's GIN arguments.

Second, our findings also show that there are elements that are equally or more important than cost down for firms to outsource their R&D functions. As we discussed above, the rise of the Chinese domestic market has led both global firms and Taiwanese IC design firms to seek to expand their market shares. The reasons why Taiwanese IC design firms have set up R&D centers and hired local engineers to engage in R&D activities have on the one hand been to use their talent to design products suitable for local markets and, on the other hand, to shorten the design period in order to quickly respond to market demand. The element of transaction cost was still very important before 2005 when most of the firms investing in China were mainly concerned with reducing production and transaction costs. Nevertheless, as China has become a very large market for consumer goods, and the wage level of engineers has risen rapidly,[5] market expansion has become the main concern in building innovation networks.

Third, and finally, our findings also show that Taiwanese foundries and IC design firms have both constructed their cross-border innovation networks in recent years, and still hold the dominant position and have coordinated all the major innovation processes. This confirms the hypothesis that proposes that firms tend to outsource those activities that are not central to their resources (Odagiri 2003). Our findings show that the critical assets and knowledge are still controlled by the headquarters in Taiwan, and the subsidiaries and teams in China are engaging in product development for the Chinese domestic market. Our findings also support the thesis that knowledge creation has an institutional basis which the national system of innovation literature has maintained (Lundvall 1990; Freeman 1992). Therefore, we have seen that Taiwanese foundries and IC design firms still keep their headquarters in Taiwan's Hsinchu Science Park, due to the cluster effect that the park has created (Mathews and Cho 2000; Chen 2004; Wang 2010). What they have outsourced are non-core activities which have utilized Chinese talent to perform non-core R&D and develop products for the local market. Indeed, the national system of innovation is still the base for innovation, and the construction of global innovation networks is not to replace the former but instead to be an auxiliary to it.

In sum, Taiwanese IC designers learned the MNCs' technologies a few decades ago, and then became fast followers in the 1990s of the processes in which China was regarded as a production site to be included in the GPNs. Now these fast followers want to upgrade again and this time they are using the rise of the Chinese domestic market to build innovation networks. As a technological fast follower, the Taiwanese ICT-related IC design industry intends to fully utilize the rise of China to build up its technological and organizational capabilities in the hope of becoming a market leader. The building of cross-border innovation networks thus involves not only the change in cross-Strait relations, but also the transformation of the economic and technological division of labor across borders.

Notes

1 Before TSMC invested in China, there were many IDM semiconductor companies in China that had been established by the Chinese government. In addition, the Chinese government also fully supported the establishment of SMIC (Semiconductor Manufacturing Industrial Company) that was founded by a Taiwanese. SMIC has become the national champion that the Chinese government has wanted to promote.
2 In order to promote the semiconductor and IC design industries, the Chinese government has since the year 2000 established eight IC design incubation bases in different cities, including Beijing, Shanghai, Xi'an, Xiamen, Wuxi, Chengdu, Hangzhou, and Jinan.
3 Faraday Technology was created by UMC in 1993 while Global Unichip was created by TSMC in 1998.
4 For example, Realtek Semiconductor Corp. acquired Avence Microelectronics in Silicon Valley in 2002 in order to access knowledge on PC-based multimedia chips.
5 The salary level of China's IC design engineer has been rising rapidly in the last decade, roughly five times higher in 2012 than its 2002 level, which was slightly behind that of the Taiwanese counterparts and about half of the US's (see Table 2.2).

Table 2.2 Annual average salary of IC design engineer compared (unit: USD/year)

Year	2002	2008	2012
Silicon Valley	<80,000[*,***]	100,000[*]	130,000[*]
Taiwan (Hsinchu)	<60,000[**]	<70,000[***]	<80,000[***]
China (Shanghai)	<12,000[***]	<40,000[***]	<60,000[***]

Source: [*]Estimated from www.indeed.com/salary/ and www.salary.com/; [**]Ernst (2004); [***]Interview data.

Note
Salary = including annual salary, benefits, equipment, office space and other infrastructure.

References

Amsden, Alice H., and Wan-Wen Chu. 2003. *Beyond Late Development: Taiwan's Upgrading Policies*. Cambridge: MIT Press.

Archibugi, Daniele, and Simona Iammarino. 1999. "The Policy Implications of the Globalization of Innovation." *Research Policy* 28: 317–336.

Brown, Clair, and Greg Linden. 2006. "Offshoring in the Semiconductor Industry: A Historical Perspective." In *Brookings Trade Forum 2005: Offshoring White-Collar Work – The Issues and the Implications*, edited by Lael Brainard and Susan M. Collins, 279–333. Washington DC: Brookings Institution.

Chen, Shin-Horng. 2002. "Global Production Networks and Information Technology: The Case of Taiwan." *Industry and Innovation* 9 (3): 247–264.

Chen, Shin-Horng. 2004. "Taiwanese IT Firms' Offshore R&D in China and the Connection with the Global Innovation Network." *Research Policy* 33 (2): 337–349.

Dedrick, Jason, and Kenneth L. Kraemer. 1998. *Asia's Computer Challenge: Threat or Opportunity for the United States and the World?* New York: Oxford University Press.

Ernst, Dieter. 2004. "Globalization of Knowledge Work – Why is Chip Design Moving to Asia?" East-West Working Paper Series, East-West Center, University of Hawaii, USA.

Ernst, Dieter. 2006. "Innovation Offshoring: Asia's Emerging Role in Global Innovation Networks." East-West Center Special Report, East-West Center, University of Hawaii, USA.

Ernst, Dieter. 2010. "Upgrading Through Innovation in a Small Network Economy: Insights from Taiwan's IT Industry." *Economics of Innovation and New Technology* 19 (4): 295–324.

Freeman, Linton C. 1992. "Social Networks and the Structure Experiment." In *Research Methods in Social Network Analysis*, edited by Linton C. Freeman, Douglas R. White, and A. Kimball Romney, 11–40. New Brunswick, NJ: Transaction Publishers.

Gereffi, Gary. 1999. "International Trade and Industrial Upgrading in the Apparel Commodity Chain." *Journal of International Economics* 48 (1): 37–70.

Gereffi, Gary, John. Humphrey, and Timothy Sturgeon. 2005. "The Governance of Global Value Chains." *Review of International Political Economy* 12(1): 78–104.

Hoecht, Andreas, and Paul Trott. 2006. "Innovation Risks of Strategic Outsourcing." *Technovation* 26 (5–6): 672–681.

Lundvall, Bengt-Åke. 1990. *From Technology as a Productive Factor to Innovation as an Interactive Process*. Cambridge, MA: Harvard University Press.

Macher, Jeffrey T., David C. Mowery, and Timothy S. Simcoe. 2002. "e-Business and the Semiconductor Industry Value Chain: Implications for Vertical Specialization and Integrated Semiconductor Manufacturers." *Industry and Innovation* 9 (3): 155–181.

Mathews, John A., and Dong-Sung Cho. 2000. *Tiger Technology: The Creation of a Semiconductor Industry in East Asia.* Cambridge: Cambridge University Press.

MIC (Market Intelligence & Consulting Institute). 2010. *Information Industry Yearbook 2010.* [Zixungongye Nianjian 2010] Taipei: MIC (In Chinese).

Odagiri, Hiroyuki. 2003. "Transaction Costs and Capabilities as Determinants of the R&D Boundaries of the Firm: A Case Study of the Ten Largest Pharmaceutical Firms in Japan." *Management and Decision Economics* 24 (2–3): 187–211.

Quinn, James Brian. 2000. "Outsourcing Innovation: The New Engine of Growth." *Sloan Management Review* 41 (4): 13–28.

Stanko, Michael A., and Roger J. Calantone. 2011. "Controversy in Innovation Outsourcing Research: Review, Synthesis and Future Directions." *R&D Management* 41 (1): 8–20.

Tseng, Sheng-Wen. 2009. "Fast Follower, Industrial Cluster, and Social Embeddedness: An Inquiry into IC Design Industry in Taiwan." [Kuaisugensui Chanyejuluo yu Shehuixiangqian: Yi Taiwan IC Sheji Chanye Weili] Ph.D. Dissertation. Graduate Institute of Development Studies, National Chengchi University (In Chinese).

Wang, Jenn Hwan. 2010. *The Limits of Fast Followers: Taiwan's Economic Transition and Innovation.* [Zhuigan de Jixian: Taiwan de Jingji Zhuanxing yu Chuangxin] Taipei: Jyu-liu Books (In Chinese).

Wang, Jenn-Hwan, and Chuan-Kai Lee. 2007. "Global Production Networks and Local Institution Building: The Development of the Information-Technology Industry in Suzhou, China." *Environment and Planning A* 39 (8): 1873–1888.

Williamson, Oliver E. 1985. *The Economic Institutions of Capitalism.* New York: Free Press.

3   Embedded trust and beyond

The organizational network transformation of Taishang's shoe industry in China

Chih-peng Cheng

Introduction: Taishang on the move

In the past several years, Taishang (Taiwanese investors) in China have been facing challenges from transformation of internal and international investment environments, labor laws, and the global financial crisis in particular. According to the report of *Taiwan Business Weekly* (Lu and Yu 2008, 140–154), Taishang in the areas of the Pearl River Delta have started to close factories and move their production sites westbound and offshore in search for cheaper labor and land. The *Business Weekly* named this phenomenon the "Big Escape of Taishang." One of the interviewees in this chapter, a shoe maker in Dongguan, estimated that almost 40 percent of the Taiwanese shoe factories have not survived the crisis since 2008. Dongguan, the world shoe capital controlled by Taishang, is in the process of transition. Recent European debt crisis further frustrated the development of Chinese export-led shoe and other industries, and Taishang is located at the eye of the storm.

However, the first business migration of Taishang has to be traced back to the beginning of the 1980s, when Taiwanese export-led manufacturers chose to move their production sites outside of the homeland, first to Southeast Asian countries, then to China. Taishang found their "second spring of career" in China, because the Chinese government was able to provide foreign investors with abundant labor and land supply and lax labor as well as environmental regulation policies, which the Taiwanese government could not offer at that time. With the assistance of southeast coastal local governments, Taishang made the Pearl River Delta a world factory, exporting consumer goods around the world. Nevertheless, a series of unfriendly trade policies to foreign investors, such as Labor Contract Law and tax reforms, began to impact the investment environment in the late 2000s. This situation has pushed Taishang to re-evaluate the possibilities of China as the world's factory. As a result, the third large-scale migration of Taishang has begun, and the next destination for them could be India and Bangladesh.

If we look at business migration from the cost concern, it is nothing new for Taishang as transnational capitalists. Taishang are just repeating the action they took in the 1980s. This is one more example of industrial nomads showing how

Taishang as original equipment manufacturers (OEMs) are embedded in the global commodity chain. However, some Taishang choose to stay in China and try to free themselves from the role as industrial nomads. Various economic, social and cultural capitals accumulated by Taishang in the past 20 years in China make it possible for them to upgrade their OEM role in the international division of labor. This was something impossible for them 20 years ago when they became transnational capitalists for the first time. Taishang in China are attempting to construct a market social space where they can end the status of rootless enterprises for a long time.

However, rooting in China will cause a great impact on the trust-mediated network of Taiwanese factories. This chapter attempts to examine why and how the enclave economy created by Taishang starts to break down, rebuild, upgrade, and what may happen to the local economy by the disintegration of Taishang's exclusive network. More importantly, the adjustment on organizational network could be the key to explore the transition from OEM to OBM (original brand manufacture), which has not answered profoundly in previous Taishang studies. As a pioneer case of foreign direct investment in China, the shoe industry will be a good example for us to observe the transformation of Taishang on organizational networks. Next, I will examine the literature of economic and organizational sociology on embeddedness and networks.

Literature review: embedded trust and beyond

First of all, this chapter will discuss why industries have good economic performance from the perspective of organizational sociology. In addition to literature emphasizing vertical integration of big enterprises (Chandler 1977), more researches began to pay attention to how network-like production organization models contributed to industry competitiveness (Piore and Sabel 1984; Powell 1990; Nohria and Eccles 1992; Saxenian 1996). This successful model of network-like organization also finds evidences in Japan (Smitka 1991; Lincoln and Gerlach 2004) and other East Asian countries, including Taiwan. Taiwan as a "boss island," which is full of small and medium-sized enterprises, is also characterized by network-like organization. Moreover, the efficiency and flexibility created by this "small but beautiful" model of network-like organization helps Taiwan find a niche in the international division of labor (Shieh 1992; Chen 1994; Cheng 2011). Even Taiwan's big enterprises, such as the integrated-circuit industry, are characterized by the network-like production organization (Chen 2003).

Nonetheless, why is this kind of network-like production organization model capable of creating efficiency and flexibility, and solving market uncertainties? In response to new institutional economics and transactional cost economics (Coase 1937; Williamson 1975; North 1990), new economic sociology argues that it is impossible for firms to eradicate opportunistic behaviors of employees and business disputes. On the contrary, it is the network consisting of social relations that helps mitigate opportunism within firms and markets, which is nothing to do with the hierarchy and laws argued by transactional cost economics (Macaulay 1963; Granovetter 1985). Most importantly, embedded trust, resulted from ongoing personal interactions in the network, will influence decision making and economic performance of actors (Coleman 1998; DiMaggio and Louch 1998; Uzzi 1996). Cheng's analysis of the export-led footwear industry (1999) and Chen's study on the bicycle industry (2002) in Taiwan and China both validate the argument of embedded trust and economic performance.

The characteristic of embedded network possessed by Taiwan's industries is further strengthened by the fact of large-scale Taishang's entry to China. China's market is full of uncertainties because of the economic transition from a socialist to a capitalist system. Studies on Taiwanese investments in China highlight the enclave economy in buffering from local disturbance to satisfy the global supply chain. This strategy directly resulted in the closure of the organization network of Taiwanese export manufacturing enterprises in China. The enclave economy can work in China because Taishang and local government together create a mechanism of "pseudo township and village enterprises, real foreign direct investments" to institutionalize rent-seeking activities of local cadres and officers (Wu 1997). However, the primary goal behind the mechanism embedded in local contexts is disembeddedness, and further to smooth away China's market uncertainties in the global supply chain (Cheng 1999). Chen (2012) calls Taishang's exclusive production network the "Fortress in the Air" from the perspective of organization. It is difficult for outsiders to get into the network because the enterprises inside of the network only trust their business partners in the fortress. Although the enterprises in the fortress are rootless ones, they are fast-movers in response to changing markets without taking the locals into consideration.

Taishang's moving westbound and offshore may support both "embeddedness for disembeddedness" and "fortress in the air" to a certain degree. New economic sociology also emphasizes that it will take a long time for economic actors to build trust relationships to solve market uncertainties, and the ethnic factor is a key ingredient of the relationships (Portes and Sensenbrenner 1993). That is why only a few Chinese local factories are included in Taishang's production network (Chen 2012). However, recent data show that more and more Taiwanese factories are incorporating local factories into their network in order to cope with the increasing challenges from the changing business environments in China. This situation highlights the need to go beyond embedded trust. In other words, embedded trust will obstruct our understanding of the transformation of production organization, especially for the network-like one.

Therefore, it is necessary to rethink the relationship between network and trust. This chapter argues that industries with network-like production structure may have superior economic performance if players can build a stable status hierarchy (Fligstein 2001). In my case, Taishang as the incumbent are capable of creating a governance structure to reproduce their interests effectively, and preventing Chinese local factories from changing the status quo as the challenger.

Furthermore, the governance structure may assist Taishang in upgrading their position in the international division of labor, just as triangle manufacturing did on buyer-driven global commodity chains. It was the triangle manufacturing that has allowed Hong Kong apparel manufacturers and Taiwan shoe makers to move beyond OEM production as a "middleman" (traders) (Gereffi 1994; Korzeniewicz 1994). Since the global financial crisis, some of the leading Taiwan shoe makers even have been trying on establishing their own brand names and retail chains in the China market; meanwhile, they still control the production via subcontracting to local factories.

In conclusion, examining the transformation of Taishang's organization network in China from the power perspective can lead us to a better understanding of Taishang's transitional strategy and its outcome. Going beyond embedded trust is a good way to start with. In the following section, I will illustrate why Dongguan is a good site for researchers to observe the transformation of Taishang's production organization network, Taiwanese shoe makers in particular.

Site selection: Dongguan and Taiwan capital

This chapter focuses on Dongguan, one of 21 medium-sized cities in the southern region of Guangdong province, in southeast coastal China. There are 32 towns and 599 villages in Dongguan, a region covering 2,465 square kilometers. Geographically, Dongguan is a transport center located in the east of the Pearl River Delta, and borders Guangzhou, the provincial capital of Guangdong, on the north and Shenzhen on the south, the first post-Mao era Chinese special economic zone set up in conjunction with the launching of the government economic reform. It is a mere 90 kilometers from Hong Kong and has become one of China's rapid economic growth areas in the past three decades. Dongguan's average rate of yearly growth was 23 percent between 1978 and 2002, much higher than the country average. Although the global financial crisis of 2008 made the economic growth rate of Dongguan drop, its GDP performance is still one of the best in Guangdong province and the whole of China. This is due to its location, which made it attractive to foreign investors from Hong Kong and Taiwan.

Taiwan capital has been the main force for the Dongguan economy since 1989. Deng's southern tour of 1992 further accelerated the trend of Taiwan capital inflow into Dongguan. According to the statistics of Taiwan Businessmen Association of Dongguan, investment items by Taishang in Dongguan are over 6,000 up to the year of 2010, accounting for nearly 10 percent of total Taiwanese investment in China. In 2011, there were 4,100 Taiwanese enterprises in Dongguan, and the amount of investment reached US$1 billion. The amount of foreign trade created by Taiwanese investors was US$47.7 billion, accounting for over 30 percent of Dongguan's foreign trade in 2011. These figures clearly explain the importance of Taiwan capital in Dongguan economic development, not to mention the position before 2008. And Dongguan is the cluster of Taiwanese manufacturing investors, in addition to Shenzhen and Kunshan.

Dongguan is a global processing and manufacturing base for Chinese exports. In addition to electronics, furniture, toys, and apparel, Dongguan is the most important and largest exporting base for footwear in the world. Pou Chen, the biggest footwear enterprise in the world, and other world famous shoe makers, such as Stella and Oriental Max, are all located in Dongguan. Hence, Dongguan earns its name of the shoe capital. Although local producers have increasingly become an emerging power in making shoes, the entire cluster of the export-led footwear industry in Dongguan is still controlled by Taiwanese footwear producers (Cheng 2008).

Nevertheless, Dongguan's investment environment for Taishang has deteriorated in recent years. First of all, in order to push forward industry restructuring (transformation and upgrade) in the areas of the Pearl River Delta, Yang Wang, the former first party secretary of Guangdong province, brought up an policy of "*Teng-Long-Huan-Niao* (騰籠換鳥)," which means pushing small and medium-sized enterprises majoring in traditional manufacturing industries out in exchange for big enterprises focusing on high-tech and low-pollution industries. Guangdong is the first province in China to do this. This policy along with the Labor Contract Law of 2008 changed Guangdong's investment environment greatly and caused Taishang in the Pearl River Delta to reconsider the possibilities of westbound or offshore migration. Furthermore, a decreasing world consumers' market caused by the global financial crisis made the Chinese export-led economy even worse. Taiwanese shoe makers in Dongguan are influenced by the great global recession and China's changing regulatory regime by the same token. In response to these challenges, Taiwanese shoe makers are in transition.

To sum up, the Pearl River Delta (and Dongguan) as a global site for OEM and an experiment site for the Chinese economy is an excellent location for us to observe and examine how Taiwan capital responds to the aforementioned challenges. The transformation of the organizational network of the Taiwanese shoe industry in Dongguan is the focus of this chapter. I have collected data through field studies in the Pearl River Delta since 2007. In addition, the investigation of the Taiwanese apparel industry since 2009 in the Yangtzi River Delta will be the material in this chapter. Before entering the analysis of the network transformation, it is necessary for us to clarify the organizational features of the Taiwanese manufacturing industry both in Taiwan and China in advance.

The production organization of Taishang: from Taiwan to China

Studies on the organizational structure of the Taiwanese manufacturing industry suggest that it consists of the small and medium-sized enterprises. This network-like organizational form with the characteristic of interpersonal trust is regarded as the primary factor in contributing to the success of the Taiwanese export-led manufacturing industry in the world, including textiles, footwear, and electronics. For example, the strong ties through face-to-face interactions result in entrepreneurs not acting in self-interest when it comes to the exchange of resources, such as payment delays (Chao 1995).

My field study also supports the significance of trust in the operation of the production network of the Taiwanese footwear industry to a certain degree. The relationship between a footwear trading company and an embroidery factory exemplifies how interpersonal connections play the key role in stabilizing cooperative relationships of both sides. These two companies have been working together since 1985. During these years, the trading company as the buyer always asked its assembly factories, as the suppliers, to subcontract the embroidering part of the shoe making to the embroidery factory. The situation hasn't changed, even after the trading company moved from Taiwan first to Vietnam and then to China. Their personal relationship continues even after the embroidery company closed its factories both in Vietnam and China in 2011.

However, trust is not as universal as the studies on Taiwanese manufacturing industry claim. As a matter of fact, the seeming trust relationship could be characterized by asymmetrical dependency. Based on my observation for years, the manager of the embroidery factory is used to spending abundant time and energy to maintain rapport with the president of the trading company for stabilizing orders. On the contrary, the trading company has been investing less in this relationship. This asymmetrical dependency shows that trading companies occupy a more advantageous position than assembly and embroidery factories in the commodity chain, and they can decide which factories to place orders with. That is where the power of trading companies as buyers comes from. In other words, though trust is an important factor in stabilizing business transaction, the crucial position economic actors occupy in the supply chain does determine which one can enjoy the fruit of this trust relationship. Cheng's study (2011) on the historical formation and transformation of the governance structure of the Taiwanese footwear industry also illustrates the importance of the power perspective, even in the network-like organizational structure in Taiwan. Accordingly, embedded trust in the organizational network of the Taiwanese manufacturing industry is characterized by asymmetrical dependency.

In addition to asymmetry-dependency trust, spatial concentration is another feature of Taiwanese network-like production organization. Spatial convergence helped the Taiwanese manufacturing industry overcome the problem of firm scale and production coordination. The small and medium-sized firms, specializing in one or two steps of production, could not survive being isolated from other firms. They had to work together in close cooperation and coordination, to finish a product. Hence, the consideration of space becomes an important factor for the smaller firms in comparison with big firms characterized by vertical integration.

Take the footwear industry as an example. According to a 1989 survey of the Taiwanese Footwear Manufacturing Association, 63 percent of the Taiwanese shoe factories were concentrated in the Greater Taichung area, including Taichung County, Nantou County, and Changhua County. Taichung city, as the core of the Greater Taichung area, has been the hub in the development of the Taiwanese footwear industry. In addition to shoe factories, trading companies and international buyers set up their offices, or branch offices in Taichung city (see Figure 3.1). Indeed, most of the companies are concentrated

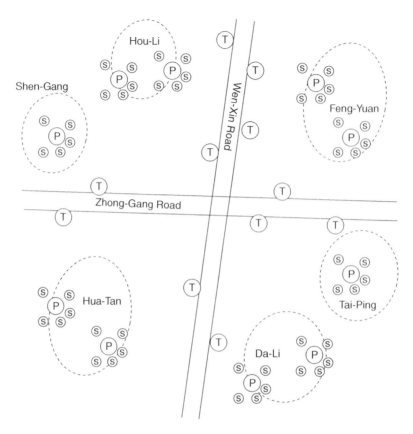

Figure 3.1 Map of the shoe factories in the Greater Taichung Area (source: Cheng (2011: 30)).

Notes
T is trading companies, P is assembly factories, and S is supporting factories. Each assembly factory has the relationship of subcontracting with other assembly factories. Multiple subcontracting relationships also exist among supporting factories, and between supporting factories and assembly factories.

in two intersecting roads in Taichung City: *Jon-Gun* Road (Taichung Harbor Road中港路) which connects downtown and the seaport, and *Wen-Shin* Road (文心路) which is close to the highway exit. Such spatial concentration provides many advantages to the Taiwanese network-organizational footwear industry, including speeding circulation of personnel, materials, and information, as well as overcoming the disadvantages of the small-scale production units.

To sum up, asymmetry-dependency trust and spatial concentration are the primary features of the relationships among small and medium-sized firms in Taiwan. This network-like production organization successfully helps the Taiwanese manufacturing industry find the niche to be OEM in the international division of labor. Although the Taiwanese manufacturing industry already moved overseas in search for cheaper labor cost in the late 1980s, the network-like organization of production seems not to change with migration of manufacturing sites. On the contrary, the production organization network of Taishang staying in China was becoming even closer in one city to overcome uncertainties of Chinese economic transition (see Figure 3.2).

Of course, the production organization would change with the relocation of its manufacturing site. For example, Taiwanese factories in China have a higher degree of vertical integration compared to their parent factories in Taiwan. That is, Taiwanese factories in China truncate the three-tired system of production organization to only two tiers, composed of parts makers and assemblers. Many processing works done by job shops in Taiwan have been incorporated into parts makers and assemblers due to cheap land and abundant labor supply in China (Chen 2012).[1] This transformation made the scale of Taiwanese factories in China bigger, especially for assemblers. For example, many assemblers in the footwear industry usually employed over

Figure 3.2 Map of the shoe factories in Dongguan.

Notes
The regions underlined, including Houjie town, Gaobu town, Dalingshan town, Dalang town, Liaobu town, Hengli town, and the Dongcheng district in Dongguan city, are where Taiwanese shoe factories are located, especially Houjie, which is called "Little Taichung," in which Taiwanese shoe factories gathered. Although the number of shoe factories is decreasing because of the global financial crisis, enterprises for shoe material and shoe machines are still located here.

ten thousand workers before 2008. Even though the production organization has transformed from a three-tiered to a two-tiered system, the core feature in the network of Taiwanese factories in China is still trust-oriented. In other words, inter-organizational trust built in Taiwan through repeated interactions gave Chinese factories difficulties in penetrating the clusters Taishang created. If Chinese factories did penetrate into the Taiwanese network successfully, they could only involve in low-end production activities (Chiu 2005). In conclusion, Taishang in China prefer partners with the same ethnic background (Hsing 1998; Cheng 1999; Chen 2012).

At the same time, the high-risk investment environment created by socialist economic transition and rampant rent-seeking activities of local officials also made the Taiwanese factories in China more integrated and reliant on each other than before. The spatial concentration of Taiwanese factories is an expected outcome. When I visited a shoe assembly factory in Dongguan in 2004, I noticed that there was a row of light orange buildings, surrounding the assembly factory, Chang Deng. Later, I realized that these buildings were parts makers and processing makers that worked as suppliers and subcontractors for the assembly factory. These parts and processing makers had a nickname, "The Little Chang Deng." The reason for this spatial concentration was that they could help each other if one of the factories had troubles with local officials. The managers of these factories held regular meetings to exchange information regarding the market and the government. They also socialized after work at Taiwanese-financed restaurants, karaoke bars, and golf clubs to release feelings of homesickness. It was the unfamiliar and unstable environment in China that accounted for the tighter trust relationship among Taishang. That is, the status of being business aliens for Taishang in China desalinated the characteristic of asymmetry-dependency within trust. Ultimately, the clusters of Taiwanese factories with trust and ethnic ingredients became an enclave in China, which was isolated from local producers.

However, the situation has changed since 2008. Facing local unfavorable trade and labor policies as well as the global financial crisis, Taishang, exported-led ones in particular, start to joke about their harsh situation in China. For example, there are three solutions for the market instabilities, namely "three turns (san zhuan: 三轉)." The first solution is "transition (zhuan xing: 轉型)," which refers to Taishang who develop their own brands and stay where they are. The second solution is "transfer (zhuan yi: 轉移)," which refers to Taishang who are incapable of developing brands and trade marketing, and therefore have to move to another location with cheaper production costs. The final solution is "career changing (zhuan hang: 轉行)," which refers to Taishang who are incapable of either brand developing or moving, and who are forced to find a different job since the factory is going to shut down. This type of joke clearly illustrates the difficult situations of Taishang in recent years.

Local embeddedness: the transformation of Taishang production network

Why is staying in China important?

Former Taishang studies mainly focused on how Taiwanese enterprises, as an invisible elbow for the international division of labor, successfully made use of various social mechanisms, such as governments, networks, and associations to reduce production cost and stabilize market environments (Wade 1990; Cheng 1999; Amsden and Chu 2003; Cheng 2011). However, the constant emphasis on the OEM role of Taiwanese enterprises restrains our perspectives on Taishang studies. Actually, it is possible for Taiwanese enterprises to escape the destiny of being an industrial nomad and upgrade to a higher position in the international division of labor. That is why I choose to focus on the first strategy of the three turns, "transition (zhuan xing: 轉型)," and examine how the process of drifting to rooting influences the transformation of Taishang's production network.

Based on my field study, there are several factors in explaining why Taishang in the shoe industry have been willing to stay in China after 2008. First of all, it will take a long time for Taishang to rebuild a manufacturing site outside of China without language and cultural affinities. Some Taiwanese shoe makers told me that it is not easy for them to build a factory in India or Bangladesh even though labor cost over there is much cheaper. Second, the footwear supply chain in China is mature and comprehensive. Buyers can easily source various components of shoes here in Dongguan. Third, managers of most Taiwanese shoe factories in China are 50 or going on 60 years old. Because of age, it is becoming more and more difficult for them to keep on moving around Taiwan, China, and any other investment locations. Besides, the second generation of Taishang in traditional manufacturing industries are not willing to take over their factories. Nevertheless, the aforementioned factors could be incomplete if we do not take the world market into consideration.

From the 1978 economic transition on, China has been embracing capitalism over 30 years. Over the past 30 years, China has been deeply embedded in the world economic system through foreign trade and foreign investments. Due to abundant labor, cheap land, and slack social and environmental policies, China became a world factory. However, social instability since the 2000s, which is caused by income inequality, an incomplete social welfare system, and environmental problems, has forced the Chinese government to reconsider the cost of being a world factory. The 11th Five-Year Plan beginning in 2006 was a turning point for the economic policies of the central government.

In the 11th Five-Year Plan, the central government redefined the contents of development. This plan was attempting to transform economic growth from being driven by industry and quantitative expansion to being driven by structural optimization and upgrading, from being driven by a large amount of resources consumption to being driven by the improvement of resources utilization efficiency, and from relying on the input of capital and substance factor to relying on science and technology advancement and human resources. Consequently, the shoe industry, with the characteristics of high resource consumption and low output, became an unfavorable target. The above-mentioned policy of "*Teng-Long-Huan-Niao*" in Guangdong province could be regarded as a response to the 11th Five-Year Plan. In addition, the 11th Five-Year Plan emphasized the balanced economic and social development, which means that economic growth should not be at the expense of social welfare of the citizens. The Labor Contract Law of 2008 would be the product of the balanced economic and social development. For the shoe industry and other traditional manufacturing ones, the Labor Contract Law not only increased their labor cost, but also forced export-led Taishang to move again.

In addition to following the blueprint of the 11th Five-Year Plan, the 12th Five-Year Plan put a great emphasis on the expansion of the domestic market so as to cope with the global financial crisis starting from 2008. The global financial crisis made it difficult for the Chinese economy to rely on foreign trade solely. The Chinese government began to accentuate the domestic market to compensate for the decreasing world consumers' market. For the central government, transforming China from world factory to world market is a cure for continuing economic growth afterward. For Taishang hoping to root, China's becoming a world market is a good opportunity to upgrade their position in the global commodity chain from OEM to ODM (original design manufacturer) and OBM. In other words, staying in China may lead them to the end of being industrial nomads. This helps explain why not all of Taishang choose to move to other countries for "better investment environments." When Taishang decided to root in China, their production network started to change at the same time.

The disorganized enclave

According to my field work, Taiwanese shoe makers have increasingly started to cooperate with Chinese local shoe factories since 2008. This corresponded with the eruption of the global financial crisis. For mainstream economists, cost incentive has explained everything already. However, economics could not tell us the details of how Taiwanese shoe makers locate local factories as their suppliers, how Taiwanese shoe makers incorporate these local factories into their network in China, and how their relationships have changed the core characteristic of Taiwanese export-led footwear network in China. That is where economic and organizational sociology can come in.

How did the Taiwanese shoe makers in China find their potential suppliers from the local factories? The referral of the third party is the most common method taken by Taiwanese shoe investors. And the colleagues who have ever subcontracted work to local factories are usually their third party. The recommendation from the experienced colleagues could reduce the costs of trial and error in locating potential local partners. Sometimes, international buyers would ask Taiwanese shoe makers to subcontract work to the local shoe factories they used to work with. However, since international buyers were not familiar with the Chinese local shoe industry, it is rare for them to do so. On the contrary, local buyers, such as Anta (安踏), Li Ning (李寧), and Aokang (奥康), do so frequently because they knew where they could find the right local suppliers for Taiwanese shoe makers. Why don't these local buyers bypass Taiwanese shoe makers? According to one of my interviewees as the president of a Taiwanese shoe trading company, good quality provided by the Taiwanese shoe factories and trading companies is the main concern. Last but not least, some Taiwanese shoe makers encouraged their talented and ambitious workers back to their hometowns and to start their own business by offering them start-up funds or lending/selling machines to them. Many parent Taiwanese shoe makers also promise these subsidiaries a certain amount of orders in keeping their new factories in work.[2]

After locating local partners, two methods are taken by Taiwanese shoe makers in Dongguan to incorporate local factories into their production network. The first strategy for them in coping with increasing labor cost is transforming themselves from shoe factories to trading companies. I call them "quasi-buyers." These Taiwanese shoe makers receive orders from international buyers as they used to do; meanwhile, they start to learn how to be a buyer to subcontract orders to local shoe factories. In other words, the role of the quasi-buyer is a subcontractor. Subcontracting is a common strategy for Taiwanese small and medium-sized enterprises to increase efficiency and reduce cost in satisfying the changing market. Nevertheless, the major discrepancy between now and then is that Chinese local shoe factories are the new contractors of Taiwanese shoe factories, rather than the previous partners with the same ethnic background. Both actors have differences in many aspects, besides ethnic background.

For example, the technical levels of local shoe factories lag behind Taiwanese shoe makers. Local factories are incapable of making complicated, delicate, and fashionable shoe types, such as high-heels, pointy-toe, and cutting die-outsole ones. In addition, the quality control is another factor highlighting their differences because local factories are seldom involved in the supply chain of the world shoe market. Furthermore, the enterprise culture between Taiwanese and Chinese local factories, such as work ethics and attitudes, is different. In recent years, these downsides of local factories have been improved via different strategies. For instance, many local factories recruit Taiwanese managers with higher pay to upgrade their equipments and management. This is an easier way for them to become a business partner with Taiwanese shoe makers. In addition, new local factories are handled by senior employees who have worked in Taiwanese factories for at least five or six years and therefore they know very well how to cooperate with Taiwanese companies. This is a common case in Dongguan. The main goal of both strategies taken by the local factories is to enter the production network of the export-led shoe industry controlled by Taishang.

However, Taiwanese managers or well-experienced local employees are not available in each local factory. Hence, Taiwanese shoe makers still need to develop standards of operation in overcoming the aforementioned technical and cultural problems of local factories. Let us take one of the Taiwanese shoe factories I visited in 2012 as an example. This factory, which has been in Dong-guan for more than ten years, produces high-end and fashionable high heels for American and European famous brands, such as Nine West, Zara, and Mango. It is also a trading company at the same time and has started to put a greater emphasis on the role of the trading company. It used to subcontract shoes to other Taiwanese factories in China when more large orders than it could handle were received. Due to cost concern, it started to subcontract its orders to local factories in 2008.[3] Up till today, almost 90 percent of its orders from inter-national buyers have subcontracted to its Chinese local suppliers. Therefore, the shoe maker who is becoming the trading company could not afford the failure of the subcontracting strategy.

In order to solve the difficulties of subcontracting and train the local factories as qualified suppliers, this shoe trading company developed a new project, called DDCP (Digital Design Center Project), so as to standardize the procedures of making shoes as much as possible.[4] According to a senior experienced manager of this company, one of the reasons for creating this project is to provide techni-cal supports for their local shoe factories:

> This is the trend for Taiwanese shoe makers to incorporate local factories into our production network. However, not all of them could qualify as sup-pliers of Taiwanese shoe makers. Accordingly, the major task of DDCP is to standardize the procedures of making shoes and to pass the standardized procedures to inexperienced local factories to satisfy the requirements of our company. Of course, the procedures of making shoes could not be standard-ized completely. This project, the DDCP, is a new experiment if we want to have local shoe factories as our partners successfully.

The interviewee running this project gave standardization a vivid metaphor, cen-tralized kitchen (中央廚房). In this centralized kitchen, all of the local suppliers become OEM for Taiwanese shoe makers. Meanwhile, Taiwanese shoe makers are also becoming quasi-buyers and upgrading their status in the global supply chain. Consequently, the Taiwanese shoe production network characterized by the enclave has started to disorganize.

In addition to being the quasi-buyer, another strategy Taiwanese shoe makers used in coping with the changing environments is insourcing. Different from the popular outsourcing, i.e., contracting work to an outside supplier, insourcing is to hire an entire team from outside to work in the factory. According to a Tai-wanese manager I interviewed in 2011, insourcing is a method to incorporate Chinese local producers into his factory. His factory provides facilities and offers two meals (lunch and dinner) and pick-up services to the hired team run by local people. Workers in the team are paid by each order, not by each month. As expected, the relationship between the Taiwanese factory and its hired team is unstable because the insourcing is a temporary strategy for rush-hour orders and seasons. That is why the Taiwanese manager called this local hired team "rescuers." Just like the quasi-buyer strategy, the rescuer strategy through insourcing also made the enclave of Taiwanese factories in China collapse. The Taiwanese manager explained the reason for doing this:

> Insourcing not only solves the problem of unstable orders but also maintains the control of critical production activities inside the factory. Furthermore, this strategy also reduces huge labor cost caused by the Labor Contract Law, international buyer audits, and deficit labor supply in China.[5] Most important of all, emerging local factories incorporated by Taiwanese export-led manufacturing industry through insourcing are able to cope with the requirement from the central government, moving toward a well-off society (奔向小康社會).[6] In recent years, local governments are also trying hard to promote their dominant areas toward moderate prosperity.

Nevertheless, most of the Taiwanese shoe makers I interviewed worried that insourcing would cause "one factory, two regimes." This is because it is not easy for Taiwanese shoe makers to manage the team workers through insourcing. Different enterprise institutions, such as labor social policies, may cause conflicts between subcontractors and contractors in the same factory. However, for the Taiwanese manager adopting an insourcing strategy, he is able to overcome the aforementioned difficulties because he only works with the local factories run by his previous experienced employees. In this case, the Taiwanese manager is the key person that encouraged his senior employees to start their own business and become his local partners.

Although new institutional sociology indicates that social ties among economic actors may reduce the conflicts of institutional differences (Nee and Ingram 1998), the phenomenon of "one factory, two regimes" through insourcing, admittedly, has increasingly changed the labor regime of the Taiwanese shoe makers in general. Let us take social insurances as an example. Taiwanese factories are usually a target of international anti-sweatshop movements. International buyers often check the labor conditions of the Taiwanese suppliers through audits. Local governments also demand Taiwanese factories to submit reports regarding the covering percentage of the labor contracts and social insurances. After adopting an insourcing strategy, Taiwanese factories improved their labor conditions in a certain way. Since the insourcing transferred the cost of social insurances from Taiwanese factories to the local teams, Taiwanese factories can save the labor costs and avoid the blame of being sweatshops, which functions similarly as the outsourcing strategy.

A president of a Taiwanese factory I interviewed in 2011 owns an apparel factory in Pinghu, a county-level city in northeast Zhejiang province, located outside of Shanghai. There were around a thousand workers in this factory by then. According to the president, the factory signed contracts with employees and covered social insurances for persons working in the factory due to the regulations of the local government. By doing so, the president called his factory a "model factory" in Pinhu Economic Development Zone. Generally, the Taiwanese factory was only responsible for 70 percent of output, and the other

30 percent was subcontracted to the local factories through either outsourcing or insourcing. In other words, the Taiwanese apparel factory at least transferred 30 percent of its extra labor cost to the suppliers, the local factories.

This situation also happened in the Taiwanese export-led shoe industry in the Pearl River Delta. A shoe interviewee told me once that local factories have great ability of solving labor social policies. A Chinese president I interviewed in 2012 also confirmed this situation. He has a shoe factory in Dongguan and there are over 400 workers in the factory. When I asked him how he handled the labor conditions of his factory, he answered:

> You don't have to set up a factory in economic or development zones. If you set up a factory in a smaller industrial park with no names, no one, what I mean is local officials, would get you into trouble. If buyers come to audit the factory, you just have to bribe all of the employees beforehand for telling the "right answers." In the case of JC Penney's audit last time, every employee in my factory can earn extra 200 RMB if they respond to the buyers' questions properly. If not, they got nothing. You know what? The fact is that this reward strategy for our employees works.

Based on the above-mentioned situation, some Taiwanese manufacturing factories in China, both shoe makers and apparel makers, completed their corporate social responsibility at the expense of workers in local factories. A transmutation of the labor regime of Taiwanese manufacturing factories is found in my field work. The repressive labor regime, which used to be the trademark of Taiwanese factories, is now becoming evident in Chinese local factories. In order to receive the orders from Taiwanese factories and trading companies, local factories themselves are also willing to do so. To sum up, Taiwanese manufacturing industries in China are incorporating local factories as new suppliers due to the transformation of Chinese internal and external business environments; consequently, the mode of its enclave economy is disorganizing. Not only the labor regime, but also the social ties used to hold the Taiwanese production network together are experiencing transforming in the transitional stage. The next question we should ask is: how do Taiwanese shoe makers interact with local suppliers with different ethnic backgrounds?

A production network of local embeddedness: the power perspective

Many Taiwanese shoe managers I interviewed argue that Taiwanese factories are better than local factories in many aspects, including factory management, technical level, human resources, labor conditions, and receiving orders, which I have mentioned in the previous sections. For example, Chinese shoe factories were criticized for cutting corners in making shoes. Taiwanese shoe managers usually complained that the percentage of B-grade shoes made by local shoe factories was higher than expected. In addition, it is common for Taiwanese shoe factories to ask for supplementary materials and parts from their suppliers.

However, Chinese local factories often disagree with this kind of request because supplements were not listed in the contract. As expected, conflicts between Taiwanese and Chinese shoe factories happened frequently. When I asked how to settle these conflicts, a Taiwanese manager answered:

> First of all, we communicate with each other as much as possible. I try to make them know how Taiwanese shoe factories do business. If this does not work, I would turn to power to make them follow my orders. Since Taiwanese shoe factories are the ones who place orders, Chinese local factories cannot ignore or deny this fact. Taiwanese factories are the boss, anyway.

The paragraph above conveyed an important message: power, rather than trust, has become the medium in illustrating the interactions between Taiwanese shoe makers and new local partners. This argument is further strengthened in my follow-up interviews with Chinese local factories. The fact that most of them received 100 percent of their orders from Taiwanese shoe makers illustrates why the Taiwanese manager above was so confident to say that "Taiwanese factories are the boss, anyway."

The power perspective not only reminds us the importance of the global commodity chain in determining economic actions, but also brings us back to the discussion regarding the relationship between foreign capital and local economy. In other words, the core question is local embeddedness of foreign direct investment. For classical dependency theory, transnational corporations, viewed as the representatives of foreign capital, are detached and detrimental to local economic development due to the enclave economy it creates in host regions. On the contrary, new economic geography stresses local embeddedness of transnational corporations in capturing the advantages the host regions can offer (Dicken et al. 1994; Dicken 2003). Previous studies on the Taiwanese case in China (Cheng 1999; Chen 2012) seemed to support the perspective of dependency theory.

However, local suppliers being new partners of Taiwanese shoe factories has changed both the Taiwanese enclave in China and its production network at the same time. The fact that local factories are included in the Taiwanese network indicates that Taiwanese shoe makers, as transnational corporations, have begun to embed themselves into the local environments and to be part of the local economy. The local embeddedness of Taiwanese enterprises in China challenges both dependency theory and new economic geography. This case is against the fatalistic perspective held by dependency theory that local embeddedness would never happen. At the same time, the time of its occurrence is 20 years later than the expectation of new economic geography. More importantly, the essence of the local embeddedness is also different from what the new economic sociology argues. Taiwanese shoe makers, which used to take embedded trust as an effective governance structure in reducing market uncertainties, have turned to put more emphasis on their position in the global commodity chain. This illustrates that Taiwanese companies in China are resorting to power in rebuilding a status hierarchy among economic actors to maintain their performance. In this status hierarchy, the incumbents, Taiwanese factories, are capable of creating effective governance structure to reproduce their interests, and making it more difficult for the challengers, Chinese local factories, to change the status quo.

In conclusion, not only trust, but also a stable status hierarchy based on power play a central role in solving market instabilities. Furthermore, this power perspective helps us understand the dynamic process of Taishang's production networks in transition in China.

Situational trust: a dynamic category

After examining the historical development of the Taiwanese shoe industry, we found that both trust and power are the main ingredients in the production network of the Taiwanese manufacturing industry in turn at various stages. Before the late 1980s in Taiwan and after the late 2000s in China, power embedded in the commodity chain is the key feature in the production network of the Taiwanese shoe industry. However, Taishang established a shoe cluster with more mutual trust in Dongguan between the late 1980s and the late 2000s. How do we explain the differences above?

Here, I want to propose a new concept, situational trust, to describe the transformations of the core feature within the production network of Taishang from Taiwan to China. What situational trust means is that trust, which is often regarded by the literature on Taiwanese manufacturing industry as a stable category (Chen 1994; Cheng 1999; Chen 2002), may change with time and space. Although trust is resulted from long-term and repeated interpersonal interactions, different institutional environments in reality may lead to variations in trust. That is, the formation of trust is a dynamic process, which is embedded in and shaped by both local and trans-border contexts simultaneously, especially in the age of globalization.

According to the aforementioned analysis, the Taiwanese manufacturing industry is characterized by the trust-oriented network intertwined with the characteristic of asymmetrical dependency. However, when Taishang began to invest in China in the late 1980s, the production network changed with transborder capital movement accordingly. Due to the risky investment environment caused by Chinese socialist economic transition and rampant rent-seeking activities of local officials, Taishang preferred working with the suppliers from the same ethnic background in stabilizing local market uncertainties. As a result, Taishang in China became more integrated and reliant on each other than before. Therefore, inter-organizational trust outranks the asymmetrical dependency in the high risky environment. The expected outcome in the production network is the Taiwanese enclave economy in coastal China, especially in the Pearl River and Yangtze River Deltas. Therefore, the institutional differences between Taiwan and China condition situational trust among Taishang.

Since 2008, Taishang in China have been forced to incorporate local producers into their production network in response to the transformation of the global financial crisis and the regulatory regime. The status hierarchy in the network once again plays an important role in explaining the interactions between Taishang and local producers. And after investing in China for 20 years, the ethnic background of the suppliers is no longer the main concern for Taishang.

Conclusion: the cross-border organization network and its next step

What is the future for Taishang? This is a question that has been bothering both Taiwanese investors and researchers for years. In the past 20 years, Taishang found their "second spring" in China and maintained the status as an invisible semi-periphery elbow in the international division of labor. Since the transformation of Chinese internal and external business environments from the late 2000s, Taishang are on the move again. As a matter of fact, not everyone is on the road for the next investment sites. Some Taiwanese shoe makers chose not to be the industrial nomads and decided to root in Dongguan, the shoe capital of the world.

There are several characteristics for those shoe makers who stay in Dongguan. First, the scale of the factory is downsizing. Second, parts of processing, such as the upper part, have moved to the inland regions with cheaper labor and land costs since they require a large number of workers to handle. Third, Taiwanese shoe makers started to subcontract orders to Chinese local factories and this is what I focus on in this chapter, the formation of cross-border organization network. Fourth, many Taiwanese shoe makers are transforming themselves into trading companies, and some leading ones I interviewed even start to create their own brands and retail stores so as to upgrade their position in the buyer-driven global footwear commodity chain. It is easy for us to understand the relationship between the first two strategies. How about the third and the fourth ones? Since cross-border organization network and own brands developing happen at the same time, what might be the link between them?

This chapter argues that the transformation of the production network could be the missing link for us to understand the process of how Taishang upgrades itself from OEM and ODM to OBM. Becoming an OBM is a long way to go, and it is difficult for Taishang to develop their own brand overnight. It is also difficult for them to give up their original advantages in OEM and ODM, because large amount of capital is needed in OBM development. The cross-border network triggered by the transformation of Chinese investment environments offer Taishang an opportunity to invest in OBM with the capital and time saved via subcontracting. And Taishang have realized that this is a one-shot opportunity for them to escape industrial nomads and become their own masters by opening up the Chinese market. This chapter provides a preliminary answer on the possible relationship between the cross-border organization network and the brand development from the organizational perspective.

During the transformation, Taishang's production network in China is not the same as the original one mainly based on trust. The asymmetrical power relationship among economic actors not only helped Taishang in rebuilding a new production order for further mobility in the global commodity chain, but also shifted the repressive labor regime from Taishang to local suppliers. Indeed, local factories and industries are emerging as a new partner with Taishang; however, the exploited situation of local workers remains unchanged. Therefore, it is power, rather than trust, that reminds us to see things from both sides. That is what beyond embedded trust means.

Notes

1 Nevertheless, there are differences among various industries. Taiwanese footwear factories in China have a higher degree of the three-tiered system because of lower automation in comparison with the bicycle and electronic industries.
2 In addition to the aforementioned three methods, self-recommendation by Chinese local factories is the fourth method that Taiwanese shoe investors search for new suppliers. However, Taiwanese investors do not prefer this method because of the high cost of trial and error.
3 As a matter of fact, many Taiwanese shoe makers have closed their factories since 2008. Hence, it is getting more and more difficult for Taiwanese shoe and trading companies to find the suppliers with the same ethnic background in Dongguan.
4 Generally, it is difficult for Taiwanese shoe makers to digitalize the shoe last and upper model, especially the shoe last. The shoe last, which consists of heel height, toe shape, and cone instep, is the soul of the shoes. It is usually manually made by the most experienced worker. And the major task of the DDCP is trying to standardize the shoe last for local shoe factories as new partners with Taiwanese shoe makers. The experiment on standardization is still continuing.
5 Insourcing and outsourcing are also the strategies of mobilizing rural labor that Taiwanese enterprises used to solve deficit labor supply in the 1970s and 1980s. The comparison between China and Taiwan would be an important issue to help us understand how industry and agriculture interact with each other in a transitional stage.
6 The 11th and 12th Five-Year Plans are the guidelines of the central government for moving toward a well-off society.

References

Amsden, Alice H., and Wan-Wen Chu. 2003. *Beyond Late Development: Taiwan's Upgrading Policies*. Cambridge, MA: MIT Press.
Chandler, Alfred D. 1977. *The Visible Hand: The Managerial Revolution in American Business*. Cambridge, MA: Harvard University Press.
Chao, Hui-Lin. 1995. "The Characters of Resource Exchange in the Network of Production of 'Hsieh-Li': The 'Social Network' of the Exchange of Economic Resources." (in Chinese) *Chinese Journal of Sociology* 18: 75–116.
Chen, Chieh-Hsun. 1994. *The Production Network of "Hsieh-Li" and Social Structure: The Socio-economic Analysis of Taiwanese Small- and Medium-sized Enterprises* (in Chinese). Taipei: Linking Books Press.
Chen, Dung-Dheng. 2003. *Making It Integrated: Organizational Networks in Taiwan's Integrated-circuit Industry* (in Chinese). Taipei: Socio Publishing.
Chen, Ming-Chi. 2002. "Industrial Distract and Social Capital in Taiwan's Economic Development: An Economical Sociological Study on Taiwan's Bicycle Industry." PhD. Diss., Yale University.

Chen, Ming-Chi. 2012. "Fortress in the Air: The Organizational Model of Taiwanese Export-manufacturing Transplants in China." *Issues & Studies* 48: 73–112.

Cheng, Chih-Peng. 2008. "Markets as Politics: The Formation and Transformation of the Chinese Export-led Footwear Industry." (in Chinese) *Taiwanese Sociology* 15: 190–163.

Cheng, Chih-Peng. 2011. "Internal Goes Before International: A Historical Analysis of the Government Structure of Taiwan Footwear Industry." (in Chinese) *Journal of Social Science and Philosophy* 23: 15–60.

Cheng, Lu-Lin. 1999. "The Invisible Elbow: Semiperiphery and the Restructuring of the International Footwear Market." (in Chinese) *Taiwan: A Radical Quarterly in Social Studies* 35: 1–46.

Chiu, Chun-Hung. 2005. "The Boundary of Trust: Taiwanese Cross-Border Bicycle Manufacturing Network in China." (in Chinese) Master's thesis. National Taipei University.

Coase, Ronald. 1937. "The Nature of the Film." *Economica* 4: 386–405.

Coleman, James S. 1988. "Social Capital in the Creation of Human Capital." *American Journal of Sociology* 94: 95–120.

Dicken, Peter. 2003. *Global Shift: Reshaping the Global Economic Map in the 21st Century*. London: Sage.

Dicken, Peter, Mats Forsgren, and Anders Malmberg. 1994. "The Local Embeddedness of Transnational Corporations." In *Globalization, Institutions, and Regional Development in Europe*, edited by A. Amin and N. Thrift, 23–45. Oxford, UK: Oxford University Press.

DiMaggio, Paul J., and Hugh Louch. 1998. "Socially Embedded Consumer Transactions: For What Kinds of Purchases Do People Most Often Use Networks." *American Sociological Review* 63: 619–637.

Fligstein, Neil. 2001. *The Architecture of Markets: An Economic Sociology of Twenty-First-Century Capitalist Societies*. Princeton: Princeton University Press.

Gereffi, Gary. 1994. "The Organization of Buyer-Driven Global Commodity Chains: How U.S. Retailers Shape Overseas Production Networks." In *Commodity Chains and Global Capitalism*, edited by Gary Gereffi and Miguel Korzeniewicz, 95–122. Westport, CO: Praeger Press.

Granovetter, Mark. 1985. "Economic Action and Social Structure: The Problem of Embeddedness." *American Journal of Sociology* 91: 481–510.

Hsing, You-Tien. 1998. *Making Capitalism in China: The Taiwan Connection*. New York: Oxford University Press.

Korzeniewicz, Miguel. 1994. "Commodity Chains and Marketing Strategies: Nike and the Global Athletic Footwear Industry." In *Commodity Chains and Global Capitalism*, edited by Gary Gereffi and Miguel Korzeniewicz, 247–265. Westport, CO: Praeger Press.

Lincoln, James R. and Michael L. Gerlach. 2004. *Japan's Network Economy: Structure Persistence and Change*. Cambridge, UK: Cambridge University Press.

Lu, Kuo-Chen, and Tzu-Yen Yu. 2008. "Big Escape of Taishang." (in Chinese) *Taiwan Business Weekly*, June 2.

Macaulay, Stewart. 1963. "Non-Contractual Relations in Business: A Preliminary Study." *American Sociological Review* 28: 55–67.

Nee, Victor, and Paul Ingram. 1998. "Embeddedness and Beyond: Institutions, Exchange, and Social Structure." In *The New Institutionalism in Sociology*, edited by Mary C. Brinton and Victor Nee, 19–45. New York: Russell Sage Foundation.

Nohria, Nitin and Robert G. Eccles, ed. 1992. *Networks and Organization: Structure, Form, and Action*. Boston, MA: Harvard Business School Press.

North, Douglass C. 1990. *Institutions, Institutional Change and Economic Performance*. Cambridge, UK: Cambridge University Press.

Piore, Michael and Charles Sabel. 1984. *The Second Industrial Divide*. New York: Basic Books.

Portes, Alejandro and Julia Sensenbrenner. 1993. "Embeddedness and Immigration: Notes on the Social Determinants of Economic Action." *American Journal of Sociology* 98: 1320–1350.

Powell, Walter. 1990. "Neither Market nor Hierarchy: Network Forms of Organization." *Research on Organization Behavior* 12: 295–336.

Saxenian, AnnaLee. 1996. "Inside-Out: Regional Networks and Industrial Adaptation in Silicon Valley and Route 128." *Cityscape: A Journal of Policy Development and Research* 2: 41–60.

Shieh, Gwo-shyong. 1992. *"Boss" Island: The Subcontracting Networks and Micro-Entrepreneurship in Taiwan's Development*. New York: Peter Lang Publishing.

Smitka, Michael. 1991. *Competitive Ties: Subcontracting in the Japanese Automobile Industry*. New York: Columbia University Press.

Uzzi, Brian. 1996. "The Sources and Consequences of Embeddedness for the Economic Performance of Organizations: The Network Effect." *American Sociological Review* 61: 674–698.

Wade, Robert. 1990. *Governing the Market: Economic Theory and the Role of Government in East Asian Industrialization*. Princeton: Princeton University Press.

Williamson, Oliver E. 1975. *Markets and Hierarchies: Analysis and Antitrust Implication*. New York: The Free Press.

Wu, Jien-Min. 1997. "Strange Bed-Fellows: Dynamics of Government-Business Relations between Chinese Local Authorities and Taiwanese Investors." *Journal of Contemporary China* 6: 315–346.

4 Taiwanese architects and post-Mao China's production of the built environment

Shiuh-Shen Chien

Introduction

Taiwanese investment has played a critical role in the Chinese industrial transition since 1978. Most research on Taiwanese investment in the industrialization of post-Mao China tends to focus on three dimensions: (1) the development and transformation of manufacturing industries (e.g., production network, technology transfer, labor conditions, and corporate strategies) (Wang and Lee 2007; Yang and Coe 2009; Chen et al. 2010); (2) the dynamics of interactions between Taiwanese firms and Chinese local governments (Hsing 1996; Wu 1997; Chien 2007); and (3) the social lives of Taiwanese businesspersons in China (family life, cultural identity, and social networking) (Shen 2008; Keng and Schubert 2010; Tseng 2011; Tseng and Wu 2011). Though it is widely agreed that industrialization has taken place along with dramatic changes in the built environment in China over the past decades (Lin and Wei 2002), what is relatively little examined in the existing literature is whether or not Taiwanese have been "directly" involved in the rampant spatial transformation. Generally speaking, the Taiwanese in the built-environment-related industry (namely, the BER industry, including real estate developers, architecture studios, planning and engineering firms, urban planners, quantity surveyors, and project managers) actually traveled to China and extended their services through different means and produced various impacts. However, those actions and their impacts have not received enough academic attention that they should deserve (Chou and Lin 2007). This chapter aims to fill this gap.

Given that some of literature on urban China has discussed western architects in post-Mao China, this chapter also focuses on Taiwanese architects and aims to extend the literature on urban China in the three following dimensions. First, global branding architects have shaped China's urban landscape by building iconic structures in many cities, such as Foster+Partners' Beijing Capital International Airport, Rem Koolhass' Chinese Central Television Headquarters (CCTV), and Paul Andres' National Theater. It is no surprise that such star architects can bring a certain amount of popularity to urban authorities as part of image marketing (Olds 2001; Cartier 2002; Smith 2008). But scholars need to ask: Why and how did most of Taiwanese architects, who have less-developed international reputations, still find opportunities to become involved in this spatial transformation process?

In addition to iconic structures, monumental mega projects, and commercial and resident buildings (Smith 2008; Sklair and Gherardi 2012), different types of architecture such as factories and hospital complexes, have been built. Taiwanese professionals have also designed certain non-iconic structures in China (described below). This brings us to the second question: How and why, and under what circumstances, did Taiwanese architects participate in the development and transformation of different professional services in China? Third, unlike the manufacturing industry, the built environment industry in general, and architects in particular, are highly regulated through state licenses and building codes, mainly out of concerns of construction safety and national security (Faulconbridge 2009). Most countries in the world set great regulations to open their BER industry to other countries, and China is no exception. It is also important to know which Taiwanese architects have been able to receive what kinds of state recognition that officially authorize these architects to practice their services in China since the 1990s.

We are aware that Taiwanese (as well as other international) architects in China have operated mainly in three categories: (1) strategic planning, (2) urban design, and (3) site planning and architectural design (Olds 2001; Ren 2011). The first two are urban-policy oriented, while the last is related to physical construction. Due to huge differences between policy and construction, as well as the length of the chapter, this chapter focuses only on those Taiwanese professionals whose architectural works have been successfully completed in China.[1] Adopting a political economy approach, the focus of our chapter is on not the spatial forms, meanings, and identity of architectural works by Taiwanese professionals, but on the process, institutions, and actors that enable Taiwanese architects to engage in China's production of the built environment within the cross-strait political context.

Other than luxury commercial and residential buildings, Taiwanese professionals have participated in the development of three other kinds of architectural products and processes: (1) architecture as part of the producer-service industry to support manufacturing operations; (2) architecture as a functional complex construction that requires high-level knowledge for quality design and construction; and (3) architecture as cultural and social practice to engage with local daily life. I argue that the participation of Taiwanese professionals in the process of China's production of the built environment reflects dynamic economic and social transformation of post-Mao China. In addition, the Chinese state plays a role in flexibly defining the service boundaries of Taiwanese professionals in response to complicated political interactions between China and Taiwan.

The rest of the chapter is divided into five sections. The first is a discussion of the transformation of China's BER industry. The second reviews the general phenomenon of overseas architects in post-Mao urban China. Third, I discuss these aforementioned three kinds of Taiwanese architects in China, including their activities and impacts. The advantages and limitations of Taiwanese architects in the border-crossing spatial transformation process are examined in the fourth part. Finally, the conclusion notes certain policy and theoretical implications.

A brief history of China's built environment industry

Relatively isolated prior to the 2000s

Historically speaking, the People's Republic of China was isolated from the West soon after it was established in 1949. In Mao's time, Russia played a role in China's built environment, as evidenced by Beijing's Top Ten Buildings in the 1960s, e.g., the Great Hall of the People (*ren min da hui tang*), Workers Stadium (*gong ren ti yu chang*), and Cultural Palace of Nationalities (*min zu wen hua gong*). Those then-famous buildings were built with the help of Russian architects and planners. However, the Russian influence abruptly ended when China broke off relations with Russia in the late 1960s. During the Cold War, China refusing to have connections with the West isolated its BER industry from the world.

After 1978, China did not have a clear policy on the built environment industry. The first regulations to institutionally allow overseas capital to enter China's built environment were established in 1992, with the condition that overseas capital was limited to joint ventures with local partners.[2] At that time, the whole housing market was divided into those for local people and those for foreign nationals. Overseas architects were permitted to extend their operations only to the foreign housing market in China. The domestic housing market, which is larger than the overseas one, was closed to overseas architects with no Chinese counterparts.[3]

More open and institutionalized after the 2000s

China began to welcome more overseas architects in the 2000s. This change in policy is attributed to three main factors. First, China joined the World Trade Organization (the WTO) in 2001, with a promise that it would open its BER industry to the world. Later, China allowed overseas architects to set up their own companies in 2005 and granted overseas survey companies permission to establish independent firms in 2007.

Second, the Olympic Games further widened the opportunities for overseas architects who were interested in the Chinese market. In 2001, Beijing was chosen to host the 2008 Olympic Games. In order to better prepare for the Olympics, Beijing welcomed (or was forced to welcome) overseas architects to design world-class stadiums and other sports-related facilities. This "mega event" factor also applied to the 2009 Shanghai World Expo and the 2010 Guangzhou Asian Games; for these events, many overseas architects were invited to submit designs (Ren 2008). Other cities and regions in China soon mimicked Beijing, Shanghai, and Guangzhou and expanded the opportunities for overseas architects.

Third, there was a growing domestic market in terms of the BER industry in China. The floor area *per capita* in China was far behind those in the West, and Chinese local leaders were keen to promote rapid spatial transformation and urbanization for land finance as extra budgetary revenue (Lin and Yi 2011). Therefore, China needed more professional architects, either domestic or international, to participate in the rise in the local BER market (Shi 2003).

Though China opened the BER industry market, it still has certain rules that constrain overseas architects. The first governs the qualifications setting up new architectural firms. For example, a single architect is not allowed to establish an architectural studio or firm. Qualified firms are required to hire three licensed architects, as well as a certain number of civil engineers, structural engineers, site managers, and so forth, in order to earn the A-level license (the business scope of which covers the whole of China). Therefore, to establish a solo company is a difficult, if not to say impossible, task for any overseas architectural firms.[4]

Second, China also has new criteria to restrict the scope of the activities of architectural firms. Overseas architects are legally permitted to participate in the construction of only the four following items: (1) construction items that are sponsored solely by foreign investment or foreign grants; (2) construction items that are projectized by foreign loans and open for international competition; (3) China–overseas joint construction items that are sponsored by either (i) overseas counterparts as the majority partner or (ii) a Chinese counterpart as the majority partner, facing certain technical difficulties that could not be overcome without overseas help; (4) construction items fully financed by Chinese domestic capital with certain technical difficulties approved by related provincial or central governments.

Foreign architects in the post-Mao urban process

Globalization of architectural practice

Overseas architects and their associates, meaning architectural firms and star architects who specialize in meeting the needs of transnational clients wherever needed, have become important agents in the formation and transformation of built environments in many developing and less-developed cities. Chinese cities are certainly no exception.

The rise of overseas architectural firms and star architects under the context of globalization is attributed to three different and interrelated factors. First, it is commonly observed that cities compete against each other in terms of image making and marketing. In order to win the image competition, cities, particularly those in developing countries, are likely to invite world famous architects to build iconic structures (Sklair 2005; Sklair and Gherardi 2012). Second is the globalization of producer service industries to generate better knowledge in accessing and processing information for those transnational manufacturing corporations that have established headquarters and factories in different cities and regions. As part of the producer-service industry, many larger architectural firms have extended their operations internationally and have dozens of overseas projects scattered worldwide (Knox and Taylor 2005). Third, the WTO has promoted free trade in the service industry, which includes architecture, spatial planning, and design. Many countries, including China, have opened up their BER industries within a few years of obtaining membership to the WTO (Ngowi et al. 2005).

Overseas architects in China since 1978

The history of overseas architects in China since 1978 can be divided into three phases: 1978–1990; 1991–2000; and after 2000 (Xue and Li 2008). First, soon after China opened up, local and central agents invited overseas architects to introduce new ideas to China. At the time, the Japanese acted as an intermediary through the channel of official development aid, and the British invested in Shenzhen, the first special economic zone geographically closest to Hong Kong. In 1982, Ieoh Ming Pei, the most famous Chinese American architect at the time, was invited to build the Fragrant Hill Hotel (*xiang shan fan dian*) on the outskirts of Beijing. In the same year, Architect Ellerbe Becket was also invited to construct the Jiang Guo Hotel Beijing, the 18-floor, 5-star, glass curtain international hotel. These two cases marked the beginning of the involvement of American architects in the changing urban landscape of post-Mao China.

From 1991 to 2000, some overseas architects began to establish local offices in China in order to improve communications and marketing with local clients. In this period, the majority of architectural works designed by overseas architects were skyscrapers and high-rise office buildings. Qingmao Building of Shanghai and the World Trade Center of Beijing are cases in point. After 2000, mega projects such as convention centers, world-class stadiums, and concert halls became the focus of policies in most cities in China, and such projects provided great opportunities for overseas architectural firms. The economic stagnation in Europe and America after the 2008 financial crisis also pushed these overseas firms to go to China to find business opportunities. Some firms sent teams from abroad, and some hired Chinese citizens who had studied either domestically or internationally.

Taiwanese architects in the dynamic cross-strait interaction

Institutional privileges

Despite the severe regulation of capital in the overseas BER industry in the 1980s and 1990s, it is believed that China treated related professionals from Hong Kong and Taiwan differently. Prior to 1992, when China first established regulations on overseas architects, J. X. Shi (史景雄) had cooperated with the Liaoning Provincial Institute of Design and then established his own Liaoning Institute of Modern Design, which was the first licensed joint-venture design institute in China. In addition, some Taiwanese architects, including C. C. Hsu (許常吉), Y. D. Chen (陳耀東), and X Zhu (朱雄), obtained a very rare permit for joint engineering consultancy, granted by the Ministry of Construction (建設部) and the Ministry of External Economic Affairs and Trade (外經貿部). In addition, China turned a blind eye to those cooperating with local partners through joint ventures (or even "license borrowing") in order to practice their professions in China.[5]

After joining the WTO, China again offered better treatment to Taiwanese architectural firms. Since 2006, China has allowed Taiwanese to participate in the Chinese state architect exams.[6] Given that the eligibility of entering state exams is a sensitive issue related to citizenship and nationality, it is clear that China allowed Taiwanese to join its state exams for political reasons. However, due to cross-strait differences in architecture education and practice environments (discussed below), as of the writing of this chapter at the end of 2012, no Taiwanese have been able to pass China's exams and receive official licenses.

In addition, China also provided even better treatment to senior and reputable Taiwanese architects. Those who were reputed to be outstanding architects were invited to join a two-day training program. Rumor has it that those joining the programs were actually recommended by the Association of Taiwanese Architects, based on the List of Outstanding Architects ranked by the Construction and Planning Agency of the Ministry of Interior, Taiwan. However, the program was offered mainly for the sake of formality. The two-day program ended with an open-book exam, and participants were not prohibited from discussing the questions in order to pass the exams. Through this special channel, 37 senior Taiwanese architects finally obtained licenses to practice in 2009. Z.-Q. Yu (俞肇川) was the first of these 37 licensed architects to successfully register his company in China, under the Shanghai Branch of the Jiamuxi Institute of Design, and to be legally allowed to assign his authorization (*qiao zhang*) to a new construction project for the Pudong Institute of Education Development.[7]

The cross-strait relationship has experienced great changes since 2008, when the pro-unification, KMT-backed Y.-J. Ma (馬英九) was elected President in Taiwan. During Ma's presidency, China and Taiwan reinitiated official talks to institutionalize cross-strait trade and commercial interactions and together signed the Economic Cooperation Framework Agreement (the ECFA). As part of ECFA, both sides made it a priority to negotiate agreements on various sectors of the agricultural and manufacturing industries, and paid little attention to the BER industry in general or the architecture industry in particular.

General skill gaps between cross-strait architects

In the end of the 1970s, Taiwan had economically "taken off," commonly referred to as the Taiwan miracle, while China, coming out of the Cultural Revolution, was very poor afterwards. The economic gap between Taiwan and China enhanced certain advantages of Taiwanese manufacturing firms, particularly those in the IT industry, to advance technologically ahead of their Chinese counterparts. Taiwanese corporations could find ways to extend their business to China (Yang and Hsia 2007; Wang and Lee 2007). However, that type of skill advancement does not apply to the Taiwanese architects in China.

I discuss the skill gaps of architectural studios or firms' operations in three dimensions: (1) design skills to make drawings; (2) business skills to promote and advertise projects; and (3) integration skills to manage resources and implement projects (McNeill 2009).[8] In terms of the last one, architects in Taiwan are responsible for the completion of architectural projects; therefore, they need to know most of the construction details, as well as how and when to coordinate related resources in time and space. In China, however, there is a clear division of labor between architects and civil engineers, structural engineers and built environment-related professionals, as stipulated by law. Generally speaking, Chinese architects are less competitive than Taiwanese architects in terms of integrated skills in project management.

However, in terms of the first two skills, Taiwanese architects may not necessarily be more experienced. The built environment industry, including the architecture sector, is mainly a market whose sales skills require certain local knowledge and personal networking, as well as public relations to generate business. Taiwanese are generally no better than their Chinese counterparts at promoting goods and projects in the domestic market of China.

Regarding design skills, partly because China eagerly welcomed Western architects after it decided to open up and partly because Western architects were keen to go to China, Chinese local architects had many more opportunities to cooperate on or jointly design new ideas and techniques introduced by Western architects (McNeill 2009; Faulconbridge 2010). In Taiwan, in contrast, it was not until the 2000s that Taiwan organized a series of international competitions. Prior to that, most public projects were exclusively limited to local state-owned engineering consultancy firms (which are allowed to manage architectural projects).[9] In this regard, Taiwanese architects in general had fewer institutional opportunities than their Chinese counterparts to learn through partnerships with top overseas architects.[10]

Moreover, over the years, little collective learning and innovation has occurred among Taiwanese architects. Mainly because of the poor operations of the Association of Taiwanese Architects, the circulation of architectural-related information such as models, texts, and photographs in a community of practice, which is important to mutual learning and innovation among related professionals (Faulconbridge 2010), is not well established in Taiwan.[11]

Last but not least, it is ironic that the faculty members of architecture departments in Taiwan are prohibited by law to have practical experience outside the campus, just as practicing architects are institutionally discouraged from holding positions as adjunct professors in schools due to discrimination in academic evaluation. Therefore, Taiwanese students are, quite unfortunately, supervised by academicians who have limited knowledge of actual industrial operations. This situation is very different from the one in China, where architecture professors are highly encouraged by the system to practice their craft through opening studios and companies off-campus to bring real projects and money back to the campus (Yang 2008). A close relationship between industry practice and school education provides more opportunities for Chinese students to acquire skills in practice.[12]

Due to a lack of advancements in sales and design skills, it was inevitable that many Taiwanese architects would fail and even suffer great financial losses in China. Therefore, it is important to examine successful strategies in order to provide sophisticated understanding of Taiwanese architects under the context of the dynamic post-Mao transformation and complicated cross-strait relations.

China strategies of Taiwanese architects

This chapter identifies four main different strategies of Taiwanese architects in China. The first one is iconic structure and luxury commercial and residential buildings. C. Y. Lee (李祖原) and Partners, the most well-known (and probably the most controversial) Taiwanese architecture firm in China, designed and/or constructed hundreds of projects of this kind in China. As probably the most famous architect in the Chinese economic sphere, Lee introduced many elements of Chinese culture into his iconic architectural works. For example, the Beijing Pangu Plaza, the only business corner in the Beijing Olympic Park, is designed to elicit the shape of a dragon. The plaza has five buildings: a 191-meter-high building as the dragon's head, three 79-meter-high residential buildings as the dragon's body, and an 88-meter-high, 7-star hotel as the dragon's tail. The Fang Yuan Building in the city of Shenyang is another case in point. With a Chinese philosophy of an "orbicular sky and rectangular earth" (*tian yuan de fang*), the Fang Yuan Building was designed as a large, round component standing on a square foundation. The round part also elicits the image of ancient Chinese coins, reflecting the function of the Fang Yuan Building as a commercial building.

In addition, other Taiwanese architects have successfully extended their practices across the Taiwan Strait by employing three entrance strategies: the Taiwanese factory strategy, the complex building strategy, and the civil architecture strategy. First, Taiwanese architects entered China by following (or being invited by) Taiwanese firms that had established factories, production lines, and headquarters in China. Manufacturing and company operations need to be established in physical constructions, and such constructions need to be designed by quality architects who possess specific know-how of the development of the industry and various production processes. In this regard, architecture in this dimension is part of a producer-service industry, which refers to those business activities that facilitate the operations of manufacturers (Moulaert and Gallouj 1993).[13] As Taiwanese manufacturing capital has moved to China over the past three decades, many Taiwanese architects have been invited by Taiwanese businesspersons to extend their practices to China.

J. J. Pan (潘冀) and Partner, an architecture firm specializing in high-tech factory-related construction in Taiwan, has offered its services to dozens of corporations in the semiconductor industry in the Hsinchu Science Park of Taiwan. High-tech industrial architecture involves industrial complications (such as fabrication, process support, bulk gas yards, and central utility units for wafer foundry) and esthetic requirements, whose quality and preciseness must meet the needs of the just-in-time global production network. Due to his quality and efficiency, Pan is famous for his repeat business from particular clients in Taiwan who established new plants or corporate compounds. When these Taiwanese high-tech firms moved to China, where Chinese local architects and construction firms unfortunately have limited experience with building industrial constructions, Pan was invited to provide cross-strait architectural services in China. The Acer (宏碁) Science Park in Zhongshan, the BenQ (明碁) Science Park in Suzhou, the ZyXEL (合勤科技) Communications Corp. Science Park in Wuxi, and the VIA Technologies (威盛) Research Center at Shenzhen are all cases in point. Acer and BenQ are two leading notebook producers originally from Taiwan, while ZyXel is a key Taiwanese manufacturer of digital subscriber lines and other networking devices. VIA Technologies is a leading Taiwanese producer of integrated circuit chips.

Second, Taiwanese architects extended their practice in China by providing functional complex designs. For example, C. C. Hsu (許常吉) and Associates Architects and Engineers specializes in hospitals and health care facilities. Hsu is a self-proclaimed pioneer and leading architect in the modernization of Taiwanese medical architecture. His works number more than 50 and cover a variety of bed sizes and medical divisions. Medical architects are experts who are able to translate hospital services into real asset solutions. Whether medical facilities are able to operate smoothly or not depends not only on the quality of medical practitioners (i.e., doctors, nurses, and medical technicians) but also the spatial layout of clinical units, medical machines, and other facilities. A best example is that architectural design for emergency rooms, where every second counts for life and death, should at least consider the following guidelines: easy access to supplies, mini televisions in reach of patients and staff, natural lighting from high clearstory windows and fewer light boxes for emergency, beside registration to have the nurse or physician be the first contact, wide alcoves and hallways to fit patient overflow, and larger mobile equipment whenever necessary, using multi-use beds to offer maximum flexibility.[14] Therefore, the great complexity of medical architecture, requiring knowledge of the functionality of medical facilities and the relationships between patients, professionals, and machines, sets a high entry-level barrier for architects.

Having designed dozens of hospitals in Taiwan, Hsu has accumulated a great amount of knowledge of medical architecture and is also a founder and chair of the Taiwan Association of Medical Architecture and Medical Management Affairs (*yiliao jianzhu ji yiwu guanli jiaoliu xiehui*), a reputable non-governmental organization encouraging professional exchanges and the promotion of medical architecture.

Hsu entered the China built environment industry in two phases. In the beginning, he was invited to China by a Taiwanese businessperson who had an interest in China's medical service market. Hsu's first medical architecture project in China was the Eastern Hepatobiliary Surgery Hospital and Eastern Hepatobiliary Surgery

Institute of the Second Military Medical University of People's Liberation Army, which was co-invested (or donated) by Samuel Yin (尹衍樑), chair of the Ruentex Financial Group (潤泰集團), and Junyuan Du (杜俊元), chair of Orient Semiconductor Electronics (華泰電子), Ltd. Then Hsu was commissioned by many Taiwanese business agglomerations to build hospitals: e.g., the Xiamen Chan Gung Hospital of the Formosa Plastics Group (台塑集團), Zhangsha Want Want Hospital of the Want Want Group (旺旺集團), the Nangjing BenQ Medical Center of the BenQ Corporation (明基集團), and the Kunshan Jen Ching Memorial Hospital of the Ford Lio Ho Motor Co., Ltd (福特六和集團).

Moreover, Hsu has extended his medical architecture practice to Chinese clients, including provincial governments (e.g., the Fujian Provincial Hospital, the Hainan Provincial Hospital), university authorities (e.g., the Hospital of Tianjin Medical University, International Hospital of Peking University), and even the military (e.g., the 301 General Military Hospital of the People's Liberation Army, the largest military hospital in China; the Chongqing Third Military Hospital). With his projects spread out across China, there is no doubt that Hsu is the most influential Taiwanese architect in China, one whose business covers wide swaths of the public and private sectors.

The third way Taiwanese architects extended their operations was by introducing new concepts and practices in community architecture. Community architects basically propose that architectural design and the building process should involve more local citizens and communities. In this regard, structures are not pure works of art designed only by architects; instead, structures are "living" buildings that people use and interact with, and therefore such buildings require more bottom-up participation, even at the beginning of design and construction. Influenced by Taiwan's democratization, more and more community architects are aware of the importance of empowerment of the people and practice the new method of community participation in the production of any built environment.

Y.-C. Hsieh (謝英俊) is a popular Taiwanese community architect in China. With the community architecture approach, Hsieh worked with the local people on reconstruction in central Taiwan after the September 21, 1999, earthquake and has received an international award. Unlike the previous two types of architects, whose works are mostly based in cities, Hsieh entered China through rural villages and remote areas in 2004 and helped the local peasants to build eco buildings by themselves with local materials and pro-poor new technologies. Unlike in urban areas, there are no strict regulations governing architect qualifications for doing business in rural areas. Though Hsieh was not among the 37 registered architects, he was able to serve in rural villages. Hsieh's "self-help" concept actually offered construction jobs, shaped local solidarity among the peasants, and used relatively small budgets during the process. The self-help idea gained further popularity in the areas affected by the 2008 Sichuan earthquake, where post-disaster relief needed to consider budget constraints, job creation, social stability, and building reconstruction. Due to his contributions in rural China, Hsieh was named one of the 2012 People of Chinese Culture in the category of architecture (*wen hua zhong guo ren wu*).

Effectiveness and limitations of cross-strait architects

In addition to the strategy of designing iconic structures and commercial and residential buildings, I have identified three main other strategies of Taiwanese architects entering China: producer-service providers, such as factory construction architects; complex building designers, such as medical facility architects; and rural and local empowerment facilitors, such as community architects. Each strategy is illustrated with one Taiwanese architect who successfully participated in China's spatial transformation over decades. It must be noted that these three architects I mentioned are not the only Taiwanese architects who have pursued similar strategies in China, and that what I have described are just some of their many architectural works in China and worldwide.

For example, Pan has also been involved in other commercial building projects. Pan's international exposure even extends to the United States, where he was invited to build the Rutgers Community Christian Church in Somerset, New Jersey. In terms of factory architecture, Chris Yao (姚仁喜) designed a factory commissioned by the YAGEO corporation (國巨電腦), and Wu Ruizong (吳瑞榮) also constructed an assembly facility on behalf of FoxxConn (鴻海電腦). In addition to Hsu, Ricky Liu and Associates (劉培森) also specialize in medical architecture and have completed Chang Gung Hospitals in Xiamen, Beijing, Fuzhou, and so on. Due to his reputation, Liu has also been invited directly to design an iconic rebuilding project of the Shaolin Sect Temple in Tianjin. Besides, Hsieh's architectural works are located not only in rural areas but also in urban areas, such as social housing in Shenzhen. H. M. Wang (王惠民), a planner originally trained by the Institute of Building and Planning of National Taiwan University, is now also practicing community planning and architecture in many rural counties of Zhejiang Province. Sinyi Realty Inc. (信義房屋) of Taiwan has also financed the first community building and participation program at Tsinghua University.

In this section, I draw generalization from these three strategies and see some of the effectiveness and limitations of Taiwanese architects within the context of the dynamic post-Mao transformation and complicated cross-strait relations. Three dimensions can be particularly discussed, as follows.

First, by using their expertise, Taiwanese architects participated in the post-Mao transition in a diverse way. China's dynamic social and economic transformation has actually facilitated in creating certain "niches" of production of the related built environments for Taiwanese professionals. Pan and many other Taiwanese architects have been invited to build IT factories, a crucial element in China becoming the world's factory for high-tech products. China planned to build thousands of modern hospitals as part of its recent medical reform, which Hsu and others took advantage of when they extended their medical-focused operations to China. With increasing social unrest occurring alongside economic changes, there is an emerging demand for the possibility of citizen participation in the decision-making process, particularly in rural and minority areas.[15] Hsieh and colleagues, employing a similar philosophy, promoted the idea of community architecture and gained attention and popularity in rural and disaster areas.

Of these three, the nature of factory architects and industrial secrets limits the number of Chinese clients for such architects, so they have far fewer clients than hospital and community architects. Architecture, as a producer-service industry, required a particular level of trust between architects and high-tech industry owners due to the possibility that corporate secrets could be leaked. Such social embeddedness explains why Taiwanese firms "outsource" their factory design projects to Taiwanese architects when they move to China, and why Taiwanese factory architects may not easily find local clients in China.

In contrast, competent hospital architects usually have a very complicated package of design know-how, which is a competitive threshold among peer professionals. And relationships between patients and hospitals in Taiwan are quite different from that in the West. Under the context of a relatively small size of population and people only keen to visit doctors if necessary, hospitals facilitated with more than a thousand beds are seldom found in Europe and the United States. This explains why Hsu could successfully find Chinese clients after following Taiwanese clients into China in the beginning and then dominate over other Western architects in the Chinese hospital design market for a while.[16] Community architects need unique communication skills and building techniques for involving local participation. Uniqueness, which is better trained in a democratic society, is an advantage that Taiwanese professionals have over their Chinese counterparts. This is why community architects are able to enter Chinese local communities directly, unlike factory and medical architects, who still need to follow Taiwanese businesspersons into the Chinese market.

Second, the various ways that Taiwanese architects have participated in China also reflect the complicated cross-strait interactions, which involve not only professional presentation but also political calculation. Even though China produces about 25,000 registered architects annually, Taiwanese are still allowed to join their state license exams. Taiwanese architects have no more experience than their Chinese counterparts in managing mega projects but they are still invited to join international competitions. The government of China offers institutional privileges specifically to Taiwanese professionals in the name of the so-called unification front (*tong zhang*) within the context of complexity cross-strait relations and domestic regulation of the BER industries.

From this perspective, the latest development that deserves attention is that the Association of Taiwanese Architects is currently negotiating with its Chinese counterpart to allow Taiwanese architects who have passed Taiwan state exams to obtain recognition of their licenses by China. Due to the huge difference in numbers of professionals, Taiwan could not possible offer mutual recognition to Chinese licensed architects. Therefore, this "unilateral recognition" program, which is clearly unfair to China, is currently at the discussion level, and it may be some time before consensus can be reached and the idea can be realized. The government of China certainly plays a role in redefining the service boundaries of Taiwanese professionals participating in the built environment process.

Third, Taiwanese architects also face two important limitations – one practical and one political. At the beginning, the BER industry in China has very different scales of time and space scales from those in Taiwan. The spatial scale of architectural projects in China un/fortunately is often 10 or 20 times greater than that in Taiwan, while the time span set by clients is often only 30–50 percent of that in Taiwan. Such differences in the scope and schedule of architectural projects actually present an obstacle to Taiwanese architects, who have relatively small studios and may not have the capability to run the financial risks inherent in operating such projects in China, which are disproportionally large and rushed as compared to their past experiences in Taiwan. On top of that, to practice their services, most Taiwanese architects are required to find Chinese local partners such as public-owned local institutes of design and planning, whose business interests are highly related to authoritarian local governments. Without the proper rule of law and checks and balances, Taiwanese architects face the uncertainty that their design ideas may be easily hijacked by local coalitions between local cadres, local planning and design institutes, and related professionals.

Conclusions

In the context of China's great economic and spatial transition since 1978, this chapter aims to answer how Taiwanese professionals participated in spatial production during the post-socialist regime. Transnational star architects and reputable architectural firms have played a role in China. Other than the iconic structure and commercial building strategies, we also found Taiwanese architects successfully entered China by employing three main strategies: architect as producer-service provider, architect as complex building designer, and architect as local empowerment activist. First, Taiwanese architects were invited by Taiwanese firm owners in China to build their factories and related facilities. Second, hospital architects provided their very complex expertise to both Chinese and Taiwanese clients. Third, community architects cooperated and interacted with the Chinese peoples. Those various strategies for Taiwanese architectural involvement in China's production of the built environment reflect the dynamic economic and social transformation of post-Mao China but also occurred within the complicated context of political interactions between China and Taiwan.

The findings of this chapter contribute to the existing literature in two ways. First, the chapter enriches the existing literature on overseas Taiwanese investment, which has paid much attention to the manufacturing-related dimension and largely ignored other producer-service industries, cultural innovations, and social activists. Our findings also partly support Chou and Lin's argument (2007) for "architects as built environment developers following the Taiwanese clients," and they also partly complement Tseng's research (in this book) on Taiwanese architects as cultural workers in China. In addition, this chapter shows how, and why, and under what circumstances, most Taiwanese architects, as non-star architects, are still able to participate in China. The findings are certainly a supplement to the existing research on transnational architects in relation to transformation of urban China (Olds 2001; Ren 2008).

At the end of the conclusion I suggest certain policy implications. The so-called Super Dutch generation, comprising Erick van Egeraat, UN Studio, Kees Christiaanse, Rem Koolhass, and similar architects who have all acquired international fame, are spatially concentrated, as most of the members can be found in Rotterdam and Amsterdam (Kloosterman 2008). The spatial proximity of these Super Dutch architects shows that the Netherlands has successfully developed its architectural practice as part of globalization of the cultural industry. Taiwan and the Netherlands have similar-sized territories and populations, and both are also located near countries with similar cultural backgrounds and huge economic hinterlands (Taiwan and China vs. the Netherlands and Europe). Based on this research, Taiwan should learn lessons from those "bittersweet" experiences of Taiwanese architects in China and reflect on how to further formulate better policies to cultivate Taiwan's own "Super Dutch generation" in the future.

Notes

1 Here, we also differentiate architectural projects from interior design ones. Though both are related to physical construction, the former has much more complicated processes than the latter. In this chapter, we discuss only architectural projects.
2 Regulation of Giving Permits to Establishment of China-Overseas Joint Venture Design Institutions (*cheng li zhong wai he ying she ji ji gou shen pi guan li de gui ding*). Documentation Code: *jian she* (1992) No. [108].
3 Interview source: CN120629.
4 Interview source: TW120817; also comments from Architect C. Y. Lee (李祖原), see news source: *lian he bao* (based in Taipei), 2009/01/08.
5 News source: Architect Magazine (*jian zhu shi za zi*), based in Taipei, 2001/May; 2002/March.
6 On Taiwanese for Qualification of Practicing Architecture in China (Taiwan *di qu ju min qu de zhu ce jian zhu shi zi ge de ju ti ban fa*). Document Code: *guo ren ba fa* (2006) [131].
7 News source: *zhong guo shi bao* (based in Taipei), 2009/01/08.
8 Kohn Pedersen Fox Associates, one of the world's pre-eminent architecture firms, is a case in point. Kohn is in charge of sales, while Pedersen focuses on design and planning and Fox shoulders all responsibility of project implementations. Interview source: TW120821.
9 The best example is Terminal Two of Taoyuan International Airport at Taiwan. The terminal was designed and built at the end of the 1990s by the architecture department of China Engineering Consultants, Inc., then the biggest state-owned civil engineering consultancy in Taiwan. Quality of the terminal was much worse than the Chep Lap Kok Hong Kong International Airport and the Singapore Changi International Airport, both of which were established around the same time by world famous architecture firms. The former was commissioned to Foster & Partners, and the latter was to Woodhead.
10 We notice that running international competitions for architectural projects has certain controversial aspects. Although a few local architects have learnt quite a lot, some, if not to say all others, are unable to improve or are even excluded from the process. Interview code: TW120822; TW120901; TW120902.
11 Interview code: TW 120817; TW120820. This is the main reason why some Taiwanese architecture reformers are organizing another non-government organization called the Architectural Reform Society (*jian zhu gui ge shi*). For more details, please visit their website: www.archifield.net/vb/forumdisplay.php?21-%E5%BB%BA%E6%94%B9%E7%A4%BE.

12 Of course, this close relationship between higher education and industrial practice also creates certain problems, such as students and faculty members who pay attention to practical skills and have no interest in theoretical concepts and philosophical debates.
13 The producer service industry includes: advertising services, human resource services, management and business consulting services, legal services, accounting and auditing services, and engineering and architectural services.
14 Interview codes: TW120718; TW120916; also official website of Emergency Physicians Monthly: www.epmonthly.com/archives/features/building-a-better-emergency-department-an-architects-perspective/.
15 Interview Code: CN120705.
16 Interview Code: TW120916.

References

Cartier, Carolyn. 2002. "Transnational Urbanism in the Reform-era Chinese City: Landscapes from Shenzhen." *Urban Studies* 39 (9): 1513–1532.
Chen, Ching-Mi., Konstantinos. A. Melachroinos, and Kang-Tsung Chang. 2010. "FDI and Local Economic Development: The Case of Taiwanese Investment in Kunshan." *European Planning Studies* 18 (2): 213–238.
Chien, Shiuh-Shen. 2007. "Institutional Innovations, Asymmetric Decentralization and Local Economic Development – Case Study of Kunshan, in post-Mao China." *Environment and Planning C: Government and Policy* 25 (2): 269–290.
Chou, Tsu-Lung., and Y.u-Chun Lin. 2007. "Industrial Park Development Across the Taiwan Strait." *Urban Studies* 44 (8): 1405–1425.
Faulconbridge, James R. 2009. "The Regulation of Design in Global Architecture Firms: Embedding and Emplacing Buildings." *Urban Studies* 46 (12): 2537–2554.
Faulconbridge, James R. 2010. "Global Architects: Learning and Innovation Through Communities and Constellations of Practice." *Environment and Planning A* 42 (12): 2842–2858.
Hsing, You-tien. 1996. "Blood, Thicker Than Water: Interpersonal Relations and Taiwanese Investment in Southern China." *Environment and Planning A* 28 (12): 362–374.
Keng, Shu, and Gunter Schubert. 2010. "Agents of Unification? The Political Role of Taiwanese Businessmen in the Process of Cross-Strait Integration." *Asian Survey* 50 (2): 287–310.
Kloosterman, Robert C. 2008. "Walls and Bridges: Knowledge Spillover Between 'Superdutch' Architectural Firms." *Journal of Economic Geography* 8 (4): 545–563.
Knox, Paul L., and Peter J. Taylor. 2005. "Toward a Geography of the Globalization of Architecture Office Networks." *Journal of Architectural Education* 58 (3): 23–32.
Lin, George C. S., and Y. H. Dennis Wei. 2002. "China's Restless Urban Landscapes 1: New Challenges for Theoretical Reconstruction." *Environment and Planning A* 34: 1535–1544.
Lin, George C. S., and Fangxin Yi. 2011. "Urbanization of Capital or Capitalization on Urban Land? Land Development and Local Public Finance in Urbanizing China." *Urban Geography* 32 (1): 50–79.
McNeill, Donald. 2009. *The Global Architect: Firms, Fame and the Urban Form*. London: Routledge.
Moulaert, Frank, and Camal Gallouj. 1993. "The Locational Geography of Advanced Producer Service Firms: The Limits of Economies of Agglomeration." *The Service Industries Journal* 13 (2): 37–41.

Ngowi, A. B., E. Pienaar, A. Talukhaba, and J. Mbachu. 2005. "The Globalisation of the Construction Industry – a Review." *Building and Environment* 40 (1): 135–141.

Olds, Kris. 2001. *Globalization and Urban Change: Capital, Culture and Pacific Rim Mega-Projects*. Oxford: Oxford University Press.

Ren, Xuefei. 2008. "Architecture and China's Urban Revolution." *City* 12 (2): 217–225.

Ren, Xuefei. 2011. *Building Globalization: Transnational Architecture Production in Urban China*. Chicago: University of Chicago Press.

Shen, Hsiu-hua. 2008. "The Purchase of Transnational Intimacy: Women's Bodies, Transnational Masculine Privileges in Chinese Economic Zones." *Asian Studies Review* 32 (1): 57–75.

Shi, Wei. 2003. "Shanghai Phenomenon: From Design Studio to Architectural Firms." (*Shanghai xian xiang dui yu jian zhu she ji gong si de diao yan*) *Time + Architecture (shi dai jian zhu)* 3: 20–23.

Sklair, Leslie. 2005. "The Transnational Capitalist Class and Contemporary Architecture in Globalizing Cities." *International Journal of Urban and Regional Research* 29 (3): 485–500.

Sklair, Leslie, and Laura Gherardi. 2012. "Iconic Architecture as a Hegemonic Project of the Transnational Capitalist Class." *City: Analysis of Urban Trends, Culture, Theory, Policy, Action* 16 (1/2): 57–73.

Smith, Christopher J. 2008. "Monumentality in Urban Design: The Case of China." *Eurasian Geography and Economics* 49 (3): 263–279.

Tseng, Yen-Fen. 2011. "Shanghai Rush: Skilled Migrants in a Fantasy City." *Journal of Ethnic and Migration Studies* 37 (5): 765–784.

Tseng, Yen-Fen, and Jieh-min Wu. 2011. "Reconfiguring Citizenship and Nationality: Dual Citizenship of Taiwanese Migrants in China." *Citizenship Studies* 15 (2): 265–282.

Wang, Jenn-Hwan, and Chuan-Kai Lee. 2007. "Global Production Networks and Local Institution Building: The Development of the Information-Technology Industry in Suzhou, China." *Environment and Planning A* 39 (8): 1873–1888.

Wu, Jieh-min. 1997. "Strange Bedfellows: Dynamics of Government–business Relations Between Chinese Local Authorities and Taiwanese Investors." *Journal of Contemporary China* 6 (15): 319–346.

Xue, Charlie Qiuli, and Yingchun Li. 2008. "Importing American Architecture to China: The Practice of John Portman & Associates in Shanghai." *Journal of Architecture* (3): 317–333.

Yang, D. Y. R., and N. M. Coe. 2009. "The Governance of Global Production Networks and Regional Development: A Case Study of Taiwanese PC Production Networks." *Growth and Change* 40 (1): 30–53.

Yang, Jingqing. 2008. "Professors, Doctors and Lawyers: The Variable Wealth of the Professional Classes." In *The New Rich in China: Future Rulers, Present Lives*, edited by David S. G. Goodman, 148–167. London: Routledge.

Yang, You-ren, and Chu-Joe Hsia. 2007. "Spatial Clustering and Organizational Dynamics of Transborder Production Networks – a Case Study of Taiwanese Information-technology Companies in the Greater Suzhou Area, China." *Environment and Planning A* 39: 1346–1363.

5 Establishing *guanxi* in the Chinese market

Comparative analysis of Japanese, Korean, and Taiwanese expatriates in mainland China

Shigeto Sonoda

Importance of *guanxi*: an East Asian commonality

It is commonly believed that utilizing *guanxi* (in English, individual relationships or connections) would be a better and even desirable policy when doing business in China (Sonoda, 2001; Gold et al., 2002; Fan, 2007; Wong, 2007; Flora et al., 2008). Foreign multinationals are no exception. On the contrary, many business-related books or academic papers put an emphasis of the effective use of *guanxi* with the Chinese government as a crucial tool for the development of business in the Chinese market (Bjorkman and Kock, 1995; Hitt et al., 2002; Standifird, 2006; Langenberg, 2007; Wu, 2007). In fact, many research results suggest that establishing good *guanxi* with government is one of the important factors for successful business for multinationals operating in the Chinese market. The following is an example.

> Guanxi, especially Guanxi with Chinese government, can assist transnational companies to obtain sources of information which mainly includes business opportunities and government policies (Davies *et al.*, 1995, pp. 207–214). With regard to business opportunities, the stronger the Guanxi network of an enterprise is, the more opportunities it has or will have.... There is little doubt that this would make it easier for these companies to reach their business objectives. Therefore, Gao (2006, pp. 119–125) has come to the conclusion that Guanxi, good relationships with Chinese government in particular, is a necessary condition for international enterprises to do business successfully in China.
>
> Another benefit that multinational companies can obtain from Guanxi is getting access to sources of resources. As a result of the scarcity of some necessities and the shortage of professionals, organizations rely on Guanxi to get access to these resources in China (Thomas, 2002). Moreover, Davies *et al.* (1995, pp. 207–214) explain that many production materials are under the control of local authorities, such as bricks, plaster and power equipment. In this regard, good relationship with relative government officials is definitely necessary for companies to make these resources obtained with higher efficiency.

Furthermore, a strong Guanxi network also can lead to a reliable supply of common production materials which is vital for a manufacturer's success.

(Yang, 2011: 164–165).

In spite of necessity, there are hesitations of foreign multinationals to establish and use *guanxi* with the local officials. Yang continues:

> On the other hand, it is perceived that Guanxi is associated with bribery and corruption although multinational companies can get many benefits from it. In addition, if any international enterprise is found involving in bribery and corruption, the company's reputation will drop sharply, large numbers of customers will be lost and then it will become uncompetitive in the market. All these imply that international enterprises, especially non-Chinese multinational companies which do not have a full understanding about Chinese business culture, should carefully handle the special item of Guanxi.
>
> (Yang, 2011: 165)

In many cases, "non-Chinese multinational companies" substantially mean "Western companies." In other words, it is sometimes claimed that companies in Greater China (Hong Kong and Taiwan) share the same tendency to use the *guanxi* network in doing business due to their cultural similarity. Again Yang claims:

> It is believed that the continuing importance of Guanxi in Hong Kong and Taiwan where the legal system has been well developed is the best proof for the continuing importance of Guanxi for doing business in China. For instance, owners of different banks in Hong Kong, including Chinese, non-Chinese and merged banks, stated that building up Guanxi with customers is their approach to deal with business in Hong Kong (Gilbert & Choi, 2003, pp. 137–146). Lin *et al.* (2006, pp. 81–93) further state that Guanxi can assist enterprises in getting more consumers in Taiwan. All these clearly show that Guanxi still plays a significant role in doing business in China, including Hong Kong and Taiwan both of which are modern, open and rule of law societies.
>
> (Yang, 2011: 166)

Some empirical researches support the idea that Hong Kong and Taiwan businessmen are still using the *guanxi* network both in their local societies and in the Chinese market though there are some differences of use of *guanxi* depending on company size and market competitiveness (Liou, 2009; Huang and Baek, 2010).

Then, how do Korean and Japanese multinationals, who are grouped as "East Asian" multinationals, adapt themselves to such circumstances? Are there any differences among these companies in terms of their adaptation to *guanxi*-oriented business circumstances?

Some claim that the Korean and Japanese show similar characteristics as the Chinese in terms of their sensitivity toward *guanxi* (Wilson and Brennan, 2001). Jin suggests that

Guanxi is a Chinese word which is also recognized in Japan and Korea. In Chinese, Guan means a door, or "to close up" with those who are inside a group, and Xi can be interpreted to mean a joined chain. Thus, together, Guanxi can be translated as relationships and connections. In all the Chinese dominated societies in Asia, people use the word Guanxi to speak of someone who knows lots of people, who is well connected, and gets things done, not necessarily through formal channels. Thus Guanxi is a social dimension and a human factor.

(Jin, 2006: 105)

Other literature emphasize minute difference of personal network in/across organizations among East Asian societies (Chen 1995; Sonoda, 2001), but no empirical researches have been conducted as to whether East Asian expatriates working in the Chinese market are really establishing a *guanxi* network with local officials in comparative perspectives.

This chapter investigates what factors are facilitating establishing *guanxi* networks with local officials by using the data set of 2nd Wave of East Asian Businessman in China Survey 2010–2011, which covers Korean, Japanese, and Taiwanese expatriates working in local subsidiaries/offices in the Chinese market.

Research design and data collection

Research design

2nd Wave of East Asian Businessmen in China Survey 2010–11 was conducted by the research group led by the author.[1] Our research group is composed of multinational members: Prof. Yasuyuki Kishi (University of Niigata) and the author are from Japan, Prof. Joon-shik Park (Hallym University) is from South Korea, Prof. Chia-ming Chang (Soochow University) and Jian-bang Deng (Tamkang University) are from Taiwan, and Prof. Minghao Fang (Dalian Institute of Technology) is from China. This multi-nationality is an indispensable factor for our research group to collect cross-national data because all the companies and expatriates show stronger trust with researchers of the same nationality and it is quite difficult for foreigners to get permission to do research on their companies. Profs. Kishi and Fang are former students of the author at Chuo University and other professors have experience in doing research collectively in the 1st Wave in 2001 (Sonoda, 2003), which made our international collaboration powerful and smooth.

Our research group collected three different types of data.

One type of data is from foreign expatriates who have been working for Korean/Japanese/Taiwanese firms operating in the Chinese market. Another form of data is from local workers working for Korean/Japanese/Taiwanese firms that we visited. Both these two forms of data are obtained from a questionnaire survey whose contents are basically the same as the one that we used at the time of the 1st Wave in 2001.[2]

The other, final sort of data is from our visiting foreign subsidiaries where we conducted interviews with the managers on the changing difficulties of doing business in Chinese market. More concretely, we visited three Japanese companies, one Korean company, and four Taiwanese companies in Suzhou, Jiangsu Province in 2010, and three Japanese companies, five Korean companies, and three Taiwanese companies in Guangdong Province in 2011. Some companies in Suzhou we visited are the same ones that we visited in 2001, but other companies, mostly Taiwanese ones, have transferred their plants to the inner area, which made it impossible to chase the same company chronologically.

Data collection

In most cases, this chapter uses the first category of the data, that is, expatriates data in 2011. As explained above, our research group chose Jiangsu and Guangdong as our research cities; we tried to collect roughly the same number of samples from Korean/Japanese/Taiwanese expatriates in Jiangsu and Guangdong. The 1st Wave included only Jiangsu and it is only in the 2nd Wave that we included Guangdong to check geographical difference within China.[3]

A total of 73 expatriate samples in Jiangsu and 42 expatriate samples in Guangdong were obtained from the subsidiaries that we visited. As it was clear that such a way is not adequate to get enough numbers of samples, our research team asked Prof. Fang to conduct a mail survey to complement the samples. We bought a foreign direct investment directory of each country, namely, *Toyo Keizai Weekly; Directory of Overseas Subsidies 2010* (2010, Toyo Keizai Shimposha) in Japan, *2009/2010 Korean Overseas Business Directory* (2010, Korea Trade-Investment Promotion Agency) in Korea, and *Membership Directory of Taiwanese Merchants in Mainland China Fourth Edition* (2008, Strait Exchange Foundation) in Taiwan, and asked Prof. Fang to collect 100 samples from each country's expatriates (50 companies in Jiangsu and 50 companies in Guangdong). He sent a questionnaire to the systematic randomly selected companies (one company out of ten) in each province by mail in 2010, but due to a low response rate, the number of samples he could collect couldn't reach the target. But we could finally obtain 150–200 samples from Korean/Japanese/Taiwanese expatriates in total, which is large enough to conduct a statistical analysis (see Table 5.1).

Table 5.1 Composition of samples: expatriates

| | | Place of research | | Total |
		Jiangsu	Guangdong	
Country	Korea	122	70	192
	Taiwan	99	66	165
	Japan	89	59	148
Total		310	195	505

Source: 2nd Wave of East Asian Businessmen in China Survey 2010–2011.

After the completion of 2nd Wave of East Asian Businessmen in China Survey, the author conducted Korean/Japanese Multinationals Headquarter Survey 2012 to compare their HRM policies on the recruitment/evaluation/promotion/education of the personnel for Chinese business in collaboration with Prof. Joon-shik Park. This chapter will use its results for the interpretation of the research results of 2nd Wave of East Asian Businessmen in China Survey 2010–2011.

Hypotheses and results of analysis

Are there any differences among East Asian companies in terms of their adaptation to *guanxi*-oriented business circumstances? In order to answer this research question, we need to make an operational definition of "adaptation to *guanxi*-oriented business circumstances" so that we can verify some hypotheses.

It is safe to say that one of the most outstanding characteristics of *guanxi*-orientedness in China is that *guanxi* with local officials is of vital importance in obtaining a lot of precious resources (information, know-how, power, and so on) in doing business in the Chinese market. In this sense, if foreign expatriates have friends in local government,[4] we can say that they are "adapted to *guanxi*-oriented business circumstances."

Hypotheses

As is frequently mentioned, Taiwan is enjoying cultural proximity to mainland China which makes Taiwanese businessmen more adapted to *guanxi*-oriented business circumstances (Liou, 2009; Huang and Baek, 2010; Yang, 2011). Therefore we can easily hypothesize,

> H_1 *More Taiwanese expatriates have friends in local government than other East Asian (namely Korean and Japanese) expatriates.*

Cultural gap with China can be overcome by language acquisition. In other words, those foreign expatriates who have a good command of Mandarin can make friends with local officials and exchange ideas more easily than those who don't, and the difference between Chinese and non-Chinese can be nominal as long as the informants have enough linguistic ability. If so,

> H_2 *Those East Asian expatriates who have better command of Mandarin have more friends in local government.*

Here again we should make an operational definition of "good command of Mandarin." In our survey of foreign expatriates, language proficiency of

Mandarin was measured by the respondent's answer to the question "How often do you use a translator in doing business in China?" The answer was scored from 4 points (No) to 1 point (Always).

In many cases, physical conditions like length of stay in local community might be a better predictor whether informants have friends in local government or not because the longer you stay, the more opportunities you might have to make friends with local officials in that community. If the length of stay of non-Chinese expatriates is longer than Taiwanese expatriates, we can see a nominal difference between Chinese and non-Chinese cultural differences in terms of their adaption to *guanxi*-orientedness. If so, we can predict that

H₃ Those East Asian expatriates who stay in China for longer have more friends in local government.

"Adaptation to *guanxi*-oriented business circumstances" might be easy or difficult depending on the conditions of the local community. Those local communities that are more *guanxi*-oriented will necessitate foreign expatriates to seek for friends in local government than those local communities that are "clean and free from corruption."

It is sometimes pointed out that Guangdong has been more economically driven and more open to "corruption" than Jiangsu (Chang, 2006: 76). Some expatriates whom we interviewed also pointed out that officials in Guangdong are "more flexible in interpreting industrial policies than Suzhou, Jiangsu, where many rules have been relatively strictly implemented."[5] If so, we can say that

H₄ More East Asian expatriates have friends in local government in Guangdong than in Jiangsu.

Results of analysis

In order to verify and prioritize the four hypotheses above, we conducted logistic regression analysis where

Y(Dummy: Friends in Local Government) = (Constant) + X_1(Dummy: Taiwan) + X_2(Necessity of Translation) + X_3(Years of Stay in China) + X_4(Dummy: Guangdong)

The result is listed in Table 5.2.

As can be seen from the table, H_3 (Years of Stay in China) is most powerful in explaining whether East Asian expatriates have friends in local government in China. On the contrary, H_2 (Necessity of Translator) and H_4 (Place of Research) are not statistically supported.

Table 5.2 Result of logistic regression analysis (1): dependent variable = friends in local government

Model	Unstandardized coefficients		Standardized coefficients	t	Sig.
	B	Std. error	Beta		
(Constant)	0.126	0.077		1.648	0.100
X_1 Taiwan (Dummy = 1)	−0.177	0.046	−0.205	−3.878	0.000
X_2 Necessity of Translator	0.016	0.021	0.041	0.758	0.449
X_3 Years of Stay in China	0.021	0.004	0.262	5.655	0.000
X_4 Place of Research (Dummy: Guangdong = 1)	−0.026	0.037	−0.031	−0.690	0.491

Source: 2nd Wave of East Asian Businessmen in China Survey 2010–11.

Note
$R^2 = .087$ (<0.001).

Surprisingly, Table 5.2 shows the completely opposite fact that H_1 presupposed. In other words, non-Taiwanese have more friends in local government than Taiwanese.

In order to clarify whether it is Korean expatriates or Japanese expatriates that have more friends than Taiwanese ones, we replace X_1 (Dummy: Taiwan) by X_{11} (Dummy: Korea) and X_{12} (Dummy: Japan) and conducted the logistic regression analysis in the following way.

Y(Dummy: Friends in Local Government) = (Constant) + X_{11}(Dummy: Korea) + X_{12}(Dummy: Japan) + X_2(Necessity of Translation) + X_3(Years of Stay in China) + X_4 (Dummy: Guangdong)

The result is shown in Table 5.3.

As is clearly shown in Table 5.3, it is Korean expatriates that have more friends in local government than Taiwanese (and Japanese). Cultural proximity of Taiwanese companies with Chinese ones is not a driving force for their establishing *guanxi* with local officials.

Korean experts are more eager to obtain "social capital" by making friends with those who are in the Chamber of Commerce, foreign competitors, and local business partners than Taiwanese and Japanese (see Figure 5.1).[6]

Interpretations

Why do Korean expatriates have more friends in local government?

Why do Korean expatriates have more friends in local government? Why did cultural proximity not encourage Taiwanese expatriates to establish more *guanxi* with the local officials than Korean expatriates? It is difficult to answer these

Table 5.3 Result of logistic regression analysis (2): dependent variable = friends in local government

Model	Unstandardized coefficients	Standardized coefficients		t	Sig.
	B	Std. error	Beta		
(Constant)	0.029	0.103		0.282	0.778
X_{11} Korea (Dummy = 1)	0.204	0.046	0.244	4.391	0.000
X_{12} Japan (Dummy = 1)	0.080	0.058	0.090	1.368	0.172
X_2 Necessity of Translator	−0.006	0.023	−0.016	−0.282	0.778
X_3 Years of Stay in China	0.020	0.004	0.257	5.589	0.000
X_4 Place of Research (Dummy: Guangdong = 1)	−0.020	0.037	−0.024	−0.544	0.587

Source: 2nd Wave of East Asian Businessmen in China Survey 2010–2011.

Note
$R^2 = 0.100$ (<0.001).

questions directly, but we can point out some evidence that might explain Korean expatriates' positive attitudes to adapt themselves to the Chinese environments, which gives us a clue to understand the reasons for Korean expatriates' strong aspiration to establish *guanxi* in the Chinese market.

As Figure 5.2 illustrates, Korean expatriates have better command of Chinese (Mandarin) than Japanese regardless of the same proportion of those who studied Chinese language before taking up their position in the subsidiaries. It is no

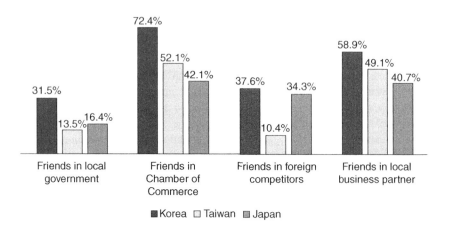

Figure 5.1 Social capital of foreign expatriates (source: 2nd Wave of East Asian Businessmen in China Survey 2010–2011).

Note
Figures show the percent of those who have friends in each category among Korean, Taiwanese, and Japanese expatriates.

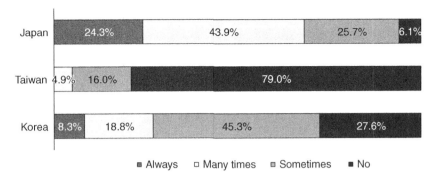

Figure 5.2 Necessity of translation (source: 2nd Wave of East Asian Businessmen in China Survey 2010–2011).

wonder that approximately 80 percent of Taiwanese expatriates do not use a translator at all when they do business in China, but it is quite surprising that more than a quarter of Korean expatriates answered so. Japanese expatriates, some of whom studied Chinese language/culture as their major when they were college students, are far behind the Korean counterparts in terms of their linguistic proficiency of Mandarin.

In fact, all of the Korean subsidiaries we visited are using Mandarin as a *lingua franca* of their communication while many Japanese subsidiaries are using Japanese especially when they talk about some crucial managerial matters with local managers.

Different language policy in subsidiaries is a reflection of different attitude toward understanding Chinese people in doing business in China. As Figure 5.3 illustrates, there is a 17–18 percent difference between Korean expatriates on one hand and Japanese and Taiwanese expatriates on the other in terms of the percentage of those who answered "Strongly agree" to the statement "To understand Chinese is important for business in China."

It is evident that Korean expatriates are spending more and effort in adapting themselves to the Chinese conditions than their Taiwanese and Japanese counterparts.

Different strategy, different mode of localization

Different language policy is also a reflection of different mode of localization policy of their headquarters. Korean/Japanese Multinationals Headquarter Survey 2012 reveals contrasting features of their HRM strategies between Korean and Japanese multinationals.

Figure 5.4 illustrates that Japanese companies are more dependent on Chinese managers hired by headquarters and local subsidiaries. Though roughly the same percentage of Korean (57.1 percent) and Japanese (59.5 percent) companies think it's difficult to recruit good personnel for China business from the local

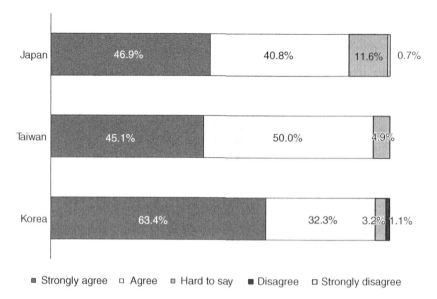

Figure 5.3 "To understand Chinese is important for business in China" (source: 2nd Wave of East Asian Businessmen in China Survey 2010–2011).

labor market, Korean companies rely more on Korean expatriates than Japanese companies to cope with the increasing importance of the Chinese market.

Though, again, roughly the same percentage of Korean companies (75.2 percent) and Japanese companies (74.2 percent) admit that their dispatching expatriates are the key actors that manage their subsidiaries. But if you look at their ideal key actor of local management, 61.8 percent of Japanese companies chose locally recruited managers/employees while 61.5 percent of Korean

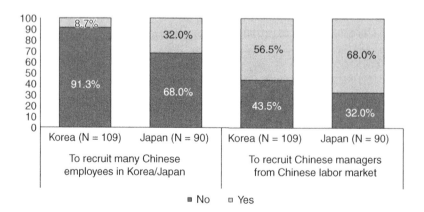

Figure 5.4 HRM strategies to cope with increasing importance of the Chinese market (source: Korean/Japanese Multinationals Headquarter Survey 2012).

companies regarded their dispatching expatriates as ideal key actors of local management (see Figure 5.5). To put it differently, expatriate-centered management in Korean subsidiaries in China is an ideal form of their localization, while Japanese companies have stronger aspirations to train locally recruited managers/employees to replace Japanese expatriates and manage their local subsidiaries.

Such different strategies of HRM will make Korean and Japanese expatriates choose different approaches to the *guanxi*-oriented Chinese market. Korean expatriates, because of their crucial role in their local management, will try to establish *guanxi* to get local information from different channels by themselves. Japanese expatriates, on the other hand, who have been regarding establishing *guanxi* with local officials as something troublesome or simply a heavy burden since early 1980s (Sonoda, 2012), will try to ask their local managers who function as a "cultural mediator" (Sonoda, 2004: 304–310) between Japanese expatriates and Chinese employees to take responsibility to manage "local affairs" including the maintenance of *guanxi* with local officials.[7]

As Lin and Keng (2008: 187) point out, Taiwanese businessmen have more channels to mobilize resources in local communities, especially from their ethnic

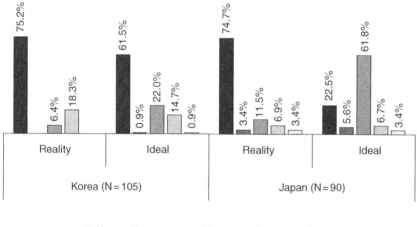

Figure 5.5 Ideal and reality of local management (source: Korean/Japanese Multinationals Headquarter Survey 2012).

Note
Figures in "Reality" show the percentage who chose each answer to the question "Who is mainly managing local offices/subsidiaries in China?" and those figures in "Ideal" show the percentage who chose each answer to the question, "Then who do you think should manage local offices/subsidiaries mainly in China in the future?"

group, which makes it less necessary to make efforts to "*la* [pull] *guanxi*" with local officials in comparison with Korean businessmen. Our data also shows that Taiwanese expatriates have less contact with local workers' families than Korean ones, which suggests that Taiwanese have their own "living sphere" and have a clearer line between expatriates and local people.

Another possible explanation for Koreans' stronger reliance on *guanxi* with local officials is that they are looking at the more positive side of establishing *guanxi* with the officials, while Taiwanese and Japanese are more cautious about the negative side. Recent research on international businessmen's perception on political risk in China suggests that Korean and German businessmen are less sensitive toward political risk, while Taiwanese and Japanese businessmen are more aware of political risk in China, which must be correlated with different attitudes of using *guanxi* with political figures in the Chinese market.[8]

Paradoxically, lack of cultural proximity seems to be functioning as a driving force for the Korean expatriates to learn Chinese language and how to "*la* [pull] *guanxi*" with local officials.[9]

Conclusion

In spite of the rapid development of the market economy, *guanxi* still matters in Chinese business. But it is quite another story whether foreign expatriates will take initiative in establishing *guanxi* with local authorities. Sometimes other local channels will help them mobilize resources they need (the Taiwanese case), and sometimes local managers who are expected to take the place of expatriates are asked to be in charge of management of *guanxi* with local officials (the Japanese case).

According to the result of logistic regression analysis, the length of stay in China is the most powerful in explaining whether East Asian expatriates have friends in local government, followed by the nationality of the expatriates. As is analyzed above, Korean expatriates, who are expected to be key actors in management of local subsidiaries by the headquarters in Korea, have more *guanxi* with local authorities than Japanese and Taiwanese expatriates. Needless to say, this result cannot be explained by cultural proximity between Korea and China.

Neither linguistic ability of Mandarin nor the place of business (whether it be Jiangsu or Guangdong), on the other hand, has any relation with whether the foreign expatriates have friends in local government or not.

Needless to say, establishment of *guanxi* is not a natural process. There is motivation behind it, and it is such a motivation that drives East Asian expatriates to seek for *guanxi* with local officials. As our research reveals, Korean expatriates make more friends with local officials, which can and should be explained by a different level of motivation.

It is in such a context that we should elaborate our comparative analysis of Japanese, Korean, and Taiwanese expatriates in China who are sometimes regarded as a single entity. Our comparative study has just begun to find out something empirically significant through our data mining.

Notes

1 The research was financially supported by the JSPS Scientific Research Grant "Coping with 'China': Comparative Sociological Analysis of Localization Process of Korean, Taiwanese, and Japanese Companies in China" (FY 2009–2012). I'm very grateful for the participants in this multinational research group who contributed to the data collection from Korean, Japanese, and Taiwanese enterprises. I'm also grateful for all the companies, expatriates, local workers who accepted our request to conduct a survey and sincerely answered our questionnaire/interview.
2 Therefore it is possible to conduct chronological analysis of the data of foreign expatriates and local workers. In this chapter, however, data of 1st Wave is not used but sometimes its results are referred to when necessary.
3 The reason of choosing Suzhou for our comparative research is because Suzhou is most convenient place for our comparison because all companies of Korea, Japan, and Taiwan are operating their business in a compact space. All the companies we visited are electric parts suppliers, which offered a good condition to control the industry of the companies we surveyed.
4 In the questionnaire, we asked, "Do you have any close and dependable friends in the following groups or organizations?" and checked whether the informants chose "Supervising sections in the local government." Those who chose this item are regarded as those who have friends in local government.
5 Interview with a Japanese manager on January 19, 2001.
6 This trend seems to be consistent during this decade because the results of 1st Wave of East Asian Businessmen in China Survey 2001 showed the same results. Though we could collect data on social capital of East Asian expatriates in China, we just focused on *guanxi* with local government simply because of its significance in managing multinationals in China (Wu, 2007: 128).
7 Such different commitment to local affairs suggests different family strategy between Korean expatriates and Japanese expatriates. According to the research result of 2nd Wave, 64.9 percent of surveyed Korean expatriates brought their families to China while only 21.6 percent of surveyed Japanese expatriates brought their families. Thus Korean expatriates regard their expatriate life as more meaningful and positive than Japanese counterparts. As to Taiwanese expatriates, the percentage of those who brought their families (37.4 percent) is between Korean expatriates and Japanese expatriates.
8 This is the tentative result of our discussion at a workshop on July 22, 2013, organized by the research project "Political Risk and Human Mobility: International Collaborative Research on the Rise of China" in Research and Information Center for Asian Studies, Institute for Advanced Studies on Asia, the University of Tokyo. More convincing empirical evidence, however, is necessary to confirm this argument.
9 Similar interpretation can be seen in Chang's analysis of 1st Wave data to compare Korean, Japanese, and Taiwanese expatriates' behavior. See Chang (2008: 162).

References

Bjorkman, I. and S. Kock. 1995. "Social Relationship and Business Networks: The Case of Western Companies in China." *International Business Review* 13 (1): 519–535.

Chang, Chia-ming. 2006. *Taiwanese Merchants in Suzhou: Analysis of Globalization and Localization.* Taipei: Laureate Publishing Company (Chinese).

Chang, Chia-ming. 2008. "Cross-border Investment and Social Adaptation in China: A Comparison of Taiwanese, Japanese, and Korean Expatriates." *East Asian Studies* 39 (1): 145–164 (Chinese).

Chen, Min. 1995. *Asian Management Systems: Chinese, Japanese and Korean Styles of Business.* London: Routledge.

Fan, Ying. 2007. "Guanxi, Government and Corporate Reputation in China: Lessons for International Companies." *Marketing Intelligence & Planning* 25 (5): 499–510.

Flora F. Gu, Kineta Hung, and David K. Tse. 2008. "When Does Guanxi Matter? Issues of Capitalization and Its Dark Sides." *Journal of Marketing* 72: 12–28.

Gold, Thomas, D. Guthrie, and D. Wank, eds. 2002. *Social Connections in China.* Cambridge: Cambridge University Press.

Hitt, Michael A, Ho-uk Lee, and Emre Yucel. 2002. "The Importance of Social Capital to the Management of Multinational Enterprises: Relational Networks Among Asian and Western Firms." *Asia Pacific Journal of Management* 19 (2–3): 353–372.

Huang, Lan-ying and H. Young Baek. 2010. "Key Drivers in Guanxi in China Among Taiwanese Small to Medium-Sized Firms." *International Business Research* 3 (1): 136–146.

Jin, Ai. 2006. "Guanxi Networks in China: Its Importance and Future Trends." *China & World Economy* 14 (5): 105–118.

Langenberg, Eike, A. 2007. *Guanxi and Business Strategy: Theory and Implications for Multinational Companies in China.* Heidelberg: Physica-Verlag.

Lin, Rui-Hua and Shu Keng. 2008. "Economic Interests and Identity Shift: A Comparative Study of Korean and Taiwanese Investors in China." *East Asian Studies* 39 (1): 165–192 (Chinese).

Liou, Dian-yan. 2009. "Globalization with *Guanxi* for Taiwanese High-Tech Industry to China: Panacea or Pandora's Box?" PICMET 2009 Proceedings. 2268–2273.

Sonoda, Shigeto. 2001. *Chinese Psychology and Behavior.* Tokyo: NHK Books (Japanese).

Sonoda, Shigeto, ed., 2003. *Cross-border Businessmen in East Asia: Comparative Analysis of Image Formation toward Business Partners (12572003).* Report to Japan Society for Promotion of Science (Japanese).

Sonoda, Shigeto. 2004. "Globalization and Increasing Function of 'Mediator': The Logic of Social Integration of Japanese Firms in Asia." In *Globalization and East Asia,* edited by Yoshimoto Kawasaki et al. Tokyo: Chuo University Press (Japanese).

Sonoda, Shigeto. 2012. "Emerging Labor Disputes in Dalian, 2005: Historical Analysis of Inter-organizational Conflicts of Japanese Companies in China in the Eyes of Japanese Expatiates." In *History of Sino-Japan Relations, 1972–2012 III Culture and Society,* edited by Shigeto Sonoda. Tokyo: The University of Tokyo Press (Japanese).

Standifird, S. Stephan. 2006. "Using Guanxi to Establish Corporate Reputation in China." *Corporate Reputation Review* 9 (3): 171–178.

Wilson, Jonathan and Ross Brennan. 2001. "Managing Chinese/Western Joint Ventures: A Comparative Analysis of the 'Interaction and Networks' and 'Chinese Management' Literature." www.impgroup.org/uploads/papers/279.pdf.

Wong, Meiling. 2007. "Guanxi and Its Role in Business." *Chinese Management Studies* 1 (4): 257–276.

Wu, Jianlian. 2007. "An Analysis of Business Challenges Faced by Foreign Multinationals Operating the Chinese Market." *International Journal of Business and Management* 3 (12): 169–174.

Yang, Fang. 2011. "The Importance of Guanxi to Multinational Companies in China." *Asian Social Science* 7 (7): 163–168.

6 Local response of "growth" and "dependency"

A case study of Taiwan businessmen in Suzhou, China

Chia-ming Chang and Ter-hsing Cheng

Introduction

The first Taiwan-funded enterprises were established beginning in 1984 in Suzhou; today, Taiwan-funded enterprises have reached more than 7,000. Taiwan's businesses have become the main source of foreign capital utilization in Suzhou, and Suzhou has also become one of the most intensive and active regions for Taiwan's investment in mainland China. Suzhou's development zone has become an important hub for Taiwan's investment, increasing the status of its business environment around the world. At present, Taiwan's investors are mainly concentrated in the Suzhou Industrial Park, Hi-tech development zone, Kunshan development zone, and Wujiang development zone, while investment projects are also increasing considerably. In particular, Kunshan city, often called "little Taipei" by Taiwanese businessmen, houses more than 40 percent of Taiwan-funded enterprises in Suzhou, thus becoming the most popular investment zone for Taiwanese businesses. Currently Taiwanese residents in Suzhou number about 50,000, nearly 30,000 of whom are in Kunshan city. Many organizations and cultural centers came into being to cater to Taiwanese residents, including Taiwanese business associations, restaurants with Taiwanese cuisine, Taiwanese schools for children of businessmen, and Taiwanese wives' associations.

Clearly development in Suzhou is inextricably linked to foreign investment, in particular Taiwan's investment. As for the global effect of foreign investments and enterprises, two opposing views currently exist in the theory of dependency and the theory of function; the former stresses the negative effects of globalization, especially the disadvantages caused by foreign investments, which leads to dependent development of local society as well as the distortion or resistance of the local various actors, while the latter focuses on the positive effects of foreign investment globalization on host society, thus bringing a better local development of the economy and society. On this point, this chapter considers the following questions: what economic and social effects does Taiwan's investment bring for Suzhou? What attitudes do local people have about these effects? And what about the social inclusion of Taiwanese residents by the local people of Suzhou? This chapter aims to understand the effect of economic globalization from Taiwan's investment in Suzhou and the following local response through the experience and evaluation of local people.

Literature review

This study is concerned with the interaction and relationship between foreign capital and the host, with a focus on the effects of globalization and the local response to Taiwan's investment in mainland China. The social inclusion of the local people is used as an empirical question for this study. The study period begins after reform and opening up in mainland China, especially the phases of actively developing the export-oriented economy throughout the past decade. Therefore, the following review will focus on the papers directly relating to the former issue.

Negative aspects toward foreign investment

Liu Yaling states that Huayang, a poor area located on the edge of the Pearl River Delta, experienced some improvement and development of society as a whole because a large amount of foreign investment flowed in after the reforms. The amount of Taiwan's investment was the highest; the investments of Hong Kong, Japan, South Korea, the United States, and other foreign investors were more sporadic. It drove local businesses in transition and development, and thus Huayang moved away from its agricultural frontier, and towards the frontier of industry and business (Liu 2000: 1–19).

In this process, the Huayang Town Government assumed the responsibility to serve the foreign enterprises, to solve difficulties for foreign investors, and to attract foreign capital in order to make foreign investment take root locally. The symbiotic relationship between local development and foreign investment slowly took shape, and repeated the dependent development of Latin America in the 1960s. In particular, foreign-funded enterprises developed completely separately from local labor-intensive industries, and became a unique enclave economy. The foreign-funded businesses did not attempt to integrate with local enterprises for production or assist local enterprises in upgrading technology through a sub-contracting system, let alone the spillover effect from technology transfer. These foreign investments were not only isolated from the local society, but also released a great deal of waste pollution in the production process in the rural environment. Otherwise, local emerging industries were mostly in the service of foreign-funded enterprises, and local industries were deeply constrained by foreign investments, and lack of autonomous development, and this led to increased social status of the foreign business staff in the eyes of the local people. Some farmers even became victims under the collusion between local officers and foreign enterprises, and received very little or no compensation for their land and belongings. Eventually some were forced to react drastically in the form of protests against their treatment. In conclusion, the development pattern constrained by the foreign capital in Suzhou is similar to the dependent development of Latin America.

Wang Xinxian discussed Chinese regional development under globalization. He states that the industry clustering resulting from foreign investments may not create a positive effect for local society; instead it resulted in careless or excessive actions to attract foreign investment. The negative consequences mainly included the following problems: (1) part of the foreign investment's "running for preferential policy" led to short-term investment, which resulted in not only a disadvantage to the development of local industry, but also decreased local employment; (2) local governments pursued performance, and used to "grab enterprise not to grab project," and many so-called high-tech development zones have "degraded" to general export processing zones; (3) many regions repeated construction and seriously wasted resources; and (4) finally all development zones mutually undermined one another's foundations and perpetuated a vicious cycle of competition in order to seek foreign investment, such as the detrimental example of competition in "Warring States" (Wang 2003: 1–22).

Chen Zhirou believes that the development of foreign investment in China has expanded social distances and inequalities, and leads to the formation of social discontent from the perspective of class structure. He borrows the concept of "the weapon of the weak" from James Scott, noting that although underprivileged farmers cannot compare to the middle class and intellectuals, who are good at organizing collective protest action, they usually adopt everyday forms of resistance to confront authority or express dissatisfaction with the government, including laziness, stealing, feigned ignorance, slander, arson, sabotage, etc. (Chen 2002).

Ye Yumin addressed the origins and negative effects of upgrading industrial structures and land use conflicts from the Pearl River Delta, one of China's three major metropolitan areas. He pointed out that the major industry structure of Pearl Triangle "three comes, one compensation" was not enough to provide a basis for the next period of industrial upgrades. In the meantime these smaller-scaled and labor-intensive industries still occupied a large number of land resources, and these industries utilized most of the collective land. In the process of development there was no effective city planning, and thus it led to dispersed and inefficient uses of land resources, and brought on a series of environmental problems (Ye 2003: 1–22).

Ye Yumin pointed out that the largest rental market and highest benefits were due to constructing plants, and in a one-sided pursuit of economic benefits, it led the Baoan district of Shenzhen city to allocate the largest percentage of industrial lands under the land structure of city construction. This situation made land issues complicated, in conjunction with the operation of society as a whole, and transformed into complex economic and social issues. Foreign investments gained cheap land which resulted in a profound economic impact on Baoan, because farmers can share in the huge economic income from the city's development of the village collective organization and in real estate construction on behalf of villagers just by virtue of the land use right. That is, farmers need not participate in any work and are able to share in the distribution of stock right on schedule solely by their land use right. Therefore, farmers turned actions of land production into a reliance on collective actions.

From the viewpoint of the urban environmental construction and functional development, the economic expansion of the Baoan district does have its side effects. It brought rapid urban expansion and disorder spread; urban planning and management lagged behind urban construction. Most towns processed construction first and then focused on planning, first disorder and then specification; therefore, the city function was ineffective and the layout is not very reasonable.

The above discourses invariably stressed the negative effects of globalization, particularly the disadvantages of the impact of foreign investments, and thus ushered in the dependent development of local society, which resulted in the resistance of various local actors. We refer to the perspectives of dependent development views for the time being. Among them, Liu Yaling's "symbiosis of interest" depicted a mutual interdependence between the local governments and foreign-funded enterprises, and resulted in the repetition of the dependent development evident in the Latin American experience. Chen Zhirou's "weapon of the weak" described underprivileged farmers using everyday forms of resistance to confront authority or dissatisfaction with the government. In the uncertain external environment, he also speculated that China is moving toward the road of the "dependent developments in Latin America." Likewise, Ye Yumin uses the logical argument of "industrial upgrade" and "land use" to expose the interdependent relationship between foreign investments and local landlords, and also further discusses the local socio-economic impact of Taiwan's investment. Thus it resulted in improper use of land resources and excessive disorder related to urban construction.

Positive aspects toward foreign investment

In contrast to the above "dependent" perspective, Chang Chiaming and Chiou Shilong went into southern Jiangsu Province in mainland China for an in-depth study and pointed out that in the late 1980s, especially after the 1990s, the Communist Party of China led the economic development strategy in Suzhou, and thus Suzhou took the route of an export-oriented economy, which included encouraging new development of foreign direct investments, and abandoning the previous model in which the township enterprises in South Jiangsu were characterized by collective leadership. This new pattern of foreign capital traction attracted large amounts of funding, advanced technologies, innovative business management, and technical talents and ideas for the Suzhou area to make up for the slow growth under continuing development of village-township enterprises, and opened a way in addition to the difficulties of the reform faced by the Sunan model (Chang and Chiu 2002: 27–75).

They also pointed out that introduction of foreign capital also shaped the development of local governments and economy and society. Throughout the process of export-oriented economic development, local governments led the design and planning of local development in Suzhou, and played an active and important role in "localization of property rights" and "corporatization of the regime." Local government is like a "company" or "enterprise," and also like a kind of "combination of political and economic" model. Their specific roles can be clearly understood from the relationship among the central government, local and foreign capital. Specifically, the local governments in Suzhou, including Suzhou, Kunshan, and Wujiang, take almost the same model of development; that is, competing to establish economic and technological development zones as the core foundation of an export-oriented economic development, and its significance has at least three points: (1) absorbing foreign investments, expanding export, and developing high-tech industry; (2) synthesized development of the city; and (3) relaxing direct control and intervention from the central or local governments, and increasing the autonomy of decision-making and management and administration.

Upholding the same position, Chang Chiaming's concern is the interaction and influence between production of Taiwan's investment and the development of local private or township enterprises. Chang examines the perspective of globalization and social embeddedness, and took Kunshan, Suzhou as a case to analyze the influence of Taiwanese enterprises' subcontracting business on the operation and management capacity of local township enterprises. He found some Taiwanese enterprises gradually began to establish cooperative relationships with local manufacturers, which helped to further social embeddedness, and implemented a policy of localization in order to lower prices and to increase competitiveness. A concentric electroplating factory was reformed by local township enterprises, and then joined as a member of a collaborative production network in a Taiwanese computer factory, Foxconn. It made substantial changes in its organization and management in response to requests of customers and manufacturers, and upgraded their skills so as to further expand the commissioned relationships of production with international companies in Europe and America. Its activities in production and marketing had yielded a considerable degree of global integration. In sum, while the precise scope and volume is uncertain, it is clear that Taiwan's businesses in mainland China promote the management and operation of local businesses (Chang 2006: 199–225).

Especially for the synthesis development of the city, Yin Cunyi points out that China began reform and opening up in 1979, and the change in the system greatly promoted the development of productivity and also accelerated the process of urbanization. The urbanization rate had reached 37.7 percent by 2001, and its speed was almost twice as fast as the 30 years before reform and opening up, especially for the areas of investment by Taiwan. Yin raised the question: Kunshan city and Dongguan city, in essence, were mostly agricultural before 1990, and what were the reasons for developing the industrial structure of these two places from agricultural to industrial in just over ten years? (Yin 2003: 1–17).

Yin noted that the answer to this question must be put back into the context of historical development. In the process of urbanization since Chinese reform and opening up, and for the problem selection according to the development target of urbanization, China has had the argument of "large city theory" and "small city theory." Although the latter theory in the policy-oriented level of government once dominated, the reality was that the trend of Chinese urbanization was toward the development in both directions. First, the large agricultural population poured into the large cities, unrelated to de-agriculturalization. Second, urbanization was realized through de-agriculturalization. However, the first situation was problematic because the urbanization pattern depended on the large influx of the rural population into big cities, and it was an unbearable burden of urbanization in mainland China. The second situation regarding the model of small cities was advocated and promoted by the government. However, the appearance of many small towns did not solve the real problem of urbanization of the agricultural population. The key point was that the township enterprises, which were relied on by most small towns, did not have the typical features of modern industry, from human resources to operational mechanisms. It resulted in the quick elimination of competition in a market economy, and led to insufficient economic power and weak growth in the small towns. It was this lack of absorption capacity to make enough of the rural population to become part of the non-agricultural population, so that the development model of the small towns failed to obtain the desired effect. This led to vast numbers of rural workers pouring into big cities in the 1990s.

In short, the large influx of the rural population to big cities is difficult to bear for lack of economic dynamism and growth in a large number of small towns. That has been the problem for nearly 20 years with the process of urbanization in mainland China. But at the same time, with a large number of Taiwanese enterprises coming to mainland China since the 1990s, it injected new growth factors of urbanization in mainland China, and drove a group of mid-sized and small cities to develop in the Pearl River Delta and Yangtze River Delta. Among them, Dongguan and Kunshan are especially significant examples of urbanization between the two areas. The development pattern and effectiveness of these smaller cities brought a certain impact to the existing administration systems in mainland China, and provided a useful model of Chinese urbanization. It is true that due to the space limitation of foreign direct investment (FDI), and the significance of the urbanization development model in Dongguan and Kunshan, it is a successful development model in the process of urbanization in mainland China, and it deserves concern and research.

From the experience of industrialization and urbanization in Dongguan and Kunshan, the trend of economic globalization makes technology proliferate and makes possible the leaps-and-bounds development of urbanization. This background and practice of opening to the outside world are also no longer limited to the supply capacity of domestic resources for economic development; meanwhile, economic subjects are also diversified and external resources and personality representatives also participate in the rapid development of local urbanization, which roughly responds to its industrial growth curve. This indicates the significance of the positive relationship between urbanization and industrialization. It can be called a special phenomenon to achieve unprecedented progress of urbanization and industrialization in about ten years with relatively little capital accumulation of industrialization and human resources in such a fundamental area of the agricultural economy. Its particularity is in the exogenous process of industrialization, and a large number of foreign industrial investments transform local economic structures, and promote the process of urbanization.

To summarize, the examples of Dongguan and Kunshan indicate that economic globalization and the transnational or across-area flows of capital can change the economic structure of a nation or area, and accelerate the industrialization and urbanization process, or even lead a regional or local society to achieve a "leaps-and-bounds" type of industrialization and city development. Thus an "internationalization of urbanization" phenomenon appears, which is a concept of "exo-urbanization" (Richardson 1992: 44–63; Gripaios et al. 1997: 579–603; Sit and Yang 1997: 647–677; Sit 2001: 11–45). This external force is the influx of Taiwanese investment. Taiwanese firms invested heavily in Dongguan and Kunshan, which shortened the historical process of industrialization and urbanization, effectively promoting the changes of economic and social structures, and successfully achieved leaps-and-bounds development of industrialization and urbanization, and possessed the corresponding material capacity and vision.

In addition, Zhou Changzheng noted that foreign investment and enterprise development promote the development of labor legalization, and also contribute to creating a large number of job opportunities for the local society (Zhou 2003: 48–49). By the end of June 2000, direct employment of personnel in foreign-invested enterprises in China had reached 19 million people. Jin Jiaoyi stressed that strong foreign investment can have positive effects on local development because foreign production leads to tax increases, foreign trade growth, adjustment of the industrial structure, and sustainable economic development (Jin 1999). Otherwise, according to customs statistics of Wujiang, the import and export trade volume broke the $10 billion mark for the first time in the city by the end of November 2004, ten times the amount in the same period in 2000, and it became the second county-level city of trade volume exceeding 10 billion dollars in Suzhou, occupying 1 percent of China's total import and export trade.

Foreign-funded enterprises continued to be the main force of foreign trade. Total import and export trade constituted 92 percent of total import and export trade in the whole city. Four Taiwan-funded enterprises, Tatung Electronic, ASKEY, ARIMA computer, and CPT Technology, ranked in the top 20 of Suzhou export businesses. The rapid growth of foreign trade continued with the quality and the continuous improvement in development, and the moving in of a large number of foreign enterprises. In addition, Taiwanese enterprises' contribution to employment not only existed in its direct investment enterprises to provide employment opportunities, but also indirectly by creating employment opportunities through stimulating the development of related industries (*Wujiang Daily*, December 13, 2004).

In summary, the above papers do not emphasize dependent views, but focus on the positive effects of foreign investment globalization on the host society, and thus the authors indicate better economic and social development in the local society. Here we call it the perspective of growth. According to this viewpoint, Chang Chiaming and Chiu Shilong raised a "development model of foreign traction," which stated that because foreign investments came to Suzhou, they introduced large and high-tech funds, technology, talents, and concepts. Chang

Chiaming took the concept of "global integration" and "social embeddedness" to examine the improved function of local enterprises' operation and management capacity due to the sub-contract business of Taiwan's enterprises. Yin Cunyi further used the concept of "export-oriented urbanization" to advocate the view that large Taiwanese investments effectively promoted economic and social changes in Dongguan and Kunshan, and successfully carried out industrialization and urbanization. Zhou Changzheng noted that foreign investment and enterprise development supported the development of labor legalization, and also created vast numbers of job opportunities for the local society.

Effect of foreign investment on social life

Deng Jianbang took qualitative research approaches to explore the relations between Taiwan's business staff and the local societies. He pointed out that the "MTPs" (Mainland Travel Permit for Taiwan Residents) is not only Taiwan's identity document for traveling to mainland China, but also a mark of a special social group in mainland China. In addition, Taiwanese businessmen were deemed as "social others" with exception to the working context, but also still through "leisure time." Along with the formation of Taiwan's communities, the Taiwanese lifestyle also came into the local society; therefore, Taiwanese dining, fishing for shrimp, Karaoke, bowling, and other leisure consumption are also copied from the Taiwanese communities in mainland China (Deng 2011: 348–351). Nevertheless, "the Taiwanese way of life" enters into mainland China by Taiwan's investments and business staff. As for Taiwanese residents, it is a very unique way of living, which can compensate for the feelings of homesickness. However, the Taiwanese way of life is similar to the social embeddedness of Taiwanese investment, which also appears to be integrated in local social life, and is broadly cognitive as the social effects of Taiwan's businessmen. This type of capital globalization enters into the operation of the local economic industry, and then becomes the representation of the localization of the Taiwanese lifestyle. Eventually it finalizes the process of social embeddedness.

The economic effects of Taiwan's capital spill over as the transformation of local society and daily life. In fact, the holistic process is quite complex, and we review the theory of dependence and the theory of growth to examine the positive and negative effects on host societies under the globalization of foreign investments, especially of Taiwan's investment. Current research mostly focuses on the foreign-oriented perspective, and ignores the local reactions and interactions, although very few studies have noted that the social reactionaries, still limited to some special statistic items for specific places, may not be able to directly display the contacts between the force of globalization and local society, and unfortunately more information cannot be collected to reflect the views of the local society. The so-called local reaction mainly indicates the cognitive thoughts and attitudes of the community residents, and currently this aspect of the studies is relatively few.

Research hypothesis

This chapter involves three theoretic propositions to respond to the economic and social effects of Taiwanese investment in Suzhou and the study of the local response. (1) In the background of globalization, capital flow goes beyond its original purpose, which spills over from the economic level to the social aspect of daily life, and further promotes holistic changes of society. This is the same and very close process for the influence of economic investment and its corresponding concept to enter the local society. (2) The influence of foreign investment on local society is very strong, especially on the degree and direction of the local people's perceptions and behaviors, and the value judgments and subjective cognitions of the public toward the social impact of foreign investments. The local effect of foreign investment is taken as a social fact; however, no matter what the economic or social impact is, the cognition of the local people must have a process, which in fact is also integrated into the localization process of foreign investments in social change. (3) Developing countries often strive for foreign investment and always envisage a positive role of foreign investment in social development; this is purely the perspective of "growth" theory. Once local development relies solely on foreign investment maintenance, local people may not completely agree with the positive social function of foreign investment, and thus dependency theory describes social anti-function of foreign capital. Therefore, people do not believe that more foreign investments must be better for local society.

Based on the above three theoretical propositions, we raise the following three research hypotheses:

Hypothesis 1: The relationship between the economic, social, and life factors of Taiwan investment is **significant**.

Hypothesis 2: The economic and social factors of Taiwan's investment **significantly** influence the social inclusion of the local people through their cognitions in daily life.

Hypothesis 3: More Taiwanese investments are not necessary to **significantly** acquire more social inclusion of the local public.

Methodology and sample structure

This chapter uses questionnaire surveys as its research methodology. The investigation period is between February and May, 2007. A total of 600 questionnaires were distributed in the urban district of Suzhou city, Kunshan, and Wujiang, and 581 successful questionnaires returned, which is a success rate of 97.5 percent: 228 successful cases in Suzhou, 160 successful cases in Kunshan, and 193 successful cases in Wujiang. Male correspondents account for 54.2

percent, female for 45.8 percent; age 35 and above occupies more than one half of the respondents (60.7 percent), ages 36 to 45 and above the age of 46 accounts for 22.4 percent and 16.9 percent; the locals account for 77.6 percent, non-locals are 22.4 percent; married correspondents 60 percent, never married, cohabitation, divorced, separated, and widowed represent 40 percent; the highest education of junior high school and beyond accounts for 22.6 percent, senior high school degree accounts for 34.6 percent, university and above for the remaining 42.7 percent; occupation as professional technicians 28.7 percent, second is office staff (21.6 percent), and workers (17.3 percent), commercial and the service personnel (12.9 percent) and the students (9.9 percent); 48.1 percent of correspondents do not reach 1,500 Rmb, 1501–3,000 Rmb for 38.1 percent, 3,001 yuan and above account for 13.9 percent (Table 6.1).

Empirical analysis

This research uses several scales of the questionnaire to process statistical methods such as factor analysis, correlation, path analysis, and logistic regression

Table 6.1 Structure of the sample

Variables	Options	N	%	Options	N	%
Sex	Male	317	54.2	Female	268	45.8
Age	18–25	124	21.2	26–35	231	39.5
	36–45	131	22.4	46–60	82	14.0
	61 and over	17	2.9			
How long have you lived here	Since born	451	77.6	1 and beyond	11	1.9
	2–3 years	23	4.0	4–5 years	23	4.0
	5 and over	73	12.6			
Marriage	Married	341	60.0	Unmarried	188	33.1
	Live together	13	2.3	Divorced	10	1.8
	Live apart	3	0.5	Spouse death	10	1.8
	Other	3	0.5			
Education	Primary	41	7.0	Junior high	91	15.6
	Senior high	202	34.6	College, higher	249	42.7
Occupation	Professional	154	28.7	State, party…	19	3.5
	Office staff	116	21.6	Service	69	12.9
	Workers	93	17.3	Students	53	9.9
	Retired	5	0.9	Workless	3	0.6
	Personal	20	3.7	Other	5	0.9
Income	0–800	38	7.9	801–1,200	99	20.6
	1,201–1,500	93	19.4	1,501–2,000	100	20.8
	2,001–3,000	83	17.3	3,001–5,000	52	10.8
	5,001 and higher	15	3.1			
Interview areas	Suzhou City	228	39.2	Wujiang City	160	27.5
	Kunshan City	193	33.2			

to examine the economic, social, and lifestyle influence of Taiwan's investment into the Suzhou area. Specifically, these statistical methods will examine the above three research propositions and hypotheses. First, we examine the reliability and validity of the scale items. The reliability examination adopts the Cronbach Alpha coefficient and the reliability standards of the overall scale must be higher than 0.7, or it still can display reliability not less than the standard of 0.6. This chapter selected several scales (scale of enterprise influence, scale of city construction, scale of social development, scale of lifestyle, and scale of social inclusion) and their Cronbach Alpha coefficients are between 0.656 and 0.770, which presents good reliability (see the Appendix Table 6A.1). Second, we continue three methods of commonality tests to analyze the constructive validity: alpha value after removal of the items, commonality, and factors loading. Among them, the alpha value after removal of the items must be less than Alpha Cronbach of each scale; commonality must be greater than 0.2, and factors loading must be greater than 0.45. Test results have removed 4 questions and retained 31 questions.

Second, according to the reliability and validity test of scale, we use the two scales of economic dimension and the social development scale of social dimension for a factor analysis in order to obtain some common factors, and name these common factors. The economic dimension scale has 0.773 of KMO value, and the Bartlett's test significance level is 0.000, which shows it is suitable for factor analysis. In addition, the KMO value of social development scale is 0.883, and the Bartlett's test significance level is 0.000, which also shows suitability for factor analysis. We then use the method of "Maximum variation of straightening of the hinge factor loading" to obtain the factors loading, commonality, and cumulative explained variation amount (Table 6.2 and Table 6.3). The analysis results display three common factors from the economic dimension: "operating effectiveness," "city construction," and "enterprise growth," and two common factors are acquired from the scale of social development: "social function" and "living environment," plus the two common factors of "lifestyle" and "social inclusion." Social dimension involves four common factors: "social function," "living environment," "lifestyle," and "social inclusion."

The scales we have adopted first process the necessary reverse scoring and thus the common factors which are extracted through factor analysis indicate higher scores and more positive results. Taiwan's investment in Suzhou operates beyond the original purpose of capital flows. The localization of capital first results in an economic effect and soon spills into social and daily life areas. The questionnaire scales examine the value judgment and cognition attaching to the influential process of economic capital. Table 6.4 presents the correlations among all factors of economic and social dimensions, which are affected by foreign (Taiwanese) investments. Despite a low to middle degree of correlation, the results of all factors are relevant, and also reach a significant level, which explains that the local cognition and value judgment toward the effects of the local economic, social, and living impact by Taiwan's investment are

Table 6.2 Summary results of economic dimension scale

Items	Maximum variation of straightening of the hinge factor loading			Commonality
	Operating effectiveness	City construction	Enterprise growth	
The operating effectiveness of Taiwan enterprises is superior to State-owned enterprises or township enterprises	0.831			0.696
The compliance level of Taiwan enterprises is superior to State-owned enterprises or township enterprises	0.792			0.662
Suzhou's enterprises often learn of Taiwan enterprises in the area of marketing or publicity methods	0.585			0.420
Taiwan investment contributes to the increase of city water and electricity utilities		0.838		0.749
Taiwan investment contributes to the increase of urban road		0.817		0.692
Taiwan investment is not conducive to the increase of urban communication facilities		0.507		0.408
Taiwan investment is against technology growth of local enterprise			0.773	0.601
Taiwan investment is not good for the financing of local enterprises			0.605	0.379
Taiwan investment helps talents cultivation of local enterprises			0.499	0.326
Taiwan investment contributes to the growth of local management knowledge			0.451	0.389
Eigenvalues	1.907	1.776	1.640	5.323
of explained variation %	19.065	17.764	16.400	53.229
cumulative explained variation amount	19.065	36.829	53.229	

Note
KMO = 0.773 Bartlett's test: chi-square = 938.548, df = 45, p = 0.000.

Table 6.3 Summary results of social development scale

Items	Maximum variation of straightening of the hinge factor loading		Commonality
	Social function	Living environment	
Increased Taiwan investment results in life being difficult for workers' families	0.728		0.543
Increased Taiwan investment results in local youth unemployment	0.712		0.540
Increased Taiwan investment worsens the local working conditions	0.685		0.492
Increased Taiwan investment results in more rural problems	0.584		0.391
More Taiwanese businessmen are unfavorable to raise local education standards	0.510		0.364
A large number of Taiwan enterprises recruitment causes community deterioration		0.697	0.487
More Taiwanese businessmen result in more serious environmental pollution		0.671	0.485
Massive Taiwan investment has worsened the social atmosphere		0.668	0.521
Large number of Taiwan enterprises recruitment causes community deterioration		0.660	0.482
Taiwan enterprises generally have environmental awareness		0.475	0.285
Eigenvalues	2.325	2.264	4.589
of explained variation %	23.248	22.635	45.883
cumulative explained variation amount	23.428	45.883	

Note
KMO = 0.833 Bartlett's test: chi-square = 1147.771, df = 45, p = 0.00.

Table 6.4 The correlation coefficient of economic and social factors

	Social function	Living environment	Lifestyle	Social inclusion
city construction	0.389**	0.327**	0.437**	0.211**
enterprise growth	0.239**	0.220**	0.343**	0.214**
operating effectiveness	0.440**	0.358**	0.472**	0.252**

Note
**p = 0.01(two tails).

comprehensive. This result supports Hypothesis 1. The results of the analysis show the positive relation between the evaluations of the economic and social dimensions, but the level of correlation is not high, which would seem to show that a sophisticated relationship between the factors of economic and social dimensions still exists.

When foreign (Taiwan) investment flows into local society, it will become a social influence on local development. The influential degree and direction of foreign investments on the concepts and actions of the local people correspond to the connection in the value judgments and subjective cognitions and attitudes of the local public. There must be a process for the public's cognition and it may be the most direct feeling from the change of daily life or lifestyle. Figure 6.1 shows the result of a path analysis which examines the local social inclusion toward Taiwanese businessmen and its relative concepts through the effects of economic and social factors; we take lifestyle as an intermediate variable. We can compare the effect of social inclusion between the factors of "enterprise growth" and "social function" and find that the direct effect of "enterprise growth" on "social inclusion" is 0.214, while the direct effect of "living environment" on "social inclusion" is 0.236. It shows that the cognitive evaluation of local people toward the social inclusion of Taiwanese businessmen may actually come from more social-oriented feelings. In addition, we take "lifestyle" as an intermediate variable and then we calculate the whole effect of "enterprise growth" and "city construction" on "social inclusion" via "lifestyle" as $(0.343 \times 0.334) + (0.437 \times 0.334) + 0.214 = 0.475$, while the whole effect of "living environment" and "social function" on "social inclusion" via "lifestyle" as $(0.356 \times 0.334) + (0.487 \times 0.334) + 0.236 = 0.518$. Those related concepts and feelings toward Taiwan's businessmen from society, community, and everyday life are relatively comprehensive and direct. Local people may not necessarily be in direct contact with Taiwan-funded enterprises, but the spillover effects of Taiwanese investment embedded in social life can result in more cognition and evaluation by the local people. Therefore, the results of the path analysis support Hypothesis 2: The economic and social factors of Taiwan's investment **significantly** influence the social inclusion of the local people also through the cognitions of daily life.

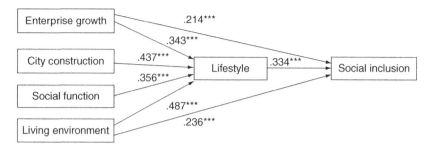

Figure 6.1 Path analysis of social inclusion.

In the examination of Hypothesis 1, we confirm the overall and compre-hensive effects of foreign (Taiwanese) investments on the local society, not only the original significance of capital flows. If we believe that foreign investment brings local society only positive features, this may not be agree-able for the local public. Therefore, we found in this research that despite a positive correlation between the factors of the economic dimension and social dimensions, the degree of correlation is not high. We then use logistic regres-sion analysis to examine whether some possible variables can explain insuffi-cient parts of this growth theory. The dependent variable is changed to the question "Are you willing to be the neighbor of Taiwanese businessmen?" Table 6.5 displays the results of the logistic regression, and we find that the degree of social inclusion toward Taiwan's businessmen in Kunshan is lower than Wujiang and Suzhou, and Kunshan actually has much more Taiwanese investment, enterprise, and businessmen than the other two cities. Therefore, this result supports Hypothesis 3: More Taiwanese investments are not neces-sary to **significantly** acquire more social inclusion of the local public. Foreign capital flows under globalization also support the arguments of dependency theory, that is, a negative social function; therefore, the degree of the local people's acceptance of Taiwanese businessmen or Taiwanese culture in Kunshan city is the lowest when compared to the other two investigation cities, and maybe this result is no surprise. Otherwise, in the examination of Hypothesis 2, we confirm that local people's evaluation of foreign (Taiwan) investments must have a process, and it is especially significant through the influence of social aspects and the factors of lifestyle. The results of logic regression analysis in Table 6.5 also show that the factors of "living environ-ment" and "lifestyle" significantly influence the social inclusion toward Tai-wanese businessmen. This fact explains that the evaluation by local people mainly comes from the social effects and daily life which has been influenced by Taiwanese investment. There is a process for foreign investment's flow from the economic aspect to the social aspect, and accordingly the cognitive appraisal of Taiwanese investment also has a process. Here is another support of Hypothesis 2.

Table 6.5 Logistic regression analysis of social inclusion

	B	Exp(β)	B	Exp(β)
age (0:35 years old and beyond)	−0.165	0.848		
marriage (0:unmarried)	0.140	1.150		
education (0:high school and beyond)	0.292	1.340		
sex (0:female)	−0.546	0.579**		
income I (1200rmb vs. 2001rmb)	0.033	1.033		
income II (1201–2000 vs. 2001)	0.088	1.092		
area I (Suzhou vs. Kunshan)	0.543	1.721*		
area II (Wujiang vs. Kunshan)	0.829	2.290***		
enterprise growth			−0.029	0.971
city construction			0.007	1.007
social function			−0.038	0.963
living environment			−0.124	0.883***
lifestyle			0.086	1.090**
constant	−0.364	0.695	0.665	1.924
	N = 461		N = 547	
	R square = 0.043		R square = 0.043	
	Chi square = 20.107*		Chi square = 24.190***	

Notes
*p = <0.05 **p = <0.01 ***p = <0.001.

Table 6.6 shows the results of this research analysis and shows that these three hypotheses are supported by the empirical analysis. The socio-economic change of foreign (Taiwan) traction in Suzhou is broad and subject to its influence, and the cognition and evaluation from local people toward foreign (Taiwan) investment has a process, in which social aspects and aspects of daily life bring more direct and comprehensive feelings. The effects of foreign (Taiwan) investments can be explained in both theories of dependence and function; however, the social judgment and evaluation of the local people may not be equal to the local governments, for the governments tend to absorb more foreign investments and maintain a positive attitude toward foreign investments, while local people may think in different ways and may not support more foreign investment. Kunshan seemingly confirms this view.

Table 6.6 Results of research analysis

	Hypothesis	Support or not
H1	The relation among the economic, social, and life factors of Taiwan investment is **significant**.	Support
H2	The economic and social factors of Taiwan's investment **significantly** influence the social inclusion of the local people also through the cognitions of daily life.	Support
H3	More Taiwan's investments are not necessary to **significantly** acquire more social inclusion of the local public.	Support

Chang Chiaming used the concept of "social embeddedness" to illustrate the localization of Taiwan's enterprises and its impact (Chang 2006). Embeddedness is a basic concept of the new economic sociology, and it originally intended to refer to the combination of a system being introduced into another object system. Contemporary economic sociologists take economic activities to a broader context of society and interpersonal relationships, and believe that economic behavior is actually embedded in social networks, or in informal social relations. Therefore, when economic and non-economic activities are mixed with each other, non-economic activities influence the cost of economic activities and available technology. This blend of such activities is known as the "social embeddedness of the economy," including the embeddedness of economic activity in social networks and in cultural, political, and religious spheres (Granovetter 1985, 2005).

Therefore, the concept of social embeddedness also alludes to a more complex meaning of social integration and localization. In the context of globalization, there must be enterprise development on the road to globalization, but it is not really workable without implementation of localization policy. If Taiwan's enterprises really want to take root in Suzhou, they must be integrated into the local culture and use the local knowledge. On the other hand, Suzhou is taken as the location of Taiwan's enterprises, it benefits from the development of Taiwan investments, and must also accept the culture and products of Taiwan's enterprises. This means we must understand the mechanism of mutual embeddedness between Taiwan's enterprises and the local people.

In addition to all dimensions of enterprise operation and management, and besides the localization of talents, funds, production, raw materials, and marketing, it is the process of Taiwanese enterprises' embedding into Suzhou society that is significant, and it is also a process of Taiwanese enterprises' production of economic and social effects on Suzhou. This research witnesses the impact of Taiwan's investment on Suzhou individuals and the concern of the local people toward Taiwan's enterprises in daily life, and their relationship with Taiwanese business staff, or even to be the neighbors of Taiwanese residents or intermarriage between Taiwanese and Suzhou citizens. These research analyses prove that the local effect of foreign investment is taken as a social fact, whether it be economic or social, it is comprehended as a process in which foreign investment also integrates into the process of social change. Conversely, the understanding, cognition, evaluation, and thoughts toward Taiwan's enterprises for local people are also an influential process of Suzhou's social culture on Taiwanese enterprises. After all, Taiwanese enterprises and businessmen also care about their images.

Chang Chiaming used the concept of "social embeddedness" to illustrate the localization of Taiwan's enterprises and its impact (Chang 2006). Embeddedness is a basic concept of the new economic sociology, and it originally intended to refer to the combination of a system being introduced into another object system. Contemporary economic sociologists take economic activities to a broader context of society and interpersonal relationships, and believe that economic behavior is actually embedded in social networks, or in informal social relations. Therefore, when economic and non-economic activities are mixed with each other, non-economic activities influence the cost of economic activities and available technology. This blend of such activities is known as the "social embeddedness of the economy," including the embeddedness of economic activity in social networks and in cultural, political, and religious spheres (Granovetter 1985, 2005).

Therefore, the concept of social embeddedness also alludes to a more complex meaning of social integration and localization. In the context of globalization, there must be enterprise development on the road to globalization, but it is not really workable without implementation of localization policy. If Taiwan's enterprises really want to take root in Suzhou, they must be integrated into the local culture and use the local knowledge. On the other hand, Suzhou is taken as the location of Taiwan's enterprises, it benefits from the development of Taiwan investments, and must also accept the culture and products of Taiwan's enterprises. This means we must understand the mechanism of mutual embeddedness between Taiwan's enterprises and the local people.

In addition to all dimensions of enterprise operation and management, and besides the localization of talents, funds, production, raw materials, and marketing, it is the process of Taiwanese enterprises' embedding into Suzhou society that is significant, and it is also a process of Taiwanese enterprises' production of economic and social effects on Suzhou. This research witnesses the impact of Taiwan's investment on Suzhou individuals and the concern of the local people toward Taiwan's enterprises in daily life, and their relationship with Taiwanese business staff, or even to be the neighbors of Taiwanese residents or intermarriage between Taiwanese and Suzhou citizens. These research analyzes prove that the local effect of foreign investment is taken as a social fact, whether it be economic or social, it is comprehended as a process in which foreign investment also integrates into the process of social change. Conversely, the understanding, cognition, evaluation, and thoughts toward Taiwan's enterprises for local people are also an influential process of Suzhou's social culture on Taiwanese enterprises. After all, Taiwanese enterprises and businessmen also care about their images.

Conclusion

First of all, people in Suzhou believe that Taiwan's enterprises play a positive role for Suzhou's economic development. In addition to capital, technology, and equipment, Taiwan's investment introduces new concepts of economic management and talents, promotes the cultivation of talents, the growth of technology and management knowledge for local enterprises, broadens the global perspective and field of vision, and is conducive to global integration of local enterprises. This process of traction follows a series of transfers of management knowledge along with capital flows; it is a natural and logical process. Therefore, in the context of globalization, capital flows have had an influence beyond their original purpose; that is, capital flows and concepts of embeddedness coexist, which attaches to the concept transfer and influential ways of capital and it can be said to have hidden and subtle characteristics.

This concept of embeddedness attaching to the capital not only occurs at the level of enterprise management, but also takes place in the formation of consumption or leisure activities. Although the Suzhou public does not entirely accept the consumption and entertainment imported by Taiwanese businessmen, it cannot be denied that the consumption patterns of "playground," "Karaoke," and "coffee shop" have generally been accepted, and have become daily activities in everyday shopping, communication, and relaxation. However, those accepted or excluded consumption and leisure entertainments, including "bath (foot bath) centers," "coffee shop," "Karaoke," "wine bar," "hotel," "porn house" are considered to be the most typical items by local residents, which are implied cultural tastes from Taiwan. The introduction of these patterns of consumption and leisure entertainment, especially as some of them are accepted into local life, confirms the effects of globalization and its local responses as Taiwanese investments came to Suzhou. These cultural aspects particularly display how foreign concepts can enter a new land and introduce new activities to the local population.

Second, Suzhou people show a more complex evaluation of the local economic and social effects of Taiwan's investments and businessmen. Broadly speaking, the local public's evaluation of the local economic and social effects of Taiwanese investments and businessmen is half positive and half negative, and of course the evaluation itself is also a form of Taiwanese businessmen's influence. However, what is the reason for this half and half evaluation? This confirms one of our research propositions: Foreign investment has a strong connection to the local society, especially the degree and direction of the local people's perceptions and behaviors, and the value judgments and subjective cognitions of the public toward the social impact of foreign investments. As for the evaluation of the socio-economic effects or individual impact of Taiwanese businessmen, the Suzhou residents have their own judgment related to their advantages and disadvantages, or the size of social influence. This is based on their life experiences and feelings, which represent a local response of the global effects of Taiwanese investment.

Finally, Suzhou people have their own immediate feelings for the evaluation of Taiwan's investments and enterprises, and according to our analysis, the local people in Kunshan city revealed the lowest degree of social inclusion toward Taiwan's businessmen. This exhibits more complex peer evaluation for the local society in judging the foreign or Taiwan's investments and enterprises. This chapter reviews the local response of Suzhou people toward Taiwanese enterprises from growth and dependence perspectives, and reveals that Taiwanese investment not only brings economic opportunities to the local society, as well as positive and negative impacts in the social life. Suzhou residents' understanding of Taiwan businessmen mainly comes from the intercultural dimension of social life, which in turn influences the social inclusion of local people toward Taiwanese businessmen. Suzhou investment policy significantly changes in

Table 6A.1 Economic and social measurement indicators and their reliability and constructive validity

	Variables	Commonality test			Decision
		Alpha value after removal of the items	Commonality	Factors loading	
Economic dimension	enterprise influence Cronbach's α = 0.669	Taiwan investment is not good for the financing of local enterprises	0.664	0.183#	0.427#	Remove
		Taiwan investment helps talents cultivation of local enterprises	0.647	0.269	0.518	Retain
		Taiwan investment is against technology growth of local enterprise	0.658	0.195#	0.441#	Retain
		Taiwan investment contributes to the growth of local management knowledge	0.625	0.386	0.621	Retain
		The operating effectiveness of Taiwan enterprises is superior to State-owned enterprises or township enterprises	0.613	0.455	0.674	Retain
		The compliance level of Taiwan enterprises is superior to State-owned enterprises or township enterprises	0.601	0.493	0.702	Retain
		Suzhou's enterprises often learn of Taiwan enterprises in area of marketing or publicity methods	0.620	0.401	0.633	Retain
City construction Cronbach's α = 0.656		Taiwan investment contributes to the increase of urban road	0.573	0.592	0.769	Retain
		Taiwan investment contributes to the increase of city water and electricity utilities	0.366	0.743	0.862	Retain
		Taiwan investment is not conducive to the increase of urban communication facilities	0.682#	0.446	0.668	Retain

Social dimension	Social development Cronbach's α = 0.770				
	More and more Taiwanese businessmen will deteriorate law and order of communities	0.758	0.244	0.494	Retain
	More Taiwanese businessmen are unfavorable to raise local education standards	0.750	0.356	0.597	Retain
	More Taiwanese businessmen result in more serious environmental pollution	0.749	0.347	0.589	Retain
	Taiwan enterprises generally have environmental awareness	0.758	0.250	0.500	Retain
	A large number of Taiwan enterprises recruitment causes community deterioration	0.746	0.379	0.616	Retain
	Massive Taiwan investment has worsened the social atmosphere	0.743	0.421	0.649	Retain
	Increased Taiwan investment is relatively easy to find a job	0.776#	0.025#	0.158#	Remove
	Increased Taiwan investment results in more rural problems	0.750	0.332	0.576	Retain
	Increased Taiwan investment results in local youth unemployment	0.748	0.390	0.624	Retain
	Increased Taiwan investment results in life being difficult for workers' families	0.749	0.362	0.602	Retain
	Increased Taiwan investment worsens the local working conditions	0.746	0.375	0.613	Retain
	Increased Taiwan investment promotes eagerness of government officials to build cities	0.776#	0.063#	0.251#	Remove
	Increased Taiwan investment results in more outsiders to Suzhou	0.772#	0.104#	0.323#	Remove

continued

Table 6A.1 Continued

Variables		Commonality test			Decision
		Alpha value after removal of the items	Commonality	Factors loading	
Lifestyle Cronbach's α = 0.656	Local products often imitate foreign products	0.602	0.422	0.650	Retain
	More and more places of entertainment serve Taiwan businessmen	0.615	0.386	0.621	Retain
	More and more places of entertainment promote my life taste	0.608	0.410	0.640	Retain
	I often buy the merchandise of Taiwan enterprises brand	0.617	0.381	0.617	Retain
	Drinking coffee becomes the new leisure style mainly under the influence of Taiwan businessmen	0.573	0.507	0.712	Retain
Social inclusion Cronbach's α = 0.796	We are willing to work in the local Taiwan enterprise	0.773	0.434	0.659	Retain
	Children are willing to work in the local Taiwan enterprise	0.769	0.462	0.680	Retain
	We are willing to work in Taiwan enterprises outside of Suzhou	0.769	0.476	0.690	Retain
	Children are willing to work in Taiwan enterprises outside of Suzhou	0.765	0.484	0.696	Retain
	We or our children are willing to marry Taiwanese	0.782	0.383	0.619	Retain
	We are willing to work in Taiwan	0.766	0.467	0.684	Retain
	Children are willing to work in Taiwan	0.767	0.468	0.684	Retain
		0.60 = <	> = 0.20	> = 0.45	

Note
not up to the pointer value.

recent years, and accordingly high-polluting manufacturing industries are not welcome. Some Taiwanese enterprises are affected and thus the socio-economic influences of Taiwan's enterprises in Suzhou need constant assessment. However, the public understanding of Taiwanese social life level should not be rapidly changed, so that this research still helps to understand current local response in Suzhou toward Taiwanese businessmen. In addition, whether the adjustment of industrial structure in the coming years has a negative effect on Taiwan and then affects the local cognition and evaluation on Taiwanese enterprises remains to be observed and explored.

Note

1 "Three" refers to material processing, sample processing, and assembling. "One" refers to compensation trade. In the beginning of reform and opening up, China tried to create a form of enterprise cooperation in trade.

References

Chang, Chiaming. 2006. *Taiwanese Businessmen in Suzhou: Globalization and Observation of Localization*. Taipei: Crown Books.

Chang, Chiaming, and Chiu Shilong. 2002. "Suzhou's Export-Oriented Economic Development and Local Government: Analysis of Four Economic and Technological Development Zones as an Example." *Sociology Journal of Soochow* 13: 21–22.

Chen, Zhirou. 2002. "Analysis of the Social Situation after the 16th Chinese Communists Party Congress." In *China's Future: Degradation of Totalitarianism*, edited by Jialong Lin and Sijian Xu, Taipei: Taiwan Think Tank.

Deng, Jianbang. 2011. "Cross-Border Life: Taiwan's Investment and Social Interaction." In *Mainland China Investment from Taiwan for 20 Years: Experience, Development and Forward*, edited by Siqin Xu and Te-Sheng Chen, 333–358. Taipei: INK.

Granovetter, Mark. 1985. "Economic Action and Social Structure: The Problem of Embeddedness." *American Journal of Sociology* 91: 481–510.

Granovetter, Mark. 2005. "The Impact of Social Structure on Economic Outcomes." *Journal of Economic Perspectives* 19 (1): 33–50.

Gripaios, Peter, Rose Gripaios, and Max Munday. 1997. "The Role of Inward Investment in Urban Economic Development: The Cases of Bristol Cardiff and Plymouth." *Urban Studies* 34 (4): 579–603.

Jin, Joy. 1999. "Big Utilization in Foreign Capital, Adjusting the Industrial Structure, Achieving Economic Sustainable Development." The Continental Midwest seminar of Leading Cadres Speak.

Liu, Yaling. 2000. "Reliance Development on Huayang, Guangdong: Common Interest between Local Government and Foreign Investment." *Issue & Studies* 29 (7): 57–72 (Japanese Edition).

Richardson, Harry W. 1992. "Urban Development Issues in the Pacific Rim." *Review of Regional Development Studies* 45: 99–126.

Sit, V.F.S. 2001. "Globalization, Foreign Direct Investment, and Urbanization in Developing Countries." In *Facets of Globalization: International and Local Dimensions of Development*, edited by S. Yusuf, S. Evelt, and W. Wu, 11–45. Washington, DC: World Bank.

Sit, V.F.S., and C. Yang. 1997. "Foreign Investment Induced Exo-urbanization in the Pearl River Delta, China." *Urban Studies* 34 (4): 647–677.

Wang, Xinxian. 2003. "Theoretical Reflections on Regional Development in Mainland China in the Era of Globalization – from the Perspective of Enterprises Clustering." published in the Conference of a Regional Economic Development in Mainland China and the Interaction of Four Places Between Cross-strait, 1–22. Taipei: Taipei Cross-Strait Economic and Cultural Exchange Association.

Wujiang Daily. 2004. December 13.

Ye, Yumin. 2003. "Upgrading of Industrial Structure in Pearl River Delta and Land Use Study – a Case of Baoan District, Shenzhen," published in the Conference of a Regional Economic Development in Mainland China and the Interaction of Four Places Between Cross-strait, 1–22. Taipei: Taipei Cross-Strait Economic and Cultural Exchange Association.

Yin, Cunyi. 2003. "Investment from Taiwan and Mainland Urbanization of Mainland China – Empirical Study on the Urbanization of Dongguan and Kunshan," published in the Conference of a Regional Economic Development in Mainland China and the Interaction of Four Places Between Cross-strait, 1–17. Taipei: Taipei Cross-Strait Economic and Cultural Exchange Association.

Zhou, Changzheng. 2003. *Studies on Globalization and Chinese Labor Legal Issues.* Nanjing University, Plexus, 48–49.

Part II
Community

7 Lifestyle migrants

Taiwanese women in China[1]

Ping Lin

Introduction

While most research on migration and China focuses on the Chinese overseas, little attention has been paid to migration into China. News from the press, and research findings, suggest that most people moving into China are professionals exploring business opportunities. In 2010, it was estimated that around 600,000 people came to China from countries in the West and around 1,000,000 from Taiwan. It is believed that most of the Westerners and Taiwanese people are well-educated and are employed by foreign (or Taiwanese) firms (Keng et al. 2012).

However, there is less literature on either Western professionals or "Chinese" people moving into China than there is on the Chinese overseas (Holdsworth 2002; Yeoh and Willis 2005; Willis and Yeoh 2008). Although Taiwanese people in China are by no means the largest group of non-Chinese citizens, their migration experiences have not yet been fully explored. Most research on Taiwanese people in China concentrates on the relocation of firms and the potential influence of this on relationships across the Taiwan Strait. Until recently there has been little research which explores the daily experiences of migrants (Keng and Schubert 2010). The limited research on their experiences tells us that most Taiwanese migrants have little intention of settling down in China, in spite of having lived there for several years (Deng 2009; Lin 2009). While most Taiwanese migrants are also ethnic Chinese, it is surprising that they do not mix with the Chinese people. Since they are treated as having an important role in the cross-Strait relationship in the previous studies, we should explore how this disparity is formed. Without further exploring their daily experiences in China, it will be difficult to predict their viewpoints on the potential disputes across the Strait.

In this chapter, I argue that there is a gap in socio-economic status between Taiwanese migrants and local Chinese people, which hinders their interaction. While the respondents are from different social standings in Taiwan, most of them occupy the higher levels of the social strata in China. This sense of "upward mobility" initially encourages migrants to move, but discourages them from associating with the "ordinary" local people after they move. Therefore, most migrants spend their daily lives with other affluent migrants and keep their interaction with local people to a minimum, so that they are like "birds living in a golden cage." The sense of upward mobility gradually turns into a sense of loneliness and depression. Before exploring the respondents' expectations and experiences, the following section reviews the literature on the migration of privileged people and the limited studies on Taiwanese people into China. Both sections provide background information for the later analysis.

International migration: from labor migrants to privileged people

Although population movement between countries is not new, research on international migration often focuses on labor migrants moving from poorer to richer countries. Most studies suggest that people move abroad for a "better life," which is defined either as obtaining economic benefit overseas or escaping economic pressure at home (Massey et al. 1993; Massey 1998). From this perspective, affluent people moving from more to less developed countries are often regarded as "tourists" or just "foreigners," with little analysis of their movement as migration but as tourism. However, this migration/tourism dichotomy may be problematic. Some people move abroad "to travel" but they do not return for years. Some people move out "to emigrate" but they return after living overseas for a certain length of time (O'Reilly 2000). In these studies, the affluent border-crossers are sometimes referred to as "privileged migrants" to illustrate their high socio-economic status in the host country, or "lifestyle migrants" to indicate their stress on "something meaningful" in their migration (Fechter 2007; O'Reilly and Benson 2009; Croucher 2012).

Lifestyle migration: privileged people on the move

The movement of these affluent people may be traced back to Europeans in Africa in colonial periods (DehKirkwood 1984; Callaway 1987). Recent studies have explored the long-distance migration of European expatriates or professionals and their family members to the Middle East and Asia (Tremayne 1984; Yeoh and Khoo 1998; Beaverstock 2002; Fechter 2007; Tzeng 2010), the short-distance emigration from Britain, Japan, and Singapore to nearby countries (O'Reilly 2000; Thang et al. 2002; Willis and Yeoh 2003, 2008; Yeoh and Willis 2005; Ono 2008; Benson 2011), and the periodic visits from some countries to particular destinations (Korpela 2009). According to these studies, most migrants initially visit the host country just as "tourists" or "language students," without planning to stay for the long term. After staying in the host country for a short period of time, they discover that their limited capital and capability at home is valued more highly in the host country. Through moving abroad, they can have more promising careers or a better quality of life with their limited resources. Therefore, a short-term visit is gradually extended into long-term residency. This type of population movement should not be understood just as "making more money overseas," but as "having a certain type of life which is unavailable at home" (Croucher 2009, 2012; O'Reilly and Benson 2009).

Although these migrants move away for various reasons, most of them have the cultural capital of the dominant class (such as language, knowledge of certain professions, and the cultural taste) of the host country. Because of the hierarchical relationship between countries, the cultural capital of the sending country is usually highly valued in the receiving country. Therefore, it is not difficult for these people to get jobs with higher pay than their comparable local co-workers. As a result, they often have a higher socio-economic status than most other people in the receiving country. This commonality of "high status" makes these affluent border-crossers different from conventional labor migrants. From this perspective, migration of privileged people is not just a movement across a geographical border because of economic incentives, but it is also a form of upward mobility. Although most privileged migrants are "upgraded" in the host country, few of them have a strong intention of settling down overseas. Most of them still think of their residency in the host country as a short-term visit even if they have lived abroad for many years.

Apart from this sense of "being upgraded," these migrants also search for "something special" in the host country. Their search for "something special" shows that lifestyle migration partially involves the cultural context. This expectation of "something special" often comes from their knowledge of or previous traveling experience in the host country. While the "something special" cultural context partially arouses their interest in moving, it also frames their actions after migration (Benson 2011). Some studies also address how the socio-economic status and the cultural context together frame a migrant's life overseas. Because most lifestyle migrants are relatively affluent and have a certain cultural expectation of the host country, they prefer to participate in certain activities with other affluent people (usually other affluent migrants), rather than become involved in the ordinary public affairs of the local society. Therefore, these migrants are sometimes referred as "birds in the golden cage," people living in "expat bubbles," or "outsiders" in the host country (Oliver 2008; Croucher 2009).

Most studies on lifestyle migration concentrate on the experiences of men. Women in these studies are usually discussed as spouses of male migrants, but not as independent individuals. Although most women who are lifestyle migrants are well-educated (and probably have their own careers at home), they are encouraged neither to have proper careers nor to associate with the local society. Without proper careers or social lives, most of them spend their daily lives with other privileged migrants. Therefore, they are sometimes described as "trailing spouses" (Coles and Fechter 2008). While their male compatriots have more opportunities to set up their careers, these female migrants are unfortunately pushed into their traditional gender role as mothers and/or wives after migration.

Apart from the experience of married women, two studies on single women (British women in China and Japanese women in Singapore) display a picture similar to that for affluent male migrants. Through moving to less-developed countries, they obtain more opportunities to follow their own careers and to change their lives. However, they also have difficulties in maintaining or pursuing romance or relationships with their male compatriots. Partly due to this difficulty over emotional issues, most of them eventually give up their careers overseas and return home (Thang et al. 2002; Willis and Yeoh 2008). Although these two studies display a picture of "being lonely overseas," they do not explain why most single women limit their romance opportunities to their fellow-countrymen. Whether and how they interact with local men for potential romance is unclear.

Taiwanese people in China: living with limited integration

As mentioned above, current studies on lifestyle migration concentrate on emigration from the West to the East. There is little research on the form of lifestyle migration from the East or within the East, except for a few fragmentary studies on the emigration of Japanese and Singaporean people (Willis and Yeoh 2003; Ono 2008). Although more than a million Taiwanese have moved to China in the past two decades, the phenomenon of Taiwanese migrants in China is often assumed to be the result of firm relocations in traditional industry, not as a phenomenon of population movement. Therefore, research on Taiwanese migrants in China is often referred to as *Taishang Yen Jiu*, which literally means "studies on Taiwanese business overseas" (Keng and Schubert 2010; Keng et al. 2012). It seems that "making money to get rich" is the best account given of why more than a million Taiwanese people have moved to China. How Taiwanese migrants interact with Chinese people is usually overlooked in these studies.

This situation has been slightly improved with recently published research. Two papers, "The Distance of Interaction" and "The Residential Segregation," discuss the interaction between Taiwanese migrants and Chinese people. The first article discusses the hierarchical relationship between Taiwanese employees (usually working as high-ranking managers) and their Chinese colleagues (usually working as ordinary staff) at the same firm. Because of this hierarchical structure, the interaction between Taiwanese migrants and their Chinese colleagues is limited. The second article discusses their interaction after work. Most Taiwanese migrants have little interest in associating with Chinese people even if they both live in the same neighborhood (Deng 2002; Lin 2009). A picture of an "expat bubble," often referred to in other studies of lifestyle migration, is easily found in both articles, but how this "bubble" is formed has not yet been discussed.

When I was drafting this chapter in 2011, two Taiwanese female celebrities had just got married to rich Chinese businessmen they had met in China. Because most intermarriage across the Strait occurs between Taiwanese men and Chinese women, this news (of marriages between Taiwanese women and Chinese men) aroused a lot of discussion in the press (Li 2011). Since intermarriage is usually regarded as a crucial step in integration, the public interest in the potential for romance between Taiwanese women and Chinese men encouraged me to explore the migration experience of Taiwanese women, especially how single Taiwanese women interact with Chinese men. Therefore, I concentrate on the experiences of Taiwanese women in this chapter. By analyzing women's experiences, this article partially addresses how the "expat bubble" of Taiwanese migrants in the previous studies is formed.

Methods

Although it is estimated that more than a million Taiwanese people live in China, few of them register officially with the local government. Without knowing the size of the population, it is impractical to do statistical sampling. Although we are not sure exactly where the Taiwanese live in China, we know that all the three Taiwanese schools in China are located in Dongguan and Shanghai Metropolis. Therefore, it is reasonable to treat Taiwanese migrants in Dongguan and Shanghai as the main targets for research.[2]

Since it is unrealistic to acquire a randomized sample, and the aim of this research is to draw out a general pattern from various respondents rather than to provide a picture with definitive and exhaustive categorizations, I took maximal variation as the sampling strategy, including respondents in two cities (Dongguan and Shanghai) who were as varied as possible (in characteristics such as age, education, marital status, length of working experience in Taiwan, and length of stay in China, etc.). As well as the interviews and ethnographical research in 2004–2005, I kept in contact with the respondents by email, phone, and MSN and re-visited the respondents in 2008–2010 in order to track the changes in their lives. Like most sampling processes in qualitative research, the sampling in this research started with typical *snowball* techniques in the early cases, but ended up with a large range of different respondents. In total, I obtained 22 respondents in Dongguan and Shanghai.

The basic features of the respondents can be summarized as follows. Among the 22 respondents, 8 were married and 14 were single; their ages ranged from 19 to 55 in 2004–2005. All had more than 14 years of school education, which is not unusual in Taiwan but is much higher than the average length of schooling for Chinese people. The respondents were college students, self-employed, dependents, expatriates working for Taiwanese firms, and employees of Chinese firms. When I met them in 2004–2005, I was also working as a part-time school teacher in Dongguan and Shanghai. Partially due to this job, I was treated as an "insider" with a certain level of trust by respondents and many Taiwanese people I encountered in both cities. This relationship helps me collect information which is not easily obtained in the field.

The basic features discussed above display something that warrants explanation. All the respondents had been educated for more than 14 years, while no more than 4 percent of the citizens of Guangdong (and less than 12 percent of the citizens of Shanghai) had received the same amount of education (Cai 2004).[3] Therefore, it is not surprising that all the respondents had a certain socio-economic status (even when they did not have full-time jobs) within the local

Chinese society. This privileged status is unusual in conventional migration but is quite typical in studies on lifestyle migration.

Because the respondents were selected by a maximal variation strategy, the findings of this study should be close to the general pattern for the whole population. However, because the respondents were not statistically selected, the variances of the respondents did not proportionally represent the whole population. All numbers cited in this chapter are just a description of frequencies unless otherwise indicated. It is possible that some features discussed in this chapter (such as the number of married respondents) are over- or under-estimates compared to the whole population.[4] However, the contribution of this chapter is that there are overlapping features and consistency among the various respondents. These common features might also be regarded as important ones for people who were not selected to participate in this study.

Findings and discussions[5]

As indicated above, most Taiwanese migrants in China are also ethnic Chinese. They are relatively resourceful and hold higher social status than most local Chinese people. This situation was often discussed in the popular narratives in the early 2000s.[6] It is also well-known to all the respondents even if they had no connection with China before their move. Therefore, all respondents to some extent expected to have something special and/or to find a better quality of life in China. Although this expectation to some extent motivated them to move, it also leads to a "snobbish" attitude towards Chinese society. The respondents usually treat the Chinese people they encounter as "inferiors" unless contradictory information is obtained in advance. Respondents' post-migration experiences at a later stage even challenge their initial assumption about "ethnic affinity across the Strait." Eventually, most respondents began to identify themselves as "less Chinese" or "Chinese with less Chinese-ness." By illustrating the respondents' pre-migration expectations and post-migration experiences, readers may understand how class works in migration.

In the following two sections, I will present the respondents' motivation for moving to China, and then their life experiences after the move. What the respondents expected before the move, what they actually encounter in China, and how they deal with the gap in between will help us to understand how class works in migration. Because the interaction between single respondents and Chinese men is one of the focal points of this chapter, the 14 single and 8 married respondents will be discussed separately. Among the 14 single respondents, those who are a bit older (more than 30 years old in 2004–2005) have expectations and experiences which are partly different from the other single respondents, so the two groups (senior singles and junior singles) are discussed separately. Although there are some differences between these three groups of respondents (married women, senior singles, and junior singles), the commonality among the various respondents provides us with a picture for analysis in conclusion.

Motivation for move: from being ordinary to being something special

Why people move is often the first question asked in migration studies. The most common explanation is that people have various economic incentives for moving. As discussed earlier, most studies on Taiwanese people in China also indicate that Taiwanese migrants move to China mainly for the economic rewards. This account does not surprise me, since Taiwan has struggled economically while China has experienced dramatic economic growth since the late 1990s.

This "making money" explanation was also clearly given by all the single female respondents and one married respondent. It seems that the married and the single respondents move for different reasons. Apart from this difference, all respondents had expected little difficulty in migration in their retrospective interviews. Although it is easy for the respondents to travel within China, it would be a more complicated matter if they regarded China as a country to move into. Why did all respondents initially regard moving to China as just a bit more difficult than moving between cities in Taiwan? There must be something in common between single and married respondents in their pre-migration expectations.

For the married respondents, all but one said that their move was for the purpose of family reunion. Their husbands had already moved as expatriate high-ranking managers or as entrepreneurs with their own businesses before the late 1990s. As their husbands had already got stable careers, these married respondents felt little pressure or concern to consider the possible costs of migration. Those without careers in Taiwan stated that before actually moving they were happily teased by their friends for "going to be a *Shao-nai-nai* [a person who is rich with few worries about daily life]." Those with their own careers in Taiwan said that they regarded moving to China as a good chance to "take a break and have a comfortable life." Although all these married respondents knew that it might not be true that they would be a *Shao-nai-nai* or "have a cosy life," they all agreed that this picture of a comfortable life to some extent lessened their worries about migration. This sense of "enjoying oneself a little" is akin to previous studies on the spouses of European expatriates in Asia (Fechter 2007). The married respondents did not purely move for the expectation of a family reunion, but were also attracted by the idea of a comfortable life overseas.

Although all the single respondents initially said that their migration was the result of economic concern, there was something different for them. All the older single ones (those aged over 30 in 2004–2005) had some years of working experience (for example as middle-ranking administrators in firms or as bosses of small businesses) in Taiwan, but they felt that they were "being trapped" in their "not so encouraging" careers. From information from friends or their personal experiences while traveling in China, they sensed that their limited education and working experience were relatively richer than those of most Chinese people and that they might have opportunities to pursue their own careers in China. This expectation of a "second chance" encouraged them to give up their "so-so" business or career and move to China. This expectation of "doing something special" with limited resources is akin to previous studies on young Europeans in Asia (Fechter 2007). Migration is treated as a strategy to enable people to have more promising careers in the future.

Apart from these "moving for a second chance" respondents, the other six respondents were under the age of 30 in 2004–2005. All of them had 12–14 years of school education and limited (or no) work experience in Taiwan. With moderate education and limited work experience, it was difficult for them to obtain proper jobs in Taiwan. Respondent Jenny clearly expressed her move to China to be the result of feeling "without a proper job, I feel like shit" in Taiwan. In order to get away from this "life is shit" situation, they moved to China. This account seems reasonable, but it does not explain how they got hired as a "personal secretary" or a "special assistant" at a Taiwanese firm when they had little work experience before migration.

After associating with them for a certain period of time, I realized that all the junior single respondents had some connections with a "somebody" in Dongguan or Shanghai. Most job vacancies like "personal secretary" or "special assistant" in Taiwanese firms are not recruited openly but are arranged for "insiders," so recommendations from these important people provided the younger respondents with these jobs. These younger respondents were actually the nieces or daughters of their employers. With help and information from their close relatives or parents, these junior single respondents knew they could work as personal secretaries or special assistants with a certain level of salary and benefits (such as free accommodation, local transport, and the reimbursement for flights to Taiwan twice a year) for their daily life. All benefits and salaries for employees are much better than these respondents could obtain in Taiwan. This is why they were confident about moving to China. This picture of moving abroad through family ties is unusual in previous studies on lifestyle migration, but is quite common for the migration of young females moving to China in the early 2000s.

In this section, a picture of enjoying/doing/being something special is clearly suggested by all the respondents. To these respondents, migration to China is not just a geographical relocation. It is also upward mobility. They expected that they would change from "life is shit/middle-level administrator/housewife/boss of small firm" in Taiwan to "personal assistant to the boss/professional manager/ *Shao-nai-nai*" in China. Although respondents had different backgrounds and detailed personal expectations before migration, they all expected to have a high socio-economic status after the move. This picture of upward mobility to some extent explains why the respondents worried little about emigrating, and it also confirms the findings of studies on social mobility. The opportunity for upward mobility may guide people to change their behavior or life plan. To people with certain resources, moving to another country is not just moving out geographically, but moving up strategically (Erickson and Goldthorpe 1993; Bertaux and Thompson 1997). Although the host societies (Dongguan and Shanghai in the late 1990s/early 2000s) were still primitive and less developed than the sending society (Taiwan) in the same period, the respondents easily found the pathway for moving up and becoming "somebody" after the move. Their life of "being somebody" will be illustrated as follows.

Life in China: being lonely at home

How are their lives after migration? While Taiwanese men in China are some-times teased as having a "Life in Paradise" to symbolize their casual affairs with Chinese women (Shen 2008), I found a strong sense of loneliness among the female respondents in both cities. Although the respondents had expected to have a cosy life, they eventually realized that the life of being *Shao-nai-nai* was not what they thought because "life is just not only eating and shopping all day." For example, respondent Lotus was a high ranking manager in Taiwan but worked as a bank clerk in Shanghai. When I asked why she accepted this job post, she said

> I am lucky [to have this job post] ... One Ma-Ma [woman with kids] is working at a Taiwanese firm as a phone operator. Her pay is only RMB 2500 per month, but she is very happy [because it is difficult to obtain a proper job in China].

Lotus's remarks illustrate the sense of loss of some respondents in China. Although they had been well-educated in Taiwan, they had few opportunities to obtain their ideal jobs in China. Although working as a bank clerk (or phone operator) is not promising, it is still better than being jobless at home.

Stories about "being a phone operator" are not openly discussed, but are often privately addressed among the Taiwanese friends I encountered in both cities. During my fieldwork, I was often asked questions by different Taiwanese friends like "how did you get your job [a part-time teacher in a Taiwanese school]?" and "can you help my friend Mrs X [to get a job like yours]?" In the beginning, I was surprised and replied that my pay as a part-time teacher was low and that Mrs X would therefore not be happy with it. Then my friends told me that Mrs X was the wife of a busy entrepreneur. She felt lonely at home and wanted to get a job to "do something" and to associate with other Taiwanese. These various Mrs Xs were all well-educated and had certain work experience (for example as schoolteachers, nurses, and middle-level administrators at firms) in Taiwan, but they could not obtain similar jobs in China. Mrs Xs cared little about the salary but rather with whom they could work. Working as a part-time teacher in a Tai-wanese school is a good job from this perspective. Without having such a job, it is difficult for them to have a new social life. Hence, being a *Shao-nai-nai* is just another way of being a lonely housewife at home.

To these married women, a proper job does not mean working hard and making money, because all of them expected to "take a break" in China. Working with other Taiwanese people in order to make new friends is more important than making money or following one's own career per se. This finding challenges our knowledge that the life of migrants is mainly composed of economic struggles and concerns (Borjas 1999), but is akin to previous studies on women in lifestyle migration. While their husbands had successful careers, these married respondents paid more attention to associating with other migrants than to making money and having their own careers. It is reasonable for them to wish to enrich their lives by associating with other resourceful migrants, but why did they not make an effort to associate with local Chinese people and gain more local knowledge? This question will be partly addressed by exploring how the single respondents perceive the local Chinese men.

While intermarriage is often treated as an important indicator to examine the integration between migrants and local people, romance or the possibility/difficulty of having a serious relationship is also one of the topics often discussed by the Taiwanese women I encountered during fieldwork. I found that most single respondents were reluctant to associate with, let alone date, Chinese men. In 2004–2005, only 4 (3 in Shanghai and 1 in Dongguan) out of the 14 respondents had experience of this. What is the barrier between single respondents and Chinese men? The statement of one respondent, Lilly (age 23 in 2004–2005), "He [one Chinese admirer she encountered in Guangzhou] wanted to bike out with me, but I don't want to sit on his bicycle…" partially answers this question.

As mentioned in the previous section, most single respondents worked as "special assistants" or "professional managers" in firms. However, most Chinese people they might encounter were just middle-and-below managers or low-skilled laborers in the firms. Due to the disparity in position between the single respondents and the Chinese people in the firms, there is a gap in income and buying power between them. This gap in buying power was one of the factors segregating the respondents and the natives. As I observed, these ladies regarded shopping, playing bowls, or eating meals at fancy restaurants at the weekend as normal recreation. They often took taxis or private cars as their main forms of transport, and thought the local public transport to be filthy and unsafe. However, most Chinese men around them were much less wealthy; they often preferred playing football, shopping at the night market, and having meals at food-stands as affordable recreation at the weekend. It is clear that most respondents had different consumption habits and lifestyle from the local people. For Lilly the taxi was the main form of transport, so it is no surprise that she did not regard "cycling together" as an activity for possible romance. Although she looked forward to some romance, she regarded her Chinese male friends as "disqualified" from being boyfriend candidates.

In 2009, I met Lilly again. She introduced Peggy, another beautiful lady, to me. Then we three had a steak dinner together. When I teased Lilly about her "bicycle story" years ago, Peggy suddenly commented, "You won't believe that during these couple of years we are not in any relationships, but the fact is, it is the truth." I subsequently told them not to behave like a "spoilt Snow White," but to be humble and low-profile if they want to have their "trustworthy Prince Charming." Then I asked what bothered them when interacting with Chinese men: the economic disparity (buying power) or the cultural disparity (values and ideas in daily life).

"You cannot explain it in this way," Peggy replied, and continued,

> It is just like having steak and wine here. Those who are not rich enough do not have dinner here. If they somehow could have dinner here, it is difficult to expect they will have appropriate table manners and the knowledge to order proper meals.

As the message from Peggy and Lilly suggests, the barrier between Chinese men and Taiwanese women is not only economically illustrated in the "bicycle problem," but also culturally illustrated as a "problem of having proper meals together." It is also the twist between economic capability and cultural capital, especially while cultural capital is developed under conditions of a certain level of economic capability.

Barrier of integration: unwilling to "move down"

While I was writing this chapter, I had known all the respondents for more than seven years. This long-term acquaintance has helped me to a deep understanding of their life before and after migration. As discussed in the earlier sections, most of the respondents were just ordinary office ladies or conventional housewives in Taiwan. Their "high level" of cultural taste in China did not originate from Taiwan, but developed when they were a "special assistant," "professional manager," or "*Shao-nai-nai*" in China. As Bourdieu suggests, people moving up from middle/lower to upper/middle status are likely to practice and display this "high level" of cultural taste. They regard it as an icon which signifies their class status and as a means of recognizing people with whom they should (not) associate (Bourdieu 1984). Since most Chinese people are not able to send out similar signals of cultural taste, they are not regarded by the respondents as potential partners for romances or for deep friendship.

To most respondents, this social disparity is not just a gap in buying power (economic capital), but also a gap in cultural taste (cultural capital) in daily life. The respondents treat their consumption at Starbucks (or Western-style restaurants with piano bars) in the evenings (or weekends) not just as part of their normal recreation, but also as a way to enrich and display their cultural taste. Although this "high level" cultural taste is developed after migration, it is also partially "internalized" as part of the respondents' habits and is practised in other forms on various occasions. The respondents not only take their practice of this internalized knowledge as a sign of status, but they also take the practice of this knowledge in Chinese people as a way of predicting their status. While some Taiwanese men told me that the Chinese women they encountered were like "a lady with a Louis Vuitton handbag but spitting out the cane bagasse while walking on the street," the respondents here laughingly referred to the Chinese men they encountered as "a man in formal dress but squatting on the pavement" or "a man in a lousy T-shirt but driving a BMW." The respondents see the gap between themselves and Chinese men as a result not just of the gap in buying power, but also of the gap in cultural tastes and habits in daily life.

Although these statements are cruel, they reflect how respondents perceive the integration gap between migrants and natives. I have no intention of checking or confirming these statements, but argue that this *awareness* of a high-level status hinders the respondents from associating with most local Chinese people. To the respondents in both cities, this gap is not only experienced in the "bicycle problem" or the "issue of steak," but is also encountered on many occasions. Although each incident is minor, various incidents taken together cause a subtle difference to become a substantial one. Therefore, the respondents had little intention of associating with Chinese people unless they were told something special about a certain Chinese individual and this was confirmed in advance.

Conclusions

While previous studies show that Taiwanese people in China have little intention of becoming involved in Chinese society, this chapter goes beyond this well-known feature to discuss how this alienation is formed. While there is only a small ethnic gap between Taiwanese people and Chinese people, I argue that class is the critical factor in their migration. Although the expectation of "upward mobility" encourages their migration, this perception of "being superior to the Chinese people" discourages them from becoming involved in Chinese society. I suggest that more stress on the influence of class in migration is necessary for future studies.

While most studies in migration highlight the importance of economic incentives and the barrier of the ethnic gap, this chapter stresses the influence of class disparity in migration. While conventional low-skilled workers move for limited economic rewards or the chance of survival, this chapter suggests that privileged people move out for the chance to move up. To these affluent people, migration is not only the geographical process of moving but also the chance of upward mobility.

Since Sorokin's original work, *Social Mobility*, social mobility has generally been conceptualized in a way concentrating on vertical movements between occupational positions within one country. With the development of methodology, most studies in social mobility concentrate on the quantitative data collected in certain countries. Although this "survey paradigm" makes social mobility research a highly specialized and technical field, it also cuts off the observation of other dimensions of social mobility, such as moving up by moving to other countries (Bertaux and Thompson 1997; Elliott 1997). If upward mobility may easily be obtained in nearby countries, it is reasonable to expect that people with relatively richer capital will move abroad. However, this "move up through moving out" feature is still ignored in mainstream studies of social mobility.

While the research on social mobility is still ethnocentric, research on migration ignores the influence of class factors. Conventional migration research is mainly based on the characteristics of immigrants from Europe in America. In this paradigm, the process of incorporation is usually viewed using the framework of assimilation, which is embedded in methodological nationalism and the idea of an alignment between "one state, one society." Therefore, the ethnic gap between immigrants and the host society is usually regarded by default as the crucial factor for explaining the integration barrier. However, migration nowadays is getting more diverse. Immigrants from the same country but having different social status may have different experiences; immigrants from different countries but having the same social status may have similar experiences (Kasinitz et al. 2004; Colic-Peisker 2008). Despite this, the influence of class is still ignored in mainstream studies of migration.

This chapter provides a good opportunity to combine research on social mobility and migration. It also provides a good chance to observe how class matters in migration, especially when the migrants are not low-skilled laborers. To people with a certain level of resource and skills, moving to countries where one will be highly valued may be a short cut to upward mobility. This phenomenon is analyzed here in our discussion of the expectations of respondents (from being ordinary workers/housewives to enjoying/being/doing something special). However, this "moving up expectation" also causes trouble. Although it is easy for immigrants to move and have a comfortable life, it is difficult for them really to appreciate their life in the host society. Eventually, most respondents do not feel like successful women with their own careers, but rather like a lonely Bridget Jones overseas.

To sum up, lifestyle migrants are people trying to move up and move out at the same time. Although it is easy for them to move abroad, it is difficult for them to have their minds at rest overseas. This "easy to move, hard to settle down" experience means that they do not belong to the host or to the home country, but rather have an identity betwixt and between the host and the home countries. It is easier to define these migrants in terms of who they are not, rather than of who they are. Therefore, it is not surprising to see that most of these migrants keep on moving between their host and home countries. We need more studies to explore the experiences of these affluent migrants in the coming future.

Notes

1 This research was partially supported by a project (The Local Response to the Taiwanese Investment in China, 100-2420-H-194-005-MY3) of the National Science Council in Taiwan. Some sections of this chapter were published by the journal *China Information* in March 2013. However, some detailed information has been revised in this chapter. I am very grateful to China Information for the consent to the use of this information in this chapter.
2 These three schools are: Dongguan Taiwanese Business School in Dongguan City of Guangdong Province, Huandong Taiwanese Business School in Kunshan City of Jainagsu Province, and Shanghai Taiwanese Business School in Shanghai City.

3 Data about the average of residents' school education in Dongguan are not available, so I used data from the whole of Guangdong province for comparison.

4 For example, I purposely overlooked information from two married respondents who were married to the Chinese men. After conducting this research for almost ten years, I believe the number of these "happy marriages" should be very limited in the whole population. In order to present my argument clearly, I do not include the experience of these two respondents in this chapter. A few discussions on the potential success of integration are available in Chapter 12 "Class or Identity Matters: The Social Assimilation of Taiwanese Sojourners in China" in this book.

5 All names are pseudonyms.

6 Literary works and TV programs in the late 1990s and early 2000s often addressed these issues, such as *Taiwan Ren Zai Da Lu* (Taiwanese People in China), *Yi Min Shanghai* (Moving to Shanghai), and *Wo De Shanghai Jin Yen* (My Experiences in Shanghai). For the limit of word length, the influence of these narratives on migration will be addressed in separate articles elsewhere.

References

Beaverstock, Jonathan. 2002. "Transnational Elites in Global Cities: British Expatriates in Singapore's Financial District." *Geoforum* 33 (4): 525–538.

Benson, Michaela. 2011. *The British in Rural France: Lifestyle Migration and the Ongoing Quest for a Better Way of Life*. Manchester, UK: Manchester University Press.

Bertaux, Daniel and Paul Thompson. 1997. "Introduction." In *Pathways to Social Class: A Qualitative Approach to Social Mobility*, edited by Daniel Bertaux and Paul Thompson, 1–31. Oxford, UK: Clarendon University Press.

Borjas, George. 1999. *Heaven's Door: Immigration Policy and the American Economy*. Princeton, NJ: Princeton University Press.

Bourdieu, Pierre. 1984. *Distinction: A Social Critique of the Judgement of Taste*. Cambridge, MA: Harvard University Press.

Cai, Fang. 2004. *Green Book of Population and Labour*. Beijing: Chinese Academy of Social Sciences.

Callaway, Hellen. 1987. *Gender, Culture and Empire: European Women in Colonial Nigeria*. Urbana, IL: University of Illinois Press.

Coles, Anne and Anne-Meike Fechter. 2008. "Introduction." In *Gender and Family among Transnational Professionals*, edited by Anne Coles and Anne-Meike Fechter, 1–20. London: Routledge.

Colic-Peisker, Vol. 2008. *Migration, Class, and Transnational Identities*. Chicago, IL: University of Illinois Press.

Croucher, Sheila. 2009. *The Other Side of the Fence: American Migrants in Mexico*. Austin, TX: University of Texas Press.

Croucher, Sheila. 2012. "Privileged Mobility in Age of Globality." *Societies* 2: 1–13.

DehKirkwood, Deborah. 1984. "Settler Wives in Southern Rhodesia: A Case Study." In *Incorporated Wife*, edited by Hilary Callan and Shirley Ardener, 106–119. London: Croom Helm.

Deng, Jian-bang. 2002. "The Distance of Interaction between Taiwanese Managers and Chinese Employees at Taiwanese Firms." *Taiwanese Sociology* 3: 211–251.

Deng, Jian-bang. 2009. "Making a Living on the Move: Transnational Lives of Taiwanese Managers in Shanghai Area." *Taiwanese Sociology* 18: 139–179.

Elliott, Brian. 1997. "Migration, Mobility, and Social Process: Scottish Migrants in Canada." In *Pathways to Social Class: A Qualitative Approach to Social Mobility*, edited by Daniel Bertaux and Paul Thompson, 198–229. Oxford, UK: Clarendon University Press.

Erickson, Robert and John Goldthorpe. 1993. *The Constant Flux: A Study of Class Mobility in Industrial Societies*. Oxford, UK: Oxford University Press.

Fechter, Anne-Meike. 2007. *Transnational Lives, Expatriates in Indonesia*. Surrey, UK: Ashgate.

Holdsworth, May. 2002. *Foreign Devils: Expatriates in Hong Kong*. Oxford, UK: Oxford University Press.

Kasinitz, Philip, John Mollenkopf, and Mary Waters, eds. 2004. *Becoming New Yorkers: Ethnographies of the New Second Generation*. New York: Russell Sage Foundation.

Keng, Shu and Gunter Schubert. 2010. "Agents of Unification? The Political Role of Taiwanese Businessmen in the Process of Cross-Strait Integration." *Asian Survey* 50 (2): 287–310.

Keng, Shu, Rayhua Lin, and Gunter Schubert. 2012. "Studies on Taishang: The Originality, Development, and Core Issues." In *Tai Shang Yen Jiu* (Studies on Taiwanese Business Overseas), edited by Shu Keng, Gunter Schubert, and Rayhua Lin, 3–51. Taipei: Wunan Publishing.

Korpela, Mari. 2009. "When a Trip to Adulthood Become a Lifestyle: Western Lifestyle Migration in Varanasi India." In *Lifestyle Migration: Expectations, Aspirations, and Experiences*, edited by Karen O'Reilly and Michaela Benson, 15–30. Surrey, UK: Ashgate.

Li, Xin. 2011. "New Trend of Intermarriage: Taiwanese Female Celebrities and Rich Chinese Businessmen." Accessed September 15, 2012. http://big5.huaxia.com/tslj/cfht/2011/12/2705458.html.

Lin, Ping. 2009. "Do They Mix? The Residential Segregation of Taiwanese People in China." Taiwanese Political Science Review 13 (2): 57–111.

Massey, Douglas. 1998. "Contemporary Theories of Migration." In *Worlds in Motion: Understanding International Migration at the End of Millennium*, edited by Douglas Massey, Joaquin Arango, Graeme Hugo, Ali Kouaouci, Adela Pellegrino, and J. Edward Taylor, 17–59. Oxford, UK: Oxford University Press.

Massey, Douglas, Joaquin Arango, Graeme Hugo, Ali Kouaouci, Adela Pellegrino, and Edward Taylor. 1993. "Theories of International Migration: Review and Appraisal." *Population and Development Review* 19: 431–466.

Oliver, Caroline. 2008. *Retired Migration: Paradoxes of Ageing*. London: Routledge.

Ono, Mayumi. 2008. "Long Stay Tourism and International Retirement Migration: Japanese Retirees in Malaysia." In *Transnational Migration in East Asia*, edited by Shinji Yamashita, 151–162. Osaka, Japan: National Museum of Ethnology.

O'Reilly, Karen. 2000. *The British on the Costa Del Sol: Transnational Identities and Local Communities*. London: Routledge.

O'Reilly, Karen, and Michaela Benson. 2009. "Lifestyle Migration: Escaping to the Good Life?" In *Lifestyle Migration: Expectations, Aspirations, and Experiences*, edited by Karen O'Reilly and Michaela Benson, 1–14. Surrey, UK: Ashgate.

Shen, Hsiu-hua. 2008. "The Purchase of Transnational Intimacy: Women's Bodies, Transnational Masculine Privileges in Chinese Economic Zones." *Asian Studies Review* 32: 57–75.

Thang, Leng Leng, Elizabeth MacLachlan, and Miho Goda. 2002. "Expatriates on the Margins: A Study of Japanese Women Working in Singapore." *Geoforum* 33: 539–551.

Tremayne, Soraya. 1984. "Shell Wives in Limbo." In *Incorporated Wife*, edited by Hilary Callan and Shirley Ardener, 120–134. London: Croom Helm.

Tzeng, Rueyling. 2010. "Cultural Capital and Cross-Border Career Ladders: Western Professional Migrants in Taiwan." *International Sociology* 25: 123–143.

Willis, Kate and Brenda Yeoh. 2003. "Gender, Marriage, and Skilled Migration: The Case of Singaporeans in China." In *Wife or Worker? Asian Women and Migration*, edited by Nicola Piper and Mina Roces, 101–120. Lanham, MD: Rowman & Littlefield.

Willis, Kate and Brenda Yeoh. 2008. "Coming to China Changed My Life: Gender Roles and Relations among Single British Migrants." In *Gender and Family among Transnational Professionals*, edited by Anne Coles and Anne-Meike Fechter, 211–232. London: Routledge.

Yeoh, Brenda and Luisa-May Khoo. 1998. "Home, Work, and Community: Skilled International Migration and Expatriate Women in Singapore." *International Migration* 36: 159–186.

Yeoh, Brenda and Kate Willis. 2005. "Singaporean and British Trans-migrants in China and the Cultural Politics of Contact Zone." *Journal of Ethnic and Migration Studies* 31 (2): 269–285.

8 Marginal mobilities

Taiwanese manufacturing companies' migration to Inner China

Jian-bang Deng

Introduction[1]

> 7-Eleven Marching to Shanghai, Taiwanese Young Masters Landing as Store Managers
>
> Taiwan-based President Chain Store Corporation opened its first convenience store in Shanghai in 2009. Now there are 101 stores under the brand of 7-Eleven there. For the purpose of widening the market, this chain-store begins its ambitious program to recruit many young masters from Taiwan as store managers in Shanghai. One of them, Cheng Hongyan, from the 80's generation with a Master's Degree in Marketing Management from Kaohsiung First University of Technology and Science, told the journalist with an exciting tone, "Shanghai, I am coming."
>
> (TVBS News, August 28, 2012)

It is quite common nowadays that many people seek jobs abroad and work as expatriates in a global network of service operations, factories or markets. The international flow of capital has reshaped the global economy, restructuring the labor market on a large scale and forming closer relationships among foreign companies, expatriates and local employees. These movements of skilled workers – foreign and local professionals in Moscow (Gritsai 2005), British highly skilled in New York City (Beaverstock 2003), Japanese women and Australian expatriates in Singapore (Thang et al. 2002; Butcher 2006), European and American expatriates in Jakarta (Fechter 2007), Taiwanese cultural workers in Shanghai and Beijing (Tseng 2012) – have emerged as a new phenomenon accompanied with the rise of global cities. Past research has even considered skilled workers and expatriates as substantial and crucial parts in the reproduction of global cities (Beaverstock 2002; Gritsai 2005).

Nevertheless, the global city literature to date has tended to emphasize skilled workers' movement to global centers, i.e., their movement as an important part to constitute "a new geography of centrality" (Sassen 2000). Relatively little research has been done to investigate other forms of mobility, which are all in directions opposite to mainstream global centers. This chapter explores the new migration process to Inner China of skilled workers in the Taiwanese manufacturing business. It aims to show a different kind of movement and mobility – which is opposite to the mainstream move to coastal cities and instead being a movement from coastal regions to inland provinces of China – that include Taiwanese factories, Taiwanese expatriates and Chinese skilled workers. The last two categories are the main type of skilled workers discussed in this chapter. The term "new" is used to describe the migration to Inner China by both Taiwanese expatriates and Chinese skilled workers as a mobility experience different to their earlier move to China's coastal regions.

Three questions will be addressed: (1) How did the process of Taiwanese manufacturing companies, moving from Taiwan to China's Pearl River Delta area, develop and also how did the development in Inner China contribute to the inward movement of these companies in recent years? (2) What kind of new relationships, in terms of the workplace regime, are created between migrant (Taiwanese and Chinese) skilled workers and local Chinese employees? (3) What is the migration experience to inland provinces of China like for Taiwanese and Chinese skilled workers?

Empirical data for this study was generated from a four-stage field research conducted during 2011 and 2012. The first two stages of fieldwork were finished in April and August 2011. The second two stages of data were conducted in July and August 2012. The author spent nearly two months in doing ethnographic fieldwork in the provinces of Henan, Hunan, Jianxi, Gaungxi and Sichuan as well as in a medium-scaled city in outer Guangdong. The author chose these provinces or areas for fieldwork mainly because there were more expanded or relocated Taiwanese manufacturing companies there and, thus, the easier the possibility to observe the workplace of factories. Three places: Zhoukou City in Henan, Xingtian County in Hunan and Lingshan County in Guangxi were twice visited in order to establish a closer relationship with interview partners and to obtain more detailed information.

The above mentioned regions of the manufacturing companies visited were chosen by the snowballing method, in which introductions to one company led to a visit to another. Among the 26 companies, nine are electronics manufacturers, seven are footwear manufacturers and five are textile manufacturers. These three industries are characterized with relatively simple technology and high labor intensity, therefore the reasons for major Taiwanese investments inland. Most of the visited factories in these three industries hire between 200 and 800 employees, only a few have more than 2,000 workers. They are, in business size, relatively smaller than similar types of Taiwanese factories in the Pearl River Delta of the last decade. The other five companies – two metal manufacturers, one plastics manufacturer, one gifts and toys company and one trading company – are all small and medium-sized enterprises.

The methodology used in this research included in-depth interviews, focus group interviews and observation. In order to gain a broad perspective on migration experience and workplace management, people holding different types of positions were interviewed, such as: Taiwanese business owners, Taiwanese expatriates, Chinese skilled workers and local Chinese employees. Two different types of interview guidelines were also developed for Taiwanese and Chinese interview partners, respectively. For the Taiwanese business owners and expatriates, a basic interview guideline with several research sub-questions was followed by each interview with questions including descriptions on the motivation for working aboard, reasons of movement by manufacturing businesses, workplace management style in the inland and in coastal factories, evaluation of migration experience from coastal regions to inland provinces, etc. Regarding Chinese skilled workers and local Chinese employees, an interview guideline was composed with questions including choices and motivations for working in Taiwanese factories, past work and migration experiences, interactions with other groups in the workplace, comparison and evaluation of working experiences between coastal regions and inland provinces. Most of the interviews took place in the offices of the visited companies, and only one interview with a Taiwanese expatriate was finished in a coffee shop near the visited factory.

There were a total of 80 in-depth interviews conducted in the field, each lasting 40 minutes to 2 hours; 41 Taiwanese expatriates and business owners, 27 migrant Chinese skilled workers and 12 local Chinese employees. Seven of them were twice conducted, and all the interviews were recorded and transcribed in word text for later analysis. Various types of field notes were also taken after each interview. Beside the interviews, the author also had several opportunities to join in on the gatherings of Taiwanese and Chinese interview partners, as well as staying in the factory with provided accommodation in order to get closer observation of the research fields.

Mobility, work and translocality

Mobility has become one of the most important values in the contemporary world. The movement of people is linked with the rapid development of the world's economy in terms of liberation of capital, goods and services (Favell et al. 2006). Not only the movement of lower and unskilled migrants, but also the migration of skilled workers and professionals, are reflecting this change taking place as a result of the restructuring world economy.

However, both studies on migration by unskilled and skilled people have tended to focus on their movement from developing areas to Europe, North America or wealthier parts of Asia (Butcher 2006; Liu-Farrer 2009). It represents, therefore, a trend that the mobility under the era of globalization toward these areas contains a character of geographic centers. The flows of people, goods, ideas, under such kind of perspective, will have a similar direction and merge into a global connectedness. In other words, the world seems to be on the way to the formation of a "Global Village."

Such imagination about the modes of mobility is more evident when referring to the movement of skilled people. Although the migration of skilled workers, under a new form of international division of labor, has increased in importance and receiving more research attention over the recent years, there lies still an assumption that skilled people are highly paid, easily moved from one city to another and, therefore, living with a cosmopolitan "global lifestyle" (Beaverstock 2003). That is, skilled people seem able to transgress boundaries easily and enjoy a borderless life. However, recent works like Favell et al. (2006) and Fechter (2007) criticize such perspectives and argue that expatriates' lives are significantly affected by boundaries in many ways. Also the theory of transnationalism provides an alternative analytical framework to study the migration of transnational professionals (Butcher 2006). However, these perspectives are more suitable for studying mobile people who participate in cross-border activities like expatriates or transnational professionals, but not for skilled workers who do not move across national boundaries. In the context of a more globalized world, there would not only be a rapid increase of mobility in people, but also an increase in their diversified forms. Thus, there remains a call for a perspective to explore a different type of skilled worker migration.

The perspective of translocality proposed by Ulrike Freitag and Achim von Oppen (2010) seems to fill the above research gap. As both authors state, translocality is both a tool for describing as well as a perspective for analyzing empirical phenomena. It refers to the outcome of concrete movements of people, goods, ideas and symbols which "span spatial distances and cross boundaries" (Freitag and von Oppen 2010, 5). This perspective is, in particular, against the "Eurocentric focus" of the world system theory and the paradigm of globalization that emphasizes flows, mobility and transgression of boundary. Instead, translocality highlights the transgression of boundaries between spaces of "very different scale" and "the (re)creation of local distinctions between spaces." From this point of view, the research focus is shifted to the attempts "to cope with transgression and with the need for localizing some kind of order" (Freitag and von Oppen 2010, 8). When Taiwanese skilled workers from the manufacturing business migrate to the inland provinces of China, they also have a need for localizing some kind of new order with the local employees in order to ensure a minimal level of smooth and efficient production. Moreover, the term translocality provides an aspect that helps to analyze mobility experiences opposed to the mainstream global centers by emphasizing "a multitude of possible boundaries," all of which help better understand the migration experience to Inner China by both Taiwanese expatriates and Chinese skilled workers. The aim of this chapter is therefore to analyze how a new order is constituted between migrant skilled workers and local employees in their inward movement and new migration processes to Inner China by Taiwanese companies in China as well as the mobility experience of skilled workers. I will argue that the migration process of both Taiwanese and Chinese skilled workers and the manufacturing business to Inner China is not a mobility to global cities or centers, but represents mobilities from the center to the periphery. These mobilities include different actors (Taiwanese factories, Taiwanese expatriates and Chinese skilled workers), and it will show various meanings for their movement from the coastal regions to Inner China, for which I termed them "marginal mobilities."

The movement of Taiwanese manufacturing companies to Pearl River Delta and its changes

At the 1978 plenum of the Chinese Communist Party (CCP), the CCP set modernization as a goal of social development, and this marked the turning point of China's reform, which was also later called the beginning of the "open-door policy." This was a significant change in China's policy after nearly 20 years of economic stagnation in the 1950s. One of the most significant successes that this policy reform achieved was to absorb foreign capital and to pave the way for foreign direct investment. The open-door policy meant, therefore, that China opened its doors to foreign enterprises. The first step of economic reform was set up in four Special Economic Zones (SEZs) in 1979. They included Shenzhen, Zhuhai, Xiamen and Shantou. The SEZs gave the central government the opportunity to experiment with capitalism without losing control in the rest of China (Knox 1997). In order to attract more foreign capital, the Chinese government adopted preferential policies with lower income taxes for foreign-funded enterprises and refunding taxes on exported goods. These policies did help China, next only to the USA, to becoming the second largest recipient of foreign investment in the world in the late 1980s. From 1980 to 1992, the annual economic growth rate of the Pearl River Delta reached a historical high of 18.5 percent (Liu 2010, 258). The reason behind this phenomenon was mainly due to foreign investments originating from Taiwan, Hong Kong, Macau, and overseas Chinese in other countries. Investors with an ethnic Chinese background contributed to the boost of China's rapid economic growth in large volumes in the past two decades. Among them, the investment of Taiwanese businesses brought a huge impact on both Taiwan and China.

Statistics from the Investment Commission of the Ministry of Economic Affairs (MOEA) of Taiwan show that China has become, on one hand, both from the approved investment and the permitted investment project cases, the most important country for Taiwan's foreign investment. On the other hand, according to the statistic of the PRC's Ministry of Commerce (MOC) in 2012, exports from Taiwan to China reached US$2,850 million and the accumulated capital of Taiwanese investment increased to US$57,050 million with 68,095 investment projects. As Yin (2009, 4) noted, Taiwanese investments have created more than 6.8 million jobs in China – each investment is estimated to have provided 100 jobs on average. If the accompanying indirect effect of setting up a factory is considered, there will be more jobs provided by Taiwanese investment than the above number shows.

However, it is only recently that the *"Taishang"* (Taiwanese businesses) phenomena has been seriously considered, not only economically but also sociologically, and is gradually being taken as an interdisciplinary studies program. The majority of Taishang studies so far have been taken in their fieldwork either in the Pearl River Delta, in the great Shanghai area, or in cities along the southeastern coast where most Taiwanese manufacturing factories are concentrated. The abundance of cheap workers, mostly from poorer rural areas in the inner provinces of China, constituted the main source of the workforce for these companies. However, both the Labor Contract Law of 2008 and the international economic crisis starting later in the same year together led to serious problems for the survival of Taiwanese businesses in China's coastal regions (Christiansen 2010).

Table 8.1 shows the statistics of Taiwan-approved investment in China in 1998, in 2011, and the time period from 1991 to 2011. Guangdong was once the province where most Taiwanese manufacturing businesses were concentrated, which attracted, among all of China's provinces, the most investment from Taiwan during the period between 1991 and 2000. It even reached a record high of 40.5 percent of all Taiwanese investments in China in 1998, but it dropped dramatically to only 15.34 percent in the year of 2011. Also the percentage of Taiwanese investment to Jiangsu and Shanghai has dropped in recent years. On the contrary, inland provinces and areas like Sichuan, Chongqing and Hubei have received more investments from Taiwan (Table 8.1).

"Going west 500 Chinese miles (approx. 155 miles) will last another ten years for the survival of business," was the title of a 2010 news report (Chien 2010). Also during the same period, the Chinese government proposed several new projects including "the Western development" and "the rise of Central China strategy" in order to reduce disparities between western and eastern regions. While the movement of manufacturing businesses from Taiwan to the Pearl River Delta in the 1980s and 1990s can be said to be "looking for the second spring of businesses" (Deng and Wei 2010), most recent movements from coastal regions to inner regions could probably be, for many manufacturing businesses, the last chance of survival in China.

Workplace regime in Taiwanese factories in Inland China

"Culture shock" of a Taiwanese businessman in Inland China

> If you live here, you will be surprised to find that the living expenses here are not cheaper than in coastal regions. Everything is expensive here. This is different to our familiar image of Inland China. We cannot expect to reduce our labor costs in making business here. In particular, people here are "lazy." They have a different work discipline compared to the people in Dongguan and Shenzhen. People here who want to earn more money, have already gone to Guangdong or to South China, and those who still stay here do not want work hard, but rather just enjoy their lives.[2]

Above is an interview excerpt from a group interview with two Taiwanese expatriates and the owner of the company in Sichuan. When asked why Taiwanese manufacturing companies developed the idea to set up a new factory or shift their main factory production inland, most of the investors gave the reason of the rapidly rising labor costs in China's coastal regions in recent years. In particular, the Labor Contract Law of 2008 and the international economic crisis mentioned

Table 8.1 Taiwan approved investment in China by area (unit: US$m, %)

Period/area	1998			2011			1991–2011		
	Cases	Amount	Percentage by amount	Cases	Amount	Percentage by amount	Cases	Amount	Percentage by amount
Jiangsu	324	694.75	34.15	204	4,425.89	30.79	6,368	37,808.20	33.85
Guangdong	522	824.42	40.52	187	2,205.07	15.34	12,503	24,247.01	21.71
Shanghai	–	–	–	108	2,175.86	15.13	5,473	16,320.76	14.61
Sichuan	23	20.15	0.99	44	927.01	6.45	452	1,920.34	1.72
Fujian	137	150.79	7.41	77	923.41	6.42	5,460	7,667.28	6.86
Zhejiang	46	85.81	4.22	52	724.46	5.04	2,076	7,158.48	6.41
Tianjin	–	–	–	9	211.87	1.47	919	2,061.03	1.85
Beijing	–	–	–	28	154.16	1.07	1,209	1,836.60	1.64
Shandong	29	63.42	3.12	25	470.72	3.27	994	2,407.65	2.16
Chongqing	–	–	–	42	448.18	3.12	251	1,729.58	1.55
Hubei	21	32.15	1.58	14	189.82	1.32	552	1,277.29	1.14
Others	156	163.13	8.02	97	1,520.20	10.57	3,315	7,263.32	6.50
Total	1,284	2,034.6	100	887	14,376.62	100.00	39,572	111,697.54	100

Source: Mainland Affairs Council, Taiwan (1998, 25; 2012, 29).

earlier, led thousands of Taiwanese companies in the Pearl River Delta to be shut down. Migrant workers returned in large number to their villages or to their hometowns. Many manufacturing companies were forced to consider gradually moving production to the inner provinces in order to seek cheaper labor. The main reason behind this movement could more probably be that the manufacturing industry in coastal regions was facing serious labor shortages.

However, why did Taiwanese business owners and managers have a perception of "lazy" toward the people of Inner China? Did people in Inner China understand the term "work discipline" differently to those who live in Southern China, Shenzhen and Dongguan? What kind of factory workers did Taiwanese investors and managers have to face during the inward movement of their factory to Inner China?

Disappearance of "rural migrant workers" in Inland Taiwanese factories

In the past two decades of rapid economic growth in the coastal regions, lower production costs by Taiwanese manufacturers were mainly based on rural migrant workers. Official statistics suggest that more than 120 million rural migrants worked in cities, and it is estimated that half of the total migrant workers moved to coastal regions and economic zones (Knox 1997, 29). The majority of migrants came from poor rural areas in the interior provinces of China, such as Hunan, Hubei, Henan, Jianxi, Gaungxi, Chongqing and Sichuan. The inward movement of Taiwanese manufacturers, however, begins to change the composition of the employees and probably their relationships. One significant change is that the employees in the factory were not coming from thousands of miles away, but were being replaced by people from the nearer areas. During the early phases, factories located in coastal regions contained most employees that were migrants and with a citizenship status of temporary residence. These city dwellers would adapt themselves to the new and usually very unfriendly environment in the coastal developed regions. Once the manufacturing firms moved to the migrant workers' hometown, most of the recruited employees in the factory were no longer rural migrant workers and became mainly local workers. As a Taiwanese clothing manufacturer in a newly set-up factory in Zhoukou City of Henan Province said,

> While our business is located in coastal regions [in Zhejiang], we recruit our workers from very different provinces out of Zhejiang. But, when we came to Henan, the city of Zhoukou, we had only workers from the near areas. People not living in the near areas and willing to work far from their hometown might have gone out immediately to the coastal cities. There is no reason for them to come here and be hired as workers in the factory. This is similar to the period of "Export Processing Zones (EPZ)" in Taiwan four decades ago. Those workers came only from the near area of the EPZ.[3]

Although the interior provinces have experienced rapid economic growth in China in the recent years, there is still a significant wage difference between coastal and inland regions. Migrant workers in the coastal cities are able to earn significantly better income than in their home villages (Christiansen 2010). Young people inland, particularly those belonging to the one child generation of the 1980s and 1990s, are still willing to go out and work in the coastal cities, but do not wish to find work in manufacturing factories. This led Taiwanese factories in Inland China to face new challenges. Paradoxically, the most distinguished difference during the inward movement process from coastal regions to Inland China for Taiwanese manufacturing companies is not the realization of the large amount of savings in labor costs, but the disappearance of "rural migrant workers." This does not necessarily mean that a large number of rural workers are disappearing in a changing China as there are still a high percentage of rural workers in China, but they do not now need to travel long distances for low-paying jobs in the coastal regions since many foreign and domestic manufacturing firms have moved to their hometown.

Is a new labor regime emerging or how is labor control produced in Inland Taiwanese factories?

What will happen when "the abundant supply of cheap (migrant) labor," on which the rapid shift of foreign manufacturing industry depends (Hsing 1997, 92), could not be found in the inland Taiwanese factories? And how is labor control in these factories possible?

In the article "Becoming *Dagongmei*: politics of identities and differences," Pun Ngai (2005) describes the process of how a rural migrant girl becomes an urban industrial operator in a developed coastal Chinese city. In order to become a female factory worker in developed Guangdong, a rural girl from an inland province has to "acquire a modern modernity." In other words, a rural girl has to change her usual rural lifestyle to become an urban industrial subject. In the factory regime of coastal developed regions, the habitus of rural life has a "bad" connotation, therefore being likely "undervalued" there (Pun 2005, 131).

However, discrimination of "rural migrant workers" in coastal developed regions is not only based on the politics of rural-urban difference but, in particular, on the hukou (house registration) system in China (Peng 2007; Wu 2009). The division between rural and urban hukou has made the Chinese hukou system limit the rights of ordinary citizens in choosing their permanent place of residence (CECC 2006). Migrants who lack a residence as a local citizen are often faced with legal discrimination in the city. Scholars like Wu (2009) utilized the term "differential citizenship" to describe an existing situation of serious inequalities in the urban-rural treatment in China. Having a local hukou in the city has always been linked with better social services. In contrast, rural migrants in the city are seen as temporary residents, and they have to face a very high threshold for changing their hukou to an urban one (Chan and Li 1999). With lack of a local hukou, rural migrant workers are often treated as "non-citizen subjects" or "second-class citizens" in the coastal cities (Lee 2007, 197; Peng 2007). Faced with the *daguofan* phenomenon ("Everyone eats in the same big rice pot") or "laziness" in factory migrant workers, a military-like management with different kinds of punishments was often emphasized in the Taiwanese factories in the Pearl River Delta area (Hsing 1997; Kung and Wang 2006).

However, a management style that frequently resorted to punishment or "military-like training" of workers was inconceivable in the inland Taiwanese factories. Many interviewees reported that many times they experienced strikes from workers when they tried to impose the management style practiced in the coastal factories. Due to factory workers mostly from the near area of the factory, Taiwanese factories inland were forced to change their former labor control practices in the coastal regions and to adapt to local society. For example, there were more flexible arrangements of working hours and vacations. A Chinese senior manager reported the regulation with flexible working hours to the workers:

> As a Taiwanese factory, we have a regular working hour system and regular vacations. Our employees work 10 hours a day. They can go home after 18:30. In addition, we adopt a piece-rate management system, in which many can go home earlier if they finished their work. We do not have overtime work so that our workers have time to take care of their families.[4]

The majority of workers in this shoe factory in Henan are female. They have an average age of 35 years old and most of them have families. Having a job and caring for their families are equally important for these factory women. Moreover, many of the factories visited in Henan have farm vacations for raising wheat and corn. Each vacation is usually for four days to a week. Even in some cases, the managers in the factory encourage their workers to help other coworkers that are busy raising crops. Such kinds of relationships between Taiwanese managers and Chinese employees are hard to find in the workplace in coastal Taiwanese factories.

Marginal mobilities: Taiwanese expatriates and Chinese migrant skilled workers

In the inland Taiwanese factories, it was found that not only Taiwanese managers but also many Chinese skilled workers worked in the positions of mid-level supervisory staff. Some of these Chinese skilled workers had geographical nearness to the business location inland, but most of them were also usually a composition of different workers from interior provinces. For example, a big shoe factory visited in Guangxi, apart from the local staff, had mostly Chinese staff from Hunan Province. The Chinese staff were paid with a lower wage than their Taiwanese colleagues. However, they usually had relatively longer working experience in factories in the coastal regions. With a recruitment channel of internal transfer, they worked in expanded or relocated Taiwanese factories inland. Although they were similar to the Taiwanese expatriates moving from the coastal regions to inland provinces, they usually had different migration experiences compared to Taiwanese expatriates.

A Chinese cadre with a Wuhan hukou reported her choice to work in the relocated factory in Henan.

> Here is more attractive for me because my job can offer me more challenges. I get a better salary than that in the coastal regions. In addition, Henan is nearer to my hometown in Hubei. As I was working in coastal cities, I can visit my parents only every three years. Now I can go back to my hometown twice or three times in a year. It makes quite a big difference.[5]

Chinese staff, during their transfer to the new factory inland, were often offered a higher salary than they received in the coastal regions. They also had higher job positions when they were assigned to work in the inland factory. All these made positive judgments toward their migration to the inland province.

However, many Taiwanese expatriates have different judgments on their experiences in Inland China. A cheer like "Shanghai, I am coming" did not happen in the interviews with Taiwanese expatriates when they received the assignment from the mother company. A young female expat, who is 36 years old and is a management manager in a multinational Taiwanese clothing manufacturing factory in Zhoukou said,

> I have been an expat in Jordan, Cambodia and Qingdao, China. This experience is quite similar to that of our deputy manager. He even changes his expat location every year. But if you ask my preference of the expat location, honestly, I prefer go back to work in Taiwan. It's still the most familiar place to me.[6]

Many Taiwanese expatriates interviewed mentioned that they still prefer working in Taiwan or in China's coastal regions rather than inland. The reasons offered were often neither convenience in traffic, nor good living facilities around the factory. "It seems back to 20 years ago, when I first worked in the Pearl River Delta," a senior Taiwanese manager said. For many Taiwanese expatriates, the assignment to Inland China represents only a transit stage in their expat career.

Conclusion

This chapter explores emerging trends in the inward movement of Taiwanese manufacturing companies as well as drawing attention to the mobility of skilled workers in their new migration process to Inner China. It shows movements opposite to the mainstream moves to coastal cities, and rather moves from coastal regions to inland provinces of China that include Taiwanese factories, Taiwanese expatriates and Chinese skilled workers.

The rapid rising of labor costs and, in particular, the shortage of labor forces in coastal regions in the recent years are reasons why many Taiwanese companies decide to relocate their assembly plants or the whole factory to the middle or western region of China (Guo 2010). Furthermore, favoring tax policies by the Chinese government and fewer restrictions in investment fields have encouraged foreign investors in central and western China. This new wave of movement shows many differences compared to the earlier investment period where Taiwanese manufacturing industries migrated to coastal China.

First, in order to cope with the transgression problem from coastal regions to inland provinces, there is a need for Taiwanese manufacturing companies to develop a new order in the factory's labor regime. Taiwanese export manufacturers in coastal China are usually described as having a despotic control over their workers or as rootless enterprises without strong embedding into local society, which sociologist Chen Ming-chi called the model of the "fortress in the air" (Chen 2012). Such a despotic factory regime is associated with a punishment-oriented labor control and a rigid discipline of factory life that often includes the demand of overtime work and centralized dormitory management by providing accommodation adjacent to the production building to facilitate a "just-in-time labor system for just-in-time production" (Lee 1997, 121; Pun 2006, 118).

One of the key factors, which made this kind of factory regime possible, is the abundant supply of rural workers, often both young and female, migrating from inland to coastal China. Scholar Ching Kwan Lee (1998: 109) described these people as *Dagonzai*, referring to rural migrant workers laboring for the usually foreign bosses. They are characterized, as a popular song among Shenzhen workers noted, as "coming from five lakes and four seas, from all places and directions, working hard to sell their strength, working extra hours and extra shifts, but have no residence in Special Economic Zone."[7] As *Dagonzai*, migrant workers are usually unorganized, under-protected by the local government, and thus discriminated or treated in many ways as the second class in the local society they migrated into (Lee 2007). However, the inward movement of Taiwanese manufacturers and a production model based mainly on employees from adjacent villages and cities have led to the disappearance of rural migrant workers and the end of the *Dagonzai* phenomenon in the factories inland.

How should the Taiwanese factories inland respond to this changing situation? Obviously the factory inland, first of all, needs to build up a more embedded relationship in the local society instead of staying as a rootless enterprise in South China. Since the manufacturing firms inland can only find workers from the near areas where the factory is located, the manufacturers now have to collaborate with local societies in order to attract people to work in the factory, which are usually rural and middle-aged women. Furthermore, a repressive measure on labor control needs to be replaced with an improvement of relationships between the factory's management staff and local employees. Since the majority of workers are not composed of unorganized and unprotected "migrant workers" and with local workers instead, workplace conflicts are impossible to solve with a military-like management style in the factory inland. A new workplace management, such as employing more negotiation with local workers, providing flexible arrangement of working hours for aged women or farm vacation for rural workers, is needed and often emphasized by both Taiwanese and Chinese supervisory staff in the factory inland. In addition, in order to cope with management problems in the workplace, Taiwanese manufacturers often send to the relocated factory more Chinese mid-level supervisory staff instead of Taiwanese managers to be in charge of skill training and let the recruited rural people become familiar with factory life. In other words, multiple embedding with the local society becomes the major model for the workplace regime in the Taiwanese factories inland.

Second, there are many studies that deal with the migration experiences of skilled workers or expatriates. However, such researches to date tend to link the mobility of skilled workers or expatriates to global cities. The migration of Taiwanese expatriates to Chinese coastal cities and rural migrant workers from their hometown to the southeast coastal region is supposed to constitute to some extent this new geography of centrality from the viewpoint of economic development. This chapter, on the contrary, shows a different approach, which explores the migration process of (both Taiwanese and Chinese) skilled workers in the manufacturing business to Inner China. Their movement inland is obviously not in the direction of global centers like Beijing, Shanghai or Guangdong, but represents mobilities from the center to the periphery. I coined the term "marginal mobilities," relying on the idea of translocality proposed by Freitag and von Oppen (2010), to describe this mode of mobility which is regarded as at odds with mainstream globalization, although there could be a very different judgment found in migration experiences towards the inland between Taiwanese expatriates and Chinese skilled workers. While Chinese staff during their transfer to the new factory inland are often offered both a higher wage and job position, working nearer to their hometown and therefore assessing their mobility as not a move to the periphery but with more challenges, many Taiwanese expatriates look at their assignment to the factory inland as not a permanent stay but rather a transit stage.

Finally, the perspective of translocality provides the study of globalizing processes from a different viewpoint. This chapter examines the inward movement of Taiwanese manufacturing companies and the mobility of Taiwanese and Chinese skilled workers in their new migration to Inner China. The movement of people and industry from coastal cities to developed cities inland constitute an important but relatively little understood category of border crossing in Greater China.

There continue to be many Taiwanese companies, like the chain store mentioned earlier, that are setting up new branches in China's global cities, attracting talent and young people to migrate for work in these global centers. Yet, the inwardly relocated Taiwanese manufacturing companies, like other newly tertiary industries set up in Shanghai and Beijing, are the products of a changing China in the globalization era. Undoubtedly, the movement from coastal regions to inner regions of China is still an ongoing process, and it still remains one of many strategies to overcome the survival of Taiwanese manufacturing businesses in the Pearl River Delta area and other coastal regions. Marginal mobilities are by definition and at first glance, those geographic movements from the center to the periphery. However, by these seemingly marginal movements, there is a new possibility opened for Taiwanese manufacturers inland to build closer relationships to the local community, giving up the enterprise organizational model of "fortress in the air." Chinese mid-level supervisory staff who are migrants with the relocated factory inland, will certainly meet more challenges related to a job promotion to higher levels, while the Taiwanese expatriates might connect this transit stage to their next career move of working aboard. The perspective translocality stimulates another important aspect that deepens our understanding of the re-embedding process of the migration of Taiwanese manufacturing companies to Inner China, leading us to see the opportunities produced for both Taiwanese and Chinese skilled workers during their peripheral movement.

Notes

1 Funding for this research derives from Taiwan's National Science Council (NSC 100–2420–H-032–001-MY3). The author is grateful to Jenn-Hwan Wang, Chih-Peng Cheng, Ruey-Ling Tzeng, Xiu-Hua Shen, Shiuh-Shen Chien, Rui-Hua Lin and two anonymous reviewers for their constructive comments.
2 Group interview, July 20, 2012, Suining City, Sichuan Province, China.
3 Group interview, July 8, 2012, Dancheng County, Zhoukou City, Henan Province, China.
4 Interview, July 11, 2012, Shangshui County, Zhoukou City, Henan Province, China.
5 Interview, July 9, 2012, Xiangcheng County, Zhoukou City, Henan Province, China.
6 Interview, July 7, 2012, Zhoukou City, Henan Province, China.
7 Cited from Lee (1998: 109).

References

Beaverstock, Jonathan V. 2002. "Transnational Elites in Global Cities: British Expatriates in Singapore's Financial District." *Geoforum* 33: 525–538.
Beaverstock, Jonathan V. 2003, "Transnational Elites in the City: British Highly-Skilled Migrants in New York City's Financial District." *GaWC Research Bulletin* 109. Leicestershire, UK: GaWC.
Butcher, Melissa. 2006. "White Collar Filipinos: Australian Professionals in Singapore." In *Mobility, Labour Migration and Border Controls in Asia*, edited by Amarjit Kaur and Ian Metcalfe, 172–192. New York: Palgrave Macmillan.
Chan, Kam Wing and Li Zhang. 1999. "The *Hukou* System and Rural-Urban Migration in China. Processes and Changes." *The China Quarterly* 160: 818–855.
Chen, Ming-chi. 2012. "Fortress in the Air: The Organization Model of Taiwanese Export-manufacturing Transplants in China." *Issues & Studies* 48 (4): 73–112.
Chien, Wei-jun. 2010. "Taiwanese labor industry moves to Inner China: Going west 500 Chinese miles to last another ten years." *TVBS News*, August 18. Accessed January 31, 2013. www.tvbs.com.tw/news/news_list.asp?no=sunkiss20100818204016.

Christiansen, Flemming. 2010. "Migrations within China." In *Diasporas: Concepts, Intersections, Identities*, edited by Kim Knott and Sean McLoughlin, 204–210. London: Zed Books.

Congressional-Executive Commission on China (CECC). 2006. "Annual Report: Monitoring Compliance with Human Rights." Accessed January 31, 2013. www.cecc.gov/pages/annualRpt/annualRpt06/ResidenceandTrave.php.

Deng, Jian-bang and Wei Ming-ju. 2010. "Family Firms and Generational Change: Taiwanese Manufacturing Business in the Pearl River Delta." *Mainland China Studies* 53 (3): 25–51 (in Chinese).

Favell, Adrian, Miriam Feldblum and Michael Peter Smith. 2006. "The Human Face of Global Mobility: A Research Agenda." In *The Human Face of Global Mobility: International Highly Skilled Migration in Europe, North America and the Asia-Pacific*, edited by Michael P. Smith and Adrian Favell, 1–25. New Brunswick, NJ: Transaction.

Fechter, Anne-Meike. 2007. *Transnational Lives: Expatriates in Indonesia*. Aldershot, UK: Ashgate.

Freitag, Ulrike and Achim von Oppen. ed. 2010, *Translocality: The Study of Globalising Processes from a Southern Perspective*, Leiden: Brill.

Gritsai, Olga. 2005. "Foreign and Local Professionals in the Moscow Offices of Global Business Service Companies." *GaWC Research Bulletin* 162. Leicestershire, UK: GaWC.

Guo, Qiang. 2010. "Labor industry moves to Inner China." *US-China Today*, June 29. Accessed January 31, 2013. www.uschina.usc.edu/w_usci/showarticle.aspx?articleID=15379&AspxAutoDetectCookieSupport=1.

Hsing, You-tien. 1997. *Making Capitalism in China: The Taiwan Connection*. New York, NY: Oxford University Press.

Knox, Angie. 1997. *Southern China: Migrant Workers and Economic Transformation*. London: Catholic Institute for International Relations.

Kung, I-chun and Wang Hong-zen. 2006. "Socially Constructed Ethnic Division of Labour: Labour Control in Taiwanese-Owned Firms in Malaysia and Vietnam." *International Sociology* 21 (4): 580–601.

Lee, Ching Kwan. 1997. "Factory Regimes of Chinese Capitalism: Different Cultural Logics in Labor Control." In *Underground Empires: The Cultural Politics of Modern Chinese Transnationalism*, edited by Aihwa Ong and Donald M. Nonini, 115–142. London: Routledge.

Lee, Ching Kwan. 1998. *Gender and the South China Miracle. Two Worlds of Factory Women*. Berkeley: University of California Press.

Lee, Ching Kwan. 2007. *Against the Law: Labor Protests in China's Rustbelt and Sunbelt*. Berkeley: University of California Press.

Liu, Xiao-xuan. 2010. *The Micro-foundation of China's Market Economy*. Singapore: Cengage Learning Asia Pte Ltd.

Liu-Farrer. Gracia. 2009. "Educationally Channeled International Labor Mobility: Contemporary Student Migration from China to Japan." *International Migration Review* 43 (1): 178–204.

Mainland Affairs Council (MAC). 1998. *Cross-Strait Economic Statistics Monthly* No. 169. Taipei: MAC. Accessed January 31, 2013. www.mac.gov.tw/public/Attachment/26510132285.pdf.

Mainland Affairs Council (MAC). 2012. *Cross-Strait Economic Statistics Monthly* No. 229. Taipei: MAC. Accessed January 31, 2013. www.mac.gov.tw/public/Attachment/26510132285.pdf.

Peng. Thomas. 2007 "Hourly Wages, Hard Workers, and a Hegemonic Regime: The Factory Regime of a Taiwanese-invested Factory in South China." *Taiwanese Sociology* 14: 51–100 (in Chinese).

Pun, Ngai. 2005. *Made in China: Women Factory Workers in a Global Workplace*, Durham, NC: Duke University Press.

Pun, Ngai. 2006. "Capital's Incorporation of Labor Rights and Corporate Codes of Conduct in a Chinese Dormitory Labor Regime." In *How China Works: Perspectives on the Twentieth-century Industrial Workplace*, edited by Jacob Eyferth, 110–123. London: Routledge.

Sassen, Saskia. 2000. "Wem gehört die Stadt? Neue Ansprüche im Rahmen der Globalisierung." In *Machtbeben: Wohin für die Globalisierungt?*, edited by Saskia Sassen, 7–37. München, DE: Deutsche Verlags-Anstalt.

Thang, Leng Leng, Elizabeth MacLachlan and Miho Goda. 2002. "Expatriates on the Margins: A Study of Japanese Women Working in Singapore." *Geoforum* 33: 539–551.

Tseng, Yen-Fen. 2012. "Creative Identities: Taiwanese Cultural Workers in China." In *Conference on Border Crossing in Greater China: Production, Community and Identity*, October 13–14, 2012, Taipei: Center for China Studies, National Chengchi University.

Wu, Jieh-Min. 2009. "Rural Migrant Workers and China's Differential Citizenship: A Comparative-Institutional Analysis." In *One Country, Two Societies: Rural-Urban Inequality in Contemporary China*, edited by Martin King Whyte, 55–81. Cambridge, MA: Harvard University Press.

Yin, Chun Yi. 2009. "Economic Trends in Cross-straits." In *Conference on Taiwanese Investment in China for two Decades: Experience, Development and the Future*, October 3–4, 2009, Taipei: Taiwan Foundation for Democracy, Center for China Studies and National Chengchi University.

9 Cross-Strait economic exchanges by night

Pleasure, work, and power in Chinese karaoke hostess bars

Hsiu-hua Shen

> We usually go for dinner first and later to a karaoke bar to sing songs and drink. Toward the end of the night, we simply call it a night and don't make any further inquiry about where people are going next. Some of us may leave together for hotels with the women we pick up from the bar. We know how to be cool and let each other do his own thing. As we get to know each other better over time, we even exchange comments and information about the women we were with.
>
> (A Taiwanese manager in a food factory, Kunshan, China)

As one wanders at night through the streets in the commercial districts of the Special Economic Zones (SEZs)[1] in Coastal China, it is impossible not to notice the abundance of bars, salons, restaurants, and neon signs, as well as the flirtation between men and women. When their shift was over, many factory workers wandered the streets near their factories and shop and ate together at the street vendors. Chinese women in their late teens or early twenties, dressed in mini-skirts or other sexy apparel, emerged from their rented apartments and strolled into karaoke bars ready to begin work. Meanwhile, Taiwanese businessmen arranged their night's activities. Thus, a zone of industry/work and toil by day became a playground for leisure, alcohol, and indulgence at night.

This chapter explores the ritual and institutionalization of heterosexual karaoke hostessing and related commercial sex in China where Taiwanese businessmen act as consumers and/or producers of the businesses. Since the late 1980s, thousands of Taiwanese capital holders and professionals have gone to China to invest and work. The majority of them have been men. Frequenting karaoke hostess bars with their clients or colleagues has been part of their business operation and leisure activity for many of those Taiwanese men, particularly during the 1990s and 2000s when Taiwanese dollars were still relatively strong in relation to Chinese yuan (Shen 2008a). The quotation at the beginning of the chapter reveals that the art of going to karaoke bars and engaging in commercial sex among Taiwanese businessmen in China is highly structured by certain patterns of ritual between Taiwanese businessmen and the organization of the industry.

This chapter has two goals. One is to reveal the highly gendered and sexualized organization of economic exchanges across the Taiwan Strait between Taiwan and China in the last three decades. The majority of Taiwanese business personnel in China have been men and their visits to hostess bars and liaisons with Chinese women have been no secret in either Taiwanese or Chinese societies. In China, Taiwanese businessmen have gained a reputation for linking to the sex industry and to extramarital affairs. In Taiwan, stories about Taiwanese businessmen's sexual liaisons are widely circulated by the Taiwanese mass media. *Ikuo Liangchi*, "One Country, Two Wives" (Chiu and Lin 1994), or the "Taiwanese first wife's club," have become common expressions in Taiwan to signify the cross-Strait liaisons between Taiwanese businessmen and Chinese women in China to marriages and families in Taiwan. The widespread lack of marital fidelity by Taiwanese businessmen in China is seen by many people in Taiwan to threaten the economic well-being of the wives and children of Taiwanese businessmen, to challenge the institution of the family as a heterosexual monogamous unit, and to pose danger to national security due to cross-Strait political disputes (Shen 2003, 2008b; Shih 1998). Yet, only limited studies have taken seriously the gendered and sexualized nature of cross-Strait economic exchanges. The other goal of this chapter is to deconstruct the associated discursive fiction among its consumers that frequenting karaoke hostess bars is about "play" rather than linked to the organization of work and to the creation of social differences and hierarchies. The chapter will show that the contemporary sexualized leisure market in China is not something emerging *naturally* as an effect of demand and supply, but highly structured and institutionalized in terms of a hierarchic organization of human labor, style of consumption, and material resources. What appears to be about masculine play and pleasure is about work that itself is based on creation and maintenance of difference and hierarchy. In this case, the difference and hierarchy are transnationally structured and significant between genders and between Taiwanese and Chinese in terms of class and nationality. Overall this chapter argues that the space of karaoke hostess bars and the phenomenon of prostitution in contemporary China both reflects and engenders the social hierarchy upon which a global political economy and uneven development depends.

In the following sections, I first discuss the related literature and methodology to this particular study. I then analyze the ritual and hierarch relations that enable and sustain the organization of karaoke hostessing in contemporary China. I finalize the chapter by discussion and conclusion.

Masculine play: a site of (re)producing social hierarchies

In his classic study, Clifford Geertz (1973) argues that the cockfight in Bali, in a form of play, is a public site of assorting and displaying social status and hierarchy and of consolidating interpersonal and intergroup relations and identities. The cockfight rarely takes place between men of the same kingroup and between different social statuses. It is attentively arranged to be a status match in terms of social membership and hierarchy. A fight between near status equals and between high status individuals is considered to be a deeper match. The deeper a match is, the greater emotion, including the owners of the cocks and the audience is absorbed in the fight and the closer the identification between men and the cockfight. Women, children, and subordinates are excluded from the deep play. In its form of deep play, the cockfight is a matter of social status, gender, and age. Social category, status, and relations are attentively organized in the so-call "play" process.

Considering that "the culture of people is an ensemble of texts," Geertz (1973, 452) treats the highly structured nature of the cockfight as a significant text for interpreting how society is built and people are put together in Bali. Play or more precisely "masculine play" in this case, becomes a site of social and cultural investigation (Shen 2008a). Masculine play can be expressed through various forms. Sexualized masculine play practiced in the form of frequenting karaoke hostess bars by transnational Taiwanese business owners and professionals in China, I would argue, is a crucial site of social investigation on how social hierarchy is organized and (re)produced, how work is hiding behind the idea of play and pleasure, how the term of play can make the institutionalization of the sex industry to be overlooked, and how the culture of making capitalism is gendered and sexualized.

Transnational corporations have been leading forces in contemporary global capitalism. Transnational capital holders and various business, political, and mass media personnel working to promote the expansion of transnational corporations are categorized by Sklair (2001) as "the transnational capitalist class" who are influential players in the contemporary global political economy. A major characteristic of the transnational capitalist class is "the transnational business masculinity" and its association with the commercial entertainment and sex industries (Connell 2000; Shen 2003, 2008a). While more women have become active in various workforces, men are still the leading actors in transnational and local business and politics. As a result, the component and the influence of the transnational capitalist class are likely to be male dominated. Studies have found that various venues, including bars and clubs, are established to provide such clients with entertaining and sexual services of female hostesses/escorts (Enole 1989; Klein 2000; Pan 2004; Shen 2003, 2008a). While the commercialization and sexualization of women by transnational business personnel is a well-acknowledged fact, limited studies have been done on the people and processes involved in the institutionalization and popularization of the industry. Where, how, and why does the commercialization and sexualization of women by transnational business personnel occur and how is it organized? What are the social backgrounds of the main actors involved and in what social circumstances do they encounter each other? And which social relations and consequences are emerging from this process?

Karaoke hostess bars or other similar places are popular places where many businessmen including Japanese, Taiwanese, or Chinese initiate their commercialization and sexualization of women and cultivate their working relations

(Allison 1994; Hwang 2003; Shen 2003, 2008a; Zheng 2004, 2006). In Japan, since the postwar economic growth period, many medium-to-large corporations frequently entertain their male employees and clients in karaoke hostess bars in order to assimilate their employees into their corporate system and culture, and to cultivate connections with their business associates (Allison 1994). In the reform era in China, collectively visiting hostess bars and developing various forms of intimacies with hostesses acts a means to select potential business partners and to establish business networks (Zheng 2006). Taiwanese businessmen also have a long history of collectively visiting hostess bars to facilitate business and establish networks (Hwang 2003). This masculine practice is deeply integrated into economic developments in these societies.

Women's emotional and sexual labor is necessary for making this close connection between masculine play and capitalist accumulation. In a typical middle-ranged hostess bar in Japan, Taiwan, or China, hostesses serve their customers drinks, food, keep them involved in conversation, flatter them and boost their spirits, and exchange flirtatious and sexual talk. Sex transactions with hostesses are not unusual in many Taiwanese and Chinese hostess bars and some Japanese hostess bars (Allison 1994; Hwang 2003; Shen 2003, 2008a; Zheng 2006). Personal and business networks are cultivated among businessmen as they share the time and experience to interact, to relax, to have fun, and to develop sexual liaisons with women together.

However, like the cockfight in Bali as a form of social exclusion, status display, and competition, frequenting karaoke hostess bars as a form of masculine play is not power neutral. My analysis in the chapter shows that women except the hostesses and men who are not interested in or disagree with this type of practice are not welcome in this type of setting. Frequenting hostess bars is also organized by social category. Different status groups of men do not usually socialize together in this type of setting. Power relations between men as consumers who pay to get emotional and/or sexual services and women as hostesses who are the workers performing emotional and bodily labor to get paid are dynamic. On the one hand, hostesses can be manipulating through the performance of their labor (Allison 1994). However, in the name of play by men, the work women perform and the organization taking to establish and promote the entertaining and sex industry are invisible. Male bonding and status performance through the consumption of women in karaoke bars are sites of creating gender and other forms of inequality (Allison 1994; Shen 2008a; Zheng 2006).

In his study on prostitution in Shanghai, French historian Christian Henriot (2001) uses the term "common prostitution" to describe the emerging historical transformation of prostitution in Shanghai from 1849 to 1949 from the high-class brothel centered on a luxury market for courtesans to the various categories of prostitution provided to the masses from all backgrounds. The hostess bars patronized by foreign businessmen and professionals, such as the Taiwanese and others, and the culture associated with visits to such bars are important parts of the landscape that constitutes contemporary "common prostitution" in China. New social categories and novel linguistic expressions, such as *k fang* (karaoke halls), *xiao jie* (miss, a term referring to women working in the sex or entertainment businesses), *ernai* (mistress), *bao ernai* (keeping mistresses), *ernai tsun* (mistress villages), *singhuila* (using sex to bribe the ones in power) are created and/or become well known in China. The entertainment and sex industries in China have proliferated and become common in recent decades. However, this should not been taken to imply that entertainment and commercial sex have been necessarily more accepted by the Chinese society. Actually, from the negative associations attached to the phenomenon and from the created categories, it shows that contemporary common prostitution has become a symbol of moral and gender corruption by the market economy in the post-socialist China. What is overlooked behind the moral discourse are the people, institutions, and power that organize the industry.

Research and background

Since the introduction of economic reform in 1978, sex and related entertainment industries have burgeoned in China's SEZs, the result of its open economic zones. Initially they catered to the increasing numbers of foreign businessmen and later to both foreign tourists and local Chinese men (Jeffreys 2004; Pan 2004; Xiao 2011, this volume; Zheng 2006). Taiwanese businessmen are prominent among these foreign businessmen. Because many of them are married with children and wives in Taiwan, they become "situational singles" (Shen 2003, 2005, 2008b, 2014) within the context of establishing intimate relations with Chinese women in China. This chapter is based on fieldwork conducted between 1999 and 2012 in Dongguan and Shenzhen in Guangdong Province, Xiamen City in Fujian Province, and Shanghai and Kunshan City in the Shanghai-Nanjing Economic Corridor. I chose these locations because they hosted large numbers of Taiwanese business people, one of the largest overseas groups in the PRC.

For the purpose of writing this chapter, I use the data gathered from more than 130 interviews with male Taiwanese investors and managers in China and four interviews with the Chinese mistresses of these businessmen, seven with Chinese hostesses, and two with the Chinese managers (the Mamas) of karaoke bars frequented by these businessmen. During my research in different coastal Chinese cities, I lived with my Taiwanese interviewees in their companies' dormitories or their personal homes and accompanied Taiwanese businessmen to karaoke bars and massage salons. These live-in arrangements within the Taiwanese business communities enabled me to observe closely Taiwanese businessmen's culture of going to karaoke bars and their associations with Chinese women. Due to the highly private and sensitive nature of the interviews and in order to protect my research subjects, except the ones directly derived from secondary sources, all the names of people given in this chapter are pseudonyms.

My overall research project was to understand Taiwanese business people's personal lives and social relations in China. As I approached my potential interviewees about my study, they understood that their associations with karaoke bars were an important part of their everyday life and as a result became an important part of my research. Except top managers of large firms and business owners of medium-to-large-sized firms, many of them voluntarily told me about this aspect of their lives and made it possible for me to visit karaoke bars with them. They were willing to reveal this part of their lives in China to me for four major reasons. The first is the knowledge that their intimacies with Chinese women were "public secrets" widely reported by both the Taiwanese and Chinese mass media, and were, therefore, very difficult to deny. The second was that the firms they worked for were usually not publicly known and they did not have to worry much that talking about their personal conduct would harm their firms' public image and reputation. The third was the fact that I did not pose a direct threat of gossiping about their personal affairs in China to their families and social circles in Taiwan because I was an outsider to them and because I promised individual confidentiality. The last and the most important reason was an awareness that they needed to talk about their sexual adventures with Chinese women in much the same way as they talked about their economic adventures and profit accumulation in China. As a result, once I was in the field, I was surprised with their quick responses and rich narratives on a matter that I initially assumed would be very private and not easily and publicly narrated. However, it is important to clarify that to protect their own personal and business images, I was unable to let top managers of large firms and business owners of medium-to-large-sized firms talk about their experiences with or their social circle of sexual play with me even I gained access to talk to them. The study, thus, is about the middle to low ranking Taiwanese businessmen's masculine play in China.

As a woman, my gender position did limit access to the more sexual aspects of interactions between these Taiwanese businessmen and their Chinese hostesses in karaoke bars. Normally, the positions of women in hostess bars are limited to hostesses, Mamas, or waitresses. Women are not seen as consumers in these settings because this business is operated upon the logic of heterosexual services to male consumers. Although sexual acts are not necessarily involved at the sites, the talk and the jokes are always heterosexually oriented. Since I was neither a worker nor a "real" consumer, my gendered presence in these masculine hostess bars disturbed the existing gendered division of service and entertainment, and reshaped the social circumstances for carrying out masculinities.

It is also important to mention the relatively low number of Chinese bar hostesses interviewed for this study. As a Taiwanese woman, I had difficulty gaining the trust of those Chinese women who were intimately associated with Taiwanese businessmen because of the publicly "dishonorable" nature of their status in these relationships, because of the "dishonourable" nature of their jobs as hostesses, and because of their perception that that I must be on the side of Taiwanese women in judging their relationships. As an academic from outside of China, I also sensed that my social/class position exacerbated the differences between these women and myself and, as a result, inhibited discussion. Nevertheless, because of my intensive encounters with Chinese women in karaoke bars, in the dormitories of Taiwanese businessmen, or in other settings where they accompanied Taiwanese businessmen, I did frequently have opportunities to observe them and have causal conversations with them.

Cross-Strait economic activities by night

The place

The typical karaoke hostess bar which Taiwanese businessmen frequent in China is a heterosexual-oriented entertainment space where female hostesses are available to serve their customers by participating in drinking, singing, and dancing, and by providing sexual favors, including sexual transactions inside or outside the bars. This type of masculine entertainment was already very popular among Taiwanese businessmen in Taiwan even before they went to China (Hwang 2003). According to many Taiwanese businessmen, there were very few leisure places available to them, except a few piano bars, when they first arrived in coastal Chinese towns or cities in the late 1980s or early 1990s. As more Taiwanese and other foreign businessmen arrived in China, some Taiwanese businessmen brought management experiences from Taiwan and put their money into karaoke bars or other types of entertainment businesses in Chinese towns and cities. In fact, many karaoke hostess bars frequented by Taiwanese businessmen were Taiwanese-owned (also see Lee 2001).[2] As investors and consumers, Taiwanese businessmen play significant roles in introducing and developing sex-related entertainment in different parts of China following the arrival of their capital (Chiu and Lin 1994; Lee 2001; Liu 2004).

To provide privacy for their customers, these hostess bars are typically furnished with a fair number of private rooms, each of which has a stereo system, a TV, a table, and comfortable couches. The bigger sized rooms are even equipped with a small dance floor and private restroom. To create a public space for their consumers to interact with each other and with the other hostesses, a big, public dance floor is usually included in some of those bars and dance music is played two to three times every night for half hour sessions. In the bars where Taiwanese are major customers, much of the dance music played in these bars is Western dance music, but inside private rooms, the most popular music is mainly Taiwanese and Hong Kong popular music.

Alcohol and food, often Taiwanese dishes served best with alcohol, are made available in these bars, especially in those Taiwanese-owned ones. Except for Chinese Mandarin, Hokkien, a language used by the ethnic majority in Taiwan, is the main language used by the Taiwanese customers regardless of their ethnic backgrounds in Taiwan.[3] The hostesses working there are usually very familiar with the popular music in Taiwan and know Hokkien songs well even though most of them do not understand or speak much of the language.[4] Indeed, once during a visit to a karaoke bar, a hostess even teased me on my incapability of finishing a Hokkien song, despite my Taiwanese background, while she sang most of songs that night in Hokkien.

Ya Lee, a Taiwanese businessman, had eight years' experience in the entertainment business in China and published a book in Taiwan in 2001 about Taiwanese businessmen's affairs with Chinese women. He explained that the reasons that Taiwanese men tend to visit Taiwanese-owned bars are because "they feel that they know how to negotiate a better price and service for themselves there and because they are more comfortable in these bars since they share the same background of coming from Taiwan" (Lee 2001, 27). Equally, to attract Taiwanese customers, the owners of and the people working in these bars consciously create a "Taiwanese environment" or, in Ya Lee's (2001, 27) words, "the taste and smell of Taiwan" in the middle of these Chinese SEZs. Taiwanese-owned bars provide senses of familiarity and security including food, language, music, and fellow-nationals-based trust that those Chinese-owned ones usually cannot offer to Taiwanese businessmen in a foreign land, China.

According to my interviews, many Taiwanese men mentioned that due to the lack of leisure activities in economic zones during their early years of arrival in China, "karaoke hostess bars served as places of relaxing and leisure for them after work." A Taiwanese owner of a shoe factory in Dongguan told me that a friend of his who is a Taiwanese businessman often said that "karaoke hostess bars are the soul food of Taiwanese [men] in China." Within the context of migration, those Taiwanese-friendly karaoke hostess bars are masculine expatriate enclaves for Taiwanese businessmen in China whereas Western expat bars in Shanghai are for Western expatriates (mainly men, but also attracting some Western expat women, see Farrer 2011).

The people

Three major categories of people are involved in the nightlife in this type of bar: the Mamas, the hostesses, and the consumers. The Mamas are important agents in promoting and running karaoke bar business at a daily basis. They are responsible for recruiting and managing hostesses, and for greeting, arranging rooms for, and checking out customers. According to my research, Mamas are usually females and many of them are former hostesses themselves since they know the business and the social circles well. For instance, a Mama to whom I talked in Dongguan in 1999 was then working in a local Taiwanese-owned karaoke bar and had worked as a hostess before she became a Mama. She was then 26 years old and had left home in Hubei Province six years earlier. A Mama's income comes from two major sources – a basic salary and a fee collected from the hostesses she manages. From the owner of the bar where she worked, the Mama mentioned above received her then basic salary, 1,000 RMB (US$125) per month, subject to a precondition related to the sale of a certain amount of alcohol to her customers. The more alcohol she sold per month, the higher her salary would be. She also earned extra money from the hostesses whom she managed, getting 20 RMB from each of their service tips and 100 RMB for each sexual service in which her hostesses engaged. The more popular her hostesses were, the more fees she could collect from them. Therefore, to be able to recruit and train qualified hostesses who are skillful at encouraging their clients to drink more, who are well liked in the bar, and who are willing to engage in sexual favors with clients is the major task that a Mama has to undertake in order to secure her success in this business. To hostesses, especially the inexperienced ones, Mama is the one bringing them into the business, bridging them with bars since most of the bars do not directly manage them, providing them with basic business trainings on how to host consumers, and help them brining in consumers by keeping close contacts with former and potential consumers.

The second main category of people in coastal Chinese karaoke bars is the hostess, locally called "*xiao jie*," or miss.[5] Indeed, hostesses are the most important factor in keeping a karaoke bar attractive to its customers and profitable to its owners. In a typical karaoke hostess bar in coastal China, there was always a room set up with long benches and there were always hostesses dressed in a sexy fashion, usually with an attempt to show their busts and legs, and waiting there to be called to work. It was very common to see from several dozen to several hundred hostesses working in medium-to-large-sized karaoke bars in coastal Chinese SEZs. Several Taiwanese businessmen repeatedly mentioned to me that they had heard that a large karaoke bar on the island of Hainan off the southern coast of China once had over a thousand hostesses who lined up along the hallway and the stairs to greet its customers. This setup was to fulfill male consumers' fantasy of desire that the bars are full of Chinese women waiting to serve them. Although the karaoke bar owners clearly benefit from the customers attracted to the bars by these hostesses, there usually is no monetary obligation between the hostesses and the bars. Because prostitution is illegal in China, not to have direct monetary relation with hostesses is a strategy that many business owners employ to avoid legal responsibility should any hostess residing in their bars be accused of engaging in prostitution.[6]

In her study of prostitution in the twentieth century in Shanghai, Hershatter (1999, 34) finds that male authors of Shanghai guidebooks constructed a hierarchy among prostitutes by "the class background of the customers, the native place of both customers and prostitutes, and the appearance and age of the prostitute." In my study, I also find that Taiwanese businessmen as consumers also generate a discursive hierarchy among Chinese women in sex-related industries according to their customers, age, look, native place, social skill, and education. According to Taiwanese businessmen, Chinese women working at the bars they frequent are ranked near the bottom in the business. In contrast, the ones work at the places mainly catering to Western or Japanese businessmen are placed by Taiwanese businessmen at the top of the hierarchy. Western and Japanese businessmen tend to occupy relatively privileged positions than other expatriate or local businessmen in China because of their influential economic and international capital. The rating of Chinese women in sex-related industries marks the hierarchy of men, including expatriate and Chinese on the stage of the emerging Chinese market.

In addition to the general hierarchy of Chinese women in sex-related industries, there is an internal hierarchy among Chinese karaoke bar hostesses who

serve Taiwanese businessmen. Age is a common reference in defining the desir-
ability of a hostess by Taiwanese businessmen. Many Taiwanese businessmen
told me that women over 25 years old were considered "too old" for this business. This corresponded to my observations that the majority of hostesses were
between 18 and 25 years old. Regional background of hostesses is closely associated with the popularity of particular types of physical characteristics. Women
from northeastern provinces of China are very popular among Taiwanese businessmen because of their fair skin and tall figures. As a Taiwanese businessman
in Xiamen told me, "I like northeastern girls. Their skin is so fair, tender, and
soft to touch; just like cotton. They are also tall; with long legs..." This businessman sounded like he was talking about a specific commodity. Similarly,
women from the inland province of Sichuan are also well liked because of their
fair skin. Shanghai women get special attention from Taiwanese businessmen
because of Shanghai's superior position in China's "spatial hierarchy" (Perkins
2008) and its associations with the "modern," "international," and "cosmopolitan." Their high status among Taiwanese businessmen is reflected in the ways
in which they are constructed by these men as "elegant," "confident," "calcula-
tive," and "difficult to 'get.'" In addition to the physical, regional criteria, a
skillful hostess who knows how to sing, drink, carry on conversations, and "open
up" herself by making sexual jokes and exposing her body to public view and
touch is on the top of welcome list.

This internal hierarchy of hostesses structured by Taiwanese businessmen, I
suggest, works as a guide for them to differentiate hostesses with various
regional, social backgrounds for the purposes of negotiating their sexual consumption of different hostess. It works as a template imposed upon hostesses to
model and to perform their body and manner into certain patterns in order to
survive and make it in this business. It also suggests that some hostesses have
more agency to get more clients and negotiate a better price for themselves when
they have more body capital and social skills even though there are standard
costs for consideration for various type of services the hostesses provide.

It is well documented that most karaoke hostesses in coastal Chinese SEZs
are not local in origin and are part of the "floating population" from rural interior
to relatively industrialized urban areas (Hershatter 1996; Perkins 2008; Zheng
2004). In hoping to gain better employment and life opportunities in the cities,
they are recruited into this business through two major channels. One is through
visits made by the Mamas and/or the "hen's heads" (male pimps) who go
directly to villages or cities to look for women. An article published by a popular
Taiwanese weekly magazine (*Taiwan Next Magazine Online*, August 30, 2001)
reported on a trip taken by a Chinese Mama, a former bar hostess herself then
working in a Shanghai karaoke bar frequented by Taiwanese businessmen, and a
male pimp to Dailien, a northeastern city, to recruit hostesses.[7] To satisfy her
customers' desire for fresh faces, this Mama travels outside of Shanghai every
three months to find a new source for hostesses. For this particular recruitment,
she contacted several local pimps about her intentions before leaving for Dailien.
Once she arrived there, she found many women attracted by these pimps already

waiting for her in a hotel room. When the reporter from *Taiwan Next Magazine* asked one of the pimps how he found these women, he responded: "I just put an ad for models in a local newspaper. Within a week, more than one hundred women, including students, factory workers, and office secretaries came. I only charged them a 100 RMB registration fee" (*Taiwan Next Magazine Online*, August 30, 2001). In the hotel room, these women lined up for this Mama to check out their faces, their figures, and their alcohol tolerance one by one. This Mama even grasped some of these women's busts to check out their sizes. At the end of this process, she selected only three women from more than fifty of them and advised them:

> Since you have decided to leave home to get into this business, you should open up yourself. The reason we leave home is to make more money. In addition to singing and dancing, you also must dare to do other things [with your clients] as well.
>
> (*Taiwan Next Magazine Online*, August 30, 2001)

Soon after they arrived in Shanghai, this Mama took these women out to purchase new clothes. The next day they started to work as hostesses in the bar.

The other main channel that many karaoke bar hostesses use to enter this business is through the introduction or persuasion of their acquaintances who have already worked in bars. For instance, a mistress of a Taiwanese businessman in Dongguan came with her older sister and her brother-in-law from Sichuan Province in 1992. Although her sister and her brother-in-law went back home after working there for more than three years, she decided to stay. For more than two years, she worked in a couple of Taiwanese- and Hong Kong-owned shoe factories, physically demanding jobs requiring repeated physical movements and a great deal of overtime. Later, through an introduction by a friend from the same hometown, she started to work as a waitress at a restaurant affiliated with a hotel. There, she got to know some women working in the entertainment industry. After working in the hotel for half a year, she changed jobs and became a hostess in a karaoke bar where she met a married Taiwanese businessman who later asked her to quit her job and become his mistress.[8] Like her, many karaoke hostesses in southeast coastal China first worked in factories or other service jobs before becoming hostesses. It is part of the process of changing jobs to seek better lives for themselves and families.

Hershatter (1996) argues that Chinese scholarship on emerging prostitution in the reform era tended to regard it as evidence of women's unequal status and to categorize prostitutes as victims. It overlooks prostitution "as work or as a phenomenon shaped in part by labor market condition..." (Hershatter 1996, 218). For migrant women, it is not easy to find good-paid jobs in urban settings. The tangible incentives offered by sex-related industries are major factors that tempt many women to enter and stay in the business in order to move up from the bottom of social, spatial hierarchy (Perkins 2008). For instance, there is a huge income disparity between factory and karaoke bar work, as exemplified by the fact that a migrant woman factory worker in Guangdong received an average monthly salary of several hundred to a couple thousand RMB in the last two decades, while, according to my research, a karaoke hostess could make several hundred RMB or more in tips from serving a client. Although not all karaoke bar hostesses contract for sex, many of these karaoke bar hostesses do provide sex services, earning another several hundred to a couple thousand RMB depending on the type and length of services (one time or staying overnight) they provide before sharing her tips with her Mama (also see Zheng 2004 for the allure of high incomes for working as hostesses in Dalian and see Perkins 2008 for arguing that sex work is the quickest route for rural-to-urban migrant women to move up in the social hierarchy in China). Schell (1994, 334) finds that a common expression among Chinese women working in the entertainment industry is the following: "entertaining just one customer brings more than half a year's salary."

A hostess I met one night in a karaoke bar in Dongguan in 1999 was a college graduate from a northeastern city. Compared to the majority of karaoke hostesses who tend to be junior high or high school graduates, her education level was much higher than her colleagues in the bar. She also fit into the image of the tall, fair skinned northeastern girls. She previously worked for a state enterprise with a monthly salary of 800 RMB. After she found out that her Chinese boyfriend cheated on her with a karaoke hostess, she was angry and decided to come south to look for different opportunities. Although she initially decided to work as a hostess because she wanted revenge on her boyfriend[9] and to hurt his feelings, she stayed in the business because of the high pay, using her appearance and her higher educational level as an advantage to negotiate with her clients. According to her, she made 180 RMB for one night's service in the bar, after she gave 20 RMB to her Mama. She usually went out with her clients for sexual transactions two to three times per week, receiving each time from her clients 1,000 RMB. She told me that, on average, she made 20,000 RMB in a month.[10]

In general, because of their disadvantaged social backgrounds, the relatively inexpensive cost of their services, and the rather large number of them in the sex-related industry, Chinese women working in the sex industry particularly and with limited economic and cultural capital generally tend to be seen as cheap, easy to get, and hungry for material gains from their intimate relations with men in Taiwanese businessmen's discursive description (Shen 2003). This negative construction of Chinese women reinforces Taiwanese businessmen's sense of normality of sexual clubbing and existing hierarchies organized by the differences based on gender, class, and nationality in the work and organization of karaoke hostess bar businesses.

Finally, Taiwanese businessmen are the consumers who make karaoke bars profitable. Most of them are married and middle aged, between 30 and 60 years of age. They were either owners or expatriate managers of Taiwanese companies and had worked in China from several months to more than two decades when I met them between 1999 and 2012. For those whose families were in Taiwan, they only got to visit their wives and children one week or so every two to three months, according to the policy of their Taiwanese companies. Generally free from family obligations, they arranged for their own leisure pleasure during their off-work time. A Taiwanese manager in Shenzhen mentioned his leisure activities during the weekends before his wife came from Taiwan to join him several months before I met him in 2000:

> Prior to my wife's relocation here, the phone in my office would ring nonstop [every Saturday afternoon].[11] My Taiwanese friends were calling me and asking: "Hey, where should we go to 'play' this time?" Every time, I just needed to go to the place where they wanted me to meet them and get into the car. The whole weekend's activities from Saturday evening to Sunday midnight were all arranged.

The "play" mentioned here usually refers to visits to hostess bars and/or to resorts with their male colleagues and friends in the company of bar hostesses. For many Taiwanese businessmen, particularly the owners of small and medium-sized companies and the marketing and sales managers, visiting karaoke bars was defended as a necessity for expanding and strengthening their business networks, something that they did in Taiwan and that they now did on a much more frequent and liberated basis in China. According to a now Taiwanese businessman and former high-ranking personnel in the shoe industry, he used to frequent karaoke hostess bars with his business associates almost every workday when he was working in Taiwan from the 1970s to the early 1990s and continued to do so to the mid-2000s after he relocated his work to China from the early 1990s.

From my fieldwork in the last few years, I have found that the practice of frequenting karaoke hostess bars among Taiwanese businessmen has declined significantly since the mid to late 2000s due to the rising cost of business operations and to the decline of Taiwanese business competition in China. Nevertheless, karaoke hostess bars have been practiced by Taiwanese business personnel as "platforms" for them to meet and get acquainted with each other. "We meet, drink, and talk with the help of alcohol and women. We feel relax, we chat, and the distance between us is shortened," a Taiwanese marketing professional told me during my 2012 fieldwork in Xiamen. Some of my interviewees made similar comments that "if we can show the most relaxing and even ugly part of ourselves [meaning the flirtation and intimate acts with hostesses] in front of each other, we have a basic understanding and trust to work together." The acquaintance and some sort of trust they gain from meet-ups at hostess bars can be beneficial to their business negotiations if their products or proposed business projects are competitive with others. As this marketing professional above described:

> If I got to know a businessman at karaoke bars before, it is easier for me to approach to him the next time when we are talking about business at table. Or at least I will know something about his personality after drinking together at bars and know how to talk or approach to him.

A Taiwanese business owner of a small-sized firm made a similar observation in a 2012 interview in Dongguan:

> People become relaxing after drink and you get to a chance to learn about their personalities. If someone is a person who likes money, next time if you have opportunity to do business with him, you can offer him money. If he likes women, you can treat him to hostess bars.... Relaxing at karaoke bars together also makes easier for negotiating some business deals or proposals which normally wouldn't have been discussed at formal business settings to take place. For instance, at that kind of setting someone can make some kind of business bribery look casual...

What is discussed above is the common justification by Taiwanese businessmen to frame their practices of frequenting karaoke hostess bars. Although one cannot totally deny the potential business implications of frequenting karaoke hostess bars for Taiwanese businessmen, it is certainly just part of the reasons for this type of clubbing as evidenced from some Taiwanese operations which do not use clubbing to expand business networks but still have good business outcomes. According to my research, for many other Taiwanese men, frequenting karaoke bars is a new thing. It was much cheaper and more affordable to visit karaoke hostess bars in China than in Taiwan particularly for low-ranking business personnel. China also provided more freedom because many of their families were not around and, since they were outsiders, the social policing they would encounter in Taiwan was less intensive. It was about being lonely away from home and physical needs. Finally, because it was very difficult to resist peer pressure, it was often easier to go along with their male Taiwanese colleagues and friends (please see Shen 2008a for discussions on the justifications of Taiwanese businessmen's sexual clubbing in China).

The way Taiwanese businessmen go about their masculine play in karaoke bars is also organized by their social status as shown by Clifford Geertz (1973) on his study of cockfights in Bali. The karaoke hostess bars I have described in this chapter are frequented by the low- to middle-ranged Taiwanese business owners and managers in China. Among them, the differences on how they club lay less on the type of Chinese hostesses they are associated with, but more on the frequency and the degree of flexibility of clubbing. The cost for an individual trip to the type of karaoke hostess bars described in this study is affordable in relation to most of Taiwanese men's financial capacity. But to be able to club and take women out frequently requires a certain degree of flexibility in terms of time and financial condition. I have found that male owners of small-sized firms are more likely to be the regular consumers of karaoke hostess bars because their firms are less structured and they have more financial capacity and control over their own time to do so. They are also more likely to be the ones who develop "keeping mistress" relations with Chinese women through clubbing. Businessmen working in marketing or sales positions are another group of Taiwanese men who visit karaoke hostess bars frequently because their works often require them to entertain their business associates in such settings. Well-established Taiwanese business owners and personnel in China, according to my study, do not normally socialize in the same circle of entertainment activities with people who are their subordinates from their firms and who are from smaller firms. As clubbing is a form of social networking, it makes sense that well-established businessmen tend to socialize with businessmen sharing similar economic and social status. In order to protect their professional and private image and reputation, the higher status the Taiwanese businessmen are, the more private their clubbing activities will be. Luxury private clubs are one of those places where those men socialize and entertain each other.

The routine – the first part of the night

When I asked Taiwanese businessmen why they frequented karaoke hostess bars, they usually responded in the following ways: "It is part of our job. Only in that kind of atmosphere can we make better connections with our clients and our business deals are much easier to settle after spending time together in karaoke hostess bars" or "I work very hard. Going to karaoke bars is a way to reward myself for my hard work" or "I feel lonely and there is nothing I can do here during my free time in this kind of economic zone and that is what we do here." Taiwanese businessmen go to karaoke bars to have fun, to reward themselves for their hard work, to make business connections, to cultivate their male friendships, to act as good members of their male peer groups, to seek sexual adventures, and to display their superior gender and transnational class status (Shen 2008a). To satisfy this type of male entertainment and association, they seek the emotional and physical services provided by another group of women, in this case, Chinese women. What Taiwanese businessmen do in karaoke bars is often based on certain routines aimed at the creation of a relaxing, fun, and sexual atmosphere.

Taiwanese businessmen visit karaoke bars in groups ranging from a few individuals to a couple of dozen. In each group, one or more of them, usually the ones who are business owners, marketing or sales managers, or high ranking, senior personnel, act as the leaders of the group. These individuals are the ones either initiating these activities in their companies to entertain their business associates and colleagues or acting as "big brothers" to the Taiwanese in China. I call them "karaoke hostess bar old hands" to refer to their leading roles in initiating and smoothing out nightlife activities for many Taiwanese businessmen in China. Many of these types make several visits to karaoke bars per week. Once when I was staying in a Taiwanese firm in Dongguan for about eight days its marketing manager and his colleagues entertained their business associates in karaoke bars on six of the nights.

When Taiwanese businessmen and their guests arrive at a karaoke bar, they are greeted by a Mama who will quickly approach the leaders of the group, address them warmly by their business titles and welcome their arrival by telling them how nice it is to see them again or how much she has missed them to imply that they should come to see her more often. She quickly leads the group to a private room and asks what they would like to drink or eat, and how many host-esses they would like to have. In general, each male customer will order one hostess to serve him. The Mama then brings a number of hostesses from the waiting room and lines them up for the customers to choose. She will continue to bring more women into the room until all of the customers are happy with their hostesses. On one occasion in Dongguan, I was with a group of Taiwanese businessmen in a karaoke bar where they were entertaining a Chinese buyer who worked for an American company in Shenzhen. Unsatisfied with all the women presented by the Mama, this Chinese man went directly to the waiting room and brought a hostess of his choice back to the room with him.

Contrary to the conventional assumption that these Taiwanese karaoke hostess bar goers would prefer to "try" different hostesses each time, many Tai-wanese businessmen to whom I talked tend to go back to a couple of familiar bars and many of them like to have some sort of "familiarity" in their associ-ations with hostesses, although now and then they still desire fresh faces. As a manager in Dongguan put it, "it takes too much work to introduce myself to a new hostess and to get to know her from zero each time I make a visit to a bar." Another manager in Dongguan who used to visit karaoke bars once per week said that "even to do that thing [having sex], it still needs some level of mutual understanding [between a client and his hostess]," implying that he often took the same hostesses out from bars for overnights. Accordingly, before Taiwanese businessmen go to visit a bar, some of them, usually the old hand type, may call the hostesses they like and ask them to reserve the night for them. They may also call the Mamas to pre-arrange some hostesses for their guests. Furthermore, Mamas and hostesses call their customers frequently, in the words of the Mama I interviewed in Dongguan, "to connect with our customers and to make sure that they come back to visit us soon." That is an efficient way for them to solicit customers. When I hung out with Taiwanese businessmen in the evenings or on weekends in China particularly before 2005, I witnessed many of them, espe-cially the old hand type, getting phone calls from Mamas or hostesses. Tempted by these phone calls, some would call other Taiwanese businessmen to set up times and places for their night's activities. Once a Mama or a hostess has good connections with these old hands, they are certain that these men will bring more business to them. In this way, these businessmen are crucial in introducing new customers to karaoke hostess bars and in developing the culture associated with it in Taiwanese business communities in China.

For Taiwanese businessmen so inclined, nightlife in Chinese SEZs starts long before the sun sets. A Taiwanese business owner who returned to Taiwan after six years in Xiamen told me:

> I miss my life on the mainland.... My days then and there were very color-ful; now my life here in Taiwan is just like black and white. When I was on the mainland, every day after three or four clock in the afternoon, I would get many phone calls from *xiao jie* and be invited to go for the dinner first and then go for drinks at the bars they work later...

The "colorful" nightlife starts to heat up when food, drinks, and hostesses are all available in the room. A round of toasts with beer or wine is a typical way to greet each other in the room.[12] For those customers who already know their hostesses, they quickly team up, select songs that they want to sing, and flirt verbally and physically with each other. For those who are served by unfamiliar hostesses, they initiate small talk and tell jokes to break the ice. Games are usually introduced at this early stage of the nightlife to encourage interactions, enliven the atmosphere, and create excitement. In my experience losers had to down a drink or sing a song; according to some stories, however, losers often had to remove some of their clothing or expose themselves to physical touching.

Similar to Allison's (1994) findings on Japanese bar hostesses, experienced Chinese hostesses should know how to involve themselves in these games and to tend constantly to their clients' needs – refilling their drinks,[13] feeding them food, keying songs into the stereo system for them to sing, and stroking their egos through conversation and humor. According to my observation, some hostesses are good at praising their clients on their social status, their looks, and their personality. They sometimes act as "the sweet girlfriend" to their returning clients – holding their hands, sitting on their laps, listening to them, telling them how much they miss them in their absence, and so on.

Unlike the professionally trained Japanese bar hostesses in an upscale bar studied by Allison (1994), many Chinese karaoke bar hostesses are migrant women who are new and inexperienced, lacking professional training before they start to work. They tend to dress more causally than the experienced ones and are more likely to be rigid in their body language. As a result, some of them look quite "innocent and shy" and, ironically, they become some of the Taiwanese businessmen's favorites because they are perceived as "purer" and "simpler" than those experienced hostesses are. In this situation the men are more likely to act as the "protectors" of these hostesses and to appear tenderer in their body language toward them. While they may appear as loving boyfriends, they are really showing the earnestness which older men often demonstrate towards the protection of younger women.

Sexual favors for their clients are very central to the role of being a hostess in the bars I visited. There, I witnessed many Taiwanese businessmen holding their hostesses tight beside them, their hands now and then wandering around their hostesses' arms, busts, butts, or legs, usually in "quiet" and "gentle" ways. On the dance floor, there were more intimate bodily touches. It is reasonable to suggest that the verbal and physical interactions between Taiwanese businessmen and their hostesses would be more "open" than what I observed when no outsiders (including me) were present.

Karaoke bars are created, artificial spaces where heterosexual men's romantic and sexual desires are meant to be fulfilled temporarily by monetary deals. If a hostess does not provide the services she is expected to give, her customer can express his dissatisfaction quite directly. On one occasion, in a karaoke bar in Kunshan, I observed a hostess who was sent out of the room by a Taiwanese businessman because she was in a bad mood and did not make any effort to please him. This businessman then ordered another hostess to serve him.

Regardless of their intentions upon entering a hostess bar with a group, Taiwanese businessmen find it difficult to resist the peer pressure. For example, a young single Taiwanese manager in his early thirties in Dongguan told me that he did not like the idea of a hostess serving him and flirting with him when he visited karaoke bars. He decided, on one occasion, not to have a hostess when he went with his Taiwanese male colleagues to visit a karaoke bar. He soon recognized the consequences of his decision. According to him:

> All my co-workers were too busy hanging out with their hostesses to talk to me. I was sitting there alone and feeling very strange. A half-hour later, I asked the Mama to send a girl to me. In this type of place, if you do not play the same game as other men do, you feel the pressure.

According to my interviewees, Friday and Saturday nights[14] were the busiest nights for karaoke bar business; Sunday was the day when Taiwanese businessmen hung out together with karaoke hostesses outside the bars, either in their dormitories, in nearby commercial districts, or in tourist resorts. Monday nights were also very busy because those Taiwanese businessmen who had wives with them in China and who were, therefore, unable to get out of their houses during the weekends, could use business needs as an excuse to go home late when they were in fact visiting bars.

In general, the eating, drinking, singing, game-playing, and flirting in karaoke bars usually lasts for a few hours. While these activities provide entertainment, they also serve as "the foreplay" for "the second half" of the night, a phrase Taiwanese businessmen use to refer to the sexual activities afterwards. If at the end of the clubbing, the clients like their hostesses, they may ask them for sex in hotels, in their own places, or in rooms provided for their customers by some karaoke bars elsewhere in the same buildings.

The second part of the night

In contemporary China, hostess bars have become one of the key settings where commercialization/sexualization of leisure is at work and where "common prostitution" is widely marketed to satisfy the needs of both Chinese and foreign men. It is also in these places where many Chinese women directly participate in the global economy by putting their bodies to work in the "night market" (Bishop and Robinson 1998). Taiwanese businessmen are important agents in expanding mass sexuality in contemporary Chinese society by investing in this business and by acting as its consumers.

An owner of a beauty supply factory in Xiamen in 2001 told me that, after a night's drinking in a karaoke bar, he often asked his hostess if she would like to "have a cup of tea" with him later. If she said yes, he would take her back to his factory and negotiate a price for her stay overnight. He told me that he was "an old hand" in this kind of deal and could easily negotiate a good price, around 800 RMB then. Once on a Saturday night in Dongguan in 1999, I went to a hostess bar with a group of four Taiwanese businessmen and the Taiwanese wife of one of these men. Four hours later, after we called it a night, I saw one of these men leave the bar with his hostess. A company driver came to pick up the rest of us. As we entered the van, I noted that three other Taiwanese businessmen whom I did not know and their hostesses rode with us back to their places. On another occasion during a weekend in 2001, I visited a recreation farm owned by a Taiwanese and located just outside the Dongguan area. There I saw some Taiwanese businessmen in the company of Chinese women who came to stay overnight. The owner of this recreation farm confirmed that most of his customers were Taiwanese men working in the area[15] and most of them brought Chinese women along with them.

There are few examples of how Taiwanese businessmen process "the second part of the night." Because of the illegal status of prostitution in China, special arrangements are required at collective and institutional levels within Taiwanese business communities to avoid the legal risks associated with sexual transactions with Chinese women. Instead of going to hotels, many Taiwanese businessmen prefer to take hostesses to private places, such as their own or other Taiwanese dormitories or apartments, as indicated in the earlier story about the three Taiwanese businessmen and their hostesses riding with me in the same van. According to the conversation I overheard in the van, two of these men wanted the driver to let them off at their dormitories and the third opted for his friend's apartment. Based on my research, some Taiwanese companies openly or quietly allow their male Taiwanese employees to take women back to their dormitories because they do not want their employees to get into legal trouble in China.[16] Some Taiwanese wives living in the dormitories complained to me that they sometimes ran into "unknown" Chinese women there. A middle-ranking Taiwanese manager in a large Taiwanese firm in Shenzhen mentioned that some of his Taiwanese colleagues would arrange to share the same apartment units because they liked to take women back to their dormitories and they could do so with more freedom because they shared the same interest. He said that the Chinese housekeepers in their dormitory would be the ones who know best which Taiwanese businessmen bring women back to their rooms because they have to clean their rooms. These institutional and collective arrangements of consuming Chinese women's sexuality by Taiwanese firms and business communities are direct evidences showing that transnational Taiwanese capitalism is masculinized.

Taiwanese businessmen help each other at an individual level as well. During my research in Xiamen, I stayed a good portion of my time there in a room over a Taiwanese businessman's home near his factory. Once during a conversation with his Chinese secretary, she told me that the bedroom in which I stayed was a guest room that her boss reserved for the overnight stays of his Taiwanese male friends and their Chinese women guests. The owners or high-ranking managers of small firms are more likely to make such arrangements to cover their friends or colleagues because they directly hold the decision power and because there is relatively less negative bureaucratic concern in small firms.

Because karaoke bars are seen as entertainment or leisure settings by Taiwanese businessmen, they actually veil their sexual orientation and operation. During my extended stays in China, I never heard Taiwanese businessmen describing their practices in hostess bars or afterwards as "prostitution" or directly calling these hostesses "prostitutes" or "sex workers."

After nightlife

As a result of the preference of some Taiwanese businessmen for the same hostesses repeatedly or wanting to have a stable sexual and/or emotional partner while they are away from home, they establish romantic relationships. Consequently, some of them ask these women to quit their jobs and to become their "stay in lovers" in return for a living expense and a regular specified amount of money. They opt, in short, to turn these causal sexual affairs into some sort of stable relationships, either as temporary wives or long-term mistresses. For Chinese hostesses, the longevity of this type of work is relatively short and rough because of the strong age discrimination and potential health risks in this occupation. Becoming their clients' longer-term partner is one of the options that many hostesses take. For some of them, emotional attachment can gradually develop toward these men as their relationships last for an extensive period of time as I have found from my talks with Chinese women in the industry. In addition, as "kept" women, they will not have to take other sex customers, potentially reducing their chances of getting sexual diseases (Yu 2004).

During my stays in China, I witnessed or heard about many Taiwanese businessmen who were involved in these more stable or long-term relationships. In one case, a manager in Doungguan broke up with his Chinese girlfriend of a year and half shortly before I visited his firm in 2000 and returned to Taiwan in an attempt to smooth things out with his wife. In another case, the owner of the recreation farm in Dongguan mentioned earlier arranged for his girlfriend to return to her hometown in Sichuan after he suggested to her to quit her job as a bar hostess. He paid for her living expenses in her hometown and for her travel expenses to come to stay with him in the farm for a couple of weeks every two months or so. In yet another case, a farm owner living outside Dongguan had maintained a relationship with a Chinese woman since 1998. He did not keep much contact with his wife and children in Taiwan after they found out about his affair in China. Consequently, he did not even know until several months after the fact that his wife had died in a huge earthquake in the central part of Taiwan in September 1999. When I re-visited them in the early part of 2005, he and his girlfriend were thinking about getting married. The Mama in Dongguan mentioned earlier in the chapter told me that, during her more than three-year career as a Mama, she had seen approximately two hundred hostesses who later became mistresses. Many of these relationships, according to her, only lasted for several months. A few of them, however, became long-term relationships after these men either divorced their wives or decided to keep two families.

Conclusion

By exploring Taiwanese businessmen's sexual play in China, this chapter shows that the operation of Taiwanese capital and the formation of expatriate Taiwanese business communities and their transnational capitalist class status in China are highly gendered and sexualized. Typical karaoke hostess bars in coastal Chinese SEZs are intended to provide entertainment and sexual services to male customers, including the many foreign businessmen working and living there. They are commercial social spaces where men's sexual and emotional needs and fantasies are well attended to, where women are often reduced to sexual beings to satisfy men's needs and their works are invisible, where the close relations between economic production and masculine play are unrecognized, and where the organization and hierarchical relations that are taken to promote the business are overlooked. What is visible is men's pleasure and women's sexuality.

What I have shown in the chapter is that karaoke hostess bars frequented by many Taiwanese businessmen in China are highly organized enterprises in which space is carefully designed to provide privacy and comfortable socialization, women as Mamas or bar hostesses whose labor is measured by their appearance, social skills, and cultural capital, and time is divided into different sections to stimulate the atmosphere and pleasure. Taiwanese businessmen mainly as consumers and some of them also as producers of the industry collectively understand that visiting hostess bars is a great masculine pleasure and business making that they enjoy and use to facilitate their male bonding, to extend their business networks, and to build their expatriate communities in China. They do this together through certain routines of "play" in and after hostess bars, they protect each other from the consequences of these activities, and they utilize subtle means to repress inside their communities other types of masculinity that disapprove of these practices. What appears to be "play" is in fact involved with lots of organization, work, hierarchies, and profit-making.

The popularity of karaoke hostess bars among Taiwanese businessmen and other men indicates that the sexual culture of common prostitution in China is highly leisurialized, commercialized, and masculine-oriented. Chinese women's bodies and sexuality are commodified and become important parts of Chinese economy. Nightlife in karaoke hostess bars and other similar places are key sites where commercialized sexual and emotional relations are established by many foreign men with local women in China. These bars are public spaces where commodified transnational intimate frontiers are occupied by many Chinese women today. Transnational hierarchical relations among gender, ethnicity/nationality, and/or class are created and reinforced. Pleasure and power relations inside karaoke hostess bars disclose that nightlife is never merely about social life at bars or at nights. It is about social, power relations at international, national, and individual levels. Cross-Strait economic exchanges by night or China by night indeed is another way to tell stories and to analyze events about complex social and power relations formed and negotiated through Taiwan's economic exchanges with China and in different corners of China.

Notes

1 Through the leadership of Premier Deng Xiaoping, China introduced economic reforms in 1978 and established numerous Special Economic Zones, first along its coastline and later inland, to attract investments. With its abundant cheap labor and a potentially huge domestic market, it has become one of the most favored countries in the world for receiving foreign direct investment and its coastal SEZs are where huge numbers of foreign investors and professionals locate. Since the last National People's Congress (NPC), these special zones have been abolished ... or at least some special rights there have ended, like the tax breaks.

2 As the entertainment and sex industry have become more established in China, local Chinese have also put more economic and human resources into the business. As a result, the importance of Taiwanese capital and managerial experiences in the industry has declined.

3 Hokkien, also called Taiwanese, and conventionally referred to as the language of Taiwan is often used by Taiwanese business people to express their Taiwanese origin among themselves in China. However, Hokkien as a common indicator of Taiwanese identity in China does not automatically apply in Taiwan's context because internal ethnic politics rather than being Taiwanese/Chinese is the primary factor of division among people.

4 The cultural and linguistic affiliation between Taiwanese and Chinese certainly plays a very significant role in facilitating interactions between Taiwanese businessmen and Chinese women.

5 Unlike in Taiwan, *xiao jie* or miss is a very common title to refer to women; because this term is used to refer to the women working in the entertainment/sex industry in China, it is considered to be disrespectful to use this term to refer to Chinese women.

6 According to a newspaper report in 2003, in some karaoke hostess bars in Shanghai hostesses had to pay 20–50 RMB to bar owners. Please see *China Times Weekly* (May, 2003, Vol. 1315. Internet version at http://forums.Chinatimes.com.tw/ctw/main/index.htm).

7 "Selling Women by NT 2000,000," from the online version of *Taiwan Next Magazine* (August 30, 2001, Vol. 14 at http://twnext.atnext.com/template/twnext/art_main.cfm).

8 Their relationship lasted for more than five years. When I re-visited them in January 2005, I heard that they separated at the end of 2003 and that this woman had married a Chinese man in her hometown two months earlier.

9 According to a popular Chinese book (Yu 2004) on the life experiences of Hong Kong men's Chinese mistresses in Shenzhen, their previous experience of being abused and betrayed in their intimate relationships with men, indeed, is a quite common factor behind many Chinese women's decision to get into the entertainment and sex industry. These women distrust love relationships and treat them as monetary deals.

10 Some Chinese hostesses do make and save money and find alternatives for their life. Some others get lost in the cycle of moving in and out between bars and men's places. Nevertheless, it is no doubt that sex-related industry and women, including those ones working at karaoke hostess bars in the industry, have contributed greatly to Chinese economic development.

11 Many Taiwanese factories I visited in coastal China, except in Shanghai, only had Sundays off because they did not really follow the five working days labor regulation.

12 When I visited karaoke bars with Taiwanese men in China, red wine mixed with soda was a popular drink for them. According to the former president of a big Taiwanese entrepreneurial association in Southern China and to other Taiwanese businessmen, Taiwanese business communities in China were promoting "mild" red wine instead of the strong Chinese alcohol among their members because there were cases where Taiwanese businessmen collapsed or died from this strong alcohol. This intervention

shows the magnitude of the problem with the drinking culture in Taiwanese business communities in China.

13 Encouraging their clients to drink is an important part of their business relationship with their Mamas and the bars in which these hostesses work. A Mama has to sell a certain quota of alcohol in order to secure her basic salary and a bar's major income comes from the sale of alcohol.

14 For instance, in Shanghai, the busiest night would be Friday night because most of the Taiwanese companies follow the five working days regulation. In the Guangdong and Xiamen areas, it is Saturday nights because most Taiwanese companies have a six working days policy for their Taiwanese employees.

15 Another source of his customers was Taiwanese male sexual tourists who usually stayed on his farm for several days to a week or so. They either went to karaoke bars directly for women to bring back to their rooms on his farm or they asked him to find the women for them.

16 This treatment is more likely to be given by smaller sized-firms because their management style is less formal. However, during my research, I found that it also happened in large Taiwanese firms.

References

Allison, Anne. 1994. *Night Work: Sexuality, Pleasure, and Corporate Masculinity in Tokyo Hostess Club*. Chicago: The University of Chicago.

Bishop, Ryan, and Lillian S. Robinson. 1998. *Night Market: Sexual Cultures and the Thai Economic Miracle*. New York and London: Routledge.

Chiu, Chang, and Tsuei-fen Lin. 1994. *Ikuo Liangchi: liangan fenin paipishu* (One Country, Two Wives: The Bluebook of Intermarriages across the Taiwan Strait). Taipei: Chin-Mei Press.

Connell, R. W. 2000. *The Men and the Boys*. Berkeley and Los Angeles: University of California Press.

Enloe, Cythia, 1989. *Bananas, Beaches, & Bases: Making Feminist Sense of International Politics*. Berkeley, CA: University of California Press.

Farrer, James. 2011. "Global Nightscapes in Shanghai as Ethnosexual Contact Zones." *Journal of Ethnic and Migration Studies* 37 (5): 747–764.

Geertz, Clifford. 1973. *The Interpretation of Cultures*. New York: Basic Books Classics.

Henriot, Christian. 2001. *Prostitution and Sexuality in Shanghai: A Social History, 1849–1949*. Cambridge, UK: Cambridge University Press.

Hershatter, Gail. 1996. "Chinese Sex Workers in Reform Period." In *Putting Class in Its Place: Worker Identities in East Asia*, edited by Perry Elizabeth, 199–224. Berkeley, CA: Institute of East Asian Studies, University of California.

Hershatter, Gail. 1999. *Dangerous Pleasures: Prostitution and Modernity in Twentieth-century Shanghai*. Berkeley, CA: University of California Press.

Hwang, Shu-Ling. 2003. "Taiwan's Flower Drinking Culture." *Taiwanese Sociology* 5: 73–132.

Jeffreys, Elaine. 2004. *China, Sex and Prostitution*. London and New York: Routledge-Curzon.

Klein, Naomi. 2000. *No Logo*. New York: Picador USA.

Lee, Ya. 2001. *Dalu de unro yixiang* (Mainland China as a Tender Strange Land). Taipei: Fu-Kuo International Publishing Co. Ltd.

Liu, C. Y. 2004. *Taishang dalu chenlun jish* (The Documentation of Taiwanese Business People's Indulgence in China). Taipei: Stardoms Publishing Co. Ltd.

Pan, Suiming. 2004. "Three 'Red Light Districts' in China." In *Sexual Cultures in East Asia: The Social Construction of Sexuality and Sexual Risk in a Time of AIDS*, edited by Evelyne Micollier, 23–53. London and New York: RoutledgeCurzon.

Perkins, Tamara. 2008. "The Other Side of Nightlife: Family and Community in the Life of a Dance Hall Hostess." *China: An International Journal* 6 (1): 96–120.

Schell, Orville. 1994. *Mandate of Heaven: A New Generation of Entrepreneurs, Dissidents, Bohemians, and Technocrats Lay Claims to China's Future*. New York: Simon & Schuster.

Shen, Hsiu-hua. 2003. "Crossing the Taiwan Strait: Global Disjunctures and Multiple Hegemonies of Class, Politics, Gender, and Sexuality." Ph.D. dissertation, University of Kansas.

Shen, Hsiu-hua. 2005. "'The First Taiwanese Wives' and 'the Chinese Mistresses': The International Division of Labour in Familial and Intimate Relations across the Taiwan Strait." *Global Networks* 5 (4): 419–437.

Shen, Hsiu-hua. 2008a. "The Purchase of Transnational Intimacy: Women's Bodies, Transnational Masculine Privileges in Chinese Economic Zones." *Asian Studies Review* 32: 57–75.

Shen, Hsiu-hua. 2008b. "Becoming 'the First Wives': Gender, Intimacy, and Regional Economy between Taiwan and China." In *East Asian Sexualities: Modernity, Gender and New Sexual Cultures*, edited by Stevi Jackson, Liu Jieyu, and Woo Juhyun, 216–235. London: Zed Books.

Shen, Hsiu-hua. 2014. "Staying in Marriage across the Taiwan Strait: Gender, Migration, and Transnational Family." In *Wives, Husbands, and Lovers: Marriage and Sexuality in Hong Kong, Taiwan, and Urban China*, edited by Deborah S. Davis and Sara L. Friedman. Stanford, CA: Stanford University Press.

Shih, Shu-mei. 1998. "Gender and a New Geopolitics of Desire: The Seduction of Mainland Women in Taiwan and Hong Kong Media." *Sign: Journal of Women in Culture and Society* 23 (2): 287–319.

Sklair, Leslie. 2001. *The Transnational Capitalist Class*. Oxford, UK: Blackwell.

Xiao, Suowei. 2011. "The 'Second Wife' Phenomenon and the Relational Construction of Class-coded Masculinities in Contemporary China." *Men and Masculinities* 14: 607–627.

Yu, Qiao. 2004. *Ko Hun* (Painful Marriages). Beijing, China: Zuo Jia Publishing.

Zheng, Tiantian. 2004. "From Peasant Women to Bar Hostesses: Gender and Modernity in Post-Mao Dalian." In *On the Move: Women and Rural-to-Urban Migration in Contemporary China*, edited by Arianne Gaetano and Tamara Jacka, 80–108. New York: Columbia University Press.

Zheng, Tiantian. 2006. "Cool Masculinity: Male Clients' Sex Consumption and Business Alliance in Urban China's Sex Industry." *Journal of Contemporary China* 15 (46): 161–182.

10 Class, gender and globalized intimacy
The second-wife phenomenon in Greater China

Suowei Xiao

Introduction

China's market reforms and opening up to foreign direct investment in the early 1980s embraced the arrival of a large number of Hong Kong and Taiwanese businessmen who took advantage of the cheap labor and huge domestic market in the mainland. As they engaged in economic activities, building factories and expanding business, they also developed extramarital relationships with Chinese women, creating a phenomenon referred to in Cantonese as "keeping a second wife" (*baao yilai*). *Yilai* was originally a vulgarism in the greater Canton Area (including Hong Kong) to refer to concubines. Since the early 1990s, the term "*baao yilai*" has been widely used in Guangdong and Hong Kong to include second households created by Hong Kong and Taiwanese businessmen in mainland China. The term has also been picked up in non-Cantonese speaking regions in China (pronounced *bao ernai* in Mandarin) to refer to a long-term arrangement between a married man and an economically dependent woman, often living in a house provided by the man.[1]

The contemporary phenomenon of "keeping a second wife" first became known in the Pearl River Delta of Guangdong Province, a region that took advantage of the earliest market reforms, absorbing a large share of foreign investment. In the ensuing decades, the geography of the phenomenon has extended to many coastal areas and major cities in China (Tam 2001). The demographic of men who keep second wives has expanded to include professionals from Hong Kong and Taiwan, salaried workers and container truck drivers who work regularly in mainland China (Shen 2005; Tam 1996, 2001, 2005; Tu 2004). Mainland Chinese men have also adopted this practice in recent years. The composition of second wives has also expanded to include rural women who migrated to economically developed regions for job opportunities and urban women with higher educational and economic status (Xiao 2011).

Marriage in Hong Kong, Taiwan and mainland China is defined as free-choice monogamy in the law, prohibiting a married person from cohabiting with a third party. Thus, the second-wife practice is neither legally nor socially sanctioned for the most part. However, in practice there is a lot of room to maneuver, particularly for cross-border liaisons. In addition to the legal difficulty in determining the nature of intimate relationships,[2] a Hong Kong or Taiwanese man's extramarital affair in the mainland generally lies in the legal vacuum of the sovereignty of Hong Kong, Taiwan or mainland China.

Although there has not been an accurate calculation of the number of cases, some estimates are available. Maria Tam, an anthropologist based in Hong Kong, estimated that one out of six Hong Kong men who work in mainland China has set up a second household with a second wife or mistress (Tam 2001). Hong Kong legislative counselors and social workers have surmised that by 1995, about 300,000 Hong Kong men had established second households in different parts of China, approximately 5 percent of the entire Hong Kong population of six million (Shih 1998; Tam 1996). A more recent 2004 survey of Hong Kong truck drivers who regularly crossed the border to transport goods between Hong Kong and the mainland revealed that over 26 percent of the 193 men who responded to the questionnaire kept a mistress in mainland China (Tam et al. 2009). In Taiwan, a 1993 survey conducted by a private Taiwanese consulting company and sponsored by the Mainland Affairs Council in Taiwan reported that more than 70 percent of married Taiwanese male investors and managers in China had extramarital relationships with women in China (Chiu and Lin 1994).

Not all but (most possibly) a small portion of men in Greater China have pursued a second wife; the phenomenon has been seen as a major social problem in Hong Kong, Taiwan and the mainland. For instance, as early as in the mid-1990s, Hong Kong society noticed an outburst of public debate concerning the issue of Hong Kong men keeping second wives in the mainland. The cross-border affairs have been widely publicized and discussed in various venues of media coverage in Hong Kong and became an important theme of many talk show programs and soap operas. Newspapers were filled with editorials, letters to the editor, local stories and feature articles on this very topic (Shih 1998; So 2003; Tam 1996). In the mainland, before the latest revision of the marriage law in 2001, there was a big public debate on whether prohibiting "keeping a second wife" (*baoernai*) should be included in the law.[3]

Drawing upon a combination of in-depth interviews, ethnographic fieldwork, media reports and works of other scholars, in this chapter I take the arrangements of "keeping a second wife" by cross-border sojourners from Hong Kong and Taiwan as a microcosm of the reconfigurations of intimate economies under globalization and transnational migration.[4] I examine the ways in which socio-cultural forces of globalization have generated stratified windows of opportunities and constraints for individuals in diverse social positions to experience intimacy and illuminate how individuals capitalize cross-border intimacy in an attempt to achieve dignity, distinction, belonging and social mobility. Specifically, by delineating the differentiated meanings that keeping a second wife have taken on for business-class Taiwan or Hong Kong sojourners and working-class Hong Kong men who travel regularly across the border, I argue that class identities and distinctions are being constructed and negotiated through intimate relations and "sexualized masculine play" (Shen 2008) in a global context. I also discuss the varied ways migrant and local women enter and navigate these relationships. Rejecting the motif of local Chinese women as mere passive objects of male desire, I examine both the broader structural conditions that shape the range of choices available to women who become second wives and their strategies of negotiating life chances in response to the macro forces of globalization and the commercialization of women's bodies, sexuality and emotions. Ultimately, the analysis unpacks how class, migration and cross-border intimacy are intertwined in shaping the motivations, trajectories and strategies of men and women who engage in intimate relationships.

Globalization and the intimate economy

One of the consequences of global capitalism is the reshaping structure, including both the opportunities and the division of labor, in the realm of love, intimacy and care that pervades social life (Boris and Parrenas 2010; Shen 2005). Innovative scholarship has been conducted on the effects of global economic restructuring on the formal and informal labor markets as well as in private lives. This global capitalist operation is deeply gendered and classed. Male entrepreneurs and professionals from the First World sojourn in developing nations to make larger profit and exercise "increasingly libertarian sexuality" (Connell 1998), taking advantage of their "flexible citizenship" (Ong 1999). Working-class men in developed economies encounter job insecurity and pay cuts as a result of the outsourcing of production to the Third World nations, which jeopardize their chances in the local marriage market (So 2003). Poor Third World women provide cheap labor as factory workers or work as hostess and bar girls catering to the erotic desires of transnational elites in developing nations (Hoang 2011a; Pun 2005; Salzinger 2003; Shen 2008) and travel to developed nations to serve middle- and upper-class families as domestic workers, service workers and sex workers (Hochschild 2002; Lan 2006; Parrenas 2008). From a macro-structural perspective, business elites, predominantly male, are conventionally perceived as agents and winners of the global capitalist expansion while working-class men and Third World women become passive objects or victims of the global economic restructuring.

Scholars paying close attention to the everyday practices and understandings which develop in response to global movement suggest people in local spaces should not be viewed as the passive objects of globalization but as actors who both resist and participate in the processes of globalization (Hoang 2011a). Some studies have demonstrated that people in local spaces engage in acts of resisting and protesting global economic restructuring (Smith and Guarnizo 1998). Others illustrate how people capitalize on exploitative global linkages in order to improve their lives. For instance, sex workers in Dominican Republic feigned emotions of love and care to dupe their clients into providing money and visas to migrate abroad to improve their position in the new global economy (Brennan 2004). Similarly, Vietnamese women often used the country's position in the global economy to exaggerate their conditions of poverty, create crises and procure large remittances from their clients (Hoang 2011b). Although

disadvantaged in the local marriage market, lower-class men in wealthy countries and regions, such as the US, Europe, Hong Kong and Taiwan, mobilized
transnational family ties and patronized international matchmaking services to
find spouses in developing countries (Thai 2008).

This chapter contributes to the scholarship on the relationship among globalization, migration and intimate life in three aspects. First, it extends the notion
that the sexual consumption of women's bodies has been at the frontier of transnational business status and masculinity (Hoang 2011a; Shen 2008) and argues
that it is not simply through men's activities of consumption, but also through
women's various forms of labor – domestic, emotional and symbolic, that the
masculine display and class manifestation is accomplished.

Second, it reveals that while globalization opened up new possibilities for
individuals in multiple means, the range of choices available to men and women
in different class positions differ sharply. Accordingly, individuals enter into
seemingly similar intimate relationships with divergent motivations, trajectories
and strategies. As revealed in the analysis that follows, businessmen and
working-class men from Hong Kong and Taiwan demanded differentiated forms
of labor from their second wives with which to achieve distinctive senses of
masculinity. Similarly, while most modern urban Chinese women entered into
the second-wife relationship as a transitional strategy to elude downward social
mobility, migrant women were more likely to interpret the intimate liaison with
Taiwan and Hong Kong men as both a springboard to a better life and an emotional anchor in an urban space.

Third, I demonstrate that as global capitalist expansion transforms the class
structure to be extended beyond national boundaries, intimate relations have
become a key venue where symbolic and emotional boundaries of class are reart-
iculated and negotiated in a global context. Businessmen achieved and consolidated their status of "transnational super elites" via the ability to attract,
domesticate and "play with" young, pretty and desirable Chinese women.
Working-class men from Hong Kong converted their First World privileges to
enjoy a higher level of love, care and respect at their second homes in a Third
World nation, which in turn mediated their feelings of emasculation due to their
low-class positions in their home society.

In the following sections, I will illustrate the second-wife arrangements of
transnational businessmen and cross-border workers from Hong Kong and
Taiwan and the varying meanings these relationships convey to these men.
Although the rest of the chapter is organized around men from two different
classes, I emphasize women's labor in helping men achieve desirable gender and
class identities and interweave the experiences of both local urban and rural
migrant women in second-wife arrangements into the analysis.

Transnational business elites

China's economic reforms and the open-door policy initiated in the late 1970s
has greatly increased the flow of capital, goods and products between mainland

China and the rest of the world. Attracted by favorable economic policies, lured by the availability of a large quantity of cheap labor and facilitated by the cultural and linguistic alliance, hundreds of thousands of Hong Kong and Taiwanese investors, managers and professionals have ventured to China since the 1980s to build factories and expand business (Hsing 1998; Lang and Smart 2002). As early as in the mid 1990s, survey data revealed that 122,200 Hong Kong residents had worked in China during the previous 12 months with more than 60 percent being white collar and managerial workers (Siu 1999). In the case of Taiwan, according to the official data from the Chinese Ministry of Foreign Trade and Economic Cooperation throughout August 2007, the number of cumulative investment cases from Taiwan in China totaled 74,036 and the cumulative capital invested amounted to more than US$44.8 billion (Shen 2008). The majority of Hong Kong and Taiwanese business people are men, many of whom relocated to China while leaving their family behind and returning to visit them with varying frequency.

For many of these traveling businessmen, they take advantage not only of the preferable investment environment and output market in China, but also of the opportunity to become involved in extramarital affairs and sexual intimacy with local Chinese women. Visits to sexually oriented karaoke bars and commercial sexual engagements with Chinese women are part of regular social activities with male Taiwanese colleagues and other male business associates (Lee 2001; Liu 2001; Shen in this volume). Second households were also set up with Chinese women for longer-term extramarital relationships (Lang and Smart 2002; Shen 2005; Tam 2005; Tam et al. 2009). As Hiu-hua Shen (2005) argues, these transnational businessmen create an international division of labor in familial and intimate relations between Chinese women and wives at home as they participate in the international division of labor in production relations. As a result, women across the geographic border are separated in "we women" and "they women" who fit into contrasting and competing roles to fulfill the patriarchal constructs of transnational business masculinity (Connell 1998; Shen 2005; Tam 2005). Sexually charged venues such as hostess bars and Chinese women's bodies in Chinese SEZs (Special Economic Zones) become intimate frontiers where many Hong Kong and Taiwanese businessmen purchase intimacy to fulfill their sexual and emotional desires and comfort and to achieve transnational elite status (Shen 2008; So 2003).

While the consumption of women's bodies and sexuality is integrated into the transnational organization of capitalist operation, it is crucial to examine women's sexual and emotional "labor" in making the masculine "play" and capitalist expansion in transnational spaces. In other words, the construction and sustaining of the male labor force and transnational business elite identity depends largely on the labor of local Chinese women who served as hostesses, girlfriends, mistresses and second wives. In the following paragraphs, I demonstrate how cross-border businessmen achieve a sense of being an upwardly mobile transnational super elite through their second wives' various forms of labor in both private and public settings.

While sojourning in the mainland without families around, Hong Kong and Taiwanese businessmen and professionals were unable to enjoy the domestic care that was offered by their wives back home. To some extent, establishing a second household with a local Chinese woman caters to their loneliness and gives them a feeling of being at home in a foreign land. Although they may order commercial sexual domestic services, it feels different to have sexual intimacy with a "girlfriend" as well as having meals prepared, shirts cleaned and ironed by a family member. The form of payment and the means through which each service is delivered mark the emotional and symbolic meanings of particular services (Zelizer 2005). As revealed in Shen's (2008) research, Taiwanese businessmen and professionals justified their extramarital affairs and commercial sexual service by suggesting having "biological needs and emotional loneliness while away from home." Second-wives generally engage in varying degrees of domestic labor for their male elite partners. However, a large portion of second wives of transnational business elites do not personally perform a large amount of the domestic chores, partly due to the fact that business elites regularly have dinner with colleagues, clients and other business associates and tend to obtain paid domestic service for their second wives. The occasional domestic labor that second wives perform conveys to the business elites is more about these men's status and authority, as they can always count on their demands being fulfilled.

Lucy, a Guangzhou native, has been with a married Hong Kong architect for three years. She explained to me that her tactic to stay attractive to her boyfriend was to make him feel significant through small things. When he was with her, Lucy made him the center of her life. She would ask if he needed anything before going downstairs to buy his favorite snacks, even though she lived on the eighth floor of an apartment building with no elevator.

In order to enhance their men's status at home, second wives also engage in different forms of emotional management (Hochschild 1983), repressing or inducing feelings to present favorable facial or bodily expressions when interacting with their partner. Lucy reported that her boyfriend lost his temper quicker once their relationship had stabilized (though during the initial dating period before they cohabited, he tended to be well behaved). Because of her economic dependence, she does not feel as if she has the leverage to fight back. She said:

> I can hardly stand his bad temper. He shouts nasty words at me when he is mad at something. At those times, I will fight back if I have money, but if I am really broke, I have to hold my breath, keep myself silent, and swallow his words. It is really hard.

In addition to tolerance for ill treatment and suppressing anger, Lucy also engaged in various "expressive" forms of emotional display that workers' second wives do not normally perform. Often she had to forge an emotion to produce contentment in her lover. For example, one day the couple went shopping together. He picked out a coat for her, and insisted on the choice even though she preferred a different style. Lucy gave him a big smile, saying, "You're right. After a second look, I think this one is better."

Lucy consciously performed emotional labor to secure her position in a legally unprotected relationship. She had a long history of being financially supported by her fiancé and other male suitors before she entered into a second-wife relationship. Many of their female friends, relatives and acquaintances were also dependent on men economically; not necessarily as second wives, but also as legal wives and girlfriends. These women shared a local gender culture in which it was natural and even desirable for a woman to be financially supported by her man. Lucy stopped working when she met her first boyfriend at the age of 18. The couple planned to marry, but their five-year relationship ended when his business went bankrupt. With only a high-school education, Lucy was unable to sustain the lifestyle she used to enjoy which was crucial to constitute a cosmopolitan femininity, i.e., looking chic and having good taste, as well as to maintain good standing in her social circle, composed of young local women whom Lucy had known for years. Fashion, luxury brands, beauty tips and leisure activities were tokens to stake her claim and membership in the group. "If you knew nothing," Lucy said, "you wouldn't even be able to talk." After many unsuccessful attempts of finding unmarried men as new boyfriends, Lucy was introduced by her friend to a married Hong Kong architect who had a crush on her. "I do not like him," Lucy confessed to me, "but I need someone to take care of me [financially]." Stigmatized as the relationship might be, it sustained her lifestyle, secured her position in her social circle and shielded her from experiencing downward mobility.

Some second wives also stimulate emotions to produce satisfying conversations for their men. For example, Ah-Ying, second wife of a Hong Kong jewelry merchant in his sixties, regarded answering her boyfriend's phone calls as one of the most difficult tasks she had to handle in the relationship. She said,

> He often calls to tell me about his business, which I am not interested in at all. But I have to be the audience for his endless boring speech, pretending to listen attentively and commenting on things he mentions as if they are funny.

With attentive listening, appreciative laughter and comments of affirmation, Ah-Ying fed her boyfriend's emotional needs for communication and sharing, as well as projecting back to him a satisfying image of an interesting and charming man.

Ah-Ying came to Guangzhou to find job opportunities and to see the world outside of her hometown. As a matter of fact, she left her family in northwest China alone against her parents' will. Having survived in a number of jobs that were physically demanding and financially demeaning in different cities, she waitressed in a small night club in Guangzhou, where she caught the eyes of a married Hong Kong merchant. Before the relationship started, the old man (*laotou*, as Ah-Ying referred to him) brought her gifts ranging from expensive suits and watches to shampoo and toothpaste; took her to cafes and restaurants to enjoy chatting with her and watching her eating; and offered advice and touching words when she needed. She said

> Nobody has ever treated me so well. He did everything for me without asking me to pay back. It felt like as long as I was happy, he would be happy ... I was partly moved by his money, partly by his personality [*yiban bei ta de qian gandong le, yiban bei ta de ren gandong le*].

For his kindness, Ah-Ying was willing to make him happy. For the generous stipend (10,000 yuan a month, about US$1,400 in 2005) she received from him, she also felt obliged to do so.

Through various types of repressive and expressive emotional work, catering to male emotional needs and repressing their own, second wives of transnational businessmen seek to make the second household secure and pleasant. It is a place where the businessmen feel admired, respected and in charge of the relationship. They also constitute in businessmen the sense of having authority, power, good taste and charm. They are entitled to give orders and expect them to be completed. This entitlement is primarily endorsed by the large amount of money they give to the second wife. However, the material space and the concept of home that the arrangements have entailed reduce the appearance of a relationship as being based upon economic exchange.

Scholars have noted that the sexual and intimate consumption of Chinese women by cross-border business elites is not simply an individual activity, but has rather become a collective ritual to constitute transnational business status and masculinity (Shen 2008). The particular sexual consumption of women is seen as an expression and display of wealth, status and manliness associated with the establishment of an economic venture in an emerging economy. For instance, an investor in a small paint production factory in Dongguan documented in Hsiu-hua Shen's study (2008), said that "men have a tendency to self-promotion. When a Taiwanese businessman sees other Taiwanese men having affairs and he has nobody, he wants to find one for himself. He wants to compete" (p. 67). Another marketing manager of the electronics manufacturing plant in Shanghai suggested that "many owners of [small to medium-sized] Taiwanese firms often compete with each other on the numbers of mistresses they have and on whose mistresses are more beautiful" (p. 67). In this manner, Chinese women as mistresses become a platform for many of these privileged cross-border businessmen to perform their masculinity and to show their economic accomplishments and status in China.

The public face that a couple puts on in front of the man's friends is thus very important in sustaining the status of individual businessman. Ah-Ying's boyfriend was impotent and never succeeded in consummating their relationship during the year they were together. Ah-Ying asked him why he wanted to keep a girlfriend if he was unable to have sex. He stated that all of his friends had second wives, so why couldn't he? He longed to show others that he was a virile, charming, wealthy and successful man who was still attractive to young women, a public image that was ultimately more important than private sexual performance. To accomplish his goal, Ah-Ying accompanied the old man to the train station each time when he left for Hong Kong, where they generally encountered a number of his friends and acquaintances. Under their gaze, the couple kissed or hugged good-bye.

Many of the second wives of businessmen and entrepreneurs invest deliberate effort in keeping an attractive public face in order to maintain the man's honor and status. These women engage in extensive bodily labor (Lan 2003) to construct a positive public profile. Many of them change their appearance to fit their men's vision of a proper mate, something that varies according to age. Contrary to expectation, not every man necessarily wants his second wife to look young or entirely fashionable. For example, Ah-Ying was often required by her boyfriend to dress in expensive formal suits and dresses rather than cheap, fashionable clothes and to wear minimal make-up. In this manner she displayed her body in ways to appear more mature, so that others would not mistake the couple for grandfather and granddaughter. She also appeared more cultured, which was to hide her rural identity as well as more respectable so that she would not be mistaken as a prostitute. In contrast, for 26-year-old Lucy, looking young is her priority. She exhibited the latest fashions, wore heavy make-up and had even resorted to plastic surgery to reduce the signs of aging. In this way, she would remain physically attractive and earn face for her boyfriend.

Cross-border working-class men

Middle-class business elites are not the only group that travels across the border on a regular basis; working-class men from Hong Kong also participated in the cross-border relocation of employment and intimate relations. With its proximity to the Pearl River Delta Region and its highly efficient container terminals, Hong Kong acts as a major entrepôt for South China, and cross-border truck drivers serve as important links for these two regions. According to the Hong Kong Port Development Council, a total of 20.4 million 20-foot equivalent units of containers were handled in Hong Kong in 2003, 78 percent of which were container traffic related to South China. A survey conducted by the Hong Kong Department of Transport in 2003 shows that the total number of goods vehicle movements at the three cross-border check points at Man Kam To, Sha Tau Kok and Lok Ma Chau had reached 31,200 trips per day, among which 40 percent were container trucks (Wong et al. 2007). A 2004 cross-sectional survey of cross-border truck drivers revealed that among 193 respondents, over a quarter (26.1 percent) reported having a "second wife/girlfriend" in the mainland, while 17 percent reported having visited prostitutes in the last six months (Fung et al. 2009).

The intimate practices of taking a second wife, however, take on a different meaning for cross-border working-class men in comparison to business elites. Working in jobs with low income and prestige in Hong Kong society, blue-collar workers suffered from low self-esteem and emasculation. Workers' second wives engage in convenient, care-laden domestic work and emotional offerings of comfort and assurance for their partner, often within the confine of their private households. Through routine yet invisible, therapeutic and partially decommodified gender labor, they help produce, consolidate and enhance their men's sense of self-worth and dignity.

In general, working-class men's second wives perform a significantly larger amount of domestic labor and household chores while receiving less allowance from their partner compared to their counterparts coupled with businessmen. According to cases I've collected, none of the workers' second wives used commercial domestic services. Rather, they performed all the housework themselves. In general, they also received a much smaller stipend from their partners, varying from a couple hundred to no more than 5,000 RMB. As many truck drivers needed daily maintenance and visited commercial sex places as a "stress reliever" as they sojourned in the mainland (Fung et al. 2009), keeping a second wife was sometimes an economically wise decision.

More important than the domestic services provided by second wives is the emotional meaning they entail. Second wives often deliver the service with personalized input, such as preparing the man's favorite meal before his arrival, feeding the man's physical needs as well as psychological satisfaction of being cared for, respected and honored. Tu Qiao, a Hong Kong based journalist, spent two months in a so-called "village" of second wives – a neighborhood in Shenzhen bordering Hong Kong where a large number of second wives of Hong Kong container truck drivers and other blue-collar workers reside (Tu 2004). In all 12 cases of Hong Kong blue workers' second-wife arrangements she collected, second wives had learned to cook their men's favorite meals. Some second wives also went to great lengths to learn how to cook tasteful dishes that were nutritious, as a way to show how much they cared about their men's health. For example, Ah-Mei, a migrant woman from rural Hubei, first became the second wife of Ah-De, a Hong Kong truck driver, when she was 16. Ah-De was very thin due to poor eating habits. In order to help him gain weight and live a healthier lifestyle, Ah-Mei made a nutritious Cantonese-style soup every time she prepared a meal.

Working men – especially those in travel-based occupations – benefit from the cheap, convenient and personalized domestic work their second wives provide. These women not only help reproduce workers' labor, but also sustain and enhance their self-image and esteem.

Mild tempers, tolerance and docility are the qualities that working-class Hong Kong men seek most in their second wives, especially when they are unable to find emotional comfort in their first homes. For example, Wang Yao worked as a booking clerk in the subway after he was fired by his old company during the economic downturn of the 1990s. His new job only paid him HK$15,000 (roughly US$$1,900) a month, much lower than the average income in Hong Kong. As he brought less money to his family, his wife became increasingly distant and unhappy with him. During a leisure trip to Shenzhen with his friends, he met Ah-Yan, a charming young woman from Hunan, in a bar. She talked to him in such a gentle and loving way, with her enchanting voice "so soft that it can calm down a maniac and make him dance," that he felt able to retrieve his sense of masculinity (Tu 2004: 36). He set up a second household with her in Shenzhen, giving her about 4,000 yuan a month. In return, she helped him rebuild his dignity as a man.

The intimate arrangement with a stable household does not only provide working-class men a feeling of being the man of the house, but also becomes an emotional anchor for their second wives. Ah-Yan commented on her involvement with Wang Yao:

> I'd been a bar girl for more than a year before I met him. I was exhausted, having been pushed around by so many men. He [Wang Yao] brought me here and rented the apartment for me … I felt I eventually had a home in Shenzhen. There is someone who thinks of me…

Before they entered into a second-wife arrangement, migrant women labored long hours on assembly lines, shop floors, restaurants and entertainment venues, lived in crowded dorms or shared rental rooms which lacked basic protection of privacy. They also experienced secondary status in the city through unfriendly looks from the urbanities and regular police harassment. The households provided by the men thus served as a physical space in which migrant women could feel at home, albeit temporarily, within a larger urban space in which they were treated as outsiders. Some migrant women also had romantic feelings for their partner. In their eyes, these men were great partners who were able to provide a stable life which previous suitors or boyfriends could not. Many of these women had had intimate relationships with migrant men, which often ended because of economic difficulty. Hong Kong men were also viewed by these women as more generous, more civilized and better mannered (as they came from a First World region) in comparison to many mainland men. Thus, some migrant women wanted to make a real "home environment" in their current setting by taking good domestic and emotional care of their men and achieving a sense of interdependency and intimacy between the couple.

Through cross-border migration, some blue-collar workers from Hong Kong succeeded in upgrading their living standards, class image and sense of self-worth in mainland China. Typically earning about HK$15,000–$20,000 (roughly US$1,900–$2,600), they belong to the lowest economic stratum in their home society. Their struggle to provide a decent apartment and support a family as well as pay for their children's education causes them to be regarded as losers by mainstream standards. Their jobs as truck drivers for example consist of long hours alone, away from the eyes of others. However, the significantly lower cost of living across the border in Shenzhen makes it possible for them to convert their limited economic resources to higher social status in mainland China. It is through their second wives' therapeutic emotional work and care-laden domestic work that their sense of retrieved masculinity is validated and consolidated.

Unlike the businessmen's second wives, as discussed in the previous section, who invest deliberate effort in maintaining men's honor by presenting a positive "face" for men in public settings, second wives of the workers are less likely to escort men in public settings. Workers' second-wife practices are more individualized and privatized rather than collectively shared and publicly celebrated. This is because in general, working-class men do not engage in institutionalized business networking where they need a woman as a showpiece; neither do they belong to a masculinized entrepreneurial culture that celebrates the practice of keeping second wives. The practice of keeping a second wife is a relatively personalized means of taking advantage of the cross-border mobility to boost their masculine egos in the transnational spaces.

Conclusion

In this chapter, I've elucidated the varying forms of labor second wives have performed for their male partners and class-distinctive meanings extramarital intimacy have taken on for cross-border Hong Kong and Taiwanese men. I argue that extramarital intimacy with mainland Chinese women not only caters to sexual, emotional and domestic needs of transnational Hong Kong or Taiwanese businessmen who left their family behind, it has become an essential ritual in constituting an collective identity and privilege of transnational business elites. By consuming the body, sexuality and emotional care of attractive mainland women who are categorized as objects of male desire, it consolidates a sense of transnational superiority and privilege in the traveling businessmen.

In contrast, for working-class Hong Kong men, their second-wife practice is more likely to be taken as a means to heal their injured masculinity associated with their low-class status in their home society. With justifications of unfulfilled masculine honor and dignity as a husband in their original homes, they seek alternatives in the mainland where their relative low income can be transferred into higher consumption power and social status. Second wives of Hong Kong truck drivers and other working-class men thus often act as surrogate wives, soothing men's egos with care-laden domestic chores, emotional care and attentiveness that men are unable to receive in their original homes.

A seemingly similar intimate practice contains different meanings and consequences for men of different class positions. Cross-border mobility has therefore expanded the social space in which Hong Kong and Taiwanese men of different class backgrounds are able to negotiate their class status and masculine honor. The gendered nature of the global expansion of capitalism intertwined with local gender structure enables men in different social positions to reconstruct their gender and class identities through economic and intimate relations.

Notes

1 To a large extent, the Chinese term *yilai/ernai* and the English term "mistress" (translated as "*qingfu*" in Chinese) are interchangeable. In popular discourse in contemporary China, however, "mistress" is more broadly used, referring to a woman involved in an extramarital relationship with a married man, regardless of her financial dependence upon the man, living arrangement or the length of the relationship. The term "*yilai/ernai*" has negative connotations in popular discourses, often reducing to a simplistic meaning of money-for-sex trade. Thus, for the sake of clarity as well as preserving the complicity of the relationship, I chose to use the relatively neutral (albeit imperfect) English translation, "second wife" in my writing.
2 For instance, as defined in the Marriage Law of the PRC, as long as the couple in the second-wife relationship does not register their relationship as marriage, hold a wedding ceremony or refer to each other as husband and wife in public, the arrangement is considered an affair rather than officially constituting bigamy which is penalized within the criminal code.

3 The debate had been focused on the issue of extramarital sexual relationships, especially on how to control the phenomenon of rich men keeping "second wives" – whether to punish the "third party" or even to make extramarital sex illegal. What finally appeared in the revised marriage law was modest, largely because it is difficult to legally define what counts as keeping a second wife in explicit terms; "banning a married person from cohabiting with someone else" was added along with a provision that would allow a person in a divorce case to sue for damages when his or her spouse was "cohabiting with someone else." In the recent Disciplinary Regulations of the Chinese Communist Party (*zhongguo gongchandang jilv chufen tiaoli*) that were revised and issued in 2004, a CCP member will be deprived of membership for committing polygamy or keeping mistresses or lovers (*baoyang qingfu/fu*). This amendment is regarded as the CCP's response to the report that 95 percent of corrupted officials kept second wives or mistresses as claimed by a representative of the people at a People's Congress meeting.
4 The data presented in this chapter are primarily derived from my dissertation research that I conducted between September 2005 and August 2006 and in the summer of 2007.

References

Boris, E. and R. Parrenas. 2010. *Intimate Labors: Cultures, Technologies, and the Politics of Care*. Palo Alto: Stanford University Press.

Brennan, D. 2004. *What's Love Got To Do With It? Transnational Desires and Sex Tourism in the Dominican Republic*. Durham: Duke University Press.

Chiu, C. and T. F. Lin. 1994. *Ikuo liangChi: liangan fenin paipishu* (One Country, Two Wives: The Bluebook of Intermarriages Across the Taiwan Strait). Taipei: Chin-Mei Press.

Connell, R. W. 1998. "Masculinities and Globalization." *Men and Masculinities* 1: 3–23.

Fung, C., W. Wong, and S. M. Tam. 2009. "Familial and Extramarital Relations Among Truck Drivers Crossing the Hong Kong-China Border." *Journal of Sex & Marital Therapy* 35 (3): 239–244.

Hoang, K. K. 2011a. "New Economies of Sex and Intimacy." Ph.D. dissertation, Department of Sociology, University of California, Berkeley.

Hoang, K. K. 2011b. "'She's Not a Low Class Dirty Girl': Sex Work in Ho Chi Minh City, Vietnam." *Journal of Contemporary Ethnography* 40: 367–396.

Hochschild, A. R. 1983. *The Managed Heart: Commercialization of Human Feeling*. Berkeley: University of California Press.

Hochschild, A. R. 2002. "Love and Gold," in *Global Woman*, edited by B. Ehrenreich and A. Hochschild. New York: Metropolitan Books.

Hsing, Y. 1998. *Making Capitalism in China: The Taiwan Connection*. Oxford: Oxford University Press.

Lan, P. 2003. "Working in a Neon Cage: 'Bodily Labor' of Cosmetics Saleswomen in Taiwan." *Feminist Studies* 29: 1–25.

Lan, P. 2006. *Global Cinderellas: Migrant Domestic Workers and Newly Rich Employers in Taiwan*. Durham: Duke University Press.

Lang, G. and J. Smart. 2002. "Migration and the 'Second Wife' in South China: Toward Cross-Border Polygyny." *International Migration Review* 36: 546–569.

Lee, Y. 2001. *Dalu de wenjo yushang* (Mainland China as a Tender Strange Land). Taipei: Fu-Kuo International Publishing Co. Ltd.

Liu, C. 2001. *Taishang dalu chenlun jishih* (The Actual Records of Taiwanese Businessmen's Indulgence in China). Taipei: Stardoms Publishing Co. Ltd.

Ong, A. 1999. *Flexible Citizenship: The Cultural Logics of Transnationality*. Durham: Duke University Press.

Parrenas, R. 2008. *The Force of Domesticity: Filipina Migrants and Globalization*. New York: New York University Press.

Pun, N. 2005. *Made in China: Women Factory Workers in a Global Workplace*. Durham: Duke University Press.

Salzinger, L. 2003. *Genders in Production: Making Workers in Mexico's Global Factories*. Berkeley: University of California Press.

Shen, H. 2005. "'The First Taiwanese Wives' and 'The Chinese Mistresses': The International Division of Labor in Familial and Intimate Relations Across the Taiwan Strait." *Global Networks* 5: 419–437.

Shen, H. 2008. "The Purchase of Transnational Intimacy: Women's Bodies, Transnational Masculine Privileges in Chinese Economic Zones." *Asian Studies Review* 32: 57–75.

Shih, S. 1998. "Gender and a New Geopolitics of Desire: The Seduction of Mainland Women in Taiwan and Hong Kong Media." *Sign: Journal of Women in Culture and Society* 23: 287–319.

Siu, Y. 1999. "New Arrivals: A New Problem and an Old Problem." In *The Other Hong Kong Report, 1998*, edited by Larry Chow and Yiu-Kwan Fan, 201–228. Hong Kong: The Chinese University Press.

Smith, M. and L. Guarnizo. 1998. *Transnationalism From Below: Comparative Urban and Community Research*. New Brunswick: Transaction Publishers.

So, A. 2003. "Cross Border Families: The Role of Social Class and Politics." *Critical Asian Studies* 35: 515–534.

Tam, S. 1996. "Normalization of 'Second Wives': Gender Contestations in Hong Kong." *Asian Journal of Women's Studies* 2: 113–132.

Tam, S. 2001. "Constructing Wives and Mistresses: Polygyny Across the Hong Kong-China Border." Paper presented at Annual meeting of the Association for Asian Studies, March 22–25, 2001, Chicago.

Tam, S. 2005. "We-Women and They-Women: Imagining Mistresses Across the Hong Kong-China Border." In *Rethinking and Recasting Citizenship: Social Exclusion and Marginality in Chinese Societies*, edited by M. Tam, H. Ku and T. Kong, 109–130. Hong Kong: Centre for Social Policy Studies, Hong Kong Polytechnic University.

Tam, S., A. Fung, L. Kam and M. Liong. 2009. "Re-gendering Hong Kong Man in Social, Physical and Discursive Space." In *Mainstreaming Gender in Hong Kong Society*, edited by F. Cheung and E. Holroyd, 335–365. Hong Kong: Chinese University Press.

Thai, H. C. 2008. *For Better or for Worse: Vietnamese International Marriage in the New Global Economy*. New Brunswick: Rutgers University Press.

Tu, Q. 2004. *Bitter Marriage* ("kuhun," in Chinese). Beijing: Zuojia Press.

Wong, W., S. M. Tam and P. Leung. 2007. "Cross-Border Truck Drivers in Hong Kong: Their Psychological Health, Sexual Dysfunctions and Sexual Risk Behaviors." *Journal of Travel Medicine* 14(1): 20–30.

Xiao, S. 2011. "The 'Second Wife' Phenomenon and the Relational Construction of Class-coded Masculinities in Contemporary China." *Men and Masculinities* 14: 607–627.

Zelizer, V. 2005. *The Purchase of Intimacy*. Princeton: Princeton University Press.

Part III
Identity

11 How do identities matter?

Taiwanese cultural workers in China

Yen-Fen Tseng

Introduction

> I think of myself as being global. I see myself participating in global activities: sitting in jets, talking to machines, eating small geometric food, and voting over the phone.
>
> (Rem Koolhaas, cited by Ian Buruma, 2003)

> Satoru Aoyama and Kei Takemura, they are both quite typical of the Seventies generation: global travelers, for whom the old issues of Japanese nationalism, and obsessions with pop culture are irrelevant, and who are difficult to place in any current fashion trends. There is nothing traditionalist about the work, and yet it finds a new way of reinventing a purpose for craft techniques and aesthetic sensibilities in a very contemporary art setting.
>
> (Carvosso 2010)

This jet-setting image, shown in the above two quotes, resembles the "transnational capitalist class," memorably described by Sklair (2001), of elites working for global corporations who profess allegiance beyond their national identities. While such identity-free images/self-portraits can be directly linked to economic interests beyond national identities, such portraits are somewhat misleading when referring to identity issues related to professional practices.

For example, Koolhaas – an architect from the Netherlands who has moved constantly between countries along with his projects and has himself become a global brand name – can be expected to reformulate his professional identities along the journey; sometimes fitting an image of "professionals without borders," while the other time, an architect from the Netherlands is emphasized, and in reality he bases his firm in Rotterdam, taking pride in the professional knowledge and practices in his home country.

This chapter focuses on investigating which identity issues are involved in putting skills into practices in a foreign land, when cultural workers move across borders. By cultural workers, this chapter refers to those working in production of goods and services, with aesthetic or semiotic contents such as film, design and art, a definition coined by economic geographer Allen Scott (2004). The case of Satoru Aoyama and Kei Takemura mentioned in the opening quote illustrates the unique interest of identity issues pertinent to cultural workers. Global travelers they are, however they have based themselves outside Japan, in Britain and Berlin, respectively. To these two Japanese artists, aesthetic skills cultivated from the Japanese tradition provide valuable assets with which to move around the globe.

This chapter is written with the purpose of demystifying the "identity-free" image of skilled migrants such as the above professionals working in cultural sectors. Two aspects of identities crucial to their work experiences are of interest here, that is, professional identity and origin identity. I analyze how identities matter to migrant cultural workers from the following sources: cultural workers' narratives, second-hand data from media reports/critics and cultural products.

Cultural workers and identities

Studies on cultural workers have found that the kind of opportunities considered important to gain critical skills are subjectively defined and hence differ for each individual. For example, Molotch (2002) found that the industrial designers' core concern over their career lies in whether they can "keep the ideas coming." Since they believe that "it [to keep ideas coming] requires fun, so fun is a more important motive than money to count to their satisfaction" (Molotch 2002: 23). This is critical aspect to evaluate the core value of cultural works and how it affects people's satisfaction and potentials about their work.

This study takes an approach different from the perspective of human capital put forward by economists. Economists tend to view professional migrants as engaging in a talent flow across border where internationally recognized human capital removes the barriers of skill mobility. However, as Favell (2008: 21) points out, the "universal" metric of skill and talent, does not, in fact, remove the challenge of incorporation. "Culture and particularistic know-how still impose all the difficulties of integration on these kinds of migrants" (Favell 2008: 21). If this thesis applies to professional workers, it is even truer for cultural workers. When culture is not only a set of rules informing actions, but also part of "factor of production" as material, it would be interesting to learn what kinds of journeys cultural workers undertake to search for cultural know-how. The issue of identity enters the scene, since the above search ultimately involves a redefinition, or reformulation of senses of what cultural workers from Taiwan mean, and whether it matters.

In researching how and in what aspects cultural workers adapt to a new environment in carrying out their activities, this study focuses on two types of identities, professional identity, defined by intrinsic motives by being in such occupation, and origin identity, the intrinsic values of coming from place of origin. In theory, these two identities have their separate sets of references and values, but cultural workers, when they move to a new country, tend to experience a process of proving their market worth by thinking through these two identities. That is, they have to tackle the question of what really matters to motivate them to do certain cultural works and what it means that they come from Taiwan. For example, does being classified and/or self-classifying as designers from Taiwan enhance or hurt their intrinsic motive and value? What groups do they identify themselves with, and what groups do they try to differentiate from? Or we can use the term of "group style" coined by Eliasoph and Lichterman (2003: 213) to decode the social identity – i.e., "people carry with them images of how their group relates to and is distinct from, other groups."

This study is also interested in the outcome of such identity search in terms of utility (income, status, fame). In such an investigation, I adopt the following thesis proposed by Akerlof and Kranton (2010):

> We talk of an individual maximizing a utility function that specifies the social norms and the individual's preferences, or tastes. This description, on its face, describes what might be called *an individualistic view of identity* [original emphasis]. An individual ... enjoys a gain in "identity utility" when she adheres to the norms for her category.

This chapter will first present findings in answering the question of professional identity – which key skills or achievements are valued as the most important ones by each individual while transplanting their professional skills? Such understandings are crucial in building skills, a supposedly continuous process in cultural works. Few studies, if any, pay attention to how migration changes skill contents among skilled workers. Just as Sennett (2008) argues that social scientists pay little attention to what it is to become and maintain being skilled, the process of acquiring, polishing and valuing skill is left unconcerned.

The following analysis is based on in-depth interviews with design professionals working in Shanghai between 2008 and 2012. In total, 22 interview notes are drawn upon for analysis. Workers involved in aesthetics, such as architectural and interior designs, are attracted to large cities with speedy new constructions, such as Shanghai (Business Next 2007; Lee 2001). I asked my interviewees to evaluate their skill developments and adaptations as an essential part of professional changes by relocating to China and how identities as self-understandings of being cultural workers and coming from Taiwan at the same time, matters in the process.

Design professions in Shanghai

The rapid transformation in China's economy has created many gaps in terms of talent supply. Given the rapid demand in an instant growth in many design sectors, the local education system is unprepared for supplying design professionals in certain fields. The shortage comes from the gap in formal training and, moreover, tacit knowledge of what good designs are. Skilled and experienced Taiwanese designers moved their careers to China mainly to fill the gaps of such talent shortage. They are part of what Olds (1997) observed, in the process of designing and building the new financial district in Pudong, elite non-Chinese design professionals, or "Global Intelligence Corps" have played a significant role. The "open-mindedness" of Shanghai's business sectors as well as government agencies towards foreign designers has been credited to build an environment converged by international designers. Shanghai has its tradition of opening cultural arms toward outside influences. That is cultural context that serves as an attraction to cultural workers from Taiwan.

Two accounts draw a background of the stream of migration of design workers from Taiwan to Shanghai over the last decade:

> Architectural sector has been experiencing drastic decline in Taiwan since mid 1990s; from then on many have moved to China to find works. I did not move right away, like most Taiwanese, I considered China a backward place until an invitation to come to Shanghai in early 2000 prompted me to join the stream. But beyond Shanghai, I would have not wanted to move.
>
> (Hu 2008/1/25)

> I used to teach landscape design in college a decade ago, at that time, most students did not consider working in China as a vital option. So initially the company's Shanghai branch I am working with had hard time recruiting workers from Taiwan. But not now, the potential candidates become younger and younger.
>
> (Chou 2008/1/23)

Cosmopolitan Shanghai

As a native Taiwanese, for a very long time before I had a chance to visit the city, Shanghai stood out for me as a metropolis coined by the term *shili yangchang* – literally, "ten-mile-long foreign zone." When Leo Oufan Lee investigated this term while writing *Shanghai Modern*, a book that attempts to remap Shanghai's urban culture in the colonial period, he found a Chinese-English dictionary that defined *shili yangchang* as a "metropolis infested with foreign adventurers, usually referring to pre-liberation Shanghai" (1999: 345). The term *shili yangchang* expresses very well the deep sense of cosmopolitanism that Shanghai urban culture has embraced. After analyzing the cosmopolitan tendencies of Chinese literary productions in pre-liberation Shanghai, Lee concluded that "the phenomenon of Chinese writers eagerly embracing Western cultures in Shanghai's foreign concessions is a manifestation of Chinese cosmopolitanism, which is *another facet of Chinese modernity*" (1999: 313, italics mine).

Through major city landscape development, government officials have been crafting Shanghai's public image of openness to all kinds of foreign participants (Fallows 1988). In Shanghai, city planning and architectural design have been heavily influenced by foreign corporations, a phenomenon unknown and unthinkable in cities such as Beijing (Olds 1997). Shanghai's skyline and city-scape consequently serve as a showcase for such openness. As Hannigan (1998) points out, the city is considered irreplaceable when it comes to lifestyle pursuit. To many of my interviewees, Shanghai is attractive precisely because of its image of being cosmopolitan, in their understanding meaning open-minded towards outside influences. To these migrants, Shanghai as an open structure linked to the outside world is an asset not only for the economic opportunities, but also for the pursuit of cosmopolitan lifestyle capital, resembling London in Favell's portrait being the most cosmopolitan among all European major cities (Favell 2006). Similarly, Florida (2002) in his study on how the characteristics of the city attract creative workers, that is, those accepting more unconventional lifestyles being the most preferable among creative workers. Many of my interviewees considered international input of capital, ideas and people as well as large domestic market among the two most important assets to facilitate their career identities in China, i.e., they take pride in being part of this international scene of architects and architectures. Also, Huang (2006) argues that Taiwanese migrants in Shanghai have participated in a discursive identity to give rise to a so-called "New Shanghai People" (*xin shanghai ren*). The following are several related interview notes:

Designers of all kinds of nationalities all wish to be part of constructing Shanghai or Beijing. China is a low-income country but design professions are willing to settle for lower design fees to get in the stage. This way, you are literally working with best talents from the world right here in Shanghai, and it has been eye-opening and stimulating for me to be here.

(Hu 2008/1/25)

There are a lot of foreigners around in landscape designing, and the degree of internationalization is unthinkable in Taiwan. This has to do with their projects, including those by public sectors, being more open to foreign competitors. They worship influences from outside as long as these are considered more modernized and better. I would say Taiwan is very parochial as compared to this.

(Chou 2008/1/23)

As a result, relocating to Shanghai is perceived by many as a way to pursue the opportunity to become more internationalized. The multinational corporations have brought in much innovative manpower and changed the work culture tremendously (Chen 2006). A fashion designer/professor reportedly said: "Since I moved to Shanghai, within three months I got much more opportunities to speak English than past 15 years spent in Taipei." (Lu Rongzhi, interview by Global Vision Magazine 遠見雜誌 2006/11/6: 169).

In evaluating the benefits of being exposed to an internationalized workforce and industry, an architect said:

Since many foreign architect firms converge in Shanghai and they tend to do a lot of architectural experiments in this new frontier, therefore, I would encourage young architects come to work in Shanghai for the purpose of widening his or her perspectives of doing things. For example, the most valuable thing I learned in Shanghai is what I learned from my previous boss, an American architect who takes extra efforts in pursuing environmental protection.

(Yang 2011/5/25)

Although Mr. Yang did not continue to work in Shanghai, rather, as a returnee to Taipei, he established a small shop selling environmentally friendly design products. He told me he continues to go back to Shanghai at least once a year to attend environmental friendly design exhibitions.

Professional identity

Professional identity as a process of forming motive and goal is very subjective, up to each worker's own definition because there is no standard to measure success. An interviewed architect illustrated such process as follows:

Design is a thinking work, the cost is invisible, so is the end product. The input of effort is also invisible and there is no firm line to divide the success and failure. The process of accomplishing a project is fulfilling, and even when the project is not realized or worse you lose money. That is why for every designer, a dream lies somewhere that someone will let you perform to your fullest and the reputation follows.

(Huang 2008/1/26)

Design profession is an art, a profession, and above all, a business. As a result, many design professions find that the business goals often run counter to the intrinsic values of pursuing aesthetics that first attracted them to the profession. To many designers, throughout their career, such dilemmas of balancing between art and commerce persist to win over each other, albeit the extent of tension varies. Therefore, it can be expected that such dilemmas would be played out differently once design professions migrate to a new country where industrial organizations and client demands constitute new environments requiring adaptation.

When skilled workers migrate, the social relations that facilitate production process of creative work would change accordingly. Since identities and norms emerge from social interactions and power relations, people in different groups adopt common values, sometimes represented by cultural signs, to differentiate themselves from those in other groups. I argue that in cultural skill development, the core of such value-sharing lies in workers' self-evaluation as to what really matters to cultivate his or her work identity, in a new set of social/industrial relations.

An interviewee, trained in the Netherlands, working for a Japanese-owned transnational company in landscape designs, elaborates the cultural demand:

In terms of job security, I think at least for the time being, I do not have to worry about being replaced by local Chinese because landscape designs require cultural bridges. Japanese think I know Chinese culture better than they do, although professionally I am a Dutch-trained designer.

(Lee 2008/1/21)

There are two major challenges/issues mentioned by my interviewees in applying skills to design projects in Shanghai. The first is the division of labor in both internal and external aspects. The second issue is the massive volume and speed from start to completion, a situation considered an exciting challenge by some, and boring repetition by others. In terms of division of labor, an interviewee, a landscape professional, pointed out:

In Shanghai, the office division of labor is more detailed so that I only have to focus on my part of design. For example, there are people specializing in drawing so I don't have to do that. However, in terms of outside linkages, I have to take care of many things I didn't have to touch in Taiwan. There are much more forward and backward linkages with suppliers and buyers ready to use in Taiwan. For example, if I design a fountain, I have to really go all the way to monitor what material the suppliers can supply. There is no ready-made supplier network who can work with you.

(Wang 2001/1/27)

Another interviewee, an architect, offers the following evaluation:

The frustration about working in architectural design in Shanghai has to do with the lack of a strong construction team. You have to pay a lot of attention along the construction phases. I have to monitor everything in order to come up with a quality building. No wonder, a lot of architectural firms in China only concentrate on doing design but leave the construction to others. However, my gain is to learn much more than I originally care to know about. I cultivate quality suppliers by visiting their factories and offer them some original ideas to work with.

(Huang 1/26/2008)

In the past decade, Shanghai has been undergoing many aggressive planning and construction projects that facilitate the growth of housing and office building projects (Wu 2000). Taiwanese architects interviewed have experienced the following distinctive challenges: larger quantity and scale of building in a much speedier time frame. Just as the China-originated MIT architecture scholar, Yung Ho Chang, pointed out that most architect firms working in China construct buildings at an excessively high speed (Ruwitch 2006). What impact does this large volume of work completed within a short time span have on design skill? The evaluations are very mixed, depending on which part of the skill people value more. A landscape designer considered it rather beneficial to work with such large volume of projects that demand a speedy delivery. She said:

The projects here are not only huge in volume but also very similar to each other, at the same time, we are often required to get the works done in much shorter time in Taiwan. I can go through many rounds of trial and error in shorter time. For example, if I made some mistakes in the last project, I will be soon given another opportunity to do a similar job again so I can correct the mistakes. This way I pick up and mature skills much rapidly. I can acquire the same skill within a year here while it would probably take three years to learn the same thing in Taiwan.

(Hsieh 2008/1/22)

However, the same situation can be evaluated very negatively by others who value the artistic part of the skill. A middle-aged architect who had worked in designing housing complexes in China and returned to Taiwan after only two years of relocation, is among this crop:

The massive building projects really bored me to death. They all look the same. One after the other, I was doing the similar works. I figured out that this was not what drew me into this field. Working in China would eventually harm my talent as an architect.

(Liao 2007/6/20)

In the above case, how workers define what really matters or the most valuable part of his or her job is put to a test by working under very different demands of design and, in the above case, the architect experienced a lack of stimulus that mattered to him. Such disappointment and lack of sense of fulfillment accounted for his cutting short his career in China. No matter how mixed the above self-evaluations are, they point to very specific issues of applying skills in a global context.

How do origin identities matter in producing "culture"?

Identities concern aspects of what really matters to each individual when they make decisions on careers and migration. What do major decisions say about who they are, in the aspects of being a worker in a certain sector? These identities have to do with where to move to and whether they can make the best use of their skills to deliver the kinds of products to match their career dreams. The career ideals for cultural workers involve the transforming or explorations of human experience that first and foremost require cultural understanding and translations from "who I am" to "whose experiences I am exploring."

Root-searching identities

Cultural goods carrying aesthetic and semiotic meanings do intend to create transformative value, in a small and large way. Hence, the cultural workers have to think through some of the areas they want to focus on transforming, those being the forms or functions, in the case of design. This section analyzes how in order to create meanings and the resulting transformative values, cultural workers are engaged in certain "root-searching" projects, a formation of origin identity, reflecting on what it means to be Taiwanese designers and how such understanding can be translated into market value.

The first type of origin identity builds around taking pride over being from Taiwan. This has to do with the belief system that Taiwan designers know how design can add better life quality than locals. Taiwanese design professionals describe their aspirations for life quality actually requiring bodily experiences and tacit knowledge beyond formal training. The informal aspect of the skill constitutes core assets valued by Taiwanese design professionals. An interviewee specialized in architectural design interpreted the shortage of local talents in her field this way:

> To design something to improve the life quality, you have to come from a society that has enjoyed affluence for quite some time because only in such societies, people care something more than survival, and concerns sensibility of living. So I think the barrier for entering this type of jobs lies not in the formal training but in the aspirations about life quality.
>
> (Huang 2008/1/26)

> Shanghai is far behind Taiwan in terms of cultural maturation. That is why I think Taiwanese should keep their way and wait for the locals to catch up.
>
> (Yee 2008/1/27)

> In terms of design, Taiwanese are still way ahead in the cultural tastes and refinement. My friends in Taiwan would bring me exemplary cases in Taiwan and I got inspirations from there.
>
> (Hu 2008/1/23)

Taiwanese designers are considered better because of their mature and original styles. One interior designer said,

> In architectural works, the locals appreciate famous and established big names, but when it comes to interior designs, they value designers' personal styles and characteristics than shining brands.
>
> (Chen 2008/1/22)

The second type of identity formation comes from a process of enlarging the boundary of "us" from a Taiwanese native identity to being an authentic version of Chinese. They take pride in knowing Chinese aesthetics traditions better, inheriting from their learning humanities and culture from China uninterruptedly, in the Taiwanese formal education system. An interviewee specialized in designing products adapting from the Chinese craft tradition catering to international customers considered her skill niche lies in bridging Chinese culture with the outside world. She said,

There are many good artifacts in Chinese crafts and art traditions, but if they are to be applied to products that appeal to outside market, there is a need to connect these aesthetics with modern need. I think this is the area we can do much better than local Chinese in terms of understanding such modern needs.

(Chiang 2008/1/21)

Another case is a team of glass artists originated from Taiwan, *Luili Crafts*, who did well in business by cultivating ancient Chinese glassware-making skills and perfecting the art to sell to China and beyond. They take pride in "reincarnating" ancient crafts like the above case.

A more famous case is Architect C. Y. Lee (李祖原), the designer of once the tallest building of Taipei 101, who goes even further, considering himself a modernized version of "reincarnation." Lee can be described as one of the most representative Taiwanese architects practicing in China. His architectural elements famously (or notoriously, depending on the judgment of tastes) incorporate Chinese cultural identity. He continues to build an architectural treatise for modern Chinese architectural design in various cities of China. However, the way he attaches nostalgic Chinese symbols that represent power and wealth to the modern skyscraper façade, causes more criticism than appreciation in China. Some of his works have even been listed as the top ten ugliest buildings in China. This case shows that in societies like China that are yearning for modernization, the nostalgic reminders of traditional symbols are not always welcomed – the fit is obviously wrong but the intention of identity awareness of a Chinese heritage to be shared is certainly highlighted.

Identity utility

This section intends to investigate how Taiwanese cultural workers build their works around *their coming from Taiwan* and hope to gain success in earnings. This is when and where Akerlof and Kranton (2010: 24) would refer to as the situation of utility gain – "an individual maximizing a utility function that specifies ... the individual's preferences, or tastes." This section asks whether Taiwanese would benefit from such identity in terms of market rewards – salary, revenues, fames and status.

First of all, if Taiwanese work for Taiwanese companies, their Taiwanese identity, regardless which type they build around, does not distinguish themselves from the rest, and their identity is either being taken for granted or devalued by their co-fellow bosses. This situation prevails in many industries. According to the manager of 104 China Human Bank, an internet job site that caters to Taiwanese workers looking for jobs in China,

In general, Taiwanese got higher pay in both foreign-owned and local-owned firms than in Taiwanese-owned firms. In foreign-owned companies, they pay by positions and job functions, disregard nationalities of employees. On the other hand, local-owned companies can offer lucrative salary package to Taiwanese if they really need you. Taiwanese companies are lowest in terms of the pay scale.

(Cheng 2008/1/26)

An example is architecture designers: if they work for a Taiwanese company, they got the lowest pay. An architecture designer hopping three jobs from Taiwanese, Chinese to American firms confirmed that the pay scale in the Taiwanese company is the lowest among the three (Yang, 2008/5/25). Mr. Yang believes that being from Taiwan, he has shortened the time span between architectural assistant and architectural designer and obtained a higher pay scale than the local workers with the same working experience. Mr. Yang also attributes such a low package offered by Taiwanese architect firms to their lower market positions as compared to European and American firms. He and others mentioned that the Chinese respect European and American firms so these firms can charge higher rates due to such admiration. Some local firms would hire European Americans (Whites) just to make presentations and/or to appear in meetings with local clients.

Taiwanese identity provides the largest utility if they work for local Chinese big companies (such as state-owned), that is because they consider Taiwanese to possess assets that local Chinese do not have and, on the other hand, they have better communication with Chinese workers than other foreigners. The landscape designer observes:

> Professionally, Chinese respect Taiwanese designers and consider them higher in standards, better in quality, because to them, Taiwan is much more developed in offering good life quality. But they are not valued as high as European and Americans are, so we can charge fees higher than the locals, but lower than the Europeans and Americans.
>
> (Chou 2008/1/25)

But then some are worried that such an advantage of both identifying oneself with and being identified as Taiwanese will lose its market reward soon. This is an area for future studies to determine whether and why Taiwanese maintain their distinctive characteristics as originating from Taiwan.

Conclusion

As the migration from Taiwan to China is found to be diversified in terms of types of works, this chapter studies Taiwanese cultural workers in China, focusing on the process of transplanting cultural skills. I found that cultural workers from Taiwan value identity – both professional and origin of place – as essential parts constituting asset-specific skills. If this process goes smoothly, I also show that Taiwanese gain identity utility in market recognition and salary rewards. In order to create meanings and the resulting transformative values, cultural workers are engaged in certain "root-searching" projects reflecting on what it means to be Chinese, Taiwanese, Taiwanese in China, Chinese from Taiwan, and so on. I also found that their pride over being more professional in adhering more rigorously to professional standards reinforces their pride in coming from Taiwan, since they often attribute such professional rigor to training and work experience in Taiwan.

Cultural workers are a new type of Taiwanese migrants working in China. Their number might still be limited, but their cases can be illustrative of today's young people's pursuit. Growing up in a relatively affluent society and era, the younger generation has more autonomy to assert their own interest and follow their creativity. That can partly explain why cultural works related majors in university, such as design, have been in greater and greater demand (Chen 2012). Just as Featherstone outlined the characteristics of cultural work as "a learning mode towards life" and a fascination with "identity, presentation, appearance, life-style and the endless quest for new experience" (Featherstone 1991: 44), we might say that migration naturally becomes an option to be part of such quests for new experiences.

Cultural workers are noted for their propensity to leave their homes, for quests of new experiences. Paul Gauguin, perhaps the most famous artist in exile, migrated to Tahiti to pursue life and art works, escaping from conventions and civilizations. In one of his works from his exile in the Tahiti era – "Where do we come from? What are we? Where are you we going?" – Gauguin meant to imply the search of life in foreign land brings new flavors to such questions. In my study, I found cultural workers often looking back to search for meanings of their unique root of identity and such identity seems to weigh still more on their work after leaving their homeland.

References

Akerlof, George, and Rachel E. Kranton. 2010. *Identity Economics: How Our Identities Shape Our Work, Wages, and Well-Being*. Princeton: Princeton University Press.

Buruma, I. 2003. "The Sky is the Limit." In *What is OMA: Considering Rem Koolhaas and the Office for Metropolitan Architecture*, edited by Veronique Patteeuw et al., 53–72. Rotterdam: Nai Publishers.

Business Next. 2007. "Riverside Creative Industrial Park in Shanghai," www.bnext.com. tw/LocalityView_4375.

Carvosso, Rachel. 2010. "Taking a Flat Approach: An Interview with Adrian Favell." http://www.tokyoartbeat.com/tablog/entries.en/2010/07/taking-a-flat-approach.html

Chen, Yi-Ping. 2012. "Guides to Finding Your Best University." *Global Vision Magazine*, February. http://www.gvm.com.tw/Boardcontent_19726.html.

Chen, Yun C. 2006. "Changing the Shanghai Innovation Systems: The Role of Multi-national Corporations' R&D Centres." *Science, Technology and Society* 11 (1): 67–107.

Eliasoph, Nina, and Paul Lichterman. 2003. "Culture in Interaction." *American Journal of Sociology* 108 (4): 735–794.

Fallows, J. 1988. "Shanghai Surprise." *Atlantic Monthly*, July: 76–78.

Favell, Adrian. 2006. "London as Eurocity: French Free Movers in the Economic Capital of Europe." In *The Human Face of Global Mobility: International Highly Skilled Migration in Europe, North America and the Asia-Pacific*, edited by Michael Peter Smith and Adrian Favell. New Brunswick: Transaction Publishers.

Favell, Adrian. 2008. *Eurostars and Eurocities*. Oxford: Blackwell.

Featherstone, Mike. (1991). *Consumer Culture and Postmodernism*. London: Sage.

Florida, Richard. 2002. *The Rise of the Creative Class*. New York: Basic Books.

Global Vision Magazine. 2006. "Lu Rongzhi interview." *Global Vision Magazine* 11 (6): 169.

Hannigan, John. 1998. *Fantasy City: Pleasure and Profit in the Postmodern Metropolis*. London: Routledge.

Huang, Michelle T. Y. 2006. "The Cosmopolitan Imaginary and Flexible Identities of Global City-regions: Articulating New Cultural Identities in Taipei and Shanghai." *Inter-Asia Cultural Studies* 7 (3): 472–491.

Lee, Leo O. F. 1999. *Shanghai Modern: The Flowering of a New Urban Culture in China, 1930–1945*. Cambridge: Harvard University Press.

Lee, T. H. 2001. "Three Hundred Thousand Taiwanese Migrating to Shanghai: Issue on Entrepreneurship." *Business Weekly* 723: 88–166.

Molotch, Harvey. 2002. "Place in Product." *International Journal of Urban and Regional Research* 26 (4): 665–690.

Olds, Kris. 1997. "Globalizing Shanghai: The 'Global Intelligence Corps' and the Building of Pudong." *Cities* 14 (2): 109–123.

Ruwitch, John. 2006. "Top MIT Architect Says China's Cities Are Hard to Live In." 2006/12/2, Hong Kong, Reuters.

Sennett, Richard. 2008. *The Craftsman*. New Haven: Yale University Press.

Scott, Allen J. 2004. "Cultural-Products Industries and Urban Economic Development: Prospect for Growth and Market Contestation in Global Context." *Urban Affairs Review* 39 (2): 461.

Sklair, Leslie. 2001. *The Transnational Capitalist Class*. Oxford: Blackwell Publishers.

Wealth Magazine. 2012. "Cover Story: Mid-Career Crisis in Taiwan." *Wealth Magazine* July issue.

Wu, Fulong. 2000. "The Global and Local Dimensions of Place-Making: Remaking Shanghai as a World City." *Urban Studies* 37 (8): 1359–1377.

12 Class or identity matters?

The social assimilation of Taiwanese sojourners in China

Ruihua Lin, Shu Keng and Richard Weixing Hu

Introduction

Most of the existing publications on cross-Strait relations are macro-level analyses. They analyze structural issues and changes at the macro level, ranging from political conflicts, economic interdependence and triangular relations (Cabestan 1995, 27–50; Wu 1995, 51–26; Clark 2001, 27–53; Clark 2002, 753–766; Clark 2003, 195–215; Keng and Lin 2011, 139–155). Although these macro-level analyses are important for policy making and making sense of major changes in cross-Strait relations, they seem to have big limitations in understanding and analyzing the attitudinal changes of ordinary people involved in cross-Strait contacts. With growing social contacts across the Strait over the last three decades, scholars are increasingly puzzled with questions such as: how do people from the both sides of the Strait perceive each other? Do they change their perception and attitude toward each other or still view each other in the "us-vs.-them" context? Because more and more people believe that these contacts are gradually and constantly reshaping the social context of the current cross-Strait relations, micro-level analyses of perception and attitudinal changes are necessary for us to make long-term forecasts of the future of cross-Strait relations.

In recent years we see some good micro-analyses focusing on the Taiwanese businesspeople in mainland China (thereafter referred to as Taishang). After Taiwan lifted the ban on traveling to the mainland in the late 1980s, the Taiwanese businessmen started moving to China. The first wave of Taishang moving to the mainland China in the later 1980s and early 1990s was largely driven by the restructuring of the global production network. Even today, these Taishang still constitute the lion share of the Taiwanese in the mainland. But as cross-Strait exchanges get more diversified, Taiwanese go to China for a variety of reasons, such as for retired life, for family reasons (spouses and kids of Taishang), for cross-Strait marriage or for further studies among others. These Taiwanese in China, because of their close contacts with the local Chinese in the mainland, are the subject of our study, and we want to find out whether they have any attitudinal changes after years of experience socializing with the local Chinese.

This chapter examines to what extent the Taiwanese in the mainland China have assimilated into the local society, that is, to what extent they consider themselves as "residents" of the places they stay and whether they view local residents as the "we-group." Originally, we were interested in studying the identity change of the Taiwanese sojourners in China. But due to the lack of an appropriate conceptual framework and the sensitivity of studying identity changes, it is difficult for us to deal with the issue in a more direct way. Also, it is still too early for a Taiwanese in the mainland to really consider himself or herself as a Chinese. This study instead focuses on the different stages of their social assimilation, ranging from family arrangement, children's education and their local social relations as they have settled down in the mainland.

This chapter also seeks to clarify what factors are instrumental in the social assimilation process. Among the major framing factors, first identified by Shu Keng (2002), "class relationships" and "primordial ties" are two very important ones. The former refers to the class distance between the Taiwanese and the local Chinese, measured by the real estate price of the communities they live in, while the latter refers to the cultural distance between the Taiwanese and the local Chinese, measured by the personal identity of the Taiwanese people in terms of whether they consider themselves as Taiwanese, Chinese or both.

Our study is based on a survey project carried out in 2009. Previous studies are mostly qualitative research with rather small sample size. Our survey project, a collaboration of Uthe niversity of Hong Kong and National Chengchi University, provides both qualitative and quantitative answers to the issue of the Taiwanese assimilation in mainland China. In this survey, we interviewed the Taiwanese living in the greater Shanghai area and the Dongguan area of Guangdong Province. We collected 214 completed samples, which is the largest ever systematic survey of the Taiwanese staying in China. The findings based on our survey suggest that "class factors" have more influences on the assimilation of the Taiwanese into local society in terms of family arrangements, while "identity factors" have more impact on their current social relations and destined home in the future.

Following the introduction, we first give a brief review of the theoretical concepts of social assimilation. After that, the third section discusses the significance of the "class factor" and "identity factor" in this study. Following that, the next two sections will describe our research methods and present our research findings. The final section wraps up the discussion with some concluding remarks.

Social assimilation: a conceptual tool to observe the Taiwanese sojourners in China

Previous studies on cross-Strait relations usually involve observations and analysis of the Taiwanese identity or identity changes of the Taiwanese who have lived and settled down in China. Among these studies, however, few have treated these Taiwanese sojourners as immigrants and thus use the socio-psychological approach to explain the identity changes of these Taiwanese. Instead of analyzing whether there is any identity and socio-psychological change, this study proposes a somewhat path-breaking approach to examine their attitudinal change in light of the assimilation theory, and we use survey data to show how they put these changes into action.

Assimilation refers to the breaking or crossing of the boundary when the members of the two social/cultural groups get in touch with each other (Yinger 1981, 249). Assimilation thus happens in dimensions such as biological, cultural, social and, finally, psychological (Gordon 1964; Barth and Noel 1972, 336). These dimensions are interdependent but conceptually separate. In the case of the Taiwanese in China, with similar ethnicity and shared culture, we just need to look at the social and psychological aspects of the assimilation. In this research, we choose to focus on the following three issues to measure the degree of their assimilation: (1) family arrangements, (2) social relations and (3) destined home. We believe that we could observe and measure the degree of their assimilation for the following reasons.

First, we rely on the family arrangements to indicate how these Taiwanese are really settling down and beginning long-term living (*an'sheng-li'ming*) in the mainland. Among different aspects of family arrangements, such as whether they bring their families with them to the mainland or whether they purchase homes in places they settled, we pick the choice for their children's education as an important indicator because it involves different choices they could make. These choices include: (1) leaving their children in Taiwan, (2) sending them to Taishang schools, (3) sending them to international schools, (4) sending them to the international division of local schools or (5) sending them to local schools so that they can get closer to the mainland society. Although the education choice really depends on various practical reasons of each family, we believe it is a very good indicator to tell whether they are willing to get their family assimilated into the local society.

Second, the social relationship of the Taiwanese in the mainland is another good indicator because it is telling in terms of the degree of socialization. If they choose to hang around with other Taiwanese more than with the local people, we can tell their pattern of socialization and the degree of assimilation. So to measure their social relationship, we cauterize them into groups of hanging around with (1) almost all Taiwanese, (2) mostly Taiwanese, (3) some Chinese and some Taiwanese, (4) mostly [mainland] Chinese and (5) almost all Chinese.

Finally, the sense of "home" is one of the main aspects in distinguishing the level of assimilation of these Taiwanese. But the idea of "home" is very vague that could cause a lot of confusion. After trying many indicators, we finally decided to use the "life plan after retirement," which catches the idea of "place to return to" (*luo'ye guigen*) to indicate the "sense of home." After years of field experiences, we have found these three aspects could be the base proxies for the concept of social assimilation of the Taiwanese sojourners in China.

Competing hypotheses of social assimilation

Social assimilation involves boundary-crossing of one social group to another in the social interactive process. There are various factors affecting the pathway and quality of social assimilation. What are the most important factors affecting the social assimilation of the Taiwanese in China? Based on our survey findings, we would argue that the "class factor" and "identity factor" are two significant ones. The reasons to use these factors in our research are as follows.

The class hypothesis

The significance of the class factor in shaping social relations is widely used and accepted by social scientists. Class, however, can take different meaning in various theoretical contexts. For example, Marx treated "class" mainly as whether people possess any means of production, while Weber used the concept more as a diversified and multi-dimensional status group. But Weber emphasized the life chances of the people who could draw products and income from the "market" (Weber 1966, 1–96). People on the same footing of the market would receive similar income, own similar consuming power and share similar taste and thus belong to the same "class." In other words, for neo-Weberian theorists, social class would manifest itself through the "pattern of consumption": people at the same class prefer the same products and favor the same lifestyle (Veblen 1918; Weber 1966, 1–96; Bourdieu 1984). This is exactly the reason why Weber conceptualizes "class" as the "status group," those who enjoy the same lifestyle, reside in the same region, perform the same ceremony and observe the same dressing code, etc. This is also the reason why he has to distinguish the concept of class based on income and the class grounded on consumption (more as status groups) (Grusky 2001).

To apply the concept of class to the study of inter-group relations in a more operational way, we propose to include both "income" and "consumption" in analyzing how the members of different groups may get along with each other and, when hanging around, how they could eliminate the prejudices each group holds against others.

Therefore, the class factor in this study is conceptualized as "status groups" who have settled in different kinds of "gated communities." The status of the residential area is evaluated by the price of the housing residents own or rent. And, in this research, the value of housing is appraised by the interviewees themselves, i.e., if they believe the price of the housing they own is far above the average, they (at least they believe) belong to the higher class. Otherwise, they belong to the lower or similar class as the average local residents. As the class theories suggests, we hypothesize that the Taiwanese that feel themselves above the locals will not blend in with them while those who consider otherwise would easily blend in, no matter in terms of lifestyle, social relations or career plans. This is because those who can afford high-priced residential areas tend to associate themselves with those with similar consuming power and tastes.

The identity hypothesis

In addition to the class factors, the significance of "self-identity" in shaping the social relations among the members of different social groups is also widely acknowledged. Self-identity here refers to the recognition of belonging to some specific social groups and the assumption of the feelings and meanings associated with such belonging (Tajfel 1978). In other words, identity refers to the relations between social groups and their members: the latter identify themselves as members of the former, whether they are nation-states, ethnicities, professional groups or gender groups (Turner 1982, 15–40).

Following this perspective, the "personal identity" of the Taiwanese refers to the way they identify themselves: whether they are "Taiwanese only" or "Chinese only" or "both as Taiwanese and Chinese" (Wang 1998, 1–45; Wu 2005, 5–39). The only problem here is how to conceptualize it. Shall we name it as ethnicity? But this concept involves both cultural and political elements, and any emphasis may miss the other part. In this research, we would like to incorporate both aspects, although our focus is on the former.

Culture-based "personal identity" could be interpreted as the subjective and selective identification of the origin of the cultural system and social customs. Based on that concept, different Taiwanese could identify themselves with some of the social categories, i.e., ethnic groups in the context. In order to clarify the influences of "personal identity" on how Taiwanese may be incorporated into the local community in China, we distinguish three social categories, (1) Chinese who clearly share affinity with the traditional Chinese culture, (2) both Chinese and Taiwanese, who accommodate the Chinese culture and Taiwanese identity and (3) Taiwanese only, who do not just identify themselves Taiwanese but also reject the assumption that Taiwan is part of China.

After some descriptive characterization of the status of the social assimilation of the Taiwanese sojourners in China, we would like to examine the factors determining the level of assimilation of these Taiwanese. In this section, we try to show that the "class factors" and "identity factors" are most critical in determining the progress in the assimilation and also the community these Taiwanese settled in and the self-identification of these sojourners are the best available proxies to check the influences of these two factors.

Data and analysis

We will describe the source of data and the methods for analyzing the data to be presented and discussed in the next section.

Source of the date: the 2009 Taishang survey

The data of the study are drawn from a collaborative project between the University of Hong Kong and the National Chengchi University, entitled "Life and Attitudes of the Taiwanese in mainland China," carried out in the summer of 2009. In this survey, 12 researchers formed six research teams and each group spent a total of six weeks interviewing the Taiwanese settling in both the greater Shanghai area and cities surrounding Dongguan. During the interview, we first asked the interviewees the questions on our semi-structured questionnaire. After filling them out, the interviewers asked further questions to clarify their answers to the questions on the questionnaire, and started more casual talks on related issues. The dialogues were recorded and turned into transcripts for the researcher to keep track of their attitude changes and the reasons why they have occurred.

Since we have little information about the Taiwanese communities in China and the population of our sampling, it was difficult for us to design any forms of random sampling on the basis of pre-existing information. What we did was the snowballing for our interviewees. We followed the rule of "maximum variation" in the sample selection to diversify our source of information. As a result, our interviewees include Taiwanese businessmen, their families, Taiwanese students, the first and second generation Taiwanese, employees from both labor-intensive and high-tech manufacturers, working for Taiwanese firms, joint-ventures, foreign firms (European, American, Japanese, Korean among others) and Chinese firms, Taiwanese sojourners with different educational status, ranging from primary school to Ph.D.s, Taiwanese affiliated with different political camps and different ethnic origins. We collected 214 cases altogether, and that made this the largest systematic survey of the Taiwanese in mainland China so far.

Models and analysis

The descriptive results of the survey are presented in Table 12.1. From this table, we can get a rough idea about the assimilation of the Taiwanese in three primary dimensions. Among the three aspects, we know that about half of the Taiwanese sojourners tend to let their children stay in Taiwan for education. Also, 59 percent choose to hang around almost entirely with Taiwanese and another 20 percent mainly but not exclusively with Taiwanese. For the their life plan after retirement, a bit less than a half vow to go back to Taiwan while only 11 percent have decided to stay in China. In other words, the overall progress of the social assimilation of the Taiwanese sojourners is still quite limited, even though they have been in China for many years.

Going beyond these descriptive statistics, we could also clarify the factors that determine the progress in the assimilation of these Taiwan sojourners. We thus put three relevant variables in three regression models. In these models, we set the three dimensions of social assimilation as dependent variables, namely, children's education, personal ties and retirement plan. Since "social class" and "self-identity" are the primary concerns of the research, we make them the independent variables in these models. We conceptualize "social class" in terms of real estate prices in comparisons with local residents while "self-identity" is the self-identification as Taiwanese or both Taiwanese and Chinese. In addition, we introduce ethnic origins, party identification, time stayed in China, profits reaped in China, employment sector and some other demographic features such as generation, education, gender as controlled variables, in case they would make confounding effects on the level of social assimilation of the respondents. And due to the nature of the variables introduced (measured as ordinal level), the methods for measuring coefficients in these models are multiple linear regression analysis.

Table 12.1 The assimilation of Taiwanese sojourners in China

Children's education			Personal ties			Retirement plan		
Categories	No.	%	Categories	No.	%	Categories	No.	%
Left in Taiwan	100	51.02	Almost all Taiwanese	126	58.88	Definitely going back	96	45.93
Taishang schools	13	6.63	Mostly Taiwanese	43	20.09	Probably going back	32	15.31
International schools	19	9.69	Both Chinese and Taiwanese	30	14.02	Haven't decided	57	27.27
Int'l division of local schools	16	8.16	Mostly Chinese	13	6.07	Probably staying on	15	7.18
Local schools	48	24.49	Almost all Chinese	2	0.93	Definitely staying on	9	4.31
	196	100.00		214	100.00		209	100.00

Source: "Life and Attitudes of the Taiwanese in China." Joint Research Project of the University of Hong Kong and National Chengchi University, 2009.

Research findings and discussions

The results of the regression analyses are presented in Table 12.2: among them, the dependent variable of Model One being children's education, Model Two personal ties and Model Three retirement plans.

Social assimilation in children's education arrangement

From Model One, the class factor is the only factor that exerts significant influences on the social assimilation in terms of the children's education. This suggests that whether these Taiwanese choose to bring over their families and settle in China, and whether they would like their children to mix with the local Chinese are dependent on their class status: the higher their status, the more likely they would send their kids to stay with local Chinese. This finding seems to be just the opposite of what we expected in our hypothesis: it was the different living standard that blocks the Taiwanese from getting along with the local Chinese.

From our interviews, however, we found there are reasons that account for such perplexing findings. The Chinese society is a highly stratified society: for those with higher economic status, they would hang around with local Chinese elites and thus tend to not to look down on the local people, reflected in their decisions to bring over their families and send their kids to stay with local kids. But also note that those local kids are mostly coming from good family backgrounds as well:

> Most of the kids go to local schools, but not just any kind of local schools. Most of the parents would send their kids to the Jing'an District to attend schools there. In that school, almost all the kids come from white-collar families and no kids of peasant workers at all. I thus feel very conformable in that school … The most important reason to send my kids to that school is to give them the chance to hang around with local people. Secondly, it has to do with the quality of education. Most kids there study hard and thus lays a firm foundation for their future.
>
> (S1896–23)

On the other hand, those without the chance to get in touch with those local elites tend to leave their kids in Taiwan or send them to Taishang schools. For them, the local Chinese are just bunches of peasant workers from rural areas or poorer provinces.

This explains why the higher class the Taiwanese attribute themselves to, the higher the probability they would bring their families to China and their kids to local schools: they have the ability to establish an enclave in the locality (e.g., gated communities in Shanghai) and to associate themselves with the right "Chinese" (local Chinese elites) but at the same time to distinguish themselves from the average Chinese. As one of our interviewee describes,

Table 12.2 Factors affecting the assimilation of Taiwanese sojourners in China

	Model One Children's education		Model Two Personal ties		Model Three Retirement plan	
	B	S.E.	B	S.E.	B	S.E.
Constant	1.429	0.973	0.765	0.464	1.284	0.598
Ethnic origins (cf. Mainlanders)						
Heklo (Hokkien)	−0.350	0.430	0.155	0.203	−0.576*	0.264
Hakka	−0.893	0.537	0.388	0.266	−0.298	0.349
Party identification (cf. Pro-DPP Id)						
Pro-KMT	0.615	0.386	−0.117	0.186	0.282	0.242
Neutral	0.511	0.360	−0.182	0.178	0.330	0.232
Social class	0.287*	0.130	0.011	0.066	0.056	0.085
Self-identity (cf. self-identified Taiwanese)						
Self-identified Chinese	0.522	0.783	1.021*	0.395	1.530**	0.507
Self-identified as both	0.485	0.336	0.365*	0.162	0.063	0.214
Time stayed (in China)	0.028	0.031	0.029	0.015	0.047*	0.069
Profits reaped (in China)	−0.145	0.109	0.076	0.053	0.078	0.070

Generation (cf. born after 1977)						
Born before 1956	-0.220	0.506	-0.472	0.243	-0.548	0.320
Born between 1957 and 1976	0.362	0.375	-0.131	0.184	-0.185	0.242
Education (cf. below high school)						
Graduated and higher	0.542	0.529	-0.050	0.257	0.052	0.333
Undergraduate	0.117	0.380	0.035	0.190	-0.121	0.245
College	0.249	0.405	-0.217	0.204	-0.099	0.262
Male (cf. female)	-0.370	0.309	0.258	0.152	0.323	0.201
Service (cf. manufacturing)	-0.223	0.302	0.566***	0.145	0.320	0.190
Sample size	196		214		209	
Adj. R²	0.065		0.146		0.147	
p	<.05		<.001		<.001	
S.E.E	1.652		0.837		1.076	
Conditional index	24.122		23.590		23.357	

Source: "Life and Attitudes of the Taiwanese in China." Joint Research Project of the University of Hong Kong and National Chengchi University, 2009.

Notes
* $p < 0.05$; ** $p < 0.01$; *** $p < 0.001$.

People only have the chance to get in touch with those who in the same class as themselves: think about it, do the Taiwanese have the chance to hang around with peasant workers? Of course not.... Take myself as an example: my closest Chinese friend is the biggest real estate contractor in Shanghai, owning a soccer club. And, I feel that we have a lot in common and thus talk in the same language. But this does not mean I can make friends with Chinese, I can deal with only a small percentage of them.

(S1810–30)

In our everyday contacts, we [Taiwanese] meet only white collar class. They are the Chinese we have the chance to get in touch. In case, I frequently meet those who used to study or work in foreign counties: you won't feel unconformable talking to them, for they have the "quality" [*suzhi*] just like you.

(S1811–31)

In other words, the Taiwanese who are in better economic conditions have been able to move around and find a nice living environment. They also have the chance to meet the Chinese elites and assess their potential rising economic power (Lin 2012).

Social assimilation in personal ties

As for the factors affecting the social relations of the Taiwanese sojourners in China, Model Two tells us that only the self-identity and employment sector are relevant. For the former, those who identify themselves as "Chinese" or "both Chinese and Taiwanese" have a higher propensity to hang around with local Chinese.

As mentioned before, identity denotes the attribution of the self in a social category, and based on that, the "we-group" and "they-group" is distinguished. Therefore, when the Taiwanese identify themselves as "Chinese" or "both Chinese and Taiwanese," they actually evaluate their assumed distance from the local Chinese: those who consider themselves Chinese share a "we-ness" while Taiwanese assume a "they-ness." This is clearly manifested in the following quote from our interviewee:

I feel myself being both Taiwanese and Chinese ... I do not feel any significant difference between me and the local Chinese. Just to give you an example, we have two business partners here, one is Taiwanese and the other Shanghainese. If we have been doing business for many years in both cases, I would say both are ok and wouldn't say which is better.

(S1803–10)

This is because the Taiwanese who identify themselves as "Taiwanese only" tend to highlight Taiwan's uniqueness, which may have something in common with Chinese culture but they are never the same. The local culture developed in Taiwan in the the post-war era is what these Taiwanese tend to identify with. As a consequence, these Taiwanese won't have the we-ness feeling when they get in touch with local Chinese. As one of the female Taiwanese businesspeople described,

> All my friends are Taiwanese ... I cannot imagine that we [Taiwanese] can marry a local Chinese: we are totally different.

> (G1725–48)

In addition, the manufacturing vs. service sector is also significant. This is probably because people employed in the service sector have to serve their customers, no matter whether they are Taiwanese or Chinese while those employed in the manufacturing sector normally meet either Taiwanese as their colleagues or Chinese as labor workers. Moreover, the manufacturing sector has to establish a monitoring system coupled with discipline and sanction. The relations between Taiwanese managerial strata and the Chinese blue-collar workers thus cannot be too close or too friendly. Under such circumstances, the Taiwanese thus do not have the incentives nor the chances to have frequent contacts with local Chinese. In fact, to maintain the managerial hierarchy, Taiwanese normally have to keep away from their subordinates. This has been confirmed by one of the Taiwanese staff,

> When I was the staff [of a Taiwanese enterprise], when I came to China, I normally lived in the factory. During those years, we had maids cooking for us, drivers giving us rides, and other stuff dealing with the workers. We really had no chance to interact with labor workers. But now I am running a restaurant, I have to deal with our customers, trying to know their favorite taste. In addition, I also have to talk to my employees regularly, teaching them how to serve our customers. Gradually, I feel like they [my employees] are just like my families.

> (G1715–12)

The sector factor thus affects the chances of the daily contacts of these Taiwanese. In other words, the structure of social relations among the Taiwanese in China is partly shaped by subject/identity factors and partly by objective/necessity factors.

Social assimilation in retirement plan

Finally, factors affecting the meaning of the destined home, measured by respondents' retirement plans, are reported in Model Three of Table 12.2. The three factors – self-identity, ethnic origins and time in China – are significant in shaping the idea of home among the Taiwanese sojourners. They seem to be similar to the pattern of social relations. The meaning of home seems deeply involved with a more sensitive side of human decisions: this has to do with how people choose the final destination of their entire life. Among all the factors, without doubt, self-proclaimed identity matters. The ethnic origin also matters because these involved the true meaning of hometown (*lao'jia*). The significance of ethnic origins can be best manifested by one of crucial cases being interviewed. The interviewee is a Taiwanese female, running a business in China for more than 20 years. She brought all her family to Dongguan and her son even married a local Chinese. In every aspect, she is the ideal case of localization and thus should maintain close ties with the locality. But when being questioned, she immediately responds by saying that

> We have apartments in both Taizhong and Zhanghua: they are empty now and waiting for us to move back. Every time I think about moving back, I would be very happy. We do have friends here but still we would like to spend the rest of our life in Taiwan.
>
> (G1721–29)

Contrary to this case, one mainlander Taiwanese demonstrates strong affiliation with the local society, which is not even his hometown, though.

> For me, Shanghai feels like the home. After all, my life, my properties, my friends and almost everything belong to me are in Shanghai. So I do not feel I am that affiliated with Taiwan. This does not mean I do not love Taiwan. But every time when I go [to Taiwan], I feel I want to come back sooner. The only reason I have to go back to Taiwan is the grave of my parents. For my own case, I still have not decided where I would bury myself.
>
> (S1806–22)

Different ethnic origins represent different affinity to their imagined "home/hometown"; this could be traced back to the early-age experiences or the memories of their parents, transmitted by stories, narratives and personal contacts. All these set the foundation for the identity of the Taiwanese being interviewed.

Finally, the time stayed in China also matters because that may shape how people look at the place they stay in. It is no surprise that these factors are relevant. Again, other factors such as party identification, profits reaped in China, employment sector and demographic features such as generation, education, gender are all irrelevant.

Comparing the three dimensions of social assimilation of the Taiwanese sojourners in China, we can find that the class factor determines whether they would live and mix with local Chinese in daily lives. But when turning to the dimensions such as social relations and meanings of home, the class factor then lose all its significance. Instead, factors such as personal identity, ethnic origin and time staying in China all become critical. In other words, class facilitates the mix-up of Taiwanese with local people while identity shapes Taiwanese close relationships and psychological acceptance with local society.

Conclusion

It takes at least two to tangle. The future of cross-Strait relations is jointly determined by both sides of the Strait, with an equally important role of the US. Since the late 1980s, Taiwan started its democratic transition and completely changed the nature of cross-Strait relations on the Taiwan side. Ever since, the Taiwanese nationalist sentiment has been widespread and a Taiwanese national identity has emerged. Also, periodical elections give the ordinary Taiwanese people a say in shaping Taiwan's Mainland policy. As a consequence, the study of cross-Strait relations cannot be limited to traditional approaches, laying all the attention on structural factors or the ideas of policy elites. When analyzing the dynamics and future of cross-Strait relations, we need to take into account the opinions of the Taiwanese people.

One approach to grasp the attitudes of the Taiwanese people is to analyze the survey data (Keng et al. 2006, 23–66; Wang et al. 2010, 159–184). But in that case, the Taiwanese settled in China would be systematically left out of our survey. Since the late 1990s, these Taiwanese have been playing a very significant role in shaping cross-Strait relations (Keng 2007, 63–80; Keng and Schubert 2010, 287–310). However, due to difficulties in studying this group of people, up to now, we have not been able to present a systematic study of these Taiwanese in China, showing us what they think and how they get along with the Chinese. Thanks to "The Life and Attitudes of the Taiwanese in China" project, for the first time, we can present a systematic survey of the personal identity and social assimilation of these Taiwanese sojourners.

From the survey, we find that the extent to which the Taiwanese assimilate to the mainland is determined by different factors: the class factor helps to explain how the Taiwanese get along with the local Chinese. It also suggests that, as China grows richer, more Taiwanese would probably maintain stable and friendly working relations with the local Chinese. But this does not mean that their relationships would be very close and the Taiwanese would easily treat the Chinese as their fellow countrymen. It takes time for their identity to be transformed, as indicated in the case of the factors shaping their ideas about their destined homes.

Other critical factors, such as ethnic origins and industrial sector, suggest that cross-Strait unification cannot be that easily achieved simply by frequent contacts or interest alignments. Based on these findings, we believe that in the study of cross-Strait relations, it is time for us to inquire into the micro-level changes and trace back the sources of these changes to provide deeper and detailed evidence about how policy-makers might reach decisions and thus offer us a better prediction about the future of cross-Strait relations. This study is merely another step in that direction.

Table 12A.1 Frequency table of the sample

Gender	Case number	Ratio (%)
Male	151	70.56
Female	63	29.44
Total	214	100.00
Ethnic origins		
Hakka	22	10.33
Heklo (Hokkien)	157	73.71
Mainlander	34	15.96
Total	213	100.00
Party identification		
Pro-KMT	92	44.02
Neutral	76	36.36
Pro-DPP	41	19.62
Total	209	100.00
Generation		
21–30	35	16.67
31–40	72	34.29
41–50	54	25.71
51–60	39	18.57
Above 61	10	4.76
Total	210	100.00
Time stay in China		
1–4 years	64	30.19
5–8 years	70	33.02
9–12 years	41	19.34
13–16 years	16	7.55
Above 17 years	21	9.91
Total	212	100.00
Industrial sector		
Sector	73	35.78
Manufacturing	131	64.22
Total	204	100.00
Educational		
Below high school	35	16.36
2 to 3 years college	57	26.64
4 years college	91	42.52
Graduate school & above	31	14.49
Total	214	100.00
Profits reaped		
Deficit	45	22.96
Breaking even	20	10.20
Gaining	131	66.83
Total	196	100.00

Source: "Life and Attitudes of the Taiwanese in China." Joint Research Project of the University of Hong Kong and National Chengchi University, 2009.

References

Barth, Ernest and Donald L. Noel. 1972. "Conceptual Frameworks for the Analysis of Race Relations." *Social Forces* 50(3): 333–348.

Bourdieu, Pierre. 1984. *Distinction: A Social Critique of the Judgment of Taste*. Cambridge, MA: Harvard University Press.

Cabestan, Jean-Pierre. 1995. "The Cross-Strait Relationship in the Post-Cold War Era: Neither Re-unification Nor 'Win-Win' Game." *Issues & Studies* 31(1): 27–50.

Clark, Cal. 2001. "Prospects for Taiwan-China Economic Relations under the Chen Shuibian Administration." *American Asian Review* 19(1): 27–53.

Clark, Cal. 2002. "The China-Taiwan Relationship: Growing Cross-Strait Economic Integration." *Orbits* 46(4): 753–766.

Clark, Cal. 2003. "Does European Integration Provide a Model for Moderating Cross-Strait Relations?" *Asian Affairs* 29(4): 195–215.

Gordon, Milton M. 1964. *Assimilation in American Life: The Role of Race, Religion, and National Origins*. Oxford, UK & New York: Oxford University Press.

Grusky, David B. 2001. *Social Stratification: Class, Race, and Gender in Sociological Perspective*. Boulder, CO & Oxford, UK: Westview Press.

Keng, Shu. 2002. "Agents of Globalization or Citizens of Taiwan? National Identity of the Taishang in Great Shanghai's IT Sector." Paper Presented at the Second Annual Conference on Politics & Information, Yilan: Foguang University, Apr. 11–12, 2002.

Keng, Shu. 2007. "Understanding the Political Consequences of People-to-People Relations Across the Taiwan Strait: Towards an Analytical Framework." *Chinese History and Society* 32: 63–80.

Keng, Shu and Ruihua Lin. 2011. "Integrating from Below: Observing the 'Linkage Communities' Across the Taiwan Strait." In *China's Quiet Rise: Peace Through Integration*, edited by Baogang Guo and Chung-Chian Teng, 139–155. Lanham, MD: Rowman & Littlefield.

Keng, Shu and Gunter Schubert. 2010. "Agents of Unification? The Political Role of Taiwanese Businessmen in the Process of Cross-Strait Integration." *Asian Survey* 50(2): 287–310.

Keng, Shu, Lu-huei Chen and Kuan-bo Huang. 2006. "Sense, Sensitivity, and Sophistication in Shaping the Future of Cross-Strait Relations." *Issues & Studies* 42(4): 23–66.

Lin, Ruihua. 2012. "Birds of a Feather Flock Together: Social Class and Social Assimilation of the Taiwanese in Mainland China." *Soochow Journal of Political Science* 30(2): 127–167.

Tajfel, Henri. 1978. *Differentiation Between Social Groups: Studies in the Social Psychology of Intergroup Relation*. London: Academic Press.

Turner, John C. 1982. "Towards a Cognitive Redefinition of the Social Group." In *Social Identity and Intergroup Relations*, edited by Henri Tajfel, 15–40. Cambridge: Cambridge University Press.

Veblen, Thorstein. 1918. *The Theory of the Leisure Class: An Economic Study of Institution*. New York: B. W. Huebsch.

Wang, Fu-Chang. 1998. "Ethnic Consciousness, Nationalist Sentiments and Party Identification: The Ethnic Politics in the 1990s." *Taiwanese Sociology* 2: 1–45.

Wang, T. Y., Lu-huei Chen and Shu Keng. 2010. "Symbolic Politics, Self-Interests and Threat Perceptions: An Analysis of Taiwan Citizens' Views on Cross–Strait Economic Exchanges." In *Taiwan's Politics in the 21st Century*, edited by Wei-chin Lee, 159–184. New Jersey: World Scientific Publishing Co., Inc.

Weber, Max. 1966. "Class, Status and Party." In *Class, Status and Power: Social Stratifi-cation in Comparative Perspective*, edited by Reinhard Bendix and Seymour Martin Lipset, 1–96. New York: Free Press.

Wu, Hsin-Hsing. 1995. "The Political Economy of ROC-PRC Relations." *Issues & Studies* 31(1): 51–62.

Wu, Nai-Te. 2005. "For Love or Bread: A Preliminary Inquiry into the Changes in the National Identity of the Taiwanese." *Taiwanese Political Science Review* 9(2): 5–39.

Yinger, J. Milton. 1981. "Toward a Theory of Assimilation and Dissimilation." *Ethnic and Racial Studies* 4: 249–264.

13 Ethnic identity of Hong Kong people

An academic question turned political[1]

Robert Chung and Edward Tai

The study of ethnic identity of Hong Kong people predates the sovereignty hand-over of Hong Kong by almost 20 years, and the dichotomy of "Hongkonger" versus "Chinese" as a research instrument was widely used by Hong Kong soci-ologists in the 1980s. In a 1985 survey, Lau and Kuan (Lau and Kuan 1988: 2) reported that "59.5 percent of the respondents identify themselves as Hong-kongese, 36.2 percent as Chinese." The researchers then considered the propor-tion of those opting for a Hong Kong identity to be "striking," and together with other findings, concluded that people's "sense of attachment to Hong Kong is tremendous."

Although the study of ethnic identity is very common in the world, it is par-ticularly relevant to societies in transition, like Hong Kong before and after the change of sovereignty in 1997. In a way, the strength of people's identity towards different cultural, social and ethnic identities reflects their political atti-tudes and underlying cultural values. For this reason, the authors working at the Public Opinion Programme at the University of Hong Kong have been tracking Hong Kong people's ethnic identity changes since 1997. Before 2012, it was basically an academic study cum community service. At the beginning of 2012, due to some high profile comments made by an officer of the Liaison Office of the Central People's Government in Hong Kong, the issue has turned political.

This chapter first examines the methodology and findings of the tracking studies, and then examines the nature of the political discourse.

Hong Kong is definitely a unique case in the world which experiences a trans-ition of sovereignty not by warfare, not through a referendum seeking independ-ence, but via a joint declaration signed by the United Kingdom and China. People living in Hong Kong during the era of transition encounter many kinds of constitutional and cultural changes, symbolized by a change of flag on July 1, 1997.

According to some studies, way before the handover, people living in Hong Kong had already begun to seek a new ethnic identity. For example, Zheng and Wong (2002) suggest that the identities of "Hong Kong people" and "Chinese people living in Hong Kong" began to differentiate in the 1960s, mainly due to the rising economic status of the local born Hong Kong generation. According to their study (Zheng and Wong 2002: 72),

...in 1961, the total population in Hong Kong is 3,168,100. Among them, 50.5% were born in China, 47.7% were born in Hong Kong, 1.8% were born in other places. According to this calculation, over 50% population at that time were immigrants (52.3%).

In the 1980s, this phenomenon attracted sociologists Lau and Kuan to conduct empirical studies on Hong Kong people's identity. Their first study was a pilot survey conducted in 1985 in Kwun Tong (Lau 1998), an industrial-cum-residential community in Hong Kong. They used a questionnaire to survey the community members whether they would identify themselves as "Hong-kongese," "Chinese" or "don't know/hard to say." The result is that more than half of the people living there regarded themselves as "Hongkongese" compared to about one-third regarding them as "Chinese." The study was later enhanced to cover a random sample of Hong Kong territory-wide residents conducted in 1988. This time, two more options, "both (identities)," "neither (identity)" were included (Lau 1998). These survey questions were then repeated in various surveys intermittently until 2007 (CUHK, "Social indicators and social development project" 2003²; Wong and Wan 2007).³

Lau (1998) also breaks down the respondents' choice of the four identities by their demographic variables, namely, gender, education attainment, income and place of birth. The study found statistically significant relationships across most surveys, in that females would identify themselves as Hongkongese more, so would people with higher educational level and higher income level. For their place of birth, there is no surprise that people born in Hong Kong would regard themselves more as "Hongkongese" than "Chinese." However, Lau (1998) also made a controversial observation that the percentage claiming of both identities would increase after the handover. Zheng and Wong were inclined to agree with this observation in 2002, but became skeptical in 2005.

According to Wong and Wan (Wong and Wan 2007), the differences between the 1997 and 2007 surveys in terms of percentages of Hong Kong people identifying themselves as "Hongkongese" and "Chinese" were very minimal.

Besides, Zheng and Wong (2002) believe that the fluctuation of identities of Hong Kong people is highly related to events happening in Hong Kong. These events change people's opinions towards the Chinese and Hong Kong governments, especially in terms of trust, confidence and satisfaction, and shape Hong Kong people's identities. While this argument may be correct, we must look at it more carefully.

Conceptually, the definition itself may be controversial, especially the meaning of "both (identities)," meaning "both Hongkongese and Chinese." This combined option is the most ambiguous part of the entire study, because without a clear understanding of what is meant by "both Hongkongese and Chinese," any time series analysis on identity change would be hard to interpret.

For example, when one orders food in a restaurant, say one is given the choice of chicken or beef or both. If one chooses "both," it does not necessarily mean one likes both dishes equally. One may just think there is not much difference between the two, or one really cannot pick any one out of the two. Back to the issue of identities, does "both Hongkongese and Chinese" really means "equally acceptable" or "does not matter"?

So, what is "Hongkongese" and what is "Chinese," what is "both (identities)"? Zheng and Wong once disagreed with this ambiguous concept and accepted Wang's (1991) simple use of "Hongkongese" or "Chinese" as a kind of self-proclamation by the respondents. They suggested that people's sense of identity is affected by both subjective self-perceptions and objective conditions (Wong and Wan 2005). In order to make such studies more meaningful, either we give a better definition for the term "both (identities)" or we avoid using it altogether.

In order to prevent any translation hassle one way to another, we will use from now on "Hongkonger" to be the English translation of "Hong Kong people" or "Hongkongese." This term is used frequently by native Chinese speakers in Hong Kong nowadays in their spoken or written English.[4]

This chapter also examines how Hong Kong people with different demographic backgrounds identify themselves differently with the identities "Hongkonger" and "Chinese." We will conclude our 15-year-long time series analyses with the observation that local Hong Kong people's identity is affected not only by the economic development within or beyond Hong Kong, but by political development in Hong Kong and China during the so-called transitional period.

Methodological framework

From dichotomy to one-in-four choices

Back to 1997, when one of the authors began to study Hong Kong people's ethnic identity, he inherited the traditional method of requesting respondents to choose one answer out of a dichotomy of "Hongkonger" versus "Chinese." However, instead of using "don't know," "hard to say," "both (identities)" or other uncertain answers as the middle choice, two more specific answers were offered, namely, "China's Hongkonger" and "Hong Kong's Chinese." Obviously, to some people the concepts of "Hongkonger" and "Chinese" overlap with each other and make it difficult for them to choose one out of the two. In many previous studies, this "conceptual difficulty" is part of the test itself. In case a lot of people find it difficult to resolve this problem, their ambivalence is itself an important indicator generated by the study.

The author accepted this reasoning, but considered it more productive to reduce some ambivalent answers by using more specific labels like "China's Hongkonger" and "Hong Kong's Chinese." Technically, the first label is interpreted as "ethnical Hongkonger living in China," meaning a stronger sense of the "Hongkonger" identity, while the latter label is interpreted as "ethnical Chinese living in Hong Kong," meaning a stronger sense of the "Chinese" identity. The study has thus expanded the traditional "Hongkonger versus Chinese" dichotomy to become a one-in-four-choices design right at the beginning. People who still find it hard to "resolve" their identity can continue to choose "don't know" or "hard to say."

In our analysis, the labels of "Hongkonger" and "China's Hongkonger" are sometimes combined to mean "Hongkonger in the broadest sense," while the other two categories of "Chinese" and "Hong Kong's Chinese" are combined as "Chinese in the broadest sense." One can of course go back to the traditional analysis of "Hongkonger" versus "Chinese," for the sake of continuity, by dropping the two new labels, but one can also use the new labels for enhanced analysis. The new design has therefore added flexibility to the traditional analysis, after 1997.

In our enhanced analysis, "Hongkonger" and "Chinese" identities can be considered as "strong and pure identities," while the other two categories can be combined to mean "mixed or ambivalent identities." The analysis of "strong and pure identities" versus "mixed or ambivalent identities" can itself be a stand-alone study. By using an array of identity labels, plus a large group of demographic variables, comprehensive time series analyses could be performed to chart the development of Hong Kong people's ethnic identity.

From one-in-four choices to strength ratings

Whatever answers one gives to the dichotomous or one-in-four choices, there is still the blind spot regarding the absolute strength of these identities. To put it simply, one may choose "Hongkonger" because one identifies very strongly with this identity, or because one feels very weak about other identities, but relatively not so weak with this identity. To fill in this methodological gap, two more rating questions were introduced in the study, which requested all respondents to rate the absolute strength of their "Hongkonger" and "Chinese" identities separately using a 0–10 scale. The two questions are conceptually different from the previous set of identity questions, because they avoid the problem of overlapping identities altogether. Besides, the separate ratings themselves can be mathematically computed to indicate one's "strong" versus "weak" identities, thereby rendering the traditional questions redundant. Nevertheless, for the sake of continuity and computational checks, the traditional categorical question is still kept for backward comparison and consistency check.

After ten years, in early 2007, the survey was further enhanced to include four more identities for strength rating, namely, "citizen of People's Republic of China," "member of the Chinese race," "Asian" and "global citizen," in order to depict a clearer picture of cultural and ethnic identities. How these identities overlap or interrelate with each other, and how Hong Kong people express themselves using all these identities, is not the focus of this study.

From strength ratings to "identity indices"

To make better sense of complicated findings arising from the more sophisticated questionnaire, towards the end of 2008, a set of "identity indices" was generated after expanding the study to include a set of "importance ratings" for different identities. The formula used was to take the geometric means of "strength" times "importance" then multiplied by 10. This formula is used because both the identity strength and importance ratings are using a 0–10 scale, so their geometric mean is also a 0–10 figure. By multiplying it by 10, the final value of all indices would become 0–100, which Hong Kong people are more familiar with.

The importance ratings were introduced in the study mainly because some people may give a high rating on a certain identity, but do not feel that the identity has too much relevance in their cultural, social or political life. Therefore, there should be some indicators or indices to show the strength of people's "feeling" towards different identities. This is the basis for generating the geometric mean of "strength" × "importance" × 10 "identity indices." With the generation of these indices, the study of ethnic identity for Hong Kong people has become more comprehensive.

To sum up, our methodology involves a one-in-four-choices categorical question to measure people's "compelled choice," another set of strength and importance ratings to measure the absolute strengths of six different identities and, finally, six "identity indices" are compiled to measure the combined effect of strength and importance ratings.

Describing the trend of ethnic identities

The following figures came from household telephone surveys conducted by the Public Opinion Programme at the University of Hong Kong by one of the authors starting as early as 1997. The target of the surveys are local Cantonese-speaking Hong Kong residents (who comprise 95 percent of the Hong Kong population) aged 18 or above. The surveys are conducted by real interviewers, and each time, at least 500 and most often 1,000 successful cases are collected. The response rate ranges from 45 percent to 68 percent. The "next-birthday rule" is applied to ensure random sampling within the household, and half-yearly aggregated figures are consolidated for presentation here. The maximum sampling errors of all percentage figures is +/–4 percentage points at 95 percent confidence level, while that for 0–10 rating figures is normally +/–0.2, and that for 0–100 ratings normally +/–2.[5]

"Hongkonger" versus "Chinese"

Using the one-in-four-choices question, Figure 13.1 shows the trend of identity changes for Hong Kong people from the second half of 1997 to the first half of 2013. In the first four years after the handover, people's sense of "Hongkonger" identity was much stronger than that of "Chinese" identity, but the gap gradually diminished until it closed down in the second half of 2001. Between the fourth and fifth anniversaries, the two curves almost overlapped with each other. After that, the "Chinese" identity surpassed "Hongkonger" for another five to six years. We believe that the closing down of this gap, and subsequently the reversing of order of these two identities was due to the surge in power of the Chinese economy. It somehow peaked in the first half of 2008 when China was organizing the first-in-China Summer Olympic Games. After that, starting from the second half of 2008, the "Hongkonger" identity rebounded, while the "Chinese" identity went down. Looking at what happened across the border, Hong Kong people's feelings of their "Chineseness" might have been affected by the cases of Liu Xiaobo (a dissident sentenced to 11 years of imprisonment in December 2009), Ai Weiwei (a liberal artist arrested for suspected economic crimes in April 2010), Chen Guangcheng (a blind activist who fled to the United States embassy from his house arrest in May 2012), Li Wangyang (a dissident labor rights activist who died "accidentally" in hospital in June 2012) and many others.

In the first half of 2013, when asked to make a choice among the four identities, 38 percent of Hong Kong people identified themselves as "Hongkonger," 23 percent as "Chinese," 24 percent as "China's Hongkonger," while 12 percent identified themselves as "Hong Kong's Chinese." In other words, most Hong Kong people identified themselves as "Hongkonger," followed by "China's Hongkonger" which in turn outnumbered "Chinese" by a small margin.

From a broad perspective, 62 percent of Hong Kong people in the first half of 2013 identified themselves as "Hongkonger in the broadest sense" (meaning either as "Hongkonger" or "China's Hongkonger"), whereas 35 percent identified themselves as "Chinese in the broadest sense" (meaning either as "Chinese" or "Hong Kong's Chinese"), 36 percent chose a mixed identity of "Hongkonger or Chinese" (meaning either as "Hong Kong's Chinese" or "China's Hongkonger").

As a matter of fact, if we only look at the trend of "strong and pure identities" versus "mixed or ambivalent identities" starting from 1997, we could see that "pure identities" almost always has the upper hand except in the second half of 2012, while "ambivalent identities" put together never fall below 30 percent.

Following this broad analysis, Figure 13.2 shows the time trend of "Hongkonger in the broadest sense" and "Chinese in the broadest sense." While it is important to study why the identities of "Hongkonger in the broadest sense" and "Chinese in the broadest sense" almost overlap between 2003 and 2008, it may be even more important to study why the two identities are pulling further apart after 2008, in light of the incidents of Liu Xiaobo, Ai Weiwei, Chen Guangcheng and Li Wangyang mentioned before. In the first half of 2013, the "Hongkonger in the broadest sense" stood at 62 percent, while the "Chinese in the broadest sense" stood at 35 percent.

Strength rating for identities – "Hongkonger" vs. "Chinese"

Figure 13.3 shows the strength ratings of "Hongkonger" vs. "Chinese" over the years since 1997. One can see that the two curves basically covary with each other, but after 2009 the absolute rating of "Hongkonger" goes up while that of

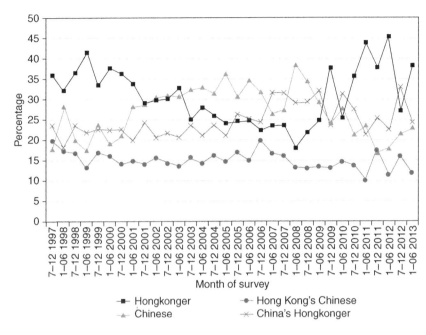

Figure 13.1 Ethnic identity (half-yearly average).

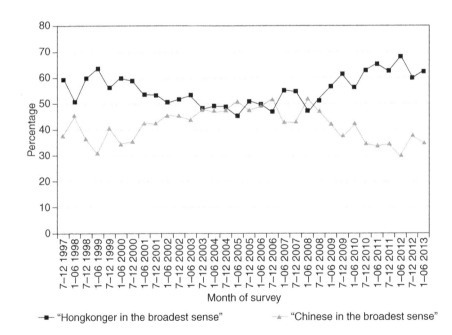

Figure 13.2 Ethnic identity (half-yearly average) – "Hongkonger in the broadest sense" vs. "Chinese in the broadest sense."

"Chinese" goes down. From our latest figure, the absolute rating for "Hong-konger" is as high as 8.1, while that of "Chinese" only stands at 6.8, a record low since our survey began in 1997. Generally speaking, "Hongkonger" ranges from 7.4 to 8.4, while "Chinese" ranges from 6.8 to 8.0. The two lines get very close to each other between 2001 and 2008, and then pull apart again. By the end of 2012, the "Hongkonger" rating reached a record high, while "Chinese" dropped to record low in the first half of 2013.

To conclude, "Hongkonger" was the dominating identity in the first four years after the handover, then there was a period of competing identities for about seven years, followed by a re-dominance of the "Hongkonger" identity again up to the writing of this book. Had anyone expected the surge in "Chinese" identity after the handover, it has not yet happened after 16 years of "one country, two systems." China's surge in economic power and international influence has not induced a parallel development in Hong Kong people's affinity to the "Chinese" identity.

"Identity indices" – all six identities gathered together

As explained before, six "identity indices" were introduced to this study series at the end of 2008, to indicate the combined effects of strength and importance of the different identity ratings. Figure 13.4 shows the profile of the six "identity indices" over the last four surveys. Other than the "Hongkonger" and "Chinese"

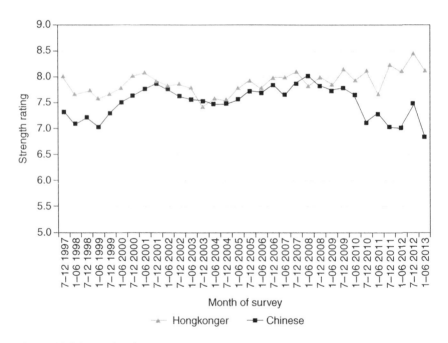

Figure 13.3 Strength rating (half-yearly average) – "Hongkonger" and Chinese.

identities, there are also identities of "citizen of the People's Republic of China," "member of the Chinese race," "Asian" and "global citizen."

"Identity indices" have numerical values ranging from 0 to 100, computed by taking the geometric mean of strength and importance ratings multiplied by 10. The higher the index, the stronger the identity. At the end of 2012, Hong Kong people felt strongest as "Hongkonger," followed by "member of the Chinese race," then "Asian," "Chinese," "global citizen" and finally "citizen of the People's Republic of China."

All in all, whether we are comparing the absolute strengths of the identity ratings, or people's categorical choices, the "Hongkonger" feeling prevails, followed by a number of cultural identities, then the political identity of PRC citizenship.

Demographics breakdown analysis

Although the general pattern is that more Hong Kong people identify themselves as "Hongkonger" than "Chinese" and give higher strength ratings to "Hongkonger" than "Chinese," thereby generating stronger identity indices for

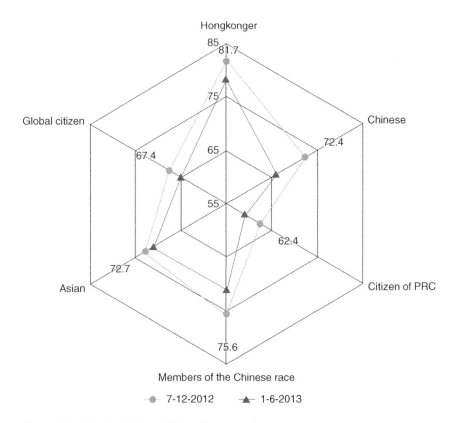

Figure 13.4 Identity indices of Hong Kong people.

"Hongkonger" than "Chinese," there are differences across demographic sub-groups. These differences are very likely related to how different groups of people perceive different events happening in Hong Kong and Mainland China.

Gender breakdown analysis

Figure 13.5 shows the percentage of the "Hongkonger" since the second half of 1997 broken down by gender. Generally speaking, females have a higher identi-fication associated with "Hongkonger" identities. Figure 13.6 shows a similar breakdown of the "Chinese" identity by gender, and we see the opposite, that males have higher identity ratings compared to females.

Figure 13.7 shows the rating of the "Hongkonger" since the second half of 1997 broken down by gender. Same as the percentages shown in the one-in-four-choices question, females gave a higher rating associated with "Hongkonger." Figure 13.8 shows a similar breakdown of the "Chinese" identity by gender and males gave higher identity ratings compared to females for most of the time except in 2009.

While it seems safe to conclude that Hong Kong males have a relatively stronger feeling of being "Chinese" and females have a stronger feeling of being "Hongkonger," the reasons remain to be studied. Is it due to the percep-tion of gender inequality across the two societies? Or due to different degrees of patriotism? Or commitment to political or social values? We do not have a hypothesis.

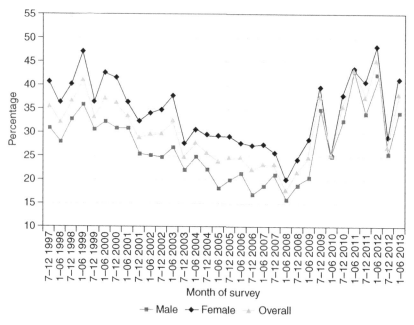

Figure 13.5 Ethnic identity (half-yearly average) – % of "Hongkonger" by gender.

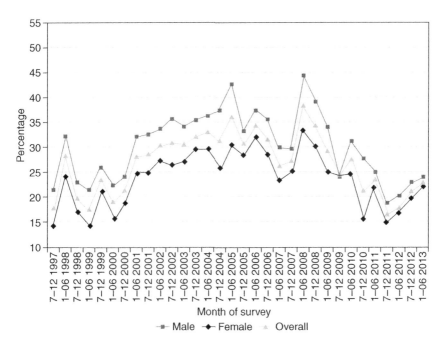

Figure 13.6 Ethnic identity (half-yearly average) – % of "Chinese" by gender.

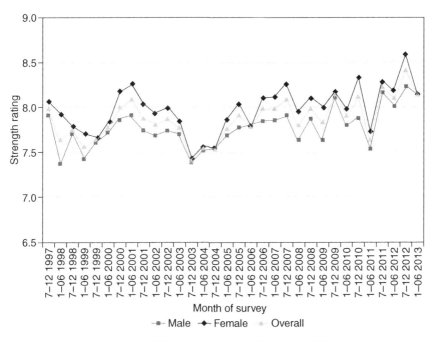

Figure 13.7 Strength rating (half-yearly average) – "Hongkonger" by gender.

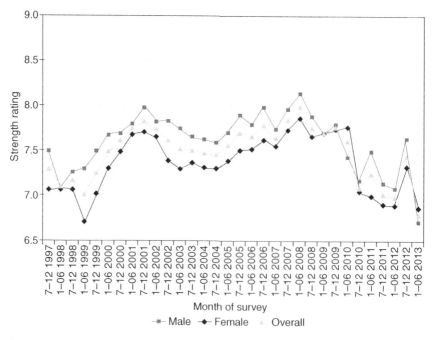

Figure 13.8 Strength rating (half-yearly average) – "Chinese" by gender.

Age group breakdown analysis

Figure 13.9 shows the percentage of the "Hongkonger" broken down by age groups of "under 30" and "30 or above." Since the survey began in 1997, the 18–29 group always identify more with the "Hongkonger" identity than the older group. On the other hand, Figure 13.10 shows that the 30 or above group always identify more with the "Chinese" identity than the younger group.

Figure 13.11 shows the strength rating of the "Hongkonger" since the second half of 1997 broken down by age groups. Generally speaking, the younger group has a slightly lower identification associated with "Hongkonger" identity. Figure 13.12 shows a similar breakdown of the "Chinese" identity by age group. It shows that the younger group has a much lower identification associated with "Chinese" identity, and the gap has widened in recent years starting from 2009. In our latest survey, the absolute rating of the 18–29 age group towards the "Chinese" identity dropped to a record low of 4.9 which can be construed as a "negative" value since we are using a 0–10 scale with 5 as the mid-point.

Immigrant breakdown analysis

Across many breakdown analyses conducted by the authors, one more analysis related to the socio-legal status of the respondents seems important – that of

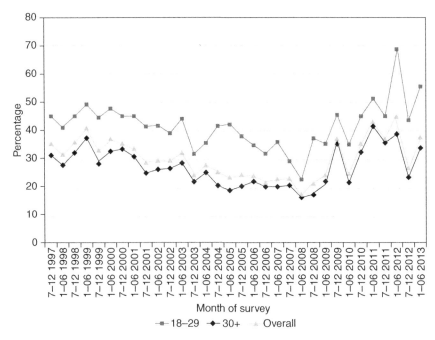

Figure 13.9 Ethnic identity (half-yearly average) – % of "Hongkonger" by age group.

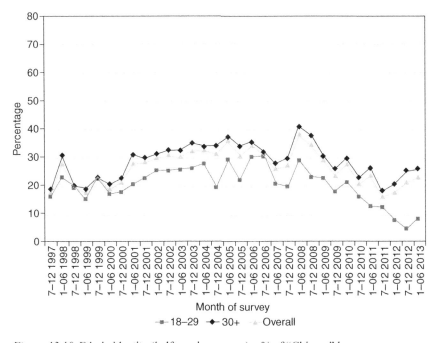

Figure 13.10 Ethnic identity (half-yearly average) – % of "Chinese" by age group.

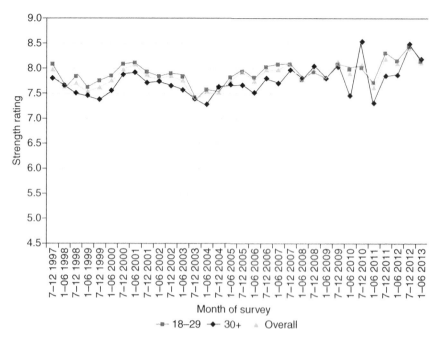

Figure 13.11 Strength rating (half-yearly average) – "Hongkonger" by age group.

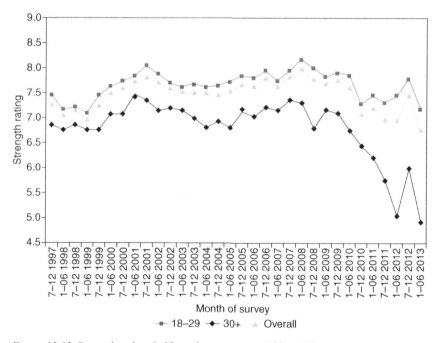

Figure 13.12 Strength rating (half-yearly average) – "Chinese" by age group.

"new immigrants" versus "permanent inhabitants" whom we will just call "non new immigrants" in our analysis. According to Immigration Ordinance (Chapter 115), Laws of Hong Kong, a Chinese citizen who has ordinarily resided in Hong Kong for a continuous period of not less than seven years before or after the establishment of the HKSAR can enjoy the right of abode in the HKSAR. We therefore would define "new immigrants" as those living in Hong Kong but without the right of abode, and "non new immigrants" as those who have lived in Hong Kong for seven years or more and have the right of abode. We want to analyze their strength of identity towards "Hongkonger" and "Chinese."

Figure 13.13 shows the percentage of the "Hongkonger" since 1999 when we first collected data related to the respondents' right of abode. Since new immigrants only account for 1–2 percent of our sample, there are lots of irregular fluctuations in the immigrant line chart due to sampling errors. However, the picture is still very clear that new immigrants generally do not identify themselves as "Hongkonger." On the contrary, many of them, sometimes as high as around 80 percent, would identify themselves as "Chinese," as shown in Figure 13.14.

Figure 13.15 shows the strength rating of the "Hongkonger" since 1999 broken down by whether respondents have the right of abode. Generally speaking, new immigrants have a lower identification associated with "Hongkonger." On the contrary, Figure 13.16 shows that they generally have a stronger feeling towards the "Chinese" identity compared to the general population.

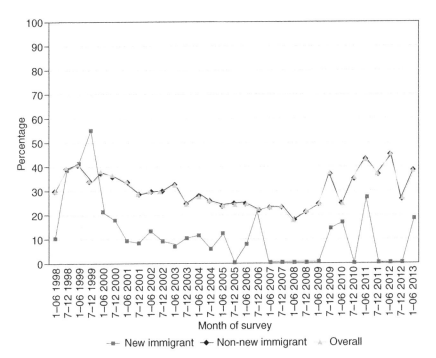

Figure 13.13 Ethnic identity (half-yearly average) – % of "Hongkonger" by immigrant.

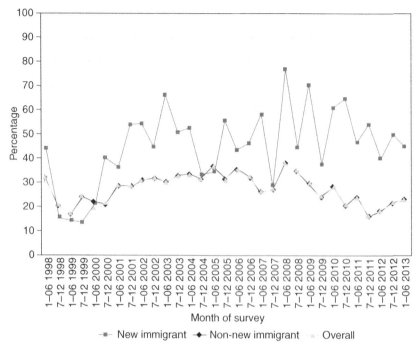

Figure 13.14 Ethnic identity (half-yearly average) – % of "Chinese" by immigrant.

To sum up, our demographics breakdown analysis has shown that females, the younger generation and non new immigrants have higher affinity for the "Hongkonger" identity, while males, the older generation and new immigrants have higher affinity to the "Chinese" identity. Perhaps both economic and political factors have played their roles differently on different demographic groups.

Ethnic identity turned political

On December 28, 2011, the Public Opinion Programme at the University of Hong Kong released its latest findings from this survey series by means of a press release which mentioned, among other things, that "in terms of absolute rating, people's identification with 'Hongkonger' has reached a ten-year high, while that of 'Chinese' has dropped to a 12-year low." One day later, Hao Tie-chuan, Director of the Publicity, Cultural and Sports Department of the Liaison Office of the Central People's Government in Hong Kong openly criticized the survey as "unscientific" and "illogical," because it uses a dichotomous measurement of "Hongkonger" and "Chinese," which is not mutually exclusive. Immediately after Hao's criticism, leftist commentators in Hong Kong used Tai Kung Pao and Wen Wei Po to launch their severest attacks on

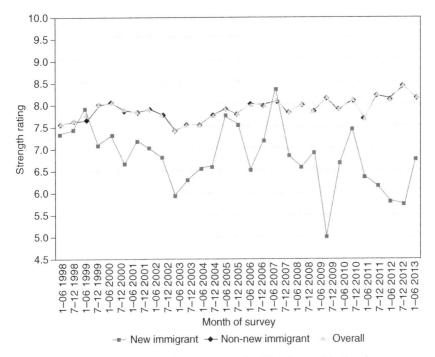

Figure 13.15 Strength rating (half-yearly average) –"Hongkonger" by immigrant.

the Programme and the author of the press release, using Cultural Revolution type rhetoric and accusations. Down to the basics, these criticisms can be summarized into three lines of arguments:

1   Because the survey requires people to choose between the identities of "Hongkonger" and "Chinese," it is unscientific and illogical.
2   The survey conducted before Hong Kong's handover was not a problem, but when carried out after the handover, it becomes "unscientific."
3   The survey advocates the independence of Hong Kong and thus has an ulterior motive.

After this wave of criticism initiated by Hao Tiechuan, the study of Hong Kong people's ethnic identity has suddenly become a political issue. Such a development was seen by some analysts in Hong Kong as a prelude to leftist commentators' attacks on the "3.23 Civil Referendum" Project proposed by the author near the end of 2011, and scheduled to take place on March 23, 2012. To many academics and human right advocates in Hong Kong, Hao's criticism constituted an infringement of academic freedom in Hong Kong by the Beijing Central Government.

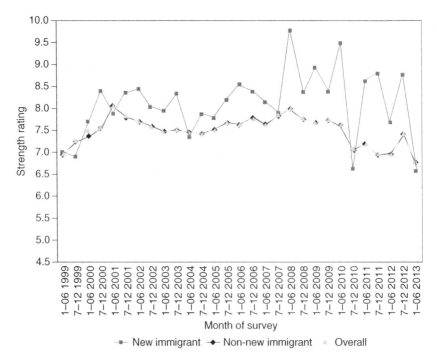

Figure 13.16 Strength rating (half-yearly average) – "Chinese" by immigrant.

At a meeting of the Panel on Education of the Hong Kong Legislative Council held in March 2012, the author officially filed his rebuttal of these criticisms with the following points:

1   In many questionnaire surveys, including those of handover anniversary surveys, respondents are asked "How do you feel?" The answers offered may include "happy, excited, worried, afraid, ambivalent, complicated" and so on. Whether the question accepts single or multiple answers, the choices offered are often overlapping and at times contradicting. In other words, it is accepted that the respondent may have a variety of overlapped and compli-cated feelings at the same time, but as long as they can point out their main or major feelings, in-depth analysis can be conducted. Therefore, asking people to choose the most desired identities among four overlapped options, namely, "Hongkonger," "Chinese Hong Kong citizen," "Chinese" and "Hong Kong Chinese citizen" is not unreasonable, even though it may have problems of "subsumption and inclusion." Survey questions are not logical tests, they are thermometers measuring people's complicated feelings, a tool for social science research.

2   Taking several steps backward, even if the above question on "Hongkonger" versus "Chinese" is inappropriate, the results released by the author at the

end of last year, showing a 10-year high in people's identity as a "Hong-konger," and a 12-year low in people's identity as "Chinese," has nothing to do with this question. They come from two separate and independent questions which even leftist commentators have dared not criticize up to this moment. The two questions require respondents to rate on a scale of 0–10 marks the strengths of their "Hongkonger" and "Chinese" identities. These are single-item questions which do not involve any "logical" problem mentioned by the Director-General Hao Tiechuan.

3   In the field of scientific research, it is impossible for a study to be changed from "scientific" before the return of sovereignty to become "unscientific" after the handover. Scientific method is a serious enquiry process. One can at most say that a certain survey has no reference value, but one cannot say that its "scientific nature" or "logical dimension" changes with the political climate.

4   For the same reason, if the above survey methodology is "unscientific" in Hong Kong, then similar surveys on ethnic identity cannot be "scientific" elsewhere in the world. What about the frequently conducted ethnic identity studies in Taiwan, which often contrast the "Taiwanese" identity with "Chinese" identity? What about the study of "Chinese" identity among overseas Chinese? What about the recent discussions over the ethnic identity of American NBA basketball player Jeremy Lin, that he is a "Taiwanese," "Chinese," "mainlander," "immigrant to Taiwan" or "American Chinese"? Why did Hao and the leftist columnists not criticize such discussions? Are "American Chinese" not "Chinese"?

5   As for the reference value of the survey, if one takes a look at the recent clashes between Hong Kong people and mainlanders on their daily lives, and also reads the result of such surveys carefully, especially the drastic drop in the strength of "Chinese identity" among the "post 80s," one would have appreciated the warning signals triggered by these surveys. Comprising 13 opinion questions plus nine demographics variables, the study is already very comprehensive and useful. Hao's complete denial of the 22-question strong survey, straddling over 15 years, with one single question which he considers "illogical," is just too arbitrary and dogmatic.

6   Finally, it is probably not worth discussing the criticisms that this series of surveys has a hidden agenda and is driven by an ulterior motive. The accusations by leftist commentators that the author has met with foreign spies and has accepted black gold are obviously false charges. However, the proposition that the author is splitting the country in the name of academic research, against all academic ethics and morals, might have induced white terror in many scholars. Academic institutions should pay attention to this, and should even consider providing appropriate legal protections for innocent academics.

Final remarks

Since December 2011 when the study of ethnic identity in Hong Kong people suddenly turned political, thanks to the concerted effort of Hao Tiechuan and leftist commentators in Hong Kong, up to the date of writing this book, the Public Opinion Programme at the University of Hong Kong has released three more waves of survey findings. As shown in this chapter, the strength of the "Chinese" identity among Hong Kong people has not gone up. On the contrary, Hao has sensitized Hong Kong people especially the younger generation on the apparent conflict between "Hongkonger" and "Chinese" especially Mainland Chinese people. Social conflicts continue to rise between local Hong Kong people and tourists, visitors and even pregnant women from Mainland China. According to the press release issued on June 18, 2013 by the Public Opinion Programme,

> the strength of "Chinese" identity has dropped ... to a new low since June 1999 ... Hong Kong people's feeling is strongest as "Hongkongers", followed by "Asians", then "members of the Chinese race", "Chinese", "global citizens", and finally "citizens of the PRC"...

Both Hao and the leftist columnists have remained quiet after their vigorous attacks in 2012. In a way, this academic question has turned back from political to academic. However, for good or for bad, the political discourse of 2012 has sensitized Hong Kong people to the social and cultural differences between the two systems under one country, on top of a political difference which the "one country, two systems" formulation tries to preserve.

Like it or not, the study of ethnic identity in Hong Kong has crossed many borders – not just crossing the border of neighboring societies, but also the border of academics and politics. Not just once, but many times.

Notes

1 The first draft of this chapter is presented in the Conference on Border Crossing in Greater China: Production, Community and Identity held by Center for China Studies, National Chengchi University, Taipei on September 13–14, 2012.
2 CUHK, "Social indicators and social development project (in Chinese)." Last modified March 12, 2003. www.cuhk.edu.hk/soc/socionexus/resources/hksoc/hksurvey/c-16.htm.
3 The survey questions were repeated in surveys conducted in 1990, 1993, 1995, 1997, 1999, 2001, 2004 and 2007.
4 Wikipedia. "Hong Kong People." Last modified December 20, 2012. http://en.wikipedia.org/wiki/Hong_Kong_people.
5 All figures can be found at "HKU POP Site" (website: http://hkupop.hku.hk).

References

Lau, S. K. 1998. "Hongkongese or Chinese." In *Hong Kong in Transition: The Continued Search for Identity and Order* (in Chinese), edited by Liu Qingfeng and Kwan Siu-chun. Hong Kong: Chinese University Press.
Lau, Siu-kai and Kuan, Hsin-chi. 1988. *The Ethos of the Hong Kong Chinese*. Hong Kong: Chinese University Press.

Wang, Gung-wu. 1991. *China and Overseas Chinese* (in Chinese). Hong Kong: Commercial Press.

Wong, Ka-ying and Wan, Po-san. 2007. *"The research study on Hong Kong people's identity" (in Chinese) The Twenty-First Century 101*. Hong Kong: Chinese University Press.

Zheng, Victor and Wong, Siu-lun. 2002. "Identity of Hong Kong Chinese: Changes Before and After 1997" (in Chinese). *The Twenty-First Century 73*. Hong Kong: Centre of Asian Studies of the University of Hong Kong.

Zheng, Victor and Wong, Siu-lun. 2005. "Identity and the Role of Government: Hong Kong as an Example" (in Chinese). *The Twenty-First Century 92*. Hong Kong: Centre of Asian Studies of the University of Hong Kong.

14 Hong Kong and diasporic China

Angelina Chin

In this postcolonial age, it is common to expect indigenous people to glorify the moments of decolonization and condemn previous colonial regimes in the name of nationalism. This logic follows from the general experience and belief that colonialism is inherently bad and humiliating. The government of the People's Republic of China (PRC) adopted a similar narrative in the 1980s and applied it to the former colony of Hong Kong, promoting the idea that fellow countrymen (*tongbao*) from the colony should embrace the nation/homeland (*zuguo*) when they were finally able to free themselves from the shackles of colonialism.

At the same time when this celebratory narrative prevailed in official announcements and patriotic discourses in mainland China, a darker narrative emerged from popular media. Ever since Hong Kong's return to China was decided in 1984, foreign reports have expressed fears of political restrictions after 1997 by emphasizing the PRC's poor human rights records and reminding the public of the miserable fate of the political dissidents during and after the notorious Tiananmen incident of 1989. These stories portray the handover of Hong Kong to China as a re-subordination of the local people to another, perhaps more evil, empire. Unlike the conventional narrative of decolonization, which associates nationalism with liberation of the local people, in this anti-PRC narrative nationalism implies political censorship and total submission of the individual to the governing state.

For the local people of Hong Kong, nationalism is a relatively new vocabulary. In the 1940s and 1950s, many migrants who escaped from the war with Japan and later from persecution by the CCP fled to Hong Kong. A large number of such migrants then settled in Hong Kong because they felt that it was a place where they could retain their wealth without being whirled into the politics of the mainland. To these early immigrants and their children, the nation of China signified chaos and deprivation. Hong Kong textbooks and government documents first referred to them as refugees. This description stresses their experience of temporary status in Hong Kong. To many of these immigrants and children, the nation of China signifies chaos and deprivation. Beginning in the 1970s, subsequent to their economic success and accumulation of wealth, these Hong Kong residents started to develop a strong local identity as "Hong Kongers" distinctive from both Britain and China. Hong Kong represented a place where they could afford to pursue dreams of getting rich and to forget about politics. It was not until the 1980s when the Sino-British declaration sealed the fate of Hong Kong that these Hong Kong residents had to face the reality that Hong Kong could no longer be a permanent political refuge and that they had to reestablish their bonds with their nation/homeland (*zuguo*) again.

The experience of colonialism has provided space for the local population to articulate their differentiation between the homeland and the political entity controlled by the CCP, and to express alternative imaginings of "citizenship," which includes the "othering" of their nation/homeland (*zuguo*) for its lag in progress compared to the city. To some extent, Hong Kongers' sense of belonging as Chinese (*Zhongguoren*) has increased since the 1990s. Nevertheless, they continue to be harsh critics of the mainland government and maintain a sense of superiority, of being a different kind of Chinese. Hong Kongers' imaginings of the mainland and their critical attitudes toward it present a challenge to the integrity of the concept of "China" and the meaning of being a "citizen of China" (*Zhongguo gongmin*).

This chapter analyzes how "China" has been represented in popular discourses in Hong Kong since the 1980s, when Hong Kong's retrocession was decided. I will first use the example of history textbooks published in Hong Kong to analyze how the historical identity of Hong Kong and a sense of national belonging have been ambiguously constructed through the contradictory grand narratives in education during and after British colonialism. Following that, I will evaluate existing strategies of resistance against "national" integration, including a "local" strategy of mobilizing people for the cause of local autonomy in Hong Kong, and the "Sinophone" approach used by literary critics who were informed by the scholarship of Cultural China. Lastly, I will explore the possibility of reclaiming "Chinese diaspora" as a political strategy to unite Hong Kong with neighboring territories.

The legend of Hong Kong in history textbooks[1]

Hong Kong's secondary school curriculum consists of two separate subjects: "History" and "Chinese History."[2] According to Flora Kan and Edward Vickers, two scholars of Hong Kong secondary school history education, the division between the two subjects can be seen as partly as "a consequence of the predominance of English as the medium of instruction in local schools," and partly "the result of a desire on the part of Hong Kong's colonial administration to conciliate local nationalist sentiment." Before the retrocession, more than half of the secondary schools in Hong Kong were Anglo-Chinese schools in which all subjects were taught in English except for Chinese language and Chinese History. Chinese History was separated out of the history subject because it would make more sense to Chinese students to learn it in Chinese. Moreover, in the 1950s the colonial government felt that bringing Chinese history into the official curriculum could offer an alternative to the anti-British and Communist elements that featured prominently in mainland textbooks.[3] Although after 1997 many

Anglo-Chinese schools began to change to Chinese as the main language of instruction, the division between the two history subjects remains.[4]

As Kan and Vickers have argued, the colonial situation of Hong Kong is peculiar in that the colonizers did not try to instill a sense of British superiority among the colonized population, because they were not ready to build a politicized sense of local or British belonging, and because they were afraid of angering the Chinese government.[5] Bernard Luk, who has done research on the postwar curriculum of Chinese Studies in Hong Kong, shows that in the 1950s, the Education Department of the Hong Kong government appointed a Committee on Chinese Studies to review the pedagogic approaches to the teaching of Chinese language, literature, culture and history. The committee strongly "identified moral education as one of the major needs" of education in Hong Kong.[6]

Chinese History textbooks

As evidenced in Chinese History textbooks from the 1950s to the 1980s, one of the main themes in history textbooks was the moral assessment of political leaders in dynastic history. Another factor contributing to the concentration on dynastic history was the political turbulence in the Mainland since the end of World War II. The Education Department was not ready to deal with such controversies in its curricula.

Qian Mu, a history scholar who migrated from China and served as the principal of the New Asia College (which later became a college of the Chinese University of Hong Kong), was one of the first Chinese History textbook authors. He authored and edited *Xinbian Zhongguo Lishi* (published in 1984) with his student, Sun Guodong, who later became a renowned historian himself. According to historian Lin Xiaoqing, Qian "used history to build a greater identification between his personal experience and historical moral experiences."[7] His belief in the discipline of history as a form of moral training for individuals is reflected in the textbook. The preface of *Xinbian Zhongguo Lishi* (hereafter *Xinbian*) states, "the objective of Chinese history education is to point out the flaws and merits of politicians so that students can learn to cultivate themselves."[8] In *Xinbian*, the authors further argue that Chinese history is where one can find "successes, failures, gains and losses" in events, "wisdom, stupidity, honesty and debauchery" in people, and "stability, chaos, prosperity and degeneration" in regimes. The role of history teachers is to analyze and point out these changes, so that "learners can broaden their knowledge" (*zhang jianshi*) and "improve their spiritual being" (*zheng xiu yang*). To these scholars as well as to the publishers of *Xinbian*, the biggest function of Chinese history education was to help individuals to become better moral beings through learning about the past. Nevertheless, the concepts of the nation (*guojia*) or citizenship (*guomin/gongmin*) were not mentioned.

As the return of Hong Kong was decided, the task of reconstructing a nationalistic history of China and Hong Kong became an urgent political and cultural task for the postcolonial Hong Kong government. In the 1990s when the return of Hong Kong came closer, some patriotic framers of Chinese history education felt that Hong Kongers' love for the nation should not be restricted to "culture" and thus proposed that Chinese history education be politicized. Ever since, identifying one's Chineseness as cultural or ethnic heritage became insufficient for the larger political agenda. In secondary school Chinese History textbooks, we see a change in the contents, with heavier emphasis on learners' sense of belonging to the PRC and more details of the achievements of leaders in the Chinese Communist Party.

Unlike earlier Chinese History textbooks authored or co-authored by one or two renowned scholars in the field, the textbooks published in the 2000s were put out by committees.[9] *Tanjiu Zhongguo Lishi* (hereafter *Tanjiu*) published by Manhattan Press in 2004 adheres closely to the "one-China" principle in its objectives. It states in the Preface:

> History education not only functions to guide students to learn about the nation's history and culture, so that they can develop a sense of identification (*rentong gan*) and belonging (*guishugan*), it also should [help students] cultivate the skills of thinking and self-learning, so that they can become lifetime active learners and national citizens (*guomin*) equipped with analytical skills. After the handover of Hong Kong to China, Chinese History has important meanings in cultivating young people's recognition of their national citizen's identity (*rentong guomin shenfen*).[10]

In contrast to *Xinbian Zhongguo Lishi* published in the 1980s, which associates the study of Chinese history with the development of an individual sense of moral judgment, in *Tanjiu* the objective of history education is to cultivate one to be a "responsible national citizen" (*guomin*) of the nation. Another Chinese History textbook, *Tansuo Zhongguoshi* (hereafter *Tansuo*), published by Ling Kee in 2006, echoes this theme. The authors quote from *Guoshi Dagang*, a prominent history textbook published by Qian Mu: "A national citizen (*guomin*) who claims to be more educated than average people should have some knowledge of his/her country's history, and should maintain a kind of humanistic feeling (*wenqing*) and respect." Then, it continues with the authors' own words: "this new curriculum also emphasizes that students should increase their understanding of the nation's circumstances (*guoqing*), and through which they can develop national/ethnic feelings (*minzu qinghuai*) and cultural belonging, as well as become responsible citizens (*gongmin*)."[11] This kind of mission statement placed in the front pages of the new textbooks conforms to Vickers's comments on the use of nationalistic history education, which is to be "pressed into service by politicians and scholars to bolster or, sometimes, to invent a national identity for the inhabitants of their states, and to foster among their population a sense of patriotic loyalty."[12] In these textbooks, the nation (*guojia*) and belonging (*rentong*) are consistently emphasized. Both generations of textbooks focus on political history and represent China as a continuous homogenous civilization, but while in the 1980s history education is regarded as a form of moral training for the individual, in the 2000s the emphasis shifts to responsibility and citizenship.[13] The change coincides with the amendments the Curriculum Development Committee made in the 1997 curriculum guide for Chinese history, which states that the aim of history is to "build a sense of belonging to China and the Chinese race."[14] They also exemplify how the Hong Kong government used the Chinese History curriculum to promote patriotic feelings after 1997.

In the overall narrative of Chinese History textbooks used today, the beginning of Western aggression witnessed the takeover of Hong Kong territories by the British after the Opium War. The return of Hong Kong represents a watershed that put an end to the history of humiliation. However, it was not until 1997 that Hong Kong history was integrated into Chinese History textbooks. The retrocession of Hong Kong and the increasing interests in local identity and history among the general public probably pushed the Curriculum Development Committee to consider the inclusion of Hong Kong history in the Chinese History curriculum. Nevertheless, as Flora Kan points out, Hong Kong history is usually "treated as peripheral to Chinese History, and merely serves to enhance students' interest and give them a sense of the relevance of Chinese History."[15] In the textbooks, the contents dealing with Hong Kong are still negligible. Hong Kong is intertwined with narratives of wars and politics, and students are encouraged to imagine themselves as citizens of mainland China. The only inclusions are in the last part of the textbooks, which narrate the signing of the Sino-British declaration and the retrocession of Hong Kong. A similar treatment is given to the retrocession of Macau.[16] Incorporating the "return" of Hong Kong and Macau in the last chapter symbolizes the grand finale of twentieth-century Chinese history. By excluding any other parts of Hong Kong history, these textbooks' authors also help construct a monolithic discourse of China through their silence about internal tensions and local histories.

History subject textbooks

While a harmonious "China" is emphasized in most Chinese History textbooks, capitalist development is the grand narrative in History textbooks. The History curriculum, which focuses on world history, is generally taught in English.[17] In the 1990s, the History subject began to incorporate local history and recent history not dealt with ever before. Form 1 to Form 3 focus on a general education of history from antiquity to contemporary history. Form 4 and Form 5 are devoted to Asian History and World History in the twentieth century respectively.[18] Like the Chinese History subject, History textbooks also attempt to construct the history of Hong Kong as a homogeneous, progressive discourse through the erasure of certain histories, but in opposite ways. While the Chinese History textbooks exclude Hong Kong till its retrocession, the narrative of Hong Kong history is told as a linear progression from a fishing village to an international prosperous city. Critiques of capitalism and urbanity, and themes such as exploitation, unequal distribution of wealth and rural everyday life, are silenced in this historical narrative.

Journey Through History: a Modern Course, published by Aristo Educational Press in 2000, is one of the most popular English textbooks taught in lower-form History classes. It consists of three books, which are devoted to Ancient and Medieval Times, Transition to Modern Times and Twentieth Century respectively. Book 3 has four chapters: "International Conflicts and Threats to Peace in the 20th Century," "Growth and Development of Hong Kong in the 20th Century," "Major Achievements in the 20th Century" and "Mini-Research on an Aspect of 20th Century." The author, Nelson Chan, has a Bachelor of Arts degree and Certification in Education from the University of Hong Kong.

One chapter in Book 3 is devoted to the history of Hong Kong, entitled, "Growth and Development of Hong Kong in the 20th century." It begins with the statement in the first paragraph, which states, "Under British rule, Hong Kong developed into an entrepot in around 1900, and then it continued to grow in the early 20th century."[19] The last section of the chapter is "Hong Kong's Contributions to China." The author states: "Under British rule, Hong Kong was closely tied to the mainland. However, the only contributions to China were the Anti-Qing movement and the war against Japan during 1937–41."[20] In regards to the Anti-Qing movement, the author argues that Hong Kong was a good place for the revolutionary movement led by Sun Yat-sen at the turn of the century because it was not under Qing rule and it gave the revolutionaries a hiding place. Here, "China" is associated with Sun's revolutionary movement, implying that the Qing government was clearly not "China." The representation of the Qing parallels that of Japan during World War II; both are foreigners invading "Chinese" territories. Under the topic of "Anti-Japanese Effort, 1937–41," the authors state, "Until Hong Kong fell to the Japanese in late 1941, local people helped Chinese refugees with food and shelter through local organizations."[21] The migrants from China are depicted as "refugees" who received help from "local people." The temporary status of "refugees" set these migrants from China apart from the "local people," who are undefined in the textbook. This use of the term "refugees" who received aid from Hong Kong also underlines the differences of these people from the immigrants since the 1950s because the latter were "productive" migrants with money or skills, which were conducive to the capitalistic development of the city. In contrast, nothing about migrations to Hong Kong is noted in the Chinese History textbooks.

The following section, "Hong Kong's Growth and Development since 1945," gives a summary of Hong Kong's transition from an entrepot to a manufacturing center, and finally to an international financial center, with one and a half pages of text accompanied by illustrations. Two main factors that "helped Hong Kong develop into a manufacturing center" in the 1950s were the Chinese civil war, which induced people to migrate to Hong Kong with "capital" and "technical knowledge," along with others who were "willing to work for low wages"; and the Korean War, during which Britain forbade Hong Kong to trade with China and thus forced Hong Kong to industrialize. Besides these brief mentions, there is nothing about the PRC or the British government in this section. No details are given about the wars aside from their positive influence on Hong Kong's economy.

The textbook then states that in the 1970s, because of competition from industries in Singapore, Taiwan and Korea, rising production costs and restrictions on trade, Hong Kong had to adapt to the new circumstances and turn itself into an international financial center. This section also lists the main categories of Hong Kong's "social developments" during the 1950s to 1980s, which were education, housing and social welfare. The social problems and political turmoil in Hong Kong during those periods, such as the riots in the 1960s, receive no attention in the textbook.

Another subsection, "China's Contributions to Hong Kong," has two topics: "Provision of things (including daily necessities and raw materials, and water)," and "Economic contributions." The economic contributions were the policies under Deng Xiaoping's economic reform "*gaige kaifang.*" The special economic zones set up at that time attracted many industrialists to move their production lines to China and increased the trade with China by a factor of 20. Following this subsection is a two-page summary of the process of retrocession, which, like the description in Chinese History textbooks, concludes the history of Hong Kong.[22] The content does not include anything beyond the return of Hong Kong. Nor does it give any details of Chinese history in the twentieth century.

Unlike the Chinese History textbooks, which downplay the importance of Hong Kong or include Hong Kong to help create a nationalistic past, the History textbook narrative emphasizes independent economic and social advancement in the twentieth century. The post-war period is described as one of development and achievement of the local people. The description implies that the success of Hong Kong is brought by British colonialism. It does not cast any moral judgment on the British government. In both Chinese History and History textbooks, Hong Kong does not appear as a subject in its own right, but is either submerged into the Chinese nationalist narrative and is represented as the shame of colonialism, or is displayed as an example of triumphal capitalism brought by colonialism.

An investigation of these various kinds of history textbooks shows that in Hong Kong secondary schools, the history of China and Hong Kong is taught in two contradictory grand narratives, appearing in Chinese History textbooks and History textbooks respectively. While the main themes of Chinese History education have not changed much over the past 20 years, after retrocession more emphasis is put on learners' identity as Chinese citizens rather than moral cultivation. History textbooks, in contrast, continue to endorse a Western capitalistic definition of progress, placing Hong Kong's status above that of its "homeland" because of Hong Kong's development under British colonialism. These history textbook examples present contesting interpretations of Hong Kong's political status in education discourse. While the PRC influence on the Chinese History curriculum appears to be stronger, authors of English History textbooks tend to take a colonial view of modernization. The contradictions in two kinds of grand narratives indicate that the construction of Chinese national identity through history education may not have been very successful.

Hong Kong autonomy movement

In the decade after Hong Kong was returned to China, there have been efforts to create better transportation networks and access that would facilitate people to cross the border between Hong Kong and the mainland. In the 2000s, the local governments in the Pearl River Delta Region have also worked together to transform the region into a mega-metropolis, spanning Hong Kong, Macau, Shenzhen, Dongguan, Foshan, Guangzhou, Huizhou, Jiangmen, Zhongshan, Zhuhai and Zhaoqing.[23] In conjunction with this project, the governments of Guangdong, Hong Kong and Macao held a liaison and agreed to jointly undertake the "Study on the Action Plan for the Bay Area of the Pearl River Estuary" in February 2009. The Bay Area of the Pearl River Estuary is "defined as comprising all 17 districts abutting the Pearl River Estuary under the administration of Guangzhou, Shenzhen, Zhuhai, Dongguan and Zhongshan, and the whole territory of Hong Kong and Macau Special Administrative Regions." It carries the

> objective to promote livability, emphasis on cooperation, innovation and services and aiming at formulating actions, the three sides are working together towards developing the Bay Area into the best "Quality Living Area" of the [Greater Pearl River Delta] and an important medium of innovation, with a view to guiding the transformation of development mode of the region.[24]

The plan covers areas such as financial services, high-tech and high-end research and development, transport, environmental matters and ecology. It aims to foster close communications between Guangdong and Hong Kong in other areas as well, including facilitation of people and cargo flows, food safety, innovation and technology, information, intellectual-property rights, culture, sports, notification of infectious diseases, social welfare, exchange of talent, emergency management and the joint promotion of cooperation in the Pearl River Delta region. From these projects, it is apparent that aggressive regional planning is underway.

Other projects related to greater integration include opening up the border areas in the New Territories of Hong Kong near Shenzhen for mainland Chinese tourists and developing new towns in northwestern New Territories to serve as new business and upper-class residential districts.[25] Many Hong Kong capitalists are in favor of these projects because such a network between South China and Hong Kong would enhance their investments and business possibilities. Real estate developers are especially strong advocates because they can reap huge profits from such development projects.

At the same time, policies that attempt to blur the border between Hong Kong and the mainland caused deep resentment among Chinese residents in Hong Kong. For example, in 2012, the Hong Kong government announced its plan to adopt Chinese "national" civic education (*guomin jiaoyu*), similar to the "patriotic" education taught in mainland China into Hong Kong's public school curriculum, while the National Education Services Centre also distributed to schools a booklet, titled "The China Model," which should form a basis for the national education curriculum to be introduced in primary schools and secondary schools in the future.[26] On July 29, 2012, tens of thousands of Hong Kongers took to the streets to protest the introduction of this form of Chinese "national" civic education in Hong Kong. Most of the protestors believe that this new curriculum would amount to "brainwashing" young minds with pro-mainland propaganda.

Overall, the speed of integration and the increasing presence of mainland Chinese in Hong Kong have caused great anxiety among local residents in Hong Kong that the city is losing its autonomy and that Hong Kongers would become indistinguishable from the mainland subjects of the PRC. A semiannual survey conducted by Dr. Robert Chung Ting-yiu, the Director of the Public Opinion Programme at the University of Hong Kong, revealed that as few as 16.6 percent of Hong Kong citizens identify themselves as Chinese – the lowest figure in a dozen years. This represents a common resistance against the top-down imposition of the concept of Greater China and the inculcation of loyalty to the state.

While government officials try to manipulate the public to acquiesce to integration, there have been counter-movements in Hong Kong calling for more local autonomy. In 2011, a group called the Hong Kong City-State Autonomy Movement was formed, and its goal is to raise Hong Kongers' local consciousness to uphold the city's autonomy and to protect the city's residents' interests and right to rule.[27] Some of its members argue that the Hong Kong government needs to prioritize and defend the interests of Hong Kongers against those of the PRC government and mainland Chinese. At the same time, they believe that Hong Kongers have no rights or duties to be critical of the PRC because Hong Kong has been, and should continue to be, under an administration separate from the rest of China. One of the previous spokespersons of the movement, Chin Wan (陳雲), even suggested that there should be a "naturalization" process in Hong Kong for mainland Chinese – only the people with the "correct" values and aspirations should be allowed to obtain permanent residency. Their rhetoric thus far places much emphasis on the peril of the mainland Chinese and the importance for Hong Kongers to defend themselves against the intrusions of mainlanders for the well-being of the city.[28] Chin Wan became a popular figure in Hong Kong because many Hong Kongers also share his sentiments against mainland Chinese.

Hong Kongers' xenophobic attitudes toward mainland Chinese especially heightened after the inception of the Individual Visit Scheme (*ziyou xing*) in July 2003, which allowed travelers from the mainland to visit Hong Kong on an individual basis. Prior to the Scheme, most mainlanders could only travel to Hong Kong on business visas or in group-tours. The purpose of the Scheme was to boost Hong Kong's economy after the SARS crisis in the spring of 2003, and travelers from the mainland did help the Hong Kong economy; but negative popular representations of mainlanders also proliferated. Such representations reveal the new anxiety of Hong Kongers about losing their sense of cultural superiority over mainlanders as decolonized British subjects. Hong Kong residents can no longer deport undesirables from the city, because the city is no longer a colony of Great Britain but a special administrative region of China, economically and politically dependent on the mainland.

However, the movement is silent about the fact that while the maintenance of Hong Kong's interests is necessary, the city has to reckon with the PRC government and it simply has no bargaining chip to ask for an autonomous status. A claim for a unique Hong Kong identity alone is weak and does not empower its residents to confront the PRC state. There have also been criticisms and public condemnations made by scholars and activists. The criticisms include its stigmatization of and its exclusionist stand toward mainland Chinese people, especially those who came from a lower-class background, characterizing mainland Chinese as unhygienic, unethical, uncivilized and greedy. While Hong Kong Autonomy Movement's rhetoric stresses the preservation of Hong Kong's identity, very few supporters of the movement are concerned about how such discriminatory attitudes and behavior undermine the key values of equity in a liberal democracy.

Moreover, while such rhetoric stirs up public hostilities against immigrants from China today, it ignores the fact that most Hong Kongers or their families were once refugees from the mainland themselves. The development of the autonomy movement was very much an outgrowth of the local identities adopted by people who were once migrants from China themselves.

Hong Kongers as cultural Chinese

Even though there seems to be rising concerns about Hong Kong being absorbed by the PRC and losing its autonomy, most Hong Kongers do have strong sentiments about being Chinese. Most Hong Kongers regardless of age acknowledge being Chinese, but one can expect a fair number of Hong Kongers would qualify their answers by saying that it is just a political fact, or indicate that this is not a matter of choice but something imposed onto them by the past colonial and current SAR regimes. However, this does not prevent them from becoming interested in Chinese history, culture and customs. Most Hong Kongers would not deny that they are Chinese (*huaren*). They might qualify this identify and call themselves Hong Kong Chinese. Here, Chineseness is signified as membership in an ethnic group (*minzu*) or as culture, not as citizenship in a nation. In a way, this echoes the idea of China represented in Chinese History textbooks published before the 1990s, when the concept of the nation-state was not yet introduced and history was taught to cultivate students' moral well-being. Rather than seeing Hong Kong identity as contradictory to the larger Chinese identity, they believe there is a way of merging these two identities, as Hong Kong scholar Lau Siu-kai argues,

> It is also likely that, despite all sorts of conflicts, the Hong Kong identity and the larger Chinese identity will become increasingly complementary inasmuch as claiming the Hong Kong identity not only does not involve denying one's Chinese identity, but also acts to reinforce it.[29]

Two scholars of overseas Chinese, Lynn Pan and Tu Wei-ming, first suggest culture as an alternative to politics in thinking about Chinese identity. Both of them discuss the term Chineseness in a celebratory manner, placing emphasis on Chinese people and their essential characteristics in different countries. Lynn Pan's *Sons of the Yellow Emperor* (Pan 1990) was one of the first histories of the Chinese diaspora. In her theory, it was "China" which occupied the "center" and people who were assimilated into other "cultures" are placed in the "periphery." In the "semi-peripheral" sphere stood the "overseas Chinese." In her model, there are four categories between the "center" and "semi-periphery," which are Hong Kong, Taiwan, (overseas) students and aspiring migrants. Pan is primarily concerned with the predicament of the loss of Chinese characteristics and does not address the hybrid composition of a diasporic identity. In addition, "authentic" Chineseness remains an essential cultural characteristic that only ethnic Chinese can maintain.

Along the same line, the theorist Tu Wei-ming also uses the term "Cultural China" to refer to a single community whose common interest in Chinese society transcends national boundaries and discourses (Tu 1991). Unlike Pan, Tu situates Taiwan, Hong Kong and Singapore along with mainland China as the core of "Cultural China." His intention is to decouple Chineseness from the geopolity "China" and yet reclaim it for the Chinese moving in global spaces. While Tu Wei-ming speaks of the insufficiency of the stereotypes and limitations in defining a Chinese, the meanings and implications of "Chineseness" remain vague in his model. Although "Cultural China" is seen as a project that can topple the national category of China, culture is mainly seen as a cultural asset that would benefit the people identified as Chinese.

The search for alternative ways to think about Chinese identity is a result of the dissatisfaction with the political hegemony, not so much of the West, but of China – the nation. "Cultural China" is seen as a project that can topple the national category of China. However, culture is a political project from the beginning when it is constructed. Tackling Pan's problematic definition of diaspora, the historian of Chinese diaspora Wang Gungwu criticizes the current focus on Chinese overseas or diaspora as too China-centered. Diaspora, in the Chinese context, has the potential for the state to build cultural nationalism that transcends the boundary of the nation-state (Wang 1993). Wang raises the point that affiliation with the homeland can expand nationalistic influences for the nation-state rather than challenge it. It re-centers the "home" – China – rather than complicating the ambiguities of belonging to two places. It also becomes complicit to the nation-state discourse and Chineseness a sign of loyalty to the state.

Sinophone

Another theory about overseas Chinese comes from the literary critic Shu-mei Shih, who launches a pertinent critique on the usage of Chinese diaspora in her book *Visuality and Identity* (Shih 2007), arguing that Chinese diaspora stands as a universalizing category founded on a unified ethnicity, culture, language, as well as place of origin or homeland.... The measure of inclusion appears to be the degree of sinicization of these ethnicities, which discloses a Han-centrism of a long-distance variety, because what often gets completely elided is the fact that the Chinese diaspora refers mainly to the diaspora of the Han people."[30]

The main problem with this is that Chineseness becomes "evaluatable, measurable, and quantifiable."[31]

In other words, Chineseness is used to measure one's authenticity and the right to represent Chinese culture, for example, Wang Gungwu's idea of "cultural spectrum of Chineseness" creates a hierarchy of "Chinese" and "disenfranchises" some people from enjoying the privileges of being *tongbao* because they cannot speak Chinese or they are too remote to Chinese culture. The main problem with the concept of "Chinese diaspora," according to Shih, is its complicity with China's nationalistic rhetoric, like the term "*tongbao*" that is used to address the people in Hong Kong, Macau and Taiwan. She feels that it is important to address "the desire of these immigrants to localize within their lands of settlement" and the term "Chinese diaspora" fails to do so.[32]

The concept that she proposes to replace Chinese diaspora is Sinophone (Shih 2007, 2010). She uses this alternative term, Sinophone, to articulate the people who engage with the culture of China but have no interests in associating with mainland China. Sinophone studies is "conceived as the study of Sinitic-language cultures on the margins of geopolitical nation-states and their hegemonic productions."[33]

It seems as though Shih's critique of "Chinese diaspora" and her concept of Sinophone works for certain kind of people in Taiwan striving for independence or people of Chinese descent who can choose to not engage with the PRC or their identity as Chinese. In other words, Sinophone might be useful for people who have a choice to disengage from the PRC. As for Hong Kong, Shih believes that Sinophone is only applicable to pre-1997 Hong Kongers, as she praises the local Cantonese movement: "The Sinophone pre-1997 Hong Kong also saw the emergence of a nativist fetishization of Cantonese against the looming hegemony of standard putonghua."[34] Unfortunately, however, in Shih's model, there is no hope for post-handover Hong Kong, as she states:

> If, for Taiwan in the late twentieth century, the Sinophone became a self-conscious category when mainland Chinese colonialism of the Guomindang was recognized and peacefully overthrown, for Hong Kong its incorporation into the Chinese polity in 1997 marked the waning of the Sinophone as its integration into China became inevitable.[35]

The political reality is that it is impossible for Hong Kongers to disown China and relinquish their ties with the PRC, even though many do want to have an autonomous Hong Kong independent from Chinese interference. Thus, the

Sinophone concept is not useful for thinking about the identities and senses of belonging for the people in Hong Kong today, nor does it really capture the sentiments of Hong Kongers in pre-1997 Hong Kong. It also fails to speak for people in Taiwan and elsewhere who are still concerned about China.

Reclaiming "Chinese diaspora" as a strategy

If both a local autonomy strategy and a Sinophone strategy cannot effectively address the problem of Hong Kong's future, what could be an alternative? While I agree with Shih's arguments on hybridity and multiple consciousness, I still would like to stress that the political expansion of Greater China has deep implications for Hong Kong, as well as the territories located on the periphery of China. Thus, I argue that re-invoking the concept of "diaspora" is still useful as a counter-movement. For example, Hong Kong, Macau and Taiwan arguably belong to the same postcolonial diasporic cluster, because all three locations were colonies in part of the twentieth century, and they were all included in the "one country, two systems" framework proposed by Deng Xiaoping, who suggested that while there could only be one "China," these former colonies could maintain their own capitalistic systems and control over domestic affairs, including immigration, currencies and public finance.[36] One of their commonalities now is that they constantly have to engage with the PRC for their survival.[37] The residents in Hong Kong, Macau and Taiwan reclaim diaspora as their political strategy, because they are located right outside of the PRC's political boundaries and yet could maintain their own administrative statuses and vantage points.

When we reconsider the concept of Chinese diaspora, we should explore how theorists have articulated in other geographical contexts since the 1990s. Most of the earlier studies of Chinese diaspora seem to have overlooked a few key themes that are explored by diaspora studies in other geographical areas. By this, I mean the attempts to use the concept not just as a sociologically descriptive term for people who escaped their "homeland," but also incorporated themes related to consciousness and sentiments of the people who left. In the following, I will point out the key ideas of diaspora that need to be incorporated into the new definition of Chinese diaspora as a political strategy.

In his article, "Re-thinking Diaspora(s); Stateless Power in the Transnational Moment" (Tölöyan 1996), the theorist Khachig Tölöyan sees the need to re-think diaspora since the term has been much exploited since the 1960s and used to signify "dispersed communities which were previously known as exile groups, overseas communities, minorities, refugees, migrant sojourners." The traditional paradigm used by the Greeks, the Armenians and the Jews placed emphasis on the acts that underwrite identity and forestall assimilation. For the Jews, the definition also implies a lamentation for the lost homeland.[38] Tölöyan uses Walter Connor's definition of diaspora – "that segment of a people living outside the homeland" – a reference for the new paradigm. To Tölöyan, what is important for the new definition of "diaspora" is the consciousness of the community or its individual members who are displaced or living outside the homeland. The emphasis is on "discursive and representational practices, on how an individual or a whole community ... feels about itself and "represents itself to itself and others."[39] The reference to "that segment of a people living outside the homeland" is crucial to understand the positionality of people living in the peripheries of China. They are displaced right outside the border of the PRC, and this allows them to have more chances to interact with the "homeland."

In *Routes* (Clifford 1997), the anthropologist James Clifford argues that diaspora is also multilocal and may not be restricted by geopolitical boundary. He summarizes William Safran's definitions of an "ideal type" of diaspora as "a history of dispersal, myths/memories of the homeland, alienation in the host country, desire for eventual return, ongoing support of the homeland, and a collective identity importantly defined by this relationship."[40]

Along the same line, the root of black diasporists lies in the common history of displacement – transportation, slavery and colonization – unifying across differences in location. In "New Ethnicities" (Hall 1996), the theorist Stuart Hall identifies two moments in which members of the black British diaspora have represented themselves in response to a common history: At first, the term "black" was used to unite people of different ethnic backgrounds for resistance. In doing so, black Britons created a "singular and unifying framework based on the building up of identity across ethnic and cultural difference between the different communities."[41] This moment was when "Africa" as an idea of home drew black people together. In the second moment, individuals start to question the existence of an essential black subject and begin to challenge the unified modes from within the communities. Diaspora identities become multiple and mobile and weaken the notion of "race." Hall triggers scholars of diaspora to think about identity in terms of fluidity and hybridity and to alter the ways in which identities are formed for all people in one location. He characterizes the process of "becoming" (or routedness) – the ruptures and discontinuities which constitute the Caribbean's "uniqueness." Similarly, China can be an idea rather than an absolute ethnicity. Perhaps by invoking the term "Chinese diaspora," individuals can come together and challenge the essentialized image of Chinese and the homogenous category of Chineseness. In other words, residents in Hong Kong, Macau and Taiwan can all imagine themselves as Chinese, and yet retain their local specificities.

The ethnographer Allen Chun in his article, "Diasporas of Mind, Or Why There Ain't No Black Atlantic in Cultural China" (Chun 2001), makes the comparison between the Black Atlantic and the Chinese diaspora as articulated by Pan, Tu and Wang. Chun points out that whereas detachment and separateness can be found in the Chinese case, the themes of suffering and social memory derived from dispersal and forced exile which feature in Jewish and black diasporas are missing.[42] While there are some commonalities between black and Chinese diasporas, there are a few major differences between the two forms of diaspora: (1) there is no sense of uprootedness and displacement in the Chinese concept under the current framework of analysis; (2) blackness in black diaspora is situated and hybridizing within Western modernity, whereas Chinese diaspora still relies on the maintenance of ethnic identity – namely, Chineseness – for its cultural distinctiveness to challenge the West politically from the outside. What remains unsatisfactory about the discussion on Chinese diaspora is the lack of consideration of the kind of diasporic consciousness that exists in black diaspora. The earlier works cling to the older formulation of diaspora and seldom explore the double consciousness of the individuals or communities in between "places."

My proposal, as stated at the beginning of the chapter, is to reclaim Chinese diaspora as a new transnational political strategy. The common interests for residents in Hong Kong, Macau and Taiwan are their concerns for the political oppression in the PRC, as well as the expansion of the PRC's political power. In a different period of post-World War II history, Hong Kong has become a refuge for political dissidents and a base for political activism against the CCP, such as the annual Hong Kong of the 1989 Tian'anmen Square social movement and street protests in support of freeing political prisoners in the PRC. I believe that this kind of peripheral activism in Hong Kong can be extended to its neighboring territories, so that an alliance can be formed to enhance the survival and protect the autonomy of these places.

So what would a strategy of reclaiming "Chinese diaspora" look like in practical terms? An example that takes the form of this approach has already formed – New School of Democracy. It was officially established in Taiwan in 2011 by Chinese, Hong Kong and foreign academics who shared the hope of ending "one-party rule" in China. Even though there have not been concrete political actions yet, the core members have been sharing their thoughts through their websites and Facebook as well as organizing lectures and discussions in Taiwan and Hong Kong. Nevertheless, the chairperson of this movement is not a Hong Kong, Macanese or Taiwanese. Rather, it is a famous political dissident and former student leader at the 1989 Tian'anmen Square movement, Wang Dan. In its launch, the movement claims that it has four primary areas of focus: "promoting democratic development in Chinese societies, solidifying the theoretical bases for democratic movements, creating a communications platform for Chinese worldwide and enabling participation in politics beyond the confines of political parties."[43] The organizers also indicate that their goal is to "rise above party politics and transnational borders, while respecting the younger generation and allowing democracy to take root through education." Such a transnational network appears to be a promising first step, and it shows how a Chinese diasporic conceptual framework can be productive in motivating more people to take initiatives or join transnational movements that raise awareness of PRC politics.

The reclaiming of the concept of Chinese diaspora and its application on the PRC periphery is best articulated by Albert Ho, the former Chairman of the Hong Kong Democratic Party and the founding board member of the New School of Democracy. When explaining that the decision to register the college in Hong Kong had special significance, he said,

> Hong Kong played a special role in the Xinhai Revolution [in 1911] which led to the formation of the Republic of China 100 years ago ... Hong Kong

had always been the place where revolutionary and reformist ideas in China came from … The demands for democracy and constitutional government that emerged from the Xinhai Revolution a century ago have yet to be met and Hong Kong's duty to history is not yet finished…[44]

Perhaps this reassertion of Hong Kong's significance as a diasporic meeting place may also allow us to rewrite the story about China in our history textbooks someday…

Notes

1 A more elaborate analysis of Hong Kong history textbooks can be found in my earlier article, "Loving Disability: 'Patriotism' in Postcolonial Hong Kong." *Asian Cultural Studies* 34 (2008). I am using segments of that article in this section.
2 For details on changes in history education curricula, see Flora Kan, *Hong Kong's Chinese History Curriculum from 1945: Politics and Identity* (Hong Kong: Hong Kong University Press, 2007) and Edward Vickers, *In Search of Identity: The Politics of History as a School Subject in Hong Kong, 1960s–2005* (Hong Kong: University of Hong Kong, Comparative Education Research Center, 2005).
3 Flora Kan and Edward Vickers, "One Hong Kong, Two Histories: "History" and "Chinese History" in the Hong Kong School Curriculum," *Comparative Education* 38, No. 1 (February, 2002), 74–75.
4 In this section, I will focus on three Chinese History textbooks published in the 1980s and the 2000s: (1) *Xinbian Zhongguo Lishi* (1984) published by Ren Ren and Ling Kee Publishing Company, which was one of the most popular textbooks used among lower-form students in the 1980s; (2) *Tanjiu Zhongguo Lishi* (2004) published by Manhattan Press; and (3) *Tansuo Zhongguoshi* (2006) published by Ling Kee Publishing Company. The latter two are Form 5 textbooks used by secondary schools today. In the comparison of their treatment of the concept of nation, I will concentrate on two aspects – the mission statements, and the depiction of Hong Kong.
5 Edward Vickers, Flora Kan and Paul Morris, "Colonialism and the Politics of 'Chinese History' in Hong Kong's Schools," *Oxford Review of Education* 29, No. 1 (March, 2003), 95–111.
6 Bernard Luk, "Chinese Culture in the Hong Kong Curriculum: Heritage and Colonialism," *Comparative Education Review* 3, No. 4 (1991), 664–665.
7 See Lin Xiaoqing, "Historicizing Subjective Reality: Rewriting History in Early Republican Early China," *Modern China* 25, No. 1 (1999), 3.
8 *Xinbian Zhongguo Lishi*, (Ren Ren and Ling Kee Publishing Company, 1984), 5.
9 The backgrounds of these committee members are not clear, but some of the contents are very similar to textbooks published in the mainland.
10 Liang Yiming, Luo Weiru, Xie Weijie and Ye Xiaobing, *Tanjiu Zhongguo Lishi* (Hong Kong: Manhattan Press Ltd., 2004), Preface.
11 Chen Hanshen, Huangzhiwen, Lu Qiming, Fan Guoji, Weng Jiangcheng, Peng Yaojun, Bu Yumin, Chen Jianhui, Guo Daliang and Chen Jierong, *Tansuo Zhongguoshi* 5 (Ling Kee Publishing Company, 2006), Preface.
12 Vickers, *In Search of Identity*, 4.
13 Not all the textbooks published in the 2000s have the same kind of prefaces, however. *Xin Linian*, published by Hong Kong Educational Publishing Company in 2004, for example, does not have a preface but an "explanation" which gives general guidance about the history syllabus and ways that the textbook can be used.
14 Curriculum Development Council (1997) *Chinese History Syllabus (Forms 1–3)* (Hong Kong, Education Department), 8.

15 Kan, *Hong Kong's Chinese History Curriculum from 1945: Politics and Identity*, 128.
16 *Tanjiu*, 215–217; *Tansuo*, 77–83.
17 The linguistic medium of instruction has been a topic of debate.
18 The World history text, *Exploring World History* for F. 5 entitled "Conflicts and Cooperation in the 20th Century World," published by Ling Kee (2004), includes nothing about China.
19 Chan, 92.
20 Chan, 110.
21 Chan, 111.
22 Chan, 112–115.
23 I have discussed in further detail the implications of this megacity project in another article. See A. Chin, "Diasporic Memories and Conceptual Geographies in Post-Colonial Hong Kong," *Modern Asian Studies*, forthcoming in 2014. I am using segments of that article here.
24 The National Development and Reform Commission, "The Outline of the Plan for the Reform and Development of the Pearl River Delta (2008–2020)," April 17, 2009.
25 "HK developers retain appetite for land banks," *South China Morning Post*, September 6, 2012.
26 The protests in July–September 2012 forced the Hong Kong government to temporarily postpone the commencement of the new subject curriculum in the academic year of 2012–2013 and let individual schools have the autonomy to decide whether and how the curriculum should be introduced. However, some activists criticize that the government can use resources and financial subsidies to affect the decisions of the schools.
27 The Basic Law of Hong Kong guarantees that the city enjoys a high degree of autonomy except in matters of defense and foreign affairs, however government officials in Hong Kong have not been active in using the Basic Law to protect the rights of the Hong Kongers.
28 Mainlanders are often referred to as "locusts" (*huangchong*) by the Hong Kong public. For reference to Chen Yun (Chin Wan), please see Chen Yun (Chin Wan). *Xianggang Chengbang Lun (The Discourse of Hong Kong City-State)* (Hong Kong, Tianchuang Chubanshe, 2011).
29 Lau Siu-kai, *Hongkongese or Chinese: The Problem of Identity on the Eve of Resumption of Chinese Sovereignty over Hong Kong* (Hong Kong: Hong Kong Institute of Asia-Pacific Studies, The Chinese University of Hong Kong, 1997), 27.
30 Shu-mei Shih, *Visuality and Identity: Sinophone Articulations Across the Pacific.* (Berkeley: University of California Press, 2007), 23–24.
31 *Ibid.*
32 *Ibid.*, 26.
33 Shu-mei Shih, "Against Diaspora: The Sinophone as Places of Cultural Production," *Globalizing Modern Chinese Literature: A Critical Reader on Sinophone and Diasporic Writing*, ed. Jing Tsu and David Wang (London: Brill, 2010), 29–48.
34 Shih, *Visuality and Identity*, 31.
35 *Ibid.*, 34.
36 While this framework is implemented in Hong Kong and Macau through the Basic Law, Taiwan rejected this framework from the beginning. Since the accession of Hu Jintao, the PRC no longer uses this framework to promote unification with Taiwan. Instead, a more gradual approach of economic integration is advocated.
37 It is worthwhile comparing Singapore with the other former colonies. Nevertheless, because of the limitations of this project, Singapore is not included in the following discussion.
38 When he examines the original Jewish-centered definition that prevailed from 2CE to around 1968, he found the following constitutive elements: (1) Coercion led to the uprooting and resettlement outside the boundaries of the homeland of large numbers of

people or of entire communities; (2) uprootedness results in the departure of a group that already has a clearly delimited identity in its homeland; (3) diasporic communities maintain a collective memory that is a foundational element of their distinct identity; (4) diasporas patrol their communal boundaries; (5) diasporic communities care about maintaining communication with each other; and (6) diasporic communities maintain contact with the homeland when it persists in identifiable form, and thus the desire to return to the homeland. See Khachig Tölöyan. "Rethinking Diaspora(s): Stateless Power in the Transnational Moment," *Diaspora* 5, No. 1 (1996).

39 Tölöyan, "Rethinking Diaspora(s)," 16.
40 James Clifford, "Diaspora," *Routes: Travel and Translation in the Late Twentieth Century* (Cambridge: Harvard University Press, 1997), 147.
41 Stuart Hall, "New Ethnicities," *Stuart Hall: Critical Dialogues in Cultural Studies*, edited by David Morley and Kuan-Hsing Chen (London; New York: Routledge, 1996), 441.
42 Allen Chun, "Diasporas of Mind, Or Why There Ain't No Black Atlantic in Cultural China," *Communal Plural* 9, No. 1 (April 2001), 97.
43 *Taipei Times*, June 1, 2011.
44 *Ibid.*

References

Chen, H., Huang, Z., Lu, Q, Fan, G., Weng, J., Peng, Y., Bu, Y., Chen, J., Guo, D. and Chen, J. 2006. *Tansuo Zhongguoshi* 5. Hong Kong: Ling Kee Publishing Company.

Chen, Y. (Chin Wan). 2011. *Xianggang Chengbang Lun* (The Discourse of Hong Kong City-State). Hong Kong: Tianchuang Chubanshe.

Chin, A. 2008. "Loving Disability: 'Patriotism' in Postcolonial Hong Kong." *Asian Cultural Studies* 34: 181–200.

Chin, A. 2014. "Diasporic Memories and Conceptual Geography in Post-Colonial Hong Kong." *Modern Asian Studies*.

Chun, A. 2001. "Diasporas of Mind, Or Why There Ain't No Black Atlantic in Cultural China." *Communal Plural* 9 (1): 95–109.

Clifford, J. 1997. *Routes: Travel and Translation in the Late Twentieth Century*. Cambridge: Harvard University Press.

Hall, S. 1996. "New Ethnicities." In *Stuart Hall: Critical Dialogues in Cultural Studies*, edited by D. Morley and K.-H. Chen. London; New York: Routledge.

Kan, F. 2007. *Hong Kong's Chinese History Curriculum from 1945: Politics and Identity.* Hong Kong: Hong Kong University Press.

Kan, F. and E. Vickers. 2002. "One Hong Kong, Two Histories: 'History' and 'Chinese History' in the Hong Kong School Curriculum." *Comparative Education* 38 (1): 73–89.

King, G and F. Owen. 2004. *Exploring World History* 5. Hong Kong: Ling Kee.

Lau, S.-K. 1997. *Hongkongese or Chinese: The Problem of Identity on the Eve of Resumption of Chinese Sovereignty over Hong Kong*. Hong Kong: Hong Kong Institute of Asia-Pacific Studies, The Chinese University of Hong Kong.

Liang, Y., Luo, W., Xie, W. and Ye, X. 2004. *Tanjiu Zhongguo Lishi*. Hong Kong: Manhattan Press Ltd.

Lin, X. 1999. "Historicizing Subjective Reality: Rewriting History in Early Republican Early China," *Modern China* 25 (1): 3–68.

Luk, B. 1991. "Chinese Culture in the Hong Kong Curriculum: Heritage and Colonialism," *Comparative Education Review* 3 (4): 650–668.

Pan, L. 1990. *Sons of the Yellow Emperor: The Story of the Overseas Chinese*. London: Secker & Warburg.

Qian, M and Sun, G. 1984. *Xinbian Zhongguo Lishi*. Hong Kong: Ren Ren and Ling Kee Publishing Company.

Shih, S. 2007. *Visuality and Identity: Sinophone Articulations Across the Pacific*. Berkeley: University of California Press.

Shih, S. 2010. "Against Diaspora: The Sinophone as Places of Cultural Production." In *Globalizing Modern Chinese Literature: A Critical Reader on Sinophone and Diasporic Writing*, edited by J. Tsu and D. Wang. London: Brill.

Tölöyan, K. 1996. "Rethinking Diaspora(s): Stateless Power in the Transnational Moment." *Diaspora* 5 (1): 3–36.

Tu, W. 1991. "Cultural China: The Periphery as the Center." *Daedalus* 120 (2): 1–32.

Vickers, E. 2005. *In Search of Identity: The Politics of History as a School Subject in Hong Kong, 1960s–2005*. Hong Kong: University of Hong Kong, Comparative Education Research Center.

Vickers, E., F. Kan and P. Morris. 2003. "Colonialism and the Politics of 'Chinese History' in Hong Kong's Schools." *Oxford Review of Education* 29 (1): 95–111.

Wang, G. 1993. "Greater China and the Chinese Overseas." *The China Quarterly* 136, December.

Index

Page numbers in *italics* denote tables, those in **bold** denote figures.

Made in the USA
Middletown, DE
31 August 2022

72759552R00157